Contents

List of Figures

List of Tables

Preface

Ever since my first fieldwork experience in a Philadelphia neighborhood among a peer group of working class African American girls in the early 1970s, I have been struck by the creativity with which girls use language to create their local social organization and police the moral order of their group. Among the girls I studied, a gossip event called the "he-said-she-said" constitutes a major political event through which preadolescent girls demonstrate their willingness to display their character; within he-said-she-said disputes, girls take action against those they construct as their offenders (parties who talk about them behind their backs). The girls' social organization consists largely of shifting coalitions of triads, rather than hierarchical structures, as occur among the boys, and gossip can be used to rearrange the social organization of the moment. Girls display intense engrossment in formulating warrants and demonstrations for their positions and exhibit determination in the pursuit of their point of view. In fact, gossip events provide an exemplar of female verbal virtuosity in orchestrating political activity. In the 1990s, in South Carolina and California, as I began to study how girls negotiate the rules of their games in hopscotch and jump rope, as well as access to the soccer field, I found that diverse groups of preadolescent girls across the United States, representing a range of social class and ethnic backgrounds, are quite articulate in producing moves that demonstrate an orientation towards a sense of justice.

Girls' ability to build a social and moral universe in which they hold one another accountable to an abstract set of rules demonstrates their social competence. Moreover, this ability contradicts many of the stereotypes that have recently dominated research on female moral development in psychology. Over the past 35 years I have been deeply concerned with images of girls in the social science literature and with the methodologies used to study them. The notion of boys as more assertive and girls as nurturing is often taken as a given.[1]

Indeed, the notion of a gender-based difference in collectivist versus individualist orientations, prominent in early cross-cultural studies of psychological anthropologists[2] as well as developmental psychologists,[3] remains an underlying premise in much psychological research today. Recently Simon Baron-Cohen, director of the autism research center at Cambridge

University, wrote in his article "The Essential Difference: The Truth about the Male and Female Brain"[4] that "males on average have a stronger drive to systemize, and females to empathize" (Baron-Cohen 2005:A19). Baron-Cohen (2003:1) asserts that, "The female brain is predominantly hard-wired for empathy. The male brain is predominantly hard-wired for understanding and building systems."

Such dualistic thinking resonates with dual cultures approaches in the social sciences. Carol Gilligan's landmark, best-selling[5] 1982 book *In a Different Voice*[6] contrasted a form of male orientation to moral development concerned with forms of justice based on rights and rules, separation and independence, with a "feminine" orientation based on caring, attachment, and dependence: "the conception of morality as concerned with the activity of care centers moral development around the understanding of responsibility and relationships, just as the conception of morality as fairness ties moral development to the understanding of rights and rules" (Gilligan 1982:19). While the male orientation in Gilligan's work was associated with the public sphere of social power, the female orientation was tied to feelings of empathy and compassion, connected to the private domestic realm.[7] The implication is that males are better positioned to participate in social and public spheres of activity.[8] Gilligan's (Brown et al. 1995:122) concern with care as a feminine ethic set the agenda for research on moral development in psychology and for research on gender and language in linguistic anthropology into the 1990s.[9] In 1996 the editors of *Time* magazine identified Gilligan as one of the 25 most influential scholars in America. *In a Different Voice* was declared to have changed the rules of psychology, the assumptions of medical research, and the conversation among parents and teachers and developmental professionals about differences between men and women, girls and boys.[10] Gilligan's work provided legitimacy for the idea that women not only reasoned about moral dilemmas in a different way from men; according to the authors of *Women's Ways of Knowing*,[11] influenced by Gilligan's work, females reasoned differently as well. Gilligan's ideas, spawning the notion of different "ways of knowing," led to a craze for creating single-sex schools, and influenced the American Association of University Women (AAUW) 1992 study *How Schools Shortchange Girls*, which pictured girls as critically suffering a loss of self-esteem during adolescence.

Feminist philosopher Susan Okin (1992:320) has argued that stereotypes such as Gilligan's "different voice" notion are detrimental to women, keeping women in their place. As long as we conceptualize women as persons lacking capacities men are endowed with, women will not be treated politically, socially, or economically the equals of men. She questions, "How are women to continue to assume all of the nurturing activities that allegedly both follow from and reinforce their 'naturally' superior virtues, and at the same time challenge men's monopoly of power in the outside world?" (1992:321). She urges policies that give incentives to both women and men to participate fully in domestic as well as non-domestic life.

The discussion of same-sex relationships in this book challenges other forms of binary thinking about gendered language behavior as well. For over three decades, since the pioneering work of Robin Lakoff (1975), the work of feminist social scientists has demonstrated concern with issues of power asymmetries in interaction and with developing political commentary about male domination. Perhaps because of a lingering dualistic association of female interaction with cooperative interaction promoted by "difference" theorists,[12] scholars have tended to associate relations of power with male groups or with male/female interaction.[13] In this book by exploring relations of power in female groups I call into question the notion that terms such as "prosocial,"[14] cooperative,[15] or polite,[16] provide adequate descriptors for female interaction. Examining how a clique of elementary school girls organize play activities such as jump rope or dramatic play, we find that girls use directives to construct hierarchically organized and socially exclusive, social relations in same-sex as well as in cross-sex interaction. To go beyond binary thinking we need to consider how females can create power asymmetries with females, and even with males.

This book documents actual events in the lives of girls' friendship groups on the playground, a setting where children interact with peers on their own terms, outside of adult supervision.[17] Previous studies of forms of children's aggression have primarily relied on questionnaires, self-reports, or diaries,[18] and have paid minimal attention to embodied language practices, absolutely critical for understanding the ways that children structure their social relations.

In this book, making use of video recordings of the mundane encounters that constitute girls' actual lives, I provide an ethnographic account of how embodied language is used to build girls' social organization. By following a particular group over a three-year period, I describe in detail the lived embodied practices through which forms of social inclusion and exclusion in a girls' peer group are achieved over time. Often this entails using symbols in talk to index one's membership in the upper middle class, a process that simultaneously makes visible the exclusion of those who lack access to these symbols. Understanding at close range the games of stance, status, and exclusion that animate the hidden lives of girls allows us to rethink what girls are made of as social, cognitive, and moral actors.

Marjorie Harness Goodwin is Professor of Anthropology at UCLA. Her work focuses on how people build their cognitive and social worlds through the use of language in interaction in a range of natural settings. An extended ethnographic study of an African American peer group formed the basis of her now classic *He-Said-She Said: Talk as Social Organization among Black Children*. She has also investigated interaction in the workplace (as part of the Xerox PARC Workplace Project), daily life in families (as a core faculty member of the UCLA Center for Everyday Lives of Families), interaction in the home of a man with severe aphasia, and is continuing to look in detail at the lives of preadolescent girls.

Acknowledgments

Scholarship is embedded in the social milieu that includes the lives of the people who I was privileged to spend time with, students and colleagues whose insights and discussion benefited me immensely, and students who were valuable participants in my fieldwork. I am very indebted to insightful discussions with many colleagues, including H. Samy Alim, John Baugh, Nancy Budwig, Michael Chandler, Penny Eckert, Ann-Carita Evaldsson, Sue Ervin-Tripp, Kris Gutierrez, Amy Kyratzis, Lourdes de Leon, Cynthia Lightfoot, Ashley Maynard, Ray McDermott, Norma Mendoza-Denton, Elinor Ochs, Sue Speer, Liz Stokoe, Barrie Thorne, and Ana Celia Zentella. During my years of teaching linguistic anthropology at UCLA my understanding of children's interactions has been invigorated by dialogue with undergraduate and graduate students. Warm thanks to my colleague Sandro Duranti, who first suggested I embark on this venture, and to my editor, Jane Huber, who provided encouragement every step of the way. I owe very special debts to Mary Bucholtz, Jack Sidnell, and Chuck Goodwin, who provided extensive and valuable comments on earlier versions of the manuscript. Financial support through grants from the Academic Senate Office, Council on Research, UCLA, made this project possible.

I am profoundly grateful to Jill Kushner Bishop and Carleen Curley Velez who provided invaluable assistance in conducting the fieldwork for this project. Without their assistance in the field, either behind the camera or serving as sound person, this project would not have been possible. Sharing observations about children's interactions with them on our way to and from the fieldsites was exhilarating. In addition, Carleen helped in transcribing the English data; Jill assisted with both the English and Spanish materials; and Maria Rivas provided invaluable assistance in translation of the Spanish data. Chuck Goodwin, Scott Phillabaum, and Erin Jacobs helped with the rendering of frame grabs and figures. I was introduced to the potential of Pitchworks for my analysis of intonation contours in the hopscotch transcripts by Mee-Jeong Park and Malcah Yaeger-Dror; they were important mentors.

Portions of this work have been previously published, in different form, in the following books and journals: "Games of Stance: Conflict and Footing in Hopscotch," in *Kids' Talk: Strategic Language Use in Later Childhood*, ed.

Susan Hoyle and Carolyn Temple Adger (New York: Oxford University Press, 1998); "Exclusion in Girls' Peer Groups: Ethnographic Analysis of Language Practices on the Playground", *Human Development* 45:392–415, 2002; "Organizing Participation in Cross-Sex Jump Rope: Situating Gender Differences within Longitudinal Studies of Activities," special edition entitled "Gender Construction in Cross-Cultural Perspective: Views from Children's Same-Sex and Mixed-Sex Peer Interactions." *Research on Language and Social Interaction* 34(1): 75–106, 2001; "Multi-modality in Girls' Game Disputes" (with Charles Goodwin and Malcah Yaeger-Dror), *Journal of Pragmatics* 34:1621–1649, 2002; "Building Power Asymmetries in Girls' Interactions. Discourse and Society," *Discourse and Society* 13 (6):715–730, 2002.

1

Introduction

It is school lunchtime and a group of eight fifth grade girls decide they will forgo their usual thirty minutes of eating and talking in favor of securing a soccer ball and beating the boys onto the field. As they begin to organize their teams on the soccer field, boys arrive, and the following debate occurs[1]:

Example 1.1

		((Ron, Miguel and Manuel approach the girls on the field.))
1	Emi:	We have it today.
2	Ron:	We play soccer every day.= okay?
3	Miguel:	It's more boys than girls.
4	Emi:	*So?* Your point?
5	Ron:	This is **our field**.
6	Emi:	It's **not** your field. Did you pay for it? **No**.
7		Your name is not written on this land.
8	Kathy:	**Mine** is. K–A–T–H–Y! *((writing in the dirt))*

Historically the soccer field had belonged to boys. In negotiating access to territory typically colonized by boys (and counter to depictions of them as silently obedient at play on the boundaries of the playground[2]), the girls not only resisted and countered the arguments of boys, but the next day challenged the very social structure of the playground. When the boys summoned a playground aide who defended the boys' rights to occupy the field, the girls declared their equally legitimate rights to the space:[3]

Example 1.2

1	Male Aide:	**GIRLS!** Go somewhere *else*.
2		The boys are coming to play
3		and you took over their field.
4		That's not cool.
5	Girls:	**NO!!** *((raucous screaming for several seconds))*
6	Melissa:	Miss Harper **said** we could!!
		[30 seconds later]
25	Male Aide:	The boys are **al**ways here playing soccer.
26		You can go over there and play soccer?

27		They *can't* go on the black top.
28		You girls can go *any*where.[4]
29		And do what you're doing.
30		Am I *right* or am I wrong.
31	Melissa:	Why can't *they* go anywhere.
32	Male Aide:	They *can't* go anywhere.
33		They can't go onto the blacktop and play soccer.
34		Somebody's gonna fall and
35		⌈break their knee.
36	Sandra:	⌊Well that means ⌈we-
37	Kathy:	⌊Well *neith*er can *we!*

Girls confronted not only the boys who prevented them from playing, but, in addition, the authority figure (summoned by the boys) who controlled local access to the playing field. The girls' concern about justice and fairness on the playground eventually resulted in reform regarding how the soccer field was used. The following year, a "safe schools" program that stressed gender equity and provided for a rotation of participants on the soccer field was put into play.

While in Examples 1.1 and 1.2 girls demonstrate through their action an intense concern with matters of justice and fairness, the next vignette involving discussion of jump rope illustrates girls' utter obliviousness to such notions. In this next lunchtime scene on the playground the same clique of girls are finishing up eating and preparing to get equipment (a jump rope) for play. Quite regularly as girls begin to play the game of jump rope they negotiate who is first, second, third, and so on, in the jumping order by calling out numbers.[5] In Example 1.3, instead of permitting girls to yell out numbers, girls tell another girl at their lunch table that she will be the last person to jump:[6]

Example 1.3

		((Girls are sitting at the lunch table))
1	Lisa:	I'm gonna go get the jump ropes.
2	Janis:	°You're *last. ((to Angela))*
3	Angela:	I'm *first.*
4	Lisa:	*No.*
5	Janis:	*NO::.*
6	Lisa:	⌈You're not *here.*
7	Aretha:	⌊You're not even *here!*
8	Angela:	°Go:d.

An explicit ranking of the girls is established. The girls tell Angela that not only is she last in the jump rope line-up (line 2), but in addition, countering her claim to any position whatsoever with loud "*NO*" responses, in choral unison (lines 6–7) they tell her that she is not even present. Angela, desperate to belong to this clique, utters a barely audible "°Go:d" in response. Rather than creating an inclusive play space for all girls, the girls collaborate in the active exclusion of one of their classmates.

Girls are able to challenge male colonization of the soccer field and argue for their rights in order to define a new moral order on their own terms. However, they are equally capable of building through their talk a form of ranked same-sex competitive social order which displays utter disdain and disgust for those they position at the bottom of their social group. These vignettes make visible features of girls' social organization and moral behavior that are often hidden from adults (teachers as well as researchers).

Methodology

In order to come to terms with the diversity of girls' experience, I con-ducted ethnographic fieldwork documenting through videotape the specific practices through which children construct their local social order. By co-ordinating their talk with others children bring their social world into being. In this book I am concerned with how girls attentively monitor their social landscape, continuously commenting on the moves others make in both conversational games (storytelling, assessing events, etc.) and playground games such as jump rope or hopscotch. In the process of such talk, particip-ants make visible for each other their perspectives on events, categorizing the behavior of others and displaying their alignments towards events.[7] I describe the public language practices girls make use of in the building of their local social organization in interactions with their peers in same- and mixed age and same- and mixed-sex groups.

I selected the playground as opposed to the classroom as the primary focus for research because not much is known about how children interact when they are apart from adult supervision.[8] While we know how children behave with peers in school and in experimental settings, how they respond when researchers ask them to reason about hypothetical moral dilemmas, or explain their conceptions of friendship (Cole et al. 2005:532), we know very little about how children in middle childhood interact with one another in the peer group. On the playground children make friends and establish alliances with children in activities that are not brokered by their parents or teachers.[9] Numerous researchers[10] have argued that children are less guarded in their behavior on the playground than in the classroom. For example, observational assessments of aggression[11] as well as student self reports[12] have shown that students have greater opportunities to observe aggression in the playground than in the classroom.[13]

In the peer setting the identities of participants are negotiated within and through talk. Unlike the identities of expert-novice, judge or plaintiff, or identities inherent in many institutional or work-related settings, roles are achieved rather than ascribed. Participants come to inhabit particular and ever-shifting positions in the local social organization of situated activity systems through interactive work.[14]

While my perspective is largely anthropological, I want to make my work accessible for researchers in a number of social science fields. While utilizing a methodology that is distinctive to a linguistic anthropologist, I engage with relevant literature in psychology, sociology, girls' and women's studies, as well as linguistic and socio-cultural anthropology, as I am also concerned with demonstrating how an ethnographically based and conversation analytic informed approach can help us to challenge some of the stereotypic views of girls which abound in work in the social sciences. My intent is to make the findings in this book available to a broad range of researchers who are concerned with the lives and well-being of girls.

Discussing the aims of feminism, Du Bois (1983:108) has argued that studies need "to address women's lives and experiences *in their own terms*, to create theory grounded in the actual experience and language of women" (emphasis in original). As early as 1920 anthropologist Bronislaw Malinowski (1959:125) urged fieldworkers to move beyond the "hearsay method of field-work" (relying on what informants report to researchers), to focus on "direct observation of the rules of custom as they function in actual life." Close ethnographic observation is needed, according to Malinowski (1959:120–121), because

> the natural impulsive code of conduct, the evasions, the compromises, and non-legal usages are revealed only to the fieldworker who observes native life directly, registers facts, lives at such close quarters with his "material" as to understand not only their language and their statements, but also the hidden motives, of behaviour, and the hardly ever formulated spontaneous lines of conduct.

Quite often we do not know how local idealizations of events gathered from interviews are related to the social practices that they are purported to describe. In this book I use as my principal data source videotaped sequences of naturally occurring interaction. I document how, through their talk with one another, girls, in same- and cross-sex interaction, build their moment-to-moment social organization on the playground.

By video and audio taping more than eighty hours of their talk at lunch and play during their hour-long lunch break over a three-year period, I was able to acquire a record of naturally occurring interaction that could later be scrutinized. Videotape captures information about the engagement and orientation in space of participants, whose actions are built through the deployment of a range of semiotic resources,[15] including the body, gesture, facial expression, and the built environment. We can examine the affective alignments and stances of participants that color the particular actions taken up. By gathering tapes primarily of the children's talk with other children, and only on rare occasions asking questions, I avoided the problem of relying on reports *to a researcher* about social identities.[16] I did not have to rely on my memory to recover what interaction had occurred. I told the children I was interested in whatever they were doing, and did not focus on gathering information about specific types of behavior. I thus diverge from psychologists who study children naturalistically, but reduce the observations they make to codes of children's interactions and provide statistical summaries of features of their interactions.

My strategy has been to investigate how participants in interaction constitute their identities for each other in the midst of ongoing interaction. As argued by conversation analyst Harvey Sacks (1995a:27):

> the trouble with [ethnography based on interviewing] is that they're using informants; that is, they're asking questions of their subjects. That means that they're studying the categories that Members use, to be sure, except at this point they are not investigating their categories by attempting to find them in the *activities* in which they're employed. [emphasis added]

Put another way, "membership categorization only amounts to anything if it can be shown to be a lay members' method, assembled and managed in members' dealings with each other and the physical world" (Silverman 1998:139).[17] Schegloff (1997:182–183) argues that if we are to analyze how issues such as power or gender connect with discursive material we need to show how such categories are "demonstrably relevant to" participants "as embodied in their conduct."

Like linguistic anthropologist Michael Moerman (1988), I find that extended ethnographic fieldwork in a particular setting where one observes what takes place in the interaction of participants without the ethnographer's intervention into the talk permits us the best starting point for seeing how talk unfolds in the everyday events of people's lives. Rather than treating talk and social organization as two separate types of phenomena, this book will demonstrate in considerable detail how talk itself constitutes a form of social action. By focusing on how talk is articulated by girls across an array of face-to-face encounters, I focus on three primary concerns: (1) how positions or stances with respect to appropriate behavior are produced in the midst of particular activities (such as games, assessments, and stories), (2) how claims to social positions are negotiated, and (3) how behavior of those who are felt to violate local norms of the group is sanctioned – all as ongoing accomplishments in the pursuit of practical activities.

Central to all girls' activity is their constant involvement in the task of monitoring or policing what is going on in their social environment. I look at how girls dispute actions in the midst of games of hopscotch and jump rope, how they position themselves with respect to other girls during storytelling or descriptions they are elaborating, and how they critique girls who attempt to place themselves above others or fail to demonstrate knowledge of or access to symbols of middle class identity. In the midst of going about their work of creating social organization, while playing games, gossiping, storytelling, and assessing one another's behavior, girls make explicit the criteria in terms of which they evaluate one another, elaborating for themselves as well as analysts the tacit norms that underlie their social order.

Situated Activities, Language Games, and Practice

In order for any human beings to coordinate their behavior with that of their coparticipants, in the midst of talk they must display to one another what they are doing and how they expect others to coordinate their talk with them. Both language and the body provide important resources for achieving this local social order. An approach to the study of social order that analyzes such local sense-making practices can be found in the field of Conversation Analysis, inaugurated in the 1960s by Harvey Sacks, Emanuel Schegloff, Gail Jefferson, and their colleagues, and in the tradition of ethnomethodology (Garfinkel 1967) from which Conversation Analysis emerged.[18] Harold Garfinkel (1991:11) has described ethnomethodology's object of inquiry as follows:

> For ethnomethodology the objective reality of social facts, in that, and just how, it is every society's locally, endogenously produced, naturally organized, reflexively accountable, ongoing, practical achievement, being everywhere, always, only, exactly and entirely, members' work, with no time out, and with no possibility of evasion, hiding out, passing, postponement, or buy-outs, is *thereby* sociology's fundamental phenomenon.

Ethnomethodology seeks to provide detailed analyses of the assemblages of practices (based on tacit knowledge) through which the work of accomplishing local social order is achieved. For conversation analysts emphasis shifts from examination of isolated sentences (the focus of study in linguistics) to how talk is embedded within sequences of action and is shaped by the immediately preceding configuration of actions.[19] By examining the sequential organization of the stream of talk-in-interaction,[20] forms of membership categorization,[21] as well as the nonvocal emotional or affective displays[22] participants provide in concert with linguistically expressed feelings, attitudes, moods, and dispositions,[23] we can investigate how participants make visible for each other the meaningfulness of a prior action. Because participants have the job of providing next moves to ongoing talk which demonstrate what sense they make of that talk, it is possible to see how group members themselves interpret the interaction they are engaged in without having to rely on accounts passed on to anthropologists through interviews. The use of videotape is crucial, as frequently next moves evaluating what someone is saying or doing involve collusive glances, eyeball rolls, high fives, or pointing gestures. Such embodied actions assist us in understanding the stances that are taken up in the midst of talk. By examining actual instances of negotiated interaction, we can document the processes through which social organization of a social group is built.

The practice of sense-making on a turn-by turn level does not occur in a vacuum, but rather takes place in the midst of a current activity or project. Within the field of microsociology, examining face-to-face interaction, Erving Goffman proposed a way of understanding the structure and function of particular locally orchestrated activities. Elaborating his definition of the "encounter" or focused gathering (Goffman 1961:18) in his article "Fun in Games," Goffman argued that encounters involve (1) a single visual and cognitive focus of attention, (2) a mutual and preferential openness to verbal communication, (3) a heightened mutual relevance of acts, and (4) an eye-to-eye ecological huddle that maximizes each participant's opportunity to perceive the other participants' monitoring of him. Within the game encounter, the basic activity is a "move" through which an actor commits himself to a position. Goffman listed love-making, boxing, dancing, and card games as instances of encounters. He added that when participants are jointly involved in sustaining a task, the term "situated activity system" (1961:18) provides a more apt and abstract notion of what is taking place. In his article "Role Distance," Goffman (1961:96) defined the "situated activity system" as involving "the performance of a single joint activity, a somewhat closed, self-compensating, self-terminating circuit of inter-dependent actions." He provided an extensive discussion of the roles of surgeons in the activity of surgery as an instance of a situated activity system. Within the situated system situated roles emerge which are "visibly meshed into the activity" that others perform.[24] This meshing of roles constitutes part of a self-compensating system. Examples of situated activity systems described in this book include the game of hopscotch, jump rope, playing house, storytelling, gossip sessions, bragging, and assessing other people's behavior.

One form of situated activity system I have discussed elsewhere (Goodwin 1990) is the gossip event "he-said-she-said." In this activity a girl accuses another of a particular infraction: having talked about her behind her back. The offended party confronts an alleged offending party because she wants to "get something straight." The statements used to initiate these confrontations are intricate, highly structured utterances. Examples include "And *Tan*ya said that *you* said that I was showin' off just because I had that *bl:ouse* on" or "Kerry said **you** said that (0.6) I wasn't gonna go around *Pop*lar no more." These declarative utterances establish the accuser's grounds (warrant) for the accusation, how she learned about the offense. Responses to the accusations are typically denials ("*Uh* uh. I ain't say anything") or accusations about the intermediary party's work in setting up the confrontation ("Well she lie. I ain't **say** that"). Indeed within a single utterance a girl can invoke a coherent domain of action, a small culture, one that includes identities, actions, and biographies for the participants within it, in addition to a relevant past that warrants the current accusation, and makes relevant specific types of next actions. Figure 1.1 provides examples.

Accusation statements which open up confrontation events can lead to serious consequences – depriving someone of her basic right to interact with others in her playgroup for a period of time (and the family's consideration of moving off the street). Phenomena within the he-said-she-said do not obtain their meaning in isolation, but rather from their position within the entire structure of the activity system.

The approach examining situated activity systems shares much with linguistic anthropologist/sociolinguist John Gumperz's (1972:16–17) notion of *speech event*, defined as an interactive unit above the level of speech act "which is to the analysis of verbal interaction what the sentence is to grammar." Important in the definitions of the appropriate unit of analysis of both Goffman and Gumperz is the idea of the interactive meshing of the

He-Said-She-Said Accusations

Annette to Benita:

> And *Tan*ya said
> that *you* said
> that *I* was showin'off
> just because I had that *bl*:ouse on.

Bea to Annette:

> Kerry said
> *you* said that (0.6)
> *I* wasn't gonna go around *Pop*lar no more.

Barbara to Bea:

> *They* say
> y'all say
> *I* wrote *e*verything over there.

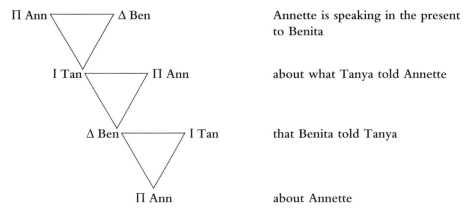

Π Ann — Δ Ben	Annette is speaking in the present to Benita
I Tan — Π Ann	about what Tanya told Annette
Δ Ben — I Tan	that Benita told Tanya
Π Ann	about Annette

Figure 1.1   He-said-she-said accusations

actions of separate participants into common social projects. Quite remarkably, this notion is similar to the idea of "operating culture" formulated by cognitive anthropologist Ward Goodenough (1981:102–103). Goodenough argued that the appropriate locus for the study of culture should be "simple clusters associated with one or only a few activities" and not social collectivities. Rather than assuming a simple correspondence between culture and social group, Goodenough argued that we should attempt to describe how the structures which members of a society use to build appropriate events change when they are involved in different activities. Finally, Wittgenstein (1958:§23) proposed the idea of "language game," in order "to bring into prominence the fact that speaking of language is part of an activity or of a form of life." As Duranti (1997:239) argues, the notion of "language game" is a working notion, rather than a category like "speech act." The concept of language game provides an invitation to the researcher to examine what speakers do with words. In order to understand how girls use language to socialize one another into a particular view of their social landscape, and to position themselves with respect to one another, the notion of language games provides an apt metaphor for capturing how through their talk girls both build meaning and hold one another accountable for their actions and statements.

The approach adopted in this book, taking as the unit of analysis situated activity systems and closely examining language games, has many resonances with "the practice turn in contemporary theory" (Schatzki et al. 2001). Practices have been defined as "embodied materially mediated arrays of human activity centrally organized around shared practical understanding" (Schatzki 2001:2).[25] Practice approaches are attempts to go beyond more static and deterministic views of social structures and systems on the one hand, and more individualistic and psychologically based accounts of human behavior on the other. Anthropologists who have engaged with practice theory have taken as the appropriate unit of analysis the "projects" or "games"[26] people are involved in – entailing the culturally constituted goals that are oriented towards, as they are defended, feared, or desired (Ortner 2003:14).[27] Ortner (in press) argues that social theorists should attempt to show how the practices of social actors articulate with the larger systems of power that constrain practices (and can be transformed by them). Inspired by the work of Raymond Williams (1977), she is concerned with how people can resist, alter, and challenge particular, historically grounded structures that are constraining their activity. Feminist conversation analysts[28] have argued that we can examine the effect of wider macro power structures that constrain people's lives by looking at what counts as power during moment-to-moment negotiations in conversation.[29] With respect to Examples 1.1–1.2, we can see the endogenous production of macro contexts[30] by examining the participant orientations of males and females in the fight over rights to play on the soccer field.

One problem that arises for practice theorists is how to view the relationships between various types of human practices or activities. Sidnell (2005:9)[31] argues that Wittgenstein's (1958:§66) concept of family resemblance provides one solution to understanding relationships between the patchworks of language games that constitute social life. Stating that a capacity for action must be understood with reference to the particular practice that it is embedded within, Sidnell proposes that we examine the structure of moves within activities to examine what possibilities for action each activity makes relevant or affords. If we examine how human practices are organized in terms of possibilities for participation, we can then look at how a series or network of resemblances are related. Sidnell (2005:206) argues that "These practices fit together to make up the accountably organized, coherent and orderly activities or language games of everyday life which, it has been suggested, can be fruitfully studied through the techniques of conversation analysis."

Extended ethnography provides a way of understanding the meaning of particular forms of action within the larger repertoire of possible actions important to the ongoing social projects of the group under study. For example, when we see how stories unfold in the everyday events of people's lives (Goodwin 1990), or how directives are used to organize a game and change over the course of a month (see chapter 4), we can view language in terms of its social functions. In Malinowski's (1959:312–313) terms language serves "as a link in concerted human activity." Examining the context of particular speech activities that bear a family resemblance across a range of encounters provides a way of looking at how language may be used in larger political processes of the group (putting someone who attempts to act as if she is superior to others in her place), or to position particular individuals as valued or despised.

Achieving Social Identity within Situated Activities

By closely describing how a specific interaction is sequentially organized, that is, how from moment to moment one turn is built upon the previous one, we can examine several notions that will be important in understanding the talk-in-interaction being analyzed in this book: *embodiment, turn taking, practice, format tying, preference, accounting,* and *moral behavior.* The terms used in the analysis of Example 1.4 will be highlighted in bold. Through a sequential analysis of talk, we can look at how participants make sense of what a prior speaker is saying, produce talk building from one turn to the next in a trajectory of action, and, in the process, work to construct local identities in the midst of a particular activity.

In the data we will examine (Example 1.4), we can also see how the identity of someone as marginal to a group is socially constructed. The notion of social construction or social construct was originally proposed by Berger and Luckman (1967) to embrace the idea that social categories (such as race, gender, or social class) are constituted through the language practices with which we represent the world in interaction with others – ways of using language that bring that world into being. While occurring on a completely different day from Example 1.3, Angela's treatment in the following sequence (Example 1.4) resembles the prior instance in which she was not permitted a role in the game. In Example 1.4 fourth graders have decided that they will have a jump rope contest between a limited number of boys and girls (3–4). Duets of one girl and one boy will jump to a rhyme until someone misses.

Angela had initiated the idea of a competition between girls and boys. Among children, it is not uncommon for particular rights to accrue to participants who provide the impetus for games.[32] However, on this occasion, Angela is told in no uncertain terms that she does not have the standing to participate in it! How she is told this, through gesture as well as talk, allows us to see the ways in which communication occurs not only in the stream of speech, but also through **embodied action** in the form of finger points and dismissive gestures. Analysis turn by turn also allows us to examine the way Angela's position in the local situated activity, as well as the more enduring children's social organization, is given shape through talk-in-interaction.

The jump rope competition can be considered a form of situated activity. Participation provides not only moves for turners and jumpers, but also for decision makers and parties taking control of the organization of the activity, specifying who is playing what role and when. For clarity the sequence has been abbreviated; however, Appendix 1.1 at the end of this chapter includes the entire larger fragment from which the sequence given here is taken.

Example 1.4

1	Ron:	Who's on the team. You, you, you,
2		*((pointing to Aretha, Lisa, Angela))*
3	Aretha:	Emi and Melissa.
4	Ron:	⌈*((looking towards Angela, arm extended towards her))*
5	Lisa:	⌊She's **NOT**. *((referring to Angela))*
6	Ron:	I know. So get her- *((waves arm to side, in*
7		*a dismissive gesture))*
8	Lisa:	Angela go out. You're not **in** this.
9	Angela:	Yes I **am**.
10	Lisa:	**No** you're **not**.
11	Angela:	If **you** guys can be in it then I **can**.
12	Lisa:	No you're **not**.
13	Angela:	Well **I'm** not leaving the rope.
14	Malcolm:	Look. There's a jump rope right there!
15	Lisa:	We'll go tell on you then.
16	Angela:	**Tell!** *((stays in rope, moves hands outwardly))*
		[20 lines omitted]
36	Lisa:	Reggie!! *((calling the male coach))*
37		*((runs towards Reggie))* I'm gonna go **tell** on her.
38	Sarah:	Angela you're not in the competition.
39	Angela:	*((walks away with blank look))*

In this sequence (lines 1–2) Ron poses the question "Who's on the team. You, you, you," while pointing to Aretha, Lisa, and Angela. The action of pointing provides an **embodied** way of indexing people being talked about and formulated as relevant participants, while opening up the possibility of those so designated to become next speakers. By producing this utterance, Ron positions himself in the role of someone who can speak on behalf of the boys' team, organizing players in the activity, and telling them what to do. The question posed in his **turn at talk** makes relevant a next action; it creates a slot for an answer from one of the parties pointed to (and indexed through the pronoun "you"). Two speakers, girls who were pointed to in Ron's initial utterance or turn, make next utterances that can be heard as responses. Aretha responds with "Emi and Melissa" (line 3). In line 5, as Ron is gazing and pointing towards Angela, Lisa states, "She's **NOT**." Her word "**NOT**" is produced with raised volume, and emphasized, as indicated by the capital letters and boldface.

Answering Lisa, Ron (line 6), like Lisa, refers to Angela in the third person rather than speaking to her directly. He states, "I know. So get her–" He waves his arm to the side, with a dismissive gesture, as if pushing something of little value to the side. Without completing his utterance, the nonvocal action he makes **embodies** the tacit meaning he wishes to convey. Indeed in Lisa's next action, she answers Ron's directive by providing a command that specifies (or elaborates) the meaning of his gesture and carries through his implied directive: "Angela go out." Lisa next supplies an explanation (a form of **accounting**) for the directive: "You're not *in* this." With her directive Lisa designates Angela as next speaker; she also ratifies Ron's right to deliver an action that should be complied with (and her position as some-one who complies with orders).

Harvey Sacks (1995b) used the terms "machinery" or "apparatus" to describe the order-producing, interactive work performed by participants on any occasion of talk. In the sequence under analysis, for example, specific procedures are made use of to tie talk from one utterance to another. Lisa's actions, her command and its justification (or **account**), set up the relevance of a response from Angela. In her next **turn** Angela refuses to comply with the directive; she remains still and steadfast next to the rope and counters the explanation with "Yes I *am*."

Lisa's next move ("No you're *not*" in line 10) is closely tied to the previous utterance, through a **practice** called "**format tying**."[33] In gener-ating a next action to a prior one, the form of a tied next utterance remains closely parallel to that of the preceding utterance, with minimal semantic shifts; "yes" changes to "no" and "am" changes to "not" in lines 9–10. **Format tying** constitutes a publicly available (rather than hidden internal) *apparatus* for tying talk in one turn to another. By maintaining the shape of the prior utterance, the new elements of the utterance are rendered salient; they stand out in opposition to the prior move's components because the rest of the utterance remains the same. Through selecting opposition that boldly states a position, here participants in conversation display a **pre-ference** towards **disagreement**. The form of ritual order that underlies this talk can be seen as contrasting with the ritual order underlying much of adult polite talk, which seeks to preserve social solidarity and inhibit conflict.[34]

In her next move (line 11) Angela provides an **account**, a justification, or rationale for the statement: "Yes I am." "If *you* guys can be in it then I *can*." When in Lisa's next move (line 12) she once more disagrees ("No you're *not*"), Angela restates her position "Well *I'm* not leaving the rope." At this point in the debate Malcolm enters the dispute, telling Angela to jump in another rope. Malcolm takes on a position not unlike the role Ron had occupied, and indeed it is Ron and Malcolm who on this occasion are ratified by others present as the participants in charge of their team. Lisa upgrades her argumentative stance towards Angela and next produces a threat to her: "We'll go tell on you then." When Angela refuses to budge, Lisa appeals to a higher authority figure, yelling to the male coach, Reggie (line 36), and shortly afterwards runs to get him.

Work in conversation analysis, speech act analysis, and politeness theory which adopts Goffman's notion of "face"[35] has argued that participants work to maintain social solidarity and avoid conflict; here just the opposite occurs as participants demonstrate an orientation toward achieving rather than avoiding conflict. Threats constitute actions taken by those who have power over someone and are intended to generate fear. In response Angela stands her ground and challenges Lisa to carry out her threat. Eventually, however, after multiple moves challenging her, Angela walks away (line 39). Frequently when someone initiates a game, she has some standing to participate in it. Here, however, the participants have selected a way of dealing with a potential participant that treats her as unworthy of any position within the local situated activity system whatsoever.

With the previous analysis we investigated how, through the forms of utterances delivered to or about Angela, both males and females collaborated in attempting to eliminate her from the game. In providing this analysis I have examined the local practices through which participants get from utterance to utterance, or produce talk built upon prior talk. Differences in social position are observable through the way in which Ron initiates a move to eliminate some players and Lisa complies, telling Angela to leave. Together Ron and Lisa's actions construct Angela as someone who is not to be included in the group. Here, without imposing analysts' categories, we can not only locate how relationships of inequality are built within moment-to-moment interaction, but also specify how differential relations of status between those constructing and ratifying Angela's position of marginality are established. Traditional concerns of sociological inquiry regarding the manifestation of power and inequality in social relationships are addressed in this analysis through a consideration of turn-by-turn interaction. We can witness the actual practices through which someone is positioned at the margins of the group. In addition, we can examine forms of resistance, the "weapons of the weak" (Scott 1985), which Angela employs to resist the position that others attempt to place her in.

Integrating Research Approaches

In comparing alternative paradigms for conducting social science research Edley and Wetherell (1997:205) have recently contrasted "bottom-up" approaches with "top-down" approaches to discursive studies. "Top-down" studies focus on "issues of power, ideological practice and social process" studying how people are "positioned by and effected through discourse" (Edley and Wetherell 1997:205).[36] Critical discourse analysts,[37] who often base many of their perspectives on the work of Foucault (1984), adopt an overt political stance in terms of both topics and the role for results of research (Woffitt 2005:139). By way of contrast "bottom-up" researchers make use of work in conversation analysis[38] and ethnomethodology[39] to examine how, within various conversational activities, identity is an achieved phenomenon.

When a conversation analysis study makes use of vernacular categories for persons (male, female, leader, etc.) the researcher is obligated to demonstrate analytically that these categories are relevantly part of the analysis performed by the participants on the scene. Social structures that are external to talk are not treated as explanations in themselves. Discursive psychologist Jonathan Potter (1996:98) argues that, "reality enters into human practices by way of the categories and descriptions that are part of those practices. The world is not ready categorized by God or nature in ways that we are all forced to accept. It is constituted in one way or another as people talk it, write it and argue it." To interpret participants' conduct with respect to pre-specified theoretical or political concerns is unacceptable for those adopting a conversation analytical approach, as it underplays and diminishes the importance of participants' own linguistic and communicative competencies.

In a recent article, Schegloff (1997:182)[40] contends that social categories should not be imposed by the analyst on materials under investigation; rather through analysis of conversational activities we ought to investigate the "forms of conduct by which persons . . . display and invoke participants' orientations to features of the interactional context" which index aspects of identity.[41] As Schegloff (1998:415) elaborates, rather than, for example, starting with ideologies about gender or power, one should begin analysis with wanting to find out what the parties to the interaction "understand themselves to be doing in it, what sort of interaction they show themselves to be collaboratively constructing."

A number of feminists and conversation analysts[42] have noted that a dilemma is posed for a researcher making use of a strict conversation analytic perspective.[43] Researchers within this tradition are obliged to show how participants are demonstrably orienting towards gender as a relevant feature in their activity.[44] On some occasions there is explicit mention of gender. For example, in the midst of a cross-sex jump rope competition children collaboratively organize the setting to provide for gender exclusivity:

Example 1.5

	((The girls have practiced several minutes))
Malcolm:	All the girls have to go bye bye.
Girls:	*((Girls start to move to another area))*
Malcolm:	Okay. Now the boys get to practice.
Ron:	This is our home field.

With the exception of contests between girls and boys (as in Examples 1.1, 1.2 and 1.5 where the terms "boy" and "girl" are used to designate positions),[45] rarely do the girls in my study make use of explicit terms to display that they are orienting to gendered categories.

Wetherell and Edley argue that we may need to look beyond the local sequence and specific lexical terms used to understand factors that influence how people are positioning themselves relative to one another. They argue that communicators make use of "interpretive repertoires . . . culturally familiar and habitual line[s] of argument comprised of recognizable themes, commonplaces, and tropes" (Wetherell and Edley 1998:400). Cameron (2005) proposes that relevance theory[46] provides a useful perspective for understanding how people mobilize particular interpretive repertoires. She argues that ignoring the cumulative knowledge of participants' past histories together, drawn from interactions outside the immediately occurring one, would be to miss something important that participants take into account when interacting in any particular moment.

Feminist conversation analysts have devoted considerable attention to explicating the issues entailed in providing grounded analyses of how gender is invoked in conversational exchanges.[47] Sunderland (2004:13) argues that conversation analysis shares with the social constructionist perspective in language and gender studies a moving away from talk of fixed "gender differences." Less common in language and gender studies is the practice of interweaving close analysis of talk-in-interaction together with extensive ethnographic fieldwork. This is the approach explicitly adopted by myself in *He-Said-She-Said*, analyzing talk-in-interaction among a working class neighborhood peer group, and by linguistic anthropologist Jack Sidnell (2005) in *Practical Epistemology: The Social Life of Knowledge in a Caribbean Community*. Ethnographic accounts permit us to examine how particular practices shape more enduring social relations and are constrained by structures of power that are brought into being in the midst of conversation.

Asymmetry in Female Social Groups

Feminism, as a social movement dedicated to political change, is concerned with putting an end to male domination of females.[48] To this end, early studies of language and gender dealing with relations of power have asked how men exert power and dominance over women.[49] Studies of how power is displayed by females in same-sex encounters were never on the agenda of earlier feminist studies of language and gender. Because many earlier cultural feminists[50] and eco-feminists[51] as *difference* theorists wanted to celebrate features of (Euro American middle class) female nature that were treated as unique, until recently[52] discussions of how relations of power can be built with females exerting dominance over other females were largely neglected.

In this book I align myself with others[53] who view gender identity not as something that is biologically given, a natural category, but rather as something that participants actively construct, a cultural artifact. Studies of gender as a social construct contrast with those emphasizing either gender *dominance* or *difference*, or theories considering gender a stable and enduring feature or trait possessed by an individual. Social constructionists, by way of contrast, view gender as "a social process"[54] and attempt to illuminate the "variability, complexity, and dynamism of linguistic behaviour in ongoing social relations" (Weatherall 1998:7).[55] Such a perspective can examine how identities are mobilized in the immediate local surround[56] as well as how people inhabit multiple "positions"[57] as they journey through the life course.[58] Children are viewed as agents in the co-construction of events rather than the passive recipients of cultural norms.[59] During the past decade feminist psychologists and linguists[60] alike have argued that social class and ethnicity need to be analyzed along with gender. While studies of language variation have linked language and social class, the tendency of many sociolinguistic studies is to describe social categories as pre-existing structures.[61] Within sociology and cultural anthropology we have descriptions of the practices used by societal members to constitute oneself as a member of a particular social class.[62] As yet, however, within linguistic anthropology there are few studies of how participants, in their moment-to-moment negotiations of status, index aspects of class identity.[63] This book examines how children make reference to activities and objects that are linked to the upper middle class in their attempts to position themselves with respect to others, putting members of another class in their place and explicitly marking their differences from parties occupying less desirable positions.

Relevance of Present Research

While the primary aim of my study is to document the everyday, taken-for-granted embodied language practices through which girls construct their social groups, I am also concerned with demonstrating how an ethnographically based and conversation analytic informed approach can help us to view the social lives of girls in new ways. I will briefly outline some of the major issues to be discussed in subsequent chapters, looking at how ethnographic description informed by a conversation analytic approach can provide insights into (1) notions of female voice, (2) studies of moral behavior and aggression, (3) features of children's peer group interaction. Situating my study with respect to these areas of focal concern I then briefly describe (4) the ethnographic studies of the peer group my work is based on, (5) how the children in the study viewed the ethnographers, and (6) the methodology used in this study. An outline of the sections of the book is then provided.

Models of female voice and moral development

Over the past 35 years I have been deeply concerned with images of girls in the social science literature and with the methodologies used to study them. Social science scholars[64] have critiqued these studies for having perpetuated a binary, dual cultures, or separate worlds view of girls' and boys' experiences, stating that girls are more "prosocial" than boys.[65] A 2004 study of "meta-analyses" of gender effects on children's language use, based on studies of gender variations in middle class Euro American children's language use,[66] argued that in same-sex groups boys are assertive and girls are prosocial: "the research literature suggests that girls are more likely than boys to use language to form and maintain connections with others, whereas boys are more likely to use language to assert their independence and to achieve utilitarian goals" (Leaper and Smith 2004:993). Contemporary psychology textbooks[67] on the family likewise recycle dualistic thinking, arguing that male personality development focuses on "agency," while women focus on "communion." The notion of boys as more assertive and girls as nurturing is taken as a given in current psychological studies; studies by Maltz and Borker (1982) as well as Maccoby (1998), which provide dualistic visions of girls' and boys' gendered play and gender-typed norms, are often cited as foundational research upon which more modern gender studies are based.[68]

Indeed, the notion of a gender-based difference in collectivist versus individualist orientations, prominent in early cross-cultural studies of psychological anthropologists[69] as well as developmental psychologists,[70] remains an underlying premise in much psychological research today. According to Brown et al. (1995:122) "Care as a feminine ethic is an ethic of special obligations and interpretations of interpersonal relationships." They argue that the feminine ethic of care is separated both politically and psychologically "from a realm of individual autonomy and freedom which is the realm of justice and contractual obligation" (1995:122). Gilligan (1982:95) argues that the "responsibility for care" involves the injunction "not to hurt." Gilligan (1982:173) provided an early version of cross-gender miscommunication, which she termed "a propensity for systematic mistranslation." She argued that "men and women may speak different languages that they assume are the same, using similar words to encode disparate experiences of self and social relationships" (Gilligan 1982:173).

Feminists, such as Patricia Hill Collins,[71] have critiqued Gilligan for promoting her positions based on an image of a generic woman who is white and middle class.[72] Systematic research has found few gender differences in levels of moral reasoning in predominantly white or African American adolescents.[73] In addition, as Tholander (2002:34) argues, moral development studies such as Gilligan's ignore a host of alternative principles not considered, such as honesty, loyalty, reverence, bravery, praise, benevolence, justice, bravery, moderation, wisdom, pity, politeness, wisdom, honesty, faith, hope, charity. Moreover, as demonstrated by the example of girls' interactions on the soccer field at Hanley School (Examples 1.1–1.2), an ethic of justice is not at all foreign to girls' ways of dealing with the world.

A dualistic conceptualization of morality fails not only to capture the multidimensionality of girls' interactions we saw in the vignettes presented above. Difference theories produce a deficit picture of female reasoning ability. Indeed, reducing moral behavior to the ways we respond to an interviewer's questions[74] provides a narrow definition of moral behavior. Instead this book investigates moral behavior through analyzing how children negotiate rules for behavior within their peer society. In the midst of the games of hopscotch and jump rope, preadolescent girls (primarily ages 10–12) across multiple groups whose interactions I analyze demonstrate the ability to regulate their own behavior according to agreed-upon (and much disputed) social rules. In Piaget's[75] terms the girls I studied make use of an autonomous morality, which contrasts with a morality based on a "mystical respect" for the rules of the game, thought to be "eternal and unchange-able" this is said to typify younger children, 8–10 year olds.

In their everyday talk with one another, as well as in the midst of games, girls' social organization is self-regulating. Girls spend inordinate amounts of time in the activity of glossing and assessing the behavior of others, defining local notions of what it is to be "rude," "geeky," "cool," "trendy," "popular," etc., and evaluating what it means to act inappropriately. The incessant monitoring of behavior that girls undertake has consequences for the type of social organization that is displayed within the group. Rather than explicitly ranking one another, girls display an orientation towards forms of similarity among group members that resembles structures that anthropologists have found in societies with an egalitarian ethos. Among the !Kung Bushmen a successful hunter should not return home and announce, as a braggart, that he killed a large animal in the bush. No matter how good the meat, the others in the camp would disparage the quality of the meat. The !Kung state in no uncertain terms that their norms are meant to prevent arrogance and to make sure that one person does not see himself as superior to others in the group:

> When a young man kills much meat he comes to think of himself as a chief or big man, and he thinks of the rest of us as his servants or inferiors. We can't accept this . . . So we always speak of his meat as worthless. This way we cool his heart and make him gentle. (Lee 1986:19)

The leveling mechanisms that have been discussed for the !Kung[76] operate in the girls' groups I have studied (working class African American girls, second generation Mexican American and Central American girls in down-town Los Angeles, and within the clique of Hanley School girls) as well. Creating a group in which one member was not marked as superior to others was accomplished only by constant monitoring of the group mem-bers. In the predominantly middle class Los Angeles clique, girls critiqued those who attempted to position themselves above others by wearing the newest fashions, producing utterances such as "She thinks she so popular because she's always up to date." Such types of utterances were similar to critiques such as "She think she cute" that occurred among the working class African American girls I studied in Philadelphia; these occurred when someone was interpreted as walking in such a way as to arrogantly exhibit stylish clothing that others could not afford. These utterances express con-cern for tacitly agreed upon notions of appropriate behavior.

In the later chapters of this book (chapters 5–7) I deal with another aspect of morality apart from the self-regulating of behavior that occurs in games and during gossip sessions. By examining practices of one-upmanship and social exclusion, I dispute the notion that an ethic of care predominates in girls' dealings with one another. I concur with Gilligan and others who feel that girls care intensely about social relationships[77] and judge themselves in terms of how they are socially positioned in terms of them. However,

I question whether an orientation towards an ideal of "attachment, loving and being loved, listening and being listened to, and responding and being responded to" (Brown et al. 1995:314) adequately describes the core of female morality.[78]

Chesney-Lind and Irwin (2004) examine the history of how American girls have been represented in popular media. While in the 1990s "bad girls" were black and Latina and often gang members or criminal, in the 2000s the focus has shifted to middle class white queen bees (Chesney-Lind and Irwin 2004:46) and "backstabbing bullies" (Harris 2004:xxi). Lyn Mikel Brown (2003:15) argues that as our views of girls as active, smart, athletic, and complicated have developed, a new ideal of "girl as fighter" has emerged. The vision of girls as socially and verbally aggressive or inherently "mean"[79] promoted in recent popular books and film (such as the 2004 "survival-of-the-fittest" film *Mean Girls*), and present in the popular press since the 1990s,[80] is overly simplistic. Nevertheless, we need to be mindful of the multiple expressions of girls' friendships and sociality that are possible. Studies among working class girls aged 16 from Glasgow, London, and Oxford, for example, found that 89 percent of the girls interviewed had been in a fight and every one of the girls had seen a fight.[81]

Chesney-Lind and Irwin (2004:49–50) note that real violence resulted from the 2003 Glenbrook High hazing incident; a few individuals of a senior high school class who disliked some juniors placed buckets on the heads of juniors and beat them. Five girls required medical attention as a result. This event was reported in the local news as demonstrating that female bullies can be as dangerous as male bullies; female bullying was identified as including fistfights as well as teasing. By examining the actual interactive practices (ways of using language in interactive settings) that make up the social world of a particular group we can investigate how girls articulate their concerns for one another and examine how morality is lodged within the actions and stances that children take up in interaction with their peers.

Much of the work in linguistics and psychology that argues for a "different voice" among females has investigated middle class Euro American groups[82] and has been conducted through interviews rather than extensive fieldwork. Descriptions of girls' psychologies, language, social organization, and play activities reported for Euro American middle class girls diverge from what I have observed while conducting fieldwork with other groups of children at play in their neighborhoods and on the playground. My early fieldwork[83] among urban working class African American children showed me that many of the popular stereotypes about "cooperative" and mitigated female speech were not supportable – particularly when we consider the ways that girls actively structure their experiences across a range of situations. Girls are capable of highly assertive ways of communicating, in both their same- and cross-sex interactions. They can orchestrate political dispute processes which are much more enduring than those of boys and far more consequential for the peer group and family.

Much of the "two cultures" or "separate worlds" ways of thinking about gender and language described in Maltz and Borker's (1982) often cited article on cross-sex miscommunication, in fact provided selective renderings of my ethnographic work among African American working class kids on Maple Street[84] (Goodwin 1980a). My fieldwork showed as many similarities as differences in the ways children used language to construct arguments.[85] Moreover, fifth grade girls on Maple Street proved equally as capable of verbal dueling as boys.[86] (This was true for the third graders at Hanley School as well, as I discuss in chapter 3.) Studies of female morality, based on experimental rather than ethnographic studies, and essentialist ideas of gendered personality, have often resulted in bifurcated and binary visions of males and females.

Towards studies of morality and conflict as social practice

Morality is lodged in the choices made by people regarding how to treat others in the midst of interaction. These are largely social choices that are intimately part of the context and the socio-political processes that constitute the lifeworlds[87] of groups. Through his early descriptions of the "presentation of self in everyday life" (Goffman 1959) outlined a field of endeavor within sociology which focused precisely on "the concerns of mundane actors with moral identity and the maintenance of face" (Bergmann 1998:185–186). As argued by Bergmann (1998:286):

> Morality is constructed in and through social interaction, and the analysis of morality has to focus, accordingly, on the intricacies of everyday discourse. Through a thorough analysis of descriptive practices and the mechanisms of everyday interaction the working of morality can be revealed.

Despite the fact that morality deals with decision-making concerning what is appropriate, fair, and right to do in a particular situation,[88] for the past 35 years the psychological study of morality has focused attention on *reasoning about* moral situations rather than on moral *action* itself. Most studies of moral development have relied on interviews, either asking subjects to discuss their own real-life moral dilemmas[89] or respond to hypothetical moral dilemmas.[90] Likewise, studies of social or relational aggression,[91] which investigate behavior that has very real moral features, have typically relied on reports, reading hypothetical vignettes, laboratory studies and question-naires, and surveys. Moreover, aggression is often treated as an internal psychological state rather than an interactional achievement.[92]

In studies of moral development as well as social aggression we have little sense of the temporal organization of social episodes; and as Shweder et al. (1987) have cautioned, the exclusive use of interviews in studies of moral development research reduces "the study of moral concepts to the study of verbal justification of moral ideas" – what people can "propositionalize."[93] That is inappropriate because what people can state is but a small part of what they know; moreover, responses to questioning about moral issues, are not always directly related to what people do.[94]

This book investigates forms of moral action empirically by examining how preadolescent girls (primarily children between the ages of 10 and 12) build their social organization and craft their local and social identities in the midst of everyday interaction on the playground. Language in interaction provides the principal means for them to articulate *for each other* what they are doing, how they expect others to participate in the activity of the moment, and how persons in their peer group are positioned and ranked vis-à-vis one another. Much of the activity of crafting social positions takes place through processes of description, storytelling, assessment (short descriptions in which evaluative commentaries occur), and argumentation.

By understanding routine forms of conflict (examined in chapters 2–3) we can put in perspective forms of aggressive interaction (examined in chapter 8) that occur when peers interact with more marginal members of the group.[95] Understanding how children who are friends conduct arguments is critical for understanding one of the most pressing issues of our time: how children create relationships implying "imbalances of power"[96] and participate in bullying. As argued by Juvonen and Graham (2004), in order to provide school-based interventions on bullying we need to first understand what conflict between friends looks like. Close ethnographic description of how children interact with other children affords an important way of understanding the role of conflict in children's social worlds.

Social practice in ethnographic studies of children's peer groups

The study of children's peer groups has been sadly neglected by anthropologists, despite the fact that as early as 1923 anthropologist Bronislaw Malinowski, in his call for the study of language as "a mode of social action," directed explicit attention to the importance of studying children's peer groups:

> In many communities we find that the child passes through a period of almost complete detachment from home, running around, playing about, and engaging in early activities with his playmates and contemporaries. In such activities strict teaching in tribal law is enforced more directly and poignantly than in the parental home. (Malinowski 1959:283)

Margaret Mead (1933:1, 15) likewise argued that anthropologists should expand the "questions all good ethnographers ask" to include children in their studies. Early on Mead noted that while there were studies of parent (in particular mother–child) interaction, there were few studies of peer group interaction, though Mead noted that "children's allegiances" and "child behavior" were as patterned as adult interaction.[97] Despite both Malinowski and Mead's early pleas for the documentation of children's lifeworlds, only lately have anthropologists taken as their mission the study of the linguistic, cultural, and social life of children – children as subjects, as actors and creators of culture.[98] As noted by Scheper-Hughes and Sargent (1998a:13) "children's voices are conspicuously absent in most ethnographic writing:"[99]

By and large, children appear in ethnographic texts the way cattle make their appearance in Evans-Pritchard's classic, *The Nuer* – as forming an essential backdrop to everyday life, but mute and unable to teach us anything significant about society and culture.

Because traditional social science views the child's world as a defective version of the more important adult world into which she will eventually be socialized,[100] studies of children's lifeworlds have been largely neglected in anthropology. Partly because of the legacy of psychological anthropology with its links to Parsonian[101] functionalist sociology, socialization within anthropology is treated as a fundamentally *psychological* rather than a social process. Children are believed to gradually *internalize* adult values, and are seen as in need of "integration into the social world."[102] The child, as an "object of social processes"[103] is defined by what she is subsequently *going to be* rather than what she presently *is*.

As James et al. (1998:94) put it, "traditional socialization theory, based as it was on social psychological models of child development . . . assumed a unidirectional flow of cultural information from competent adult to incompetent and passive child." By way of contrast, sociologist Barrie Thorne (1993:13) has argued, "children don't necessarily see themselves 'being socialized' or 'developing.'" Schwartzman (2001:28) has argued that children have been viewed as "'targets' of training – passive, imitative, conservative, and accepting of adult socialization practices" rather than as creators and interpreters of their social worlds, or capable of resisting adults. Recent analysis by Bucholtz (2002), stressing young people as cultural agents, views the anthropology of youth as concerned less with restrictive notions of culture and more actively involved with collections of ideologies and the practices through which culture is produced. In the traditional adult-centered socialization model adults were the active agents,[104] and there was little conceptual space for the possibility of child-to-child socialization. A radical paradigm shift would move children from the margins to the center of anthropological inquiry through detailed empirical studies of children displaying their social competence during the actual social moments of their lives.

One perspective considering childhood a stage in which children were active in the process of socializing each other, was taken by folklorists Iona and Peter Opie, editors of *The Lore and Language of School Children* (1959) and *Children's Games in Street and Playground* (1969). These researchers took seriously the child's ability to create culture and pass on songs, games, and lore from one generation to the next in a setting separated both spatially and conceptually from adults. As a result of the Opies' studies we have a rich archive of cultural forms produced by children for children; they studied over 5,000 children attending 70 primary, secondary modern, and grammar schools, in different parts of England, Scotland, and Wales (including one school in Dublin) in cities as well as rural districts. Their work includes not only riddles, rhymes, pranks, codes of oral legislation (by which they mean bets, bargain making, swapping, etc.), but also epithets, jeers, intimidations, tortures (for cry babies, cowards, sneaks, etc.), ways of getting even with a bully, and so on. While a feature with this work was that the Opies viewed the stage of childhood as timeless and labeled it "tradition's warmest friend,"[105] they elaborated specific practices, including sanctioning behavior, through which peers built their local social organization.

Within social anthropology Charlotte Hardman (1973:87) was among the first to argue that children are "people to be studied in their own right and not just as receptacles of adult teaching." Cultural anthropologist Bluebond-Langner's (1978) *Private Worlds of Dying Children* was ground-breaking for her presentation of children's agency: she argued that children are "willful, purposeful individuals capable of creating their own world as well as acting in the world others create for them" (1978:7).

Several important streams of research investigating the sociology of childhood, focusing explicitly on children interacting with other children rather than children interacting with adults, converged in the 1980s and 1990s.[106] James and Prout (1990:8) argue that out of multiple and convergent interdisciplinary concerns has come a new "emergent paradigm for the study of childhood."[107] According to James (1993:85) the paradigm "begins with a construction of the child as an active participating presence in the social world, rather than a mere passive spectator, and envisages children as having some part in determining the shape which their own lives take." While active agents in building and continuing culture, children are, however, both constrained and enabled by the structural contexts in which they find themselves (James et al. 1998:83). In order to examine how children reproduce culture these authors call for detailed analysis of children's social relations rather than their folklore.

In the process of investigating children interacting with other children anthropologists, linguists, and sociologists embracing an ethnographic approach have largely made use of participant observation and interviews to investigate children's social worlds. Researchers within the paradigm of the sociology of childhood call for an analysis of childhood as a discursive formation,[108] not unlike the social constructionist approach of discursive psychology.[109] Frequently, however, the procedures by which children organize and make sense of their activities in a given social context are not themselves analyzed.[110]

Recently a "competence paradigm"[111] has emerged within the disciplines of anthropology as well as sociology to account for children's agency in building social order. Within sociology William Corsaro,[112] working in Italian *scuola materna* settings as well as the United States, Donna Eder, focusing on working class Midwestern Euro American girls, and Barrie Thorne, studying working class multi-ethnic children's groups, were pioneers combining ethnography with recording naturally occurring interactions to examine how children establish friendships. In the past decade linguists,[113] researchers in education studies,[114] psychologists,[115] anthropologists,[116] as well as sociologists,[117] have also made use of video recordings of children at play to examine the moment-to-moment work entailed in the negotiation of peer relationships.

In this book ethnographic description is coupled with analysis of talk-in-interaction to explicate how children interact with peers. By examining recordings of children's naturally occurring interactions we can investigate how members of children's peer groups collaboratively construct their social worlds. In my own work, I have blended the methodologies of ethnographic description and analysis of talk-in-interaction in order to focus directly on children's own social practices and also give voice to the children I studied. The approach of conversation analysis differs from other methodologies based primarily on ethnography; rather than relying on interview data or observations carried out by the ethnographer, "conversation analysis stresses the importance of *recording* behavior in naturally occurring settings and basing analytic accounts on the observable details of participants' jointly constructed activities."[118] My approach seeks to understand the practices through which children organize and make sense out of their activities in specific contexts apart from the researcher's interaction with children.

My fieldwork among peer groups

Over the past 35 years the central groups among which I have conducted extensive fieldwork include (a) African American working class children (studied from 1970–71) in their Philadelphia neighborhood, (b) two different groups of second generation Spanish/English Central American and Mexican girls in downtown Los Angeles (studied in 1993 and 1998) on the playground and in the classroom, and (c) a group of children of mixed ethnicities and social classes in a progressive southern California school (studied in the late-1990s). In addition, for shorter periods of time I have investigated (d) playground interaction of children from an ESL (English as a Second Language) class in Columbia, South Carolina during the spring of 1996, and (e) African American children of migrant laborers during the summer of 1996 in rural South Carolina. Throughout the book I make reference to the first three principal groups (a–c) I have studied in my discussion of various language practices. However, the bulk of my analysis (chapters 3–8) draws from extended ethnographic research (three years) with the multi-ethnic group of girls in Southern California. The elementary school where I conducted extended fieldwork, which I call Hanley School, is a school that has roots in the progressive moment. It draws children from various parts of the city, though the children studied here are primarily middle class.

I observed a number of different third through sixth grade children's groups at recess and in class, in all over 30 children. For one month I observed without filming. During my second month of fieldwork I filmed a range of different third to sixth grade groups. During my third month of fieldwork, I started paying more attention to a particular group of fourth graders, a group that seemed to be quite cohesive and involved in multiple types of activities. In order to understand the ebb and flow of children's activities in some depth, to grasp how talk at one point of time influenced subsequent social processes, I focused on a core group of six girls of mixed ethnicities and classmates who interacted with them. These girls regularly ate lunch and played together. I observed the group over a three-year period as they passed from fourth to sixth grade, videotaping and audiotaping their interaction with one another; over 80 hours of videotape and 20 hours of audiotape form the corpus of the study. Because I studied children over a three-year period, I was able to observe language practices over time, as well as investigate how the composition of group members or the activity under way influenced language usage. The composition of the group was somewhat fluid, depending on who was available for lunch on any particular day. Most of the girls had attended the school since kindergarten, and were considered the most popular girls at the school. During the fourth grade members of the group included three Asian American middle class girls, two Euro American girls, one middle class and one working class, and an African American middle class girl. While it is possible to specify the ethnicity of the children, this feature of the girls' identity was seldom oriented to by them as a relevant feature within social interaction.

Jill Kushner Bishop, Carleen Curley Velez, Tracey Lovejoy, Sarah Meacham, and Fazila Bhimji assisted me in the field. One of these researchers and I were in the field at any particular time. We traded off positions of filming with the video camera and holding a highly directional microphone mounted on a pole and placed often over the heads of the girls. Essential to my project of investigating how embodied talk is used to organize peer interaction was obtaining excellent sound, which the carefully placed shutgun microphone provided.[119] Critical to my use of videotape was the notion that my focus was on situated forms of activity[120] as a unit of analysis; more specifically, my concern is with understanding the structure of participation[121] in peer interaction. C. Goodwin (in press, (a)) has defined participation as "a temporally unfolding process through which separate parties demonstrate to each other their ongoing understanding of the events they are engaged in by building actions that contribute to the further progression of these very same events." I wanted to investigate how language, as well as a range of semiotic modalities[122] through which children constructed meaning – including gesture, gaze, posture, clothing, are made relevant in the midst of the ordinary events that constitute the lifeworlds of the girls.

Children's visions of the ethnographers

Generally participants did not orient their talk to the camera. However, when taboo subjects would be brought up, the girls would be sensitive about the process of videotaping and the presence of the microphone. When girls were talking about *Girls' Life* magazines dealing with body "changes" in adolescence, one of the girls (Angela) felt this was something that the girls should be guarded about (though her apprehension was not shared by any of the others in the group). When swear words were used, girls would put their hands over their mouth or touch the microphone. Attention to the microphone occurred when Lisa reported to another girl "She called me a *fuck*in' *les*bian." When the unusual word "snickerdoodles" was used in the midst of lunchtime, Aretha glanced upwards towards the mike and repeated "snickerdoodles." When the girls were singing "The Bedroom Song"[123] they changed the lyrics so that "on the playground" replaced "in the bedroom." At other points, however, the girls acted as if they were unconcerned about more private aspects of their lives, such as their relations with boys, being captured on videotape. Commentaries such as the following occurred, for example, in the midst of singing a popular song "Torn" by Natalie Imbruglia with the lyrics "Lying naked on the floor":

Example 1.6

Girls:	*((singing))* Lying naked on the floor
	This is how it changed // into something real.
Angela:	Excuse me, but we're getting video // taped.
Aretha:	So what Angela, (0.4)
	We talked about boys in front of them,
	(1.0)
	At least *I* did,

In the following Janis reports to her volleyball team mates what a sixth grader had said about the fact that the girls were being videotaped while playing volleyball:

Example 1.7

Janis:	The girl said- She goes- "We're on TV."
	It's like- "Well that's what they want to know.
	What we do all day. That's what we do all day."
	That's what I was thinking in my head.

The camera was always visible to the girls. In the midst of a he-said-she-said in which the older sixth grade girls were saying that the fourth graders had been talking about one of their classmates behind her back, fourth grade girls in the clique provided their version of our activity:

Example 1.8

Janis:	Angela we're not trying to be mean to you.
	We're just trying to get back at Dionne.= okay?
	'Cause I *know* you told her.
6th grader:	There's a microphone on you guys.
Janis:	Wow.
Aretha:	We know that already.
	We said that it was okay to follow us.
	To videotape us.
	Because they wanna know what girls do during the week.
Janis:	We know you're talking about us. *((to 6th graders))*

At points the girls would attempt to enlist the ethnographers' help in telling off the older girls who often tried to insult them. Once at lunch Janis asked the ethnographers the meaning of "half wit" because she wanted to insult Dionne, one of the sixth graders, by calling her a name.

Example 1.9

((*talking to the ethnographers*))

Janis: I want you to walk over there and say something really mean?
Um, if they walk over to us and say something really mean?
Will you guys say something mean back to them?
If they walk over to us and say something really mean
Will you say "You guys prove a lot saying mean things to little girls."
Say "We're videotaping **them** not **you**!"

In response our stance was that we were not going to be involved in any of the conversations between groups. We explained we were only there to film what was going on. I generally interacted little with the girls, preferring to remain neutral and record their activities without my disturbance. However, I was open to talking to them, as mentioned above, when they asked for a definition of a word (i.e., "half wit", which they wanted to use to insult Dionne). Talking with the girls was not disruptive when other activities such as competitions or ball games were not on the day's agenda. Talking with particular girls, however, on one occasion was interpreted as talking about other girls, and led to my being ostracized from a particular clique (the "Blondies"). It had been my intention to talk with children about their play after the play period was over, before entering the classroom after lunch break. However, I was not able to talk with children after the recess bell rang (when their naturally occurring activities would not be interrupted) because teachers wanted students to return promptly to class.

Plan of the Book

This book documents how language and embodied action (including the use of gesture, body position, facial expression) is central to the multi-dimensional lives of preadolescent girls. By examining some of the specific language practices used to build their social world apart from adults, my intent is to document, through the voices of the girls themselves, important features of their lives often ignored or overlooked by adults. I take as the important unit of analysis not the individual girl and her psychological traits or personality, but rather the situated activities (Goffman 1961) girls participate in with others and forms of social organization which emerge through interaction.

Making use of transcripts of video and audiotaped conversations, in chapter 2 I show that across a range of different ethnic and social class groups girls display an intense engagement in rule-governed behavior and the ability to argue positions within the structure of games. In the midst of children's games, such as hopscotch, jump rope (as well as dramatic play, discussed in chapter 3) disputes are common. I describe the major debates in current research in studies of children's peer groups related to issues of gender, language, and conflict. I investigate the shape of moves and embodied practices used to accomplish negotiation and take stances or alignments in such disputes. I look at how children across a range of different groups, including an ESL group that includes boys, orchestrate moves in the game of hopscotch. It is important to establish that disputes constitute taken-for-granted features of the social worlds of children in order to examine how aggressive actions differ in shape and in intent from everyday disputes with one's friends. While commonly viewed as simple turn-taking games lacking in complexity, and reflecting cooperative female language styles, on close inspection we find that hopscotch provides exemplars of highly litigious language practices which speak to girls' active involvement and engrossment in both rule-governed behavior and confrontational interaction.

In chapter 3 and the remaining chapters of the book I investigate how preadolescent girls in a same-sex friendship group at a progressive elementary school in Southern California (Hanley School) build their social organization through talk and delineate the boundaries of their group. The playground provides a site where children can be observed apart from adults. By observing a range of diverse third through sixth grade groups of boys as well as girls, and following a particular group of girls over a three-year period from fourth to sixth grade, I was able to investigate in detail the language practices that girls made use of to formulate in-group and out-group members, rank one another, and sanction those who violate the implicit norms of the clique. Chapter 3 introduces the particular children whose interactions I am most concerned with in this book. In addition I present descriptions that emerged from interviews with the children. I look at how girls view their friendships and social relations and how boys who regularly interact with the girls talk about the social roles in their peer group. I examine how members of the clique orchestrate relationships between in-group and out-group members of their cohort in the course of playing house, and how play roles reflect friendship roles.

Asymmetrical relationships of power in both mixed sex and all female groups are examined as well. I investigate how groups on the playground attempt to assert and negotiate dominance over other groups. While a particular group may lay claim to a designated space or activity, children have ways of resisting and even transforming their local social order. I examine the language resources through which such processes occur as (1) girls in a fifth grade group challenge the boys' right to dominate the soccer field and (2) when as fourth graders girls fend off a sixth grade girl who attempts to lay claim to the contents of the girls' lunch boxes. Ways in which older girls assert their power over younger girls are explored.

In chapter 4 I examine directives that are used to orchestrate activity in the midst of a game that was common to both boys and girls' groups in the Los Angeles progressive school, jump rope. By comparing directive use across same and cross-sex interaction I am able to investigate the role that gender and level of skill might play in how the activity is organized. I look at how the forms of action used by different gender groups can change over time as members of the group gain expertise in the activity.

Numerous researchers investigating the social organization of girls' groups have argued that girls spend more time talking than actually playing games. Talk at lunchtime provided an important spate of time during which girls had extended periods to evaluate persons and events in their talk. Stories provide opportunities for differentiated forms of participation to emerge; as in games, an egalitarian or more hierarchical form of social organization can emerge, given who has tacit rights to chain a next story to a prior one (and who remains silent). In chapter 5 I discuss ways in which girls constructed a world of value and played games of status in the midst of storytelling. I discuss procedures used by girls to index their access to activities and privileges of the upper middle class. Descriptions and stories alluding to features of upper middle class culture make relevant the participation of those who have access to such events. Sequences of comparisons and bragging provide ways that girls articulate how group members stand with respect to the chosen dimensions of contrast.

Within the play realm girls not only project and articulate their own views of female identity and social roles, but also subtly put girls who fail to understand the important symbols that define middle class consumer culture in their place. The activity of making assessments[124] is discussed in chapter 6. Assessments are evaluative commentary that occurs across a range of different speech activities, including descriptions, stories, and return and exchange sequences, providing lively contests in which divergent perspectives are presented. Girls position themselves with respect to others in the peer group (sometimes absent parties) and differentiate group members with respect to who has access to privileges of the upper middle class as well as who is tuned into a local culture of hipness. Children make use of the symbols of the larger culture to create distinctions between peers. By examining assessment sequences we can look at how the larger cultural context in which the girls live, Los Angeles, Hollywood, and a consumer-oriented lifestyle, impacts their local practices for establishing relative rank.

Processes of negatively evaluating the behavior of someone in the group can provide ways of sanctioning an offending party, and in addition the means of constituting someone as a deviant member of the group. While the popular media has lately produced a number of accounts of aggressive behavior of individual girls, primarily through narratives told to a psychologist, chapter 7 examines the embodied language utilized by members of a peer group to sanction and also to victimize peers. The ways that someone is greeted, ostracized from games, addressed with bald imperatives, or depicted as occupying a degraded status can construct marginality.

Chapter 8 elaborates the significance of the analysis in the book. This book has obvious relevance to readers concerned with what "social aggression" (behavior which intends to harm someone socially) or "moral development" looks like "on the ground" and "in the flesh." While the children I studied were preadolescent, in the same school children as young as four draw from their experiences in the family and knowledge of consumer culture to position those who they view as different as marginal (Johnson 2004). The everyday practices of exclusion that take place routinely on the playground are often opaque to teachers and others who could design programs based on ideas of social justice for change. By providing transcripts of the practices through which children construct difference, I intend to contribute to a greater awareness of forms of everyday gender and class-based social exclusion that victimize children. In addition, I explore and articulate new methodologies for investigating issues of peer victimization that psychologists have traditionally addressed through questionnaires and interviewing and that sociologists concerned with children's worlds have investigated largely through participant observation. Such an understanding can assist in contributing to programs for promoting social justice among children.

Appendix 1.1

Example 1.2

1	Male Aide:	***GIRLS!*** Go somewhere ***else***.
2		The boys are coming to play
3		and you took over their field.
4		That's not cool.
5	Girls:	***NO!!*** ((*raucous screaming for several seconds*))
6	( ):	Miss Harper ***said*** we could!
7		I think I'm gonna go and just tell Miss Harper.
8	Male Aide:	Is Miss Harper out here right now?
9		Hey! Be quiet!
10		Listen up girls. ***Lis***ten.
11		Can you guys listen? Can you guys listen?
12		***Lis***ten. Turn around and ***lis***ten.
13		When the boys are coming out here to play soccer
14		Okay? You have ***no*** right to kick them off the ***field***.
15		***Lis**TE:N!* (0.8) Oka::y?
16		I've seen it happen more than once?
17		It happened the other day?
18		I asked you not to come over here
19		And yet you guys ***still*** came over and ***kicked*** the boys ***off***.
20		You did it to***day***?
21		I didn't know about this whole Miss Harper thing.
22		So as far as ***I'm*** concerned,
23		you guys can go over ***there*** ((*pointing to jungle gym area*))
24		Or the boys can play ***with*** you.= okay?
25		The boys are ***al***ways here playing soccer.
26		You can go over there and play soccer?
27		They ***can't*** go on the black top.
28		You girls can go ***any***where.
29		And do what you're doing.
30		Am I ***right*** or am I wrong.
31	Melissa:	Why can't ***they*** go anywhere.

32	Male Aide:	They **can't** go anywhere.
33		They can't go onto the blacktop and play soccer.
34		Somebody's gonna fall and
35		⌈break their knee.
36	Sandra:	⌊Well that means ⌈we-
37	Kathy:	⌊Well **neith**er can **we!**

Example 1.4

1	Ron:	Who's on the team. You, you, you,
2		*((pointing to Aretha, Lisa, Angela))*
3	Aretha:	Emi and Melissa.
4	Ron:	⌈*((looking towards Angela, arm extended towards her))*
5	Lisa:	⌊She's **NOT**. *((referring to Angela))*
6	Ron:	I know. So get her- *((waves arm to side, in*
7		*a dismissive gesture))*
8	Lisa:	Angela go out. You're not **in** this.
9	Angela:	Yes I **am**.
10	Lisa:	**No** you're **not**.
11	Angela:	If **you** guys can be in it then I **can**.
12	Lisa:	No you're **not**.
13	Angela:	Well **I'm** not leaving the rope.
14	Malcolm:	Look. There's a jump rope right there!
15	Lisa:	We'll go tell on you then.
16	Angela:	**Tell!** *((stays in rope, moves hands outwardly))*
17	Lisa:	There's five people allowed in the rope.
18		and we're five people.
19	Angela:	**Tell**. I don't really care. **Tell**.
20	Malcolm:	Ed. He's not complaining about anything.
21		**You're** the only **stub**born one.
22	Lisa:	Reggie-
23	Lisa:	Well Reggie- *((calling the coach))*
24	Ron:	Next time you'll be in the competition.
25		Work on your jumping.
26	Angela:	I **know** how to jump.
27	Malcolm:	Look. It's wasting all our time.
28	Angela:	*((moves a bit out of way, as Aretha, Lisa, and Melissa*
29		*take position in the rope))*
30	Lisa:	Move Angela.
31	Malcolm:	If you're in the competition get in.
32	Angela:	I'm in.
33	Lisa:	No you're not.
34	Brian:	Then move! *((sweeping motion with rope he holds))*
35		It's a competition. Go get another rope.
36	Lisa:	Reggie!! *((calling the coach))*
37		*((runs towards Reggie))* I'm gonna go tell on her.
38	Sarah:	Angela you're not in the competition.
39	Angela:	*((walks away with hand in mouth))*

2

Multimodality, Conflict, and Rationality in Girls' Games

In the analysis of talk in interaction, agreement has become an ambiguous term. It is used to refer to processes that operate on quite different levels of organization. First and most basic, agreement about relevant practices is central to the production of joint collaborative action; building courses of action in concert with each other requires some shared understanding and agreement about the nature of the activities participants are engaged in, and what each other is doing. The importance of agreement on this level is well illustrated by Wooton's (1997) analysis of the mental and moral development of the young child as she learns to build her action with reference to shared understandings. In my own analysis of how children build sequences of opposition (Goodwin 1990), I have argued that cooperation is central to the building of argument.

Conversation analysts as well as feminist sociolinguists have discussed how a preference for agreement[1] in conversational interaction is closely related to practices entailed in face-saving.[2] Lerner (1996:304) argues that "matters of face, on the one hand, and preference organization in conversational interaction, on the other, are intimately connected." Mills (2003:203) notes, "women's linguistic behaviour is often characterized as being concerned with co-operation (more positively polite than men) and avoidance of conflict (more negatively polite than men)." Working to avoid overt disagreement is thus argued to be central to female interaction. Building on Brown and Levinson's work on politeness, Holmes (1995:6) argues that "women's utterances show evidence of concern for the feelings of the people they are talking to more often and more explicitly than men's do" and "women are much more likely than men to express positive politeness or friendliness in the way they use language" (Holmes 1995:86).

While face-saving and the avoidance of discord has been a major theme in research on female speech,[3] key work in contemporary social theory stresses the importance of the pursuit of conflict[4] for the organization of social life. Anthropologists argue that "interpersonal conflict, disagreements, and moral dilemmas are at the heart of social life" (White and Watson-Gegeo 1990:3). According to developmental psychologists Marilyn Shantz and William Hartup (1992:11) "the virtual 'dance' of discord and accord, of disaffirmation and affirmation . . . is critical to the comprehension of development":

No other single phenomenon plays as broad and significant a role in human development as conflict is thought to. Many different functions – cognition, social cognition, emotions, and social relations – are thought to be formed and/or transformed by conflict. (Shantz and Hartup 1992:2)[5]

Dispute for children provides a way for playing with language, asserting one's position, for displaying affective stance and, consequently, character, sanctioning violators, and rearranging the social order. Rizzo (1992) finds that through disputes children work out problems and learn what they could expect from each other in a friendship exchange relationship. Despite theoretical interest in conflict, we know little about the basic turn-by-turn features or the effects of conflict taking place among naturally occurring groups in an ethnographic context.

Findings from lab and ethnographic studies differ considerably regarding the nature of conflict. Eisenberg and Garvey (1981:150), studying children in lab settings, looked at "adversative episodes" among dyads. The dyads of children Eisenberg and Garvey studied ended arguments with resolutions, in part because this was part of the task in the experimental setting. Children observed in multiparty participant frameworks,[6] by way of contrast, display an orientation towards sustaining and promoting rather than dissipating dispute. Corsaro and Rizzo (1990) find that the start of a fight among US middle and upper middle class nursery school boys may serve to initiate friendship relationships rather than to thwart them. Indeed psychologists[7] have argued that conflict is constitutive of children's dealings with one another.

Another problem with lab studies is that we do not really know how forms of friendship studied under experimentally controlled conditions compare with friendships that develop under naturally occurring conditions, where competition could occur with friends or classmates. Rizzo (1992:94) argues, "Relational processes such as conflict are best studied via a historical analysis of naturally occurring, daily interactions among relationship partners." Adopting a similar stance Jean Briggs (1992:48) states that by assuming a "natural history" approach to understanding socialization (as opposed to a more experimental framework) one can see "how actively emotions, values, and attitudes, as well as behavior, are negotiated in the learning of them through question and answer, response and counter-response."

Dispute is an interactional accomplishment, and one of the most important loci for the development of friendships and peer relationships.[8] Neither an aberration nor something to be avoided at all costs, it is, rather, constitutive of children's dealings with one another,[9] establishes group cohesiveness,[10] and provides a primary way that activities are constituted. Despite such recognition of the importance of conflict in everyday life, and in particular among peers, most contemporary feminist scholarship has not only avoided analyzing conflicts between women, but actively promoted a view of women as essentially cooperative.[11]

In this chapter I explore the embodied linguistic resources children make use of on the playground to organize conflict in the midst of the game of hopscotch. I will initially examine the shape of arguments across a range of children's groups. In subsequent chapters I will examine the role of conflict in the activities of a particular group of children, a clique of elementary school girls (of various ethnicities), comparing conflict among friends and more aggressive interactions towards a girl constructed as a social misfit.

Problems with the Deficit View of Girls' Games

Girls' games have often been described as devoid of strategic forms of interaction and the negotiation of rules. As such, they are viewed as lacking the intellectual complexity and intricate division of labor characteristic of boys.[12] Much of the work on games is primarily based on verbal reports,[13] or hypothetical studies of conflict, rather than turn-by-turn close-up observations of how a game unfolds. Deficit views pervade the work of Piaget (1965:77) who argues that "the legal sense" is not as developed in girls as in boys:

> The most superficial observation is sufficient to show that in the main the legal sense is far less developed in little girls than in boys. We did not succeed in finding a single collective game played by girls in which there were as many rules and, above all, as fine and consistent an organization.

Building on Piaget's work, Kohlberg's (1976) sequence of moral development proposed that females were less concerned than males with abstract independent rules. Challenging Kohlberg, Gilligan (1987:22) argued that equating moral development with concern for justice based on rights and rules rather than a morality of care, which focuses on relationships and responsibility to others, reflects a male bias. While males search for abstract principles, females are concerned with particular situations, relationships and people. She argues that "one voice speaks of connection, not hurting, care, and response: and one speaks of equality, reciprocity, justice, and rights" (1988:8). Gilligan characterizes the two ethics as different ways of understanding the world that organize both thinking and feeling.[14]

Work such as *Meeting at the Crossroads* (Brown and Gilligan 1992), was produced because of a discomfort with "dichotomies such as women are powerless and men are powerful" (Brown 1994:385). However, Gilligan's argument that males and females speak from different moral perspectives is quite congruent with dualistic pictures of male and female behavior predominant in the sociology of Talcott Parsons (Parsons and Bales 1955), who viewed women as relational and men as instrumental and rational. In research on gender in sociology dualistic pictures of gendered activities appear in the work of Janet Lever (1978:472), who claims that, "the play activities of boys are more complex than those of girls, resulting in sex differences in the development of social skills potentially useful in childhood and later life." Lever (1978:479) argues, "because girls play cooperatively more than competitively, they have less experience with rules per se, so we should expect them to have a lesser consciousness of rules than boys."

There are at least three problems with this line of research pursued by Gilligan and Lever. First, Gilligan, arguing that females are deviant from the more reason-based male standard, presents a dualistic[15] deficit model – a view that girls lack the capacity to participate in the basic political and legal institutions that structure our society. Presenting women as caring not only romanticizes them (Broughton 1993); it also presents a stereotypic notion of difference that fits the needs of oppressive patriarchal societies (Blum et al. 1976). A second problem involves the nature of the data. Gilligan is often cited as being contrastive with Kohlberg because she makes use of "real life" rather than "hypothetical" dilemmas. However, she and her colleagues[16] are in fact quite similar to Kohlberg, in their reliance on interviews[17] rather than investigation of the actual scenes that make up the lived social worlds of girls and women. The 1992 study *Meeting at the Crossroads*, made use of a "Listener's Guide," an open-ended interview "designed to encourage people to take [the researchers] into their psychological world."[18] Despite the use of this more responsive interview protocol, as argued by Luria (1993:203), Gilligan's links to Kohlberg's methods does not give her "a sound basis for talking about people's behavior, only for analyzing what they say." Moreover, as pointed out by Davis (1994:359), the narratives in interviews are not analyzed as "situated discursive productions" or interactional accomplishments between the interviewer and interviewee." According to Davis (1994:360) this stems from a view of femininity as a psychological entity rather than a social construction.

A final problem with Gilligan's work is that there is a very strong class and ethnic bias in her work, in that her population is primarily middle class Caucasians.[19] In the 1992 study of girls at a private day school 20 percent of the girls were from working class families and 14 percent were girls of color (Brown and Gilligan 1992:5); most of the girls came from middle or upper middle class families. This focus on a particular social class contrasts with Brown's (1998) subsequent work on girls "raising their voices," which draws on work on poor and working class white girls from a rural community in Maine, and a middle and upper middle class community in a mid-sized Maine city, and her book on *girlfighting* (Brown 2003), that draws from interviews with girls who were diverse in terms of race, social class, area of the country, and from rural, urban, and suburban, as well as private and public schools.

The data I will present includes fourth and fifth graders from the following groups:

1   A peer group that includes primarily second generation Central American and Mexican bilingual Spanish/English speakers and three Asian girls (Chinese, Korean-Brazilian, Vietnamese) in a working class area of downtown Los Angeles (this was 1993 fieldwork I conducted alone and 1997–98 fieldwork conducted with Carleen Curley Velez and Jill Kushner Bishop).

2   An ESL class in Columbia, South Carolina which includes children from Saudi Arabia, Vietnam, China, Mexico, Puerto Rico, Korea, and Azerbaijan (1996).

3   Mexican and Puerto Rican children in an ESL class in Columbia, South
     Carolina (1996).
4   African American children of migrant farmworkers in rural South
     Carolina (Ridge Spring, South Carolina, 1994).
5   African American working class children in Philadelphia (1970–71).
6   A peer group that includes mixed social classes and ethnicities in a
     southern California elementary school (during the late 1990s).

In this chapter through the use of ethnographically based fieldwork I will
problematize the idea that girls display little concern with an ethic of justice.
I examine how children, across a range of different working class ethnic
groups, argue positions within the structure of games. We will see that girls
display an intense engagement in rule-governed behavior.

I begin the exploration of how the moves in the game of hopscotch and
jump rope are both constituted and debated by diverse children's groups to
illustrate the rational practices made use of in arguing positions within games.
Specifically, we will examine the multimodal practices that are made use of
to articulate a position, considering turn shape, prosody, body positioning,
and alignment. We will look at several all girls' groups as well as one
mixed-sex group (in an ESL class) playing hopscotch.

Constituting the Game of Hopscotch

Hopscotch provides a prototypical example of a girls' game. Generally its
rules are described in terms of a simple pattern of rotation, as one girl after
another tries to move her token and her body through a grid without
hitting a line. According to Lever (1978:479), games such as hopscotch and
jump rope are examples of eventless turn-taking games that "progress in
identical order from one situation to the next. Given the structure of these
games, disputes are not likely to occur." This view of hopscotch is seriously
flawed. First, in this model, rules are viewed as mechanical instructions. The
girls I observed treated rules as resources to be probed and played with and
actively competed for first place in a round of hopscotch, as they did in
other games and activities as well. Second, by focusing only on the actions
of the jumper, the model ignores the active work of other parties who act
as judges, checking to see if any fouls have been committed.

Hopscotch as a situated activity system

Games such as hopscotch, jump rope, Chinese jump rope (a jumping game
played with elastic bands or woven rubber bands), or four square constitute
different forms of *situated activity systems* in Goffman's (1961:96) sense: "a
somewhat closed, self-compensating, self-terminating circuit of interdependent

actions." Sacks (1995a:492) has argued that games provide "central environments" for learning about "interchangeability of personnel" (as compared to the stability of categories) as well as "activity-relevant positions." The category set of the game is not a set of personal names, but rather categories relevant to the activity at hand (Sacks 1995a:490). The local categories of jumper and judge are featured in hopscotch. Concerned with looking at games as activities, Garfinkel (1963:190) argued, "The basic rules of a game define the situation and normal events of play for persons who seek to act in compliance with them (a player)."[20]

Hopscotch entails the coordinated activity of movement of a player through the playing field and commentary on that player's performance during her turn. In the US game of hopscotch, a player systematically moves through a grid of squares drawn in chalk or painted on the sidewalk, street, or playground. (In other countries lines are drawn in the earth with a stick.) The marks on the grid construct a visible field of action, which orients those who know how to read it to the sequence of moves through space that must be traversed while playing the game. Though there are many different types of grids, the one painted on a cement schoolyard in downtown Los Angeles where I did fieldwork looked like that in Figure 2.1.

The rules for hopscotch provide participants with possible as well as recognizable actions to perform and constitute means for producing turns in the game. One person jumps at a time through the grid. The order is decided by calling out numbers. The jumper is expected to move from square to square, in the pattern displayed by the numbers in the diagram. (Frequently the numbers are not actually written in the squares.) The object of the game of hopscotch is to be the first player to advance her token, commonly a stone, a stick, or a beanbag, from the lowest to the highest square and back again. From behind the start line (below square one), a player tosses her beanbag into a square and jumps from one end of the grid and back again on one foot, without changing feet and without jumping on squares where beanbags lie. Violations to the game can be argued to occur when someone

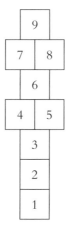

Figure 2.1   Hopscotch grid

steps on a line, steps in squares which are occupied by tokens, advances through the grid in the wrong sequential order, or moves inappropriately through space – changing feet, or walking or running rather than jumping – or hopping the wrong number of times or with the wrong number of feet (for example, hopping on one foot in the game cycle of "Two Feet"). Where there are two unoccupied squares next to each other, the jumper's feet should land in the two adjacent blocks. If a person falls down, steps on a line, or steps outside the appropriate square, she must forfeit her turn.

The shape of moves in hopscotch

Onlookers do not passively watch as someone takes her turn. Rather, hoping to detect mistakes, to call "outs," girls intensely scrutinize a jumper's body as she moves through socially inscribed space. The body, as well as the words spoken, are important in the performance of the *Out*-cry. A participant assuming the role of judge can color her critique of the jumper's move in various ways. In the next example as Marisol steps on two lines

Figure 2.2   Carla: PISASTE LA DE AQUÍ

while jumping, Carla cries "**OUT! OUT!**" This is followed by an account or justification[21] for her foul call "PISTATE LA DE A**QUÍ**, Y LA DE ACÁ." Carla justifies her *Out*-cry by running to the grid and using her own body to replay the activity just seen. In much the way that a speaker can report another's speech, the feet of the judge, Carla, both replay, and comment upon, the errors made by Marisol's feet.

Example 2.1

Marisol:	*((jumps and lands on some lines))*	**Problematic move**
Carla:	**OUT! OUT!**	**Out**! *((finger point))*
	((replays Marisol's move on grid))	
	PISASTE LA DE A**QUÍ**	**Explanation**
	You stepped on this one	
	((steps on square))	**Demonstration**
	Y LA DE AC**Á**.	
	and this one.	
	((steps on square))	

Judges not only state verbally their objections to a player's moves in the game. In addition, in conjunction with their talk, they may provide nonvocal accounts which consist of replaying past moves, to add further grounding

Figure 2.3   Carla: Y LA DE ACÁ

for their positions. In challenging the player Marisol's move, Carla animatedly provides a rendition of Marisol's past mistake. As she states that Marisol had stepped on "this one" (*la de aquí*) and "this one" (*la de acá*), Carla re-enacts Marisol's movement through space, challenging the player's prior move. The demonstration – involving a fully embodied gestural performance in an inscribed space – could not have been done without the grid, as it provides the relevant background – the necessary tool – for locating violations. Here the indexical term in the stream of the speech, the gesture and the grid, as a semiotic field in its own right, mutually elaborate each other.[22]

By examining a range of actions across several groups one finds that an orientation towards highlighting rather than mitigating opposition is clearly evident in each of the examples; the point of the game is to find someone in the wrong so that those on the sidelines get a turn. Multiple semiotic fields are entailed in the expression of children's adversarial talk during spontaneous play. These include oppositional markers (expressed through a range of different intonation contours), accounts or explanations, address terms, demonstrations, and body positions articulated on the game grid. In order to show how these are integrated in the construction of action, we will now examine the *Out*-cry in Carla's turn in more detail.

Displaying Stance in Opposition Turns

In constructing an *Out*-move the body as well as the words spoken are important in the performance of the *Out*-cry. A participant acting as judge can take up different types of footing, defined by Goffman (1981:128) as one's "stance, or posture or projected self." Turn shape as well as prosody and body positioning and turn shape are important to the construction of alternative types of alignments or stance; these are embodied displays of how one affectively positions herself with respect to ongoing interaction. In Example 2.1 the word "**OUT!**" is accompanied by a quite vivid embodied affective alignment as the finger of the judge points accusingly at the offender (while the player laughs at her own attempt to pull something over on the girl acting as judge). Figure 2.4 illustrates the accusatory point of the judge and the humorous stance of the player. The accusation can be found not only in her talk, but also visibly in the gesture she uses. In short, affect is lodged within embodied sequences of action. Moreover, the phenomena that provide organization for both affect and action are distributed through multiple media within a larger field of action.

Carla uses not only verbal means, but also posture and gesture, to accuse another girl, Marisol (at the left of the frame grab), of having landed on a line while making a jump in hopscotch. The way in which an *Out* is defined by embodied action occurring at a particular location in space provides organization for the body of the judge prior to the call. In order to assess the success or failure of the player's move she positions herself so that she can clearly see the player's feet landing on the grid. By virtue of such

Figure 2.4   Carla: OUT! OUT!

positioning Carla's talk is heard as an evaluation of Marisol's performance. A moment before the jump Carla has moved to just such a position. Indeed, the reason she is pointing with her accusing finger from a crouch is that she has bent down to look carefully at the place where the jumper will land.

Carla vividly displays heightened affect as she accuses her opponent of being *out*. Some of the organizational frameworks that make such emotion visible and relevant will be briefly described. First, Carla's action occurs in a particular sequential position: immediately after Marisol's jump, the precise place where an assessment of the success or failure of that jump is due. Second, Carla's evaluation is produced immediately, without any delay after the jump. Through such quick uptake, and the lack of doubt or mitigation in the call, there is an unambiguous assertion that a clear violation did in fact occur. Third, the two *Out*-calls are spoken with markedly raised pitch and extended vowels (Figure 2.5).

While the normal pitch of the girls is between 250 and 350 hertz, here Carla's voice leaps dramatically from 465 hertz to 678 hertz to 525 hertz over the first "*Out!*" and from to 630 hertz to 684 hertz to 585 hertz on the second "*Out!*" While 200 milliseconds is considered extended vowel length for adult speakers, the duration of the first vowel of "OUT" is 412 milliseconds, while the duration of the second is 296 milliseconds. The talk is produced with a LHL (low high low or rising–falling) contour. According to Sosa (1991:153), the LHL contour is common in "dialecto mexicano." Examining comparable 26-minute periods of games of hopscotch for working class Latina and African American girls (Goodwin et al. 2002), this contour

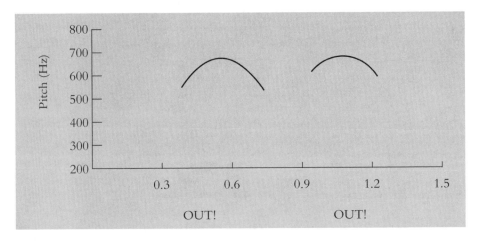

Figure 2.5   Out out pitch

was found to be distinctive to the Latina group, which included second generation Guatemalan, Salvadoran, and Mexican girls and different from that of a comparable group of working class African American girls, who produced much shallower contours. Across diverse groups we find variation in the ways of expressing affective stance.

The Shape of Opposition Moves in Game Disputes

With the previous example we find that children display a serious orientation towards forms of *aggravated correction* (Goodwin 1983a). When calling an out or a foul in the game of hopscotch – as might be expected in a game that requires locating someone as out in order to next take a turn, as in baseball when the umpire calls "Strike!" – opposition occurs immediately, positioning the affective stance at the earliest possible place with respect to the prior turn. Among the Spanish/English speaking bilingual girls I observed in downtown Los Angeles in 1993, an initial **expression of polarity**, such as "*No!*", or a **response cry** (Goffman 1978), such as "*Ay!*", is frequently followed by an emotionally charged **pejorative categorization** or **negative person descriptor** targeting the party who committed the offense, for example, *Chiriona* ("cheater").

Example 2.2

Gloria:	*((jumps from square two*	
	to one changing feet))	**Problematic move**
Carla:	**NO** CHIRIONA!	**Polarity expression +**
	No Cheater!	**Negative person descriptor**
	YA NO SE VALE ASÍ.	**Explanation**
	That way is no longer valid!	

Example 2.3

Gloria:	*((takes a turn out of turn))*	**Problematic move**
Carla:	*AY:* TÚ CHIRI*ON*A!	**Response cry +**
	Hey You Cheater!	**Negative person descriptor**
	EH NO PISES AQUÍ	**Explanation**
	Hey don't step here	
	PORQUE AQUÍ YO *VOY*!	
	Because I'm going here	

Example 2.4

Gloria:	*((Jumps from square 3 to 2*	
	changing feet))	**Problematic move**
Carla:	*EY::!* !CHIRI*ON*A!	**Response cry +**
	Hey! Cheater!	**Negative person descriptor**
	!*MI*RA!	
	Look!	
	TE VENISTES DE	**Explanation**
	You came from here	
	AQUÍ A*SÍ*::!	**Demonstration**
	like this. ((demonstrating how Gloria jumped changing feet))	

With these examples we see that the display of a form of affect is made relevant by the structure of practices for performing the *Out*-call – that is, within a specific sequential position in the midst of an activity: reacting to a violation. Emotion is conveyed through affective intensity[23] or highlighting,[24] as indicated through dramatic pitch excursions, vowel lengthening and raised volume. Unlike delayed disagreement observable in adult conversation,[25] the girls, through their intonation and gestures (such as extended finger points) display in a forceful, integrated manner that opposition is occurring, thus countering many of the stereotypical views of female language use.

For example, in Example 2.2 above, Carla begins her turn with a strong polarity marker "*NO*" followed immediately by a negative person descriptor "CHIRI*ON*A!" and then an explanation for why the move is illegal. Variants of this same pattern are found as well in Examples 2.3 and 2.4. Here the turns begin with response cries or exclamatory interjections, not full-fledged words, which take up a position with regard to a prior action: "*AY:*" and "*EY::!*"

With negative person descriptors referees argue not simply that an infraction has occurred, but that what the player is doing is something morally wrong. Girls use the term "chiriona"[26] meaning "cheater," derived from the English word "cheat" and "ona," a Spanish agentive nominalizer (or intensifier).

Cheat   + *ona*

English verb + Spanish agentive nominalizer

"Chiriona" (in Examples 2.2–2.4) provides an explicit characterization of the person who produced the move being opposed. The term "cheater" not only implies that a violation has occurred, but also implies that the target knows it and is trying to get away with it.[27] Note that the use of the pronoun "Tú" in Example 2.3 provides an additional way that the action is intensified, in that Spanish is a pro-drop language and subject pronouns are not required.[28] By using a term such as "chiriona," a judge argues only that an infraction has occurred, but that the person who committed the foul is accountable in a very strong way for its occurrence. Following the opposition preface, a referee further explicates why the move is invalid by providing a reason, often through a *demonstration*.[29] Here intonation and gestures (such as extended hand points) display in no uncertain or mitigated terms that opposition is occurring.

Negative person descriptors or categorizations such as "chiriona" (cheater) and "cheater" permit referees to argue not simply that an infraction has occurred, but that what the player is doing constitutes something morally wrong. Other address terms used by the Latina girls in this group are *"niña,"* *"niña burra,"* (silly girl), and *"zorilla"* (skunk). Among a group of Puerto Rican and Mexican second generation fifth graders I recorded in Columbia, South Carolina, address terms used while playing hopscotch included *"tramposa"* (cheater), *"embustera"* (liar), *"chapusera"* (big cheater), *"huevona"* (lazy), and *"cabrona"* (bitch). Address terms used by African American children in the rural south included "honey," "child," "woman," "fat hog," "quarter pound bacon," and first or last names of girls.

To summarize, in most argumentative moves the very first thing said, the turn preface, occupies a particularly important position. Retrospectively, it classifies the action being opposed, and prospectively it provides a guide for interpreting the position being stated in the accounts and embodied demonstrations to follow. Following the initial part of the turn an explanation for the call is given. Pejorative person descriptors provide additional ways in which opposition can be displayed.

Opposition Move Components across Groups

The range of opposition turn features we have examined, including markers of polarity, response cries, and *Out*-calls, will now be examined across various groups other than the bilingual Spanish/English speakers in downtown Los Angeles studied in 1993. Specifically, we will look at the organization of turn components as well as body positioning within these calls. We will see that very similar structures are used among diverse groups: (1) primarily fifth grade Spanish/English bilingual speakers from downtown Los Angeles (identified as S/E); (2) fifth grade African American migrant children in rural South Carolina (AA); (3) fifth grade children of diverse ethnicities in an ESL class in Columbia, South Carolina (ESL) – the ESL group included two Mexican boys and a Korean boy in addition to girls from Saudi Arabia, Vietnam, China, and Azerbaijan; (4) a fourth grade group of multicultural children in a progressive Los Angeles school (Mu); and (5) fifth grade

Puerto Rican and Mexican American girls in an ESL class in Columbia, South Carolina (PR/M). Among children in the ESL classroom, both boys and girls play hopscotch. Each example is marked with initials indicating the group speaking.

In each of the following opposition turns an explanation follows the initial turn preface of opposition. Many of the explanations are accompanied by embodied demonstrations. We will consider each of four different types of turn prefaces.

(1) **Out!-cries**, which can be produced with varying pitches and durations:

Example 2.5 (S/E)

Gloria:	*((hops with one foot outside grid, one foot on line))*
Carla:	Out.
Maria:	Out.
Gloria:	Ay::::!
Carla:	Pisistes la **ra**ya! *((hops where Gloria stepped))*
	(You stepped on the line.)

Example 2.6 (AA)

Lucianda:	*((jumps in a square two times*
	and then in a square occupied by a token))
Latifa:	You out. You **to**tally out.

Example 2.7 (ESL)

Nazrine:	*((moves to take her turn.*
	She walks to the side of the grid to throw her marker
	but it misses the square.))
Jaime:	Out out.
Ning:	Out. *((points with arm))*

An alternative to "Out" with the ESL group was the word "Ping" or "Bim"[30]:

Example 2.8 (ESL)

Ning:	*((At the far end of the grid she jumps around to start*
	jumping back from square 10.
	She touches a line as she turns around.))
Jaime:	Bim.
Nazrine:	Ping **Ping**. Ping **ping**.
	You go like **this**. *((demonstrates Ning's body position and*
	points towards her foot))
Ning:	Where.
Jaime:	Here. Here.
	((points foot next to Ning's foot responsible for the mistake))
Ning:	Where. Where. **NO**.
Nazrine:	**YES! YES!** *((hopping up and down))*
Jaime:	You out. You out. You out!

(2) Opposition signaled by an expression of **polarity** (Halliday and Hasan 1976:178) such as "No:"

Example 2.9 (S/E)

Marisol:	*((takes baby steps to throw to square 3,*
	a practice which is only permitted on 7 and above))
Carla:	**No** niña.

Example 2.10 (AA)

Lucianda:	*((steps twice in a square))*
Joy:	**No**. You stepped in number six there–
	two times. You said *((jumps two times, performing a*
	demonstration)).

Example 2.11 (ESL)

Joo-Soung:	*((hops on one foot as he picks up token, but puts one foot on*
	the line Then hops on two feet as he moves out of the grid))
	Yes! *((self congratulatory))*
Maja:	**NO!** *((positions body on the line where Joo-Soung was*
	And redoes the moves)) No. He does like this?
	((puts two feet on line))
	And he– *((jumps on two feet lifting one foot off the grid))*

Example 2.12 (Mu)

Emi:	*((takes a turn and lands on two feet where it's a one-*
	foot square))
Janis:	**No**. You landed two feet.
Melissa	You– you only can land on **one** foot.
	((demonstrates how the move should have been
	executed))
Emi:	Fine. Fine
	((she exits and takes it over from the top of grid))

(3) **Response cries** (Goffman 1978), nonlexicalized, discrete interjections such as (*Ah, Ay, Hey* and *Eh* among Latinas; *Oh, Uh,* and *Oo* among African Americans and ESL children:

Example 2.13 (S/E)

Gloria:	*((throws beanbag and it hits a line))*
Maria:	**Ah:** tocastes.
	Ah: You hit.

Example 2.14 (AA)

Lucianda:	*((steps on line))*
Latifa:	**Oh:** Lucianda. You step be**tween** the line.
	Not **in** it.

Example 2.15 (Mu)

Juan:	*((steps on the square with his stone))*.
Isabel:	⌈*Ah:*
Orna:	⌊*Ah::* You messed up.
	You stepped on this square. *((points with foot))*

Example 2.16 (ESL)

Jaime	*((steps on lines))*.
Ning:	Jaime did.
Joo–Soung:	**Oh**. You got ding.
	You do like **this**.
	And like **this**.
	Come like **this**.
	And **come** like this.
	((Joo-Soung demonstrates Jaime's mistakes
	by replaying stepping on lines of grid.))

(4) "I see," "Look!" and "Mira!" In addition to response cries and polarity markers (and combinations of these prefaces), expressions such as "I see" and directives such as "Mira!" (in Spanish) meaning "Look!" are used as opposition turn prefaces. Such actions summon players to witness the infraction that has occurred. In Example 2.17 Joo-Soung (who introduced the game to the ESL class at recess), jumps and lands on a line. Immediately Hien indicates that a violation has occurred through the use of the response cry "*Ah!*"+ a polarity marker "*Uh* uh" and an account: "I see. I see now" (lines 2–4). Hien uses both a finger point as she produces her opposition move and a foot point on the square where the mistake was made (line 6).

Example 2.17 (ESL)

1	Joo-Soung:	*((steps on a line))*
2	Hien:	***Ah!*** *((eyebrow flash, finger pointing))*
3		***Uh*** uh.
4		I see. I see now.
5	Jaime:	Yeah.
6	Hien:	I see. Right here. *((goes to square where Joo-Soung's*
		foot is on a line and points with foot))

While "Out", "No", or a response cry constitute perhaps the most prototypical and frequent types of opposition prefaces for children who are familiar with the game, among girls who are newcomers to the United States or newcomers to the game, other types of calls are used. The following provides an illustration of combinations of such forms. Response cries such as "Ah:" are followed by polarity markers "**No!**" and subsequently by an expression using "See" ("Mira!" in Spanish) among Spanish/English bilinguals in downtown Los Angeles:

Example 2.18 (S/E)
  Gloria: *((steps on a line))*
  Maria: Ah: **No!** Le hiciste así. Mira! Yo te **ví**. **No**.
          Ah no. You did it like this. Look! I saw you. No!

Among a group of ESL students in Columbia, South Carolina, Mexican American and Puerto Rican girls aged 10–11 (girls who had only been in the US for a little more than two months) Spanish was used extensively when playing hopscotch in their peer group. Rather than saying "Out!" the term "Mira!" (Look!) was used to indicate a violation. This was followed by an account accompanied by pointing to the problematic move.

Example 2.19 (M/PR)
  Priscilla: *((when she jumps she lands on a line))*
  Roxabel: **Mir**a! TO**Có** línea. *((pointing))*
          Look! She touched the line.
          Tocaste allí.= Moviste el pie.
          You touched there. You moved your foot.
          ((touches the line pointing))

Among the Mexican and Puerto Rican girls the expression, "*Mira!*" is used quite frequently, for example, in "*Mira. Pues mira. Fíjate*" (Look. Look. Well look. Imagine). "*Mira!*" can also occur with other components: "*Out!*" and accounts of the violation, as in "*Mira. Out. Mira. Vés, ya pisastes aquí*" (Look. Out. Look. See you already stepped here) or "*Mira. Mira. Si ahorita lo acabes de pisar allí en el mío*" (Look. Look. Right now you just stepped there in mine), or "*Mira. Mira. Mira. Mira. Te la mandaste a la raya blanca*" (Look. Look. Look. Look. You sent it to the white line); "*Ay chiriona. Mira tú lo pusistes aquí!*" (Aye cheater. Look you put it here.); "*No. Mírate!*" (No Look!); "*Mira. Out. Mira. Vés ya pisas aquí*" (Look, Out. Look. You see you already have stepped here. *You touched here. You moved your foot).* Finally, among African American girls the preface "See?" was also used, as in "See there. *((pointing))* See didn't you see it? Look over here" or "See that?" followed by an account: "You had both foots in the box! Get out of there!" "Mira!" and "See?", as forms of multimodal action, explicitly invoke looking at a particular configuration of the body and the grid to locate the violation. The turns initiated with "Mira" or "Look" call attention to the activity of making publicly available to others a witnessing of an infraction that has occurred.

The Course of a Multimodal *Out*-cry

The course of an *Out*-cry is not static, but instead something that happens through time. The following example demonstrates how players make use of multiple modalities to build their counter moves. In these data we first see a successful jump – a player leaping over squares already occupied with tokens and landing inside a square, not touching any lines. The player herself marks the successful execution of a difficult move with a bow and her statement "I made it!" (line 1). What follows in the continuation of her turn is an unsuccessful jump (line 3).

Example 2.20 (S/E)

		((Sylvia executes a difficult move and does a bow when she completes it successfully. She is in the midst of a sequence in which she must jump on two feet. When she jumps on one foot rather than two feet she is called "out."))
1	Sylvia:	I made it! *((bows))*
2	Ariana:	Dale.
		Go.
3	Sylvia:	*((jumps on one foot rather than two.))*
4	Ariana:	'stás out.
		You're out.
5	Thelma:	**OU:: [T.** *((clapping))*
6	Ariana:	**[OUT!**
7	Sylvia:	*((positions herself facing Ariana))*
8	Thelma:	[*((shows two fingers))*
9	Ariana:	[Two two! *((demos how the move should have been done jumping with two feet rather than one foot))*
10	Sylvia:	[**Ay:: Agai::n.**
11	Jun:	[*((hops on two feet))*

In the midst of a pattern ("*two feet*") in which all the moves must be executed jumping on both feet, the jumper hops on one foot rather than two. As soon as the jumper begins hopping on one foot, a spectator produces an *Out*-call: "'stás out" (line 4). The *Out*-call is a process that happens through time. Here the jumper continues moving through the grid when the initial *Out*-call occurs. In response a second *Out*-call – "**OUT!**" is made by two players, yelled, with increased volume and heightened pitch, challenging the jumper (lines 5 and 6).

While the first "Out" notes that something inappropriate has occurred, the second, with its increased volume, marks that the player continues after she has failed. When the jumper turns around and is positioned to see the girl who issued the initial out call, different modalities are used to mark the out: a nonvocal gesture indicating "two" (Thelma's holding up two fingers in line 8), and a demonstration of what the appropriate move should have looked like (jumping on the grid two times while saying "Two two"). Subsequently the player accepts the *Out*-call (with its warrant) and moves back to the front of the grid.

We see from this example the ways in which the *Out*-call is a product of an interaction between speaker and recipient, player and judge. The player may comment on her performance with a positive assessment midway through her move (with a bow and statement "I made it!"), and this can be affirmed with a judge saying "Go", indicating her turn may proceed, in the absence of mistakes. However, as soon as a problem occurs judges will vocally call the player on her move (with *Out*-calls in keeping with the severity of various moves.) After a mistake is made, only when player and judge are situated within a common facing formation (when jumper turns so that she is positioned vis-à-vis those acting as referees) judges demonstrate through nonvocal accounts their reasons for their calls that the jumper is out.

Public Witnessing: The Grid as a Public Assessment Space and Pointing as Situated Practice

The examples we have examined in brief demonstrate that the activity system of the game creates an assessment space where the moves of a player can be evaluated. Throughout all of these examples, a particular social organization of attention is required to construct a point of common focus. Players evaluating performances attend not only to a particular place (a geographic space), the game grid, but also monitor for particular types of events that are supposed to occur in that place (a form of conceptual space). The game with its oriented-to grid makes possible the forms of action and local identities that constitute the game; for example, throwing one's token or stepping on or outside a line counts as a consequential event, an "out" in which the player loses her turn. The situated activity system provides both a place to look and a particular category of event to look for.

By remaining in a frozen position a player collaborates in making her move available so that others can examine and scrutinize it. In the following (Example 2.21) the jumper lands on a line. The jumper and the other girls gathered closely around her create a forum for the public witnessing of her body as it is linked to a particular field of action, the grid (Figure 2.6). In providing a justification for their *Out*-calls, two girls quote the past action of the jumper, mimicking her movement into her current position:

    11   Ariana: Si pero le hicistes así?=pero
                   No but you went like this? but
    12   Donna: Uh **huh**. You did'it'l–
    14   Ariana: Cuando le hicistes así?
                   When you went like this?

In addition to the *Out*-calls, an action designating, or locating, through pointing, occurs. Ariana states (lines 23–24), "Ví como es. Ira. Ves? Si pisa" (*I saw how it is. Look. You see? It really is touching*) and points to the spot where jumper Sylvia's foot is supposedly touching (Figure 2.7).

Several players, including the jumper, ratify the event of the foot touching the line of the grid as constituting an "out." Agreeing with the *Out*-cry, the jumper moves back to the start of the grid. The following provides the complete transcript:

Figure 2.6 The grid as a public assessment space

Figure 2.7 Point to feet on the line (line 24 of Example 2.21)

Example 2.21

((Sylvia has just completed jumping through the entire grid successfully, jumping over many squares occupied with tokens. She is starting her second turn))

1	Sylvia:	Yeah! *((congratulating herself))*
2	Ariana:	Ay: Mona:::::
		Hey Cutie ((sarcastically complimenting))
3	Thelma:	Sigo. Sigo.
		I'm next, I'm next.
4	Th:/D:	Out. Out.
5	Jun:	Out.
6	Ariana:	*((runs to see how Sylvia is positioned on the grid))*
7	Ariana:	A ver cuando le hicistes asi?
		Let's see, when did you did it like this?
8	Sylvia:	⌈Looky.
9	Donna:	⌊Yeah girl.
10	Sylvia:	⌈I'm on the end.
11	Ariana:	⌊Si pero le hicistes // así?=pero
		No but you went like this. But
12		*((she gets down on the ground and does demo of hitting hands on the lines))*
13	Donna:	Uh **huh**. You did'it'l-
		((she gets down on the ground and does demo of hitting hands on the lines))
14	Ariana:	Cuando le // hicistes a**sí**?
		When you went like this ((putting both hands on the grid))
15	Jun:	It's out! // It's out! *((kneeling))*
16	Ariana:	Así.
17	Ariana:	⌈It's still out.
18	Thelma:	⌊Woo::oo::.
19	Ariana:	⌈It's **out**.
20	Thelma	⌊It's **out**.
21	Donna:	⌈**Out**.
22	Sylvia:	⌊Now look. *((continuing in her crouched position))*
23	Ariana:	Ví como es.
		I saw how it is.
24	Ariana:	Ira. Ves? Sí pisa. *((pointing))*
		Look. You see? It really is touching.
25	Ariana:	⌈It's out.
26	Jun:	⌊See?
27		Look. It's out.
28	Sylvia:	*((moves to home position on the grid))*

The way in which public witnessing of and calling of "Outs" occurs is remarkably similar across groups of children playing hopscotch. The game of hopscotch, as a form of situated activity with a set of game identities, makes relevant a series of moves by a player and responses to those moves by those acting as judges. Consider the following ways in which fifth grade immigrant children in an ESL fifth grade class three thousand miles away

Figure 2.8   Pointing to feet on line

in Columbia, South Carolina locate outs. In the next set of examples the children are (1) Puerto Rican and Mexican Spanish-dominant children in an ESL class, (2) a Vietnamese girl calling a Korean boy out, (3) a Korean boy calling a Saudi girl out.

In the following as Priscilla lands on a line, Roxabel yells "**Mi**ra! TO**Có** línea" (*Look! She hit a line*) while pointing to the line near Priscilla's feet (Figure 2.8).

Example 2.22 (M/PR)

Roxabel:	Mira! TOCó línea. *((pointing))*
	Look! She touched the line.
	Tocaste allí.= Moviste el pie.
	((touches the line pointing))
	You touched here. You moved your foot.
Priscilla:	No porque te pusiste-
	Because you put-
	Ira otra línea acá.
	Look another line here.
	⌈Ella ( )
Roxabel:	⌊Sí pero tocó esa parte aquí.
	Yes but she touched this part here.

Esa es la misma.
That's the same.
Mira lo obscuro.
Look at the dark.
Embustera. Síguele, síguele
Liar. Go on. Go on.

In the next example Hien calls Jaime out. She prefaces her turn with "Ah!" and an eyebrow flash, while pointing with her finger (Figure 2.9).

Example 2.23 (ESL)

1	Hien:	**Ah!** *((eyebrow flash, finger pointing))*
2		Uh **uh**.
3		I see. I see now.
4	Jaime:	Yeah.
5	Hien:	I see. Right here. *((pointing with foot))*
6	Joo-Soung:	Go. (0.6) Cheating!
7	Hien:	**I'm** not **cheat**ing! *((falsetto))*

Figure 2.9   Pointing to feet

Through her utterance "I see. I see now," Hien indicates how she has knowledge of the mistake by making reference to her seeing the move. Though she does not provide a complete sentence explaining the mistake that was made, the meaning of her utterance is clear. She provides a

Figure 2.10   Foot point

response cry immediately upon the execution of the problematic move, and follows it with a polarity marker "*Uh* uh." She then uses a deictic tapping with her foot as she states, "I see. Right here," in order to indicate the problematic move her explanation is referencing (Figure 2.10). The grid is used as a template against which mistakes can be noted.[31] In fact, in many of the explanations discussed here, judges explicitly point to marks on the pavement, or to feet over lines, as Examples 2.19–2.24 demonstrate.

Boys and girls in the mixed gender ESL group make use of remarkably similar moves. Joo-Soung, a Korean boy, introduced his version of the game to the group. In a third example of the use of pointing a Mexican boy checks the feet of a Saudi girl, Maja, to see if her feet are on the line, after shouting "Bim" to mark an "out" (Figure 2.11).

Example 2.24 (ESL)

1	Maha:	*((jumps and turns around at end of grid))*
2	Jaime:	BIM BIM! Bim bim bim *((singing, calling out))*
3	Maha:	Why. *((not moving))*

Figure 2.11   Pointing to feet

4	Joo-Soung:	Let me see it. *((goes to inspect))*
5	Nazrine:	*((nods head))*
6	Joo-Soung:	Let me. Don't move.
7		*((positions himself low, points))*
8		No. *((indicating she is not on the line))*
9	Jaime:	⌈No.
10	Ning:	⌊No.
11	Maha:	°Lemme see. *((preparing to resume jumping))*

Pointing,[32] a semiotic resource indexing a particular event, constitutes an important feature of marking an out. It indexes the responsible feet and the place on the grid where the "out" occurred. Ervin-Tripp (1986) has argued that for second language learners the situated use of language and activity structure in games makes it possible for children with limited language skills to participate. As she notes, "They use their activity knowledge as though there were no language barrier" (Ervin-Tripp 1986:354).[33] While lacking the ability to produce complete sentences, through various types of opposition turn prefaces, including forms of "out" (such as "Bim"), response cries such as "Ah", calls to attention such as "Mira!" and terms of polarity English language learners can mark opposition to a prior turn. In addition, they make use of quotative deictic terms such as "like this," "right here," and pointing (with hands and feet) to places on the grid in order to mark inappropriate moves of the prior speaker. Note that in the examples presented here there is little gender difference in the way that moves are executed.

Demonstrations

Players not only point to jumpers and spaces when they call outs, but they also provide demonstrations of appropriate and inappropriate moves. Because the grid is available in a permanent form, it makes possible the replaying of past actions as in instant replays in sports. We will examine more extended forms of disputes among a range of different groups in order to see the similarity in practices of disputes across diverse groups.

Demonstrations among Latina players

In the next example (2.25) we see the jumper returning to home position jumping from the far end of the grid, from square nine to seven rather than eight. When she is called "out" and asks "why" she is told her move was "backwards." In response she points to the squares on the grid and argues that the numbers go in a particular order (as she indicates four and five on the grid). The first out-caller, also pointing, argues that precisely because the squares are sequentially ordered she has done the move inappropriately: "You have to do it *back*wards." A second out-caller adds, "Because you're going backwards." and provides an in-place demonstration of the inappropriate move. Next, the first out-caller provides a second demonstration, this time on the grid. She replays the jumper's past inappropriate move (jumping from nine to seven) and then provides the move that should have been executed (jumping from nine to eight): "You come from here − right here. Es pa'acá par' allá" (*It's from here to there*).

Example 2.25

1	Ariana:	((*jumps from square nine to square seven*))
2	Sylvia:	Out.
3	Ariana:	Porqué.
		Why.
4	Sylvia:	It's backwards. ((*points to squares nine and seven on grid*))
5	Ariana:	No ese es four- cuatro, cinco, ((*points to four and five*))
		No that one's four − four, five
6	Sylvia:	I know. That's why.
7	Ariana:	Por eso. // Pise allá lo hi-
		That's why. I stepped over there.
		I did it.
8	Jun:	You have to do it backwards ((*demos jumping*))
9	Donna:	⌈°English
10	Sylvia:	⌊Yeah but you have to do it *back*wards.
11	Jun:	⌈Because you're *go*ing backwards.
12	Sylvia:	⌊You come from here − right here.
		((*demos the way Ariana did it, jumping from seven to eight*))

13	Sylvia:	Es pa'acá par' all**á**.
		It's from here to there. ((jumping from eight to seven))
14	Ariana:	Entonces pues.
		Oh well then.
15	Thelma:	⌈Backwards.
16	Sylvia:	⌊Now.
17	Sylvia:	Here. *((handing token to Ariana))*
18	Ariana:	Thank you.

Much like reported speech, players can replay and reconstruct a jumper's actions through *demonstrations*. This occurred in lines 12–13, where Sylvia demonstrated the way that Ariana jumped inappropriately from square seven to eight, rather than eight to seven, as she provided an account: "You have to do it **back**wards" (line 10).

An even more dramatic recasting of the jumping event occurs in the next example (Spanish-dominant speakers in South Carolina). When a player turns around in place rather than jumping, an onlooker yells "Ah. Per**dió**" ("*You lost*") and points to the player. In the next part of her turn the player calling out replays the jumper's activity – walking rather than jumping through the grid – providing a meta-pragmatic commentary using truncated rather than fluid movements.

Example 2.26 (M/PR)

1	Roxabel:	*((turns around on grid by walking rather than jumping))*
2	Viviana:	Ah. Per**dió**. *((pointing at player))*
		Ah. She lost.
3	Roxana:	Ah ah *((pointing at player))*
4	Roxabel:	Ah ah
5	Viviana:	Estaba así,
		She was like this
6		Estaba así,
		She was like this
7		Y luego le hizo. *((exaggerated demo of walking in grid))*
		And then she went ((exaggerated walking in grid))
8	Viviana:	⌈Así le **hi**zo!
		⌊*That's how she did it!*
9	Roxabel:	⌊Ah ah Embustera.
		Ah ah ah ah big liar.
10		Yo no le hice así.
		I didn't do it like that.
11	Viviana:	Oh **sí**. Oh **sí**.
		Oh yes. Oh yes.

An important feature of this turn is the categorization that is used: "embustera." As a form of retort to an accusation a participant charged with having committed a foul may counter-accuse her accuser by calling her a liar or cheater as Joo-Soung does in Example 2.23 after a foul was called on him: "Go. (0.6) Cheating!"

Demonstrations: An African American example

Working class African American girls, children of migrant workers in the rural South, make use of many of the same practices for highlighting opposition and building explanations. The following provides an example:

Example 2.27 (AA)

1	Lucianda:	((takes turn jumping twice in square two and possibly putting her foot on the line of square one))
2	Joy:	You out.
3	Lucianda:	⌈No I'm **not**. ((shaking head no))
4	Joy:	⌊You hit the line.
5	Crystal:	**Yes** you did.
6		⌈You hit the line. ((with hand pointing at line))
7	Joy:	⌊You hit the line.
8	Lucianda:	I **AIN'T** HIT NO LI:NE! ((leaning towards Crystal))
9	Alisha:	**Yes** you did.
10	Crystal:	((smiling, shaking head, goes to the spot)) °You did. You s-
11	Lucianda:	**No** I didn't.
12	Alisha:	Yes you did.
13	Crystal:	Didn't she go like this.
14	Lucianda:	((does a challenge hit towards Alisha))
15	Alisha:	You hit me.
16	Crystal:	You did like this ((stepping on the line as she replays the jump))
17	Lucianda:	Shut up with your old fashioned clothes. ((to Alisha))
18	Crystal:	You did like that.
19	Joy:	Yeah you hit that line right there honey. ((as she goes up and uses her foot to index it, tapping it twice.))
20	Lucianda:	((throws the rock and it lands outside))
21		My feet.
22	Latifa:	Y- you out **now!**

In this game of hopscotch referees state unequivocally "You out" (line 2), followed by an explanation ("You hit the line") (lines 4, 6, 7). As in oppositional sequences in the talk of African-American working class girls in Philadelphia (Goodwin 1990:1469), here polarity markers such as "No" (line 3, 11) and "Yes" (lines 5, 9, 12) preface opposition moves. The foul call – "You hit the line" – is emphatically opposed by the player with "I **AIN'T** HIT NO LINE!" (line 8). The low rise is a distinctively African American final contour (Figure 2.12).[34]

The pitch on Lucianda's negative, "*AIN'T*" reaches a dramatic 780 hertz. Her denial ends in a low rise over the word "line." The final vowel goes from 450 hertz to 552 hertz and lasts 960 milliseconds, so that even the low end of the utterance is well above her normal pitch range. In addition, her expression of righteous indignation at having been called out is accompanied by a strong body stance – a challenge position in which the player extends

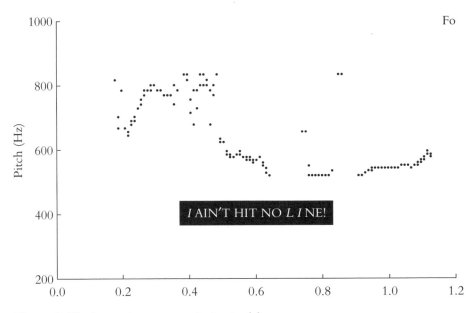

Figure 2.12   Intonation contour in Lucianda's turn

her chest towards one of the judges (line 8). While in the other examples in this chapter the onlookers accuse the jumper, here the jumper constructs her accusers as the offenders with her oppositional move.

In Example 2.27 the larger number of persons present can ratify the observer's point of view and multiple judges counter the player's position about her move. Girls who play judges re-enact the moves of the party committing the foul as a form of demonstration. For example, replaying a player's stepping on a line, Crystal states, "You did like this" (line 16) as she re-enacts Lucianda's prior move. The judges also highlight their positions by stomping the place where the line was touched (line 19). In Example 2.23, as in 2.21, 2.23, and 2.25, the grid is used as an area that can be tapped, (line 19) pointed to (line 6), and jumped upon (line 16) to further explicate the proofs judges are offering. Girls formulate their logical proofs by making use of a number of components in an integrated manner – the material game grid, their own bodies, and accounts. In the midst of this sequence the player produces a personal insult with a challenge gesture towards one of the referees (line 17). However, despite rather direct oppositional moves, girls do not break up the game.

Demonstrations among second language learners

In Examples 2.8, 2.16, and 2.24 we saw earlier that children with minimal language skills are highly competent in the art of playing hopscotch. As Ervin-Tripp (1986) has argued, for second language learners the situated use of language and activity structure in games makes it possible for children with limited language skills to participate. In the following example of ESL children playing hopscotch the primary moves of opposition are constructed through terms of polarity ("*Yes*" and "*No*"); in this way they can mark disagreement with a prior turn. In addition they make use of deictic terms such as "like this" and pointing (with hands and feet) to places on the grid in order to mark inappropriate moves of the prior speaker. Despite their paucity of language the children in the ESL class provide quite elaborate accounts. Making use of an ecology of sign systems[35] children of limited English proficiency, as the bilingual speakers, can provide a public witnessing regarding which position is more persuasive.

In Example 2.28 children provide similar readings of how Nazrine's foot touched the pavement by collaboratively re-enacting the touching of her foot. Onlookers construct Nazrine as having made a mistake through a number of moves which are countered by her in turns marked by polarity markers, *Yes*, and *No*, over several turns. Ning initiates the *Out*-call through "*LOOK*!" (line 3) and pointing to Nazrine. Maja then provides a reenactment with the framing, "You say like this" (line 5).

Example 2.28

```
1   Nazrine:      ((at the end of the grid she balances herself on one foot. The foot
                  touches the pavement and she quickly raises her foot for the
                  remainder of the time))
2   Joo Soung:    That's o⌈kay
3   Ning:               ⌊LOOK! ((points at Nazrine))=
4   Nazrine:      N⌈o!((lifts one foot up off pavement))=
5   Maja          ⌊See you ⌈say like this? ((lifts foot from pavement))
6   Ning:                  ⌊You go like this? ((lifts foot from pavement))
7   Jaime:        ((goes up to line and re-enacts her move, tapping pavement))
8   Ning:         ⌈YE:S.
9   Maja:         ⌊YE:S.
10  Nazrine:      Nuh ⌈uh::.
11  Ning:              ⌊((moves leg up in imitation of Nazrine))
12  Jaime:        ⌈YES.
13  Ning:         ⊢YES. ((nodding))
14  Maja:         ⌊YES.
15  Nazrine:      No::⌈::.
16  Ming:            ⌊We see ⌈it.
17  Jaime:                  ⊢Ye::s:
18  Maja:                   ⌊Yes. ((pointing at Nazrine))
19  Joo-Soung:    Let me see. ((points to Maja, Jaime and Ning)) One.
20  Jaime:        Let's see. ((begins approaching Nazrine))
21  Maja:         Like this? Like- ((lifts up leg, while approaching Nazrine))
22  Ning:         ((runs to Nazrine's spot, lifts leg, points foot on ground))
23  Ning:         Like this?
24  Maja:         ⌈You go like this? ((lifts up leg, pointing with foot on ground))
25  Jaime:        ⌊((does enactment near Nazrine's spot, pointing with foot on ground))
26  Joo-Soung:    Out.=
```

27	Nazrine:	**No. No**.
28	Maja:	Yes. ⌈Yes. *((nods))*
29	Ning:	⌊Yes. Yes. *((falsetto))*
30	Jaime:	Out. *((jumps))* **You're** out.
31	Joo-Soung:	Out.
32	Nazrine:	Ning. You are **crazy**. *((as she moves off grid))*

Both Maja (line 5) and Ning (line 6) in concert re-enact Nazrine's move of dropping her foot to the pavement. Turns indicating polarity persist for several turns (lines 8–18). Joo-Soung (line 19) calls for a re-enactment and three of the witnesses go up and reconstruct what the move that she made looked like, though she continues to deny that she in fact made that move. Next, several of the participants line up on the line where Nazrine is stationed and re-enact what they feel she had done, lifting up their legs, though she continues to deny that she is guilty (line 27). Orienting to the relevance of the line as the field for the enactment of the move, all of the children position themselves on the line at once (lines 20–25; see Figure 2.13).

When several individual players have converged on the space and have re-enacted her move, there exists a kind of public consensus against her. The "yes/no" debate shifts when Jaime provides a more definitive *out*-cry: "Out. **You're** out" (line 30), and Joo-Soung aligns with him with "Out"

Figure 2.13 Demonstrations among ESL children

(line 31). The public consensus leads to Nazrine's acceptance of the ruling, and the termination of the dispute. As Nazrine moves off the grid, she provides a comeback: "Ning. You are *crazy*" (line 32). Nazrine provides an assessment of her assessors, in the same way that, in Example 2.23, Joo-Soung had when he responded to Hien's *Out*-call with "Cheating" or when the accuser was dubbed an "embustera" (liar) in Example 2.22.

Demonstrations in the games of the fourth grade LA group

The moves we have examined thus far provide examples of how children who are primarily working class construct moves of opposition. The girls' clique at Hanley School, girls who were (with one exception) middle class, made use of remarkably similar moves. Among this group hopscotch was played far less than the more popular game of jump rope in the fourth grade, and many of the players were far less familiar with the rules than children in the other groups. Though they used polarity markers to signal opposition, unlike the other groups, they did not call "Out!" or provide response cries. In other ways the turns were quite similar to those of the other opposition turns we have looked at.

In Example 2.29 a judge provides explicit instructions to the jumper on how to proceed through the grid (line 2). Lisa is jumping from the far end of the grid back to home position. Before she jumps to home position, Janis (line 2) demonstrates how she is supposed to bend from squares four and five (a two square block) to pick up her stick in square one because squares two and three are occupied with tokens. Rather than bending to pick up her token, however, Lisa jumps on two squares that have tokens. Immediately two parties acting as judge state a loud "*NO:::::::!*" (lines 4–5) in the very first part of their turn, presenting a stance of opposition.

Example 2.29

1 Lisa: *((jumping from the far end of the grid.*
   She hops onto square number four and five; her token is on one))
2 Janis: Y- y- you have- you have to bend- *((bends over as she*
   demonstrates bending to pick up token from the side of the grid,
   avoiding squares occupied with tokens))
3 Lisa: *((she jumps on two squares that already contain tokens*
   She picks up her token when she returns home))
4 Janis: ⌈**NO:::::::!**
5 Aretha: ⌊**NO:::::::!** *((Aretha has arms up at chest level- fingers of*
   hands extended))
6 Aretha: ⌈*((flips hands))*
7 Janis: ⌊*((claps))*
8 Lisa: *((hits arms to legs as a form of response cry))*
9 Aretha: You're supposed to- stand- *((reaching arm out pointing to*
   square where she should be standing))=
10 Lisa: I *know.*

11   Aretha: You're supposed to
12   ⌈stand- on the **two!**
13   Janis: ⌊*((demonstrates bending and leaning to get token))*

The vowel in Janis and Aretha's "**NO:::::::!**" is extended to enhance the intensity of the move (and in fact is equally as extended as in response cries of bilingual Spanish/English speakers; the contour in fact resembles quite closely the contour in Figure 2.14, one that is more than 1460 milliseconds). Both Aretha and Janis (lines 6–7) use gestural intensifiers (Aretha with hands extended and Janis with clapping) with the extended vowel to mark that Lisa has made a mistake. Lisa herself does a response cry by hitting her arms to her legs. As the next component of the turn Aretha states the rule "You're supposed to- stand-", "You're supposed to stand- on the **two!**" (lines 9, 11–12). She points to the square where Lisa should have stood to pick up her token (line 9), rather than jumping through the grid. Janis also replicates the action. In line 13 Janis demonstrates bending, leaning and reaching to get a token. In this example a polarity marker (lines 4–5), an explanation (lines 9–12), and a demonstration (line 13) provide components of the turn remarkably similar to those we have examined thus far for working class second generation Mexican and Central American children, African American children, and English language learners.

Playing with the Rules

The model of girls' play in the current literature argues that turn-taking games such as hopscotch progress in identical order from one situation to the next, thus proposing that they operate within what Hart (1951:125) has called a world of "mechanical jurisprudence." However, to the contrary, when actual play is examined we find that girls regularly test the rules, disputing what can count as a proper application of one, and seeing how far they can extend certain rules to work to their advantage. Rather than following rules they learn how to work and play with them.

Girls in the position of judge respond to infractions of players with face-threatening acts formulated with negatives. This occurs in the following example of a game of hopscotch among second generation bilingual speakers, in which one player violates one of the rules about how to move one's feet before propelling her beanbag to the squares at the far end of the grid. According to the rules of ABC a player may take three baby steps on the side of the hopscotch grid before throwing her beanbag into a square above the number six.

In the following as Marisol is learning how to do "ABC," she looks towards the other players and starts laughing. Marisol persistently takes steps that are slightly larger than those permitted, playfully probing what she can get away with. The referees counter her tests with polarity markers: "**NO::**"

(lines 2, 4), and response cries: "***AY::***" (lines 3, 11). These turn prefaces of opposition occur immediately after Marisol laughingly produces her first set of "ABC" moves. The opposition turns contain negative person descriptors: "***NO*** chiri**O**na!" (line 4) and "Cheater!" (line 7) as well. Through these categorizations the judges explicitly accuse the player of knowingly having violated implicit rules, and attempted to get away with it.

Marisol begins her turn again (signaled with "Okay" in line 5) and once again takes large steps. This time Gloria produces her opposition move "***NO:::***" (line 9) accompanied by a dramatic lowering of her body. In response Marisol's wide smile signals that she indeed is attempting to get away with something with her move. Carla's next move makes use of "***AY::***", another turn preface which signals opposition through a response cry (line 11). This move is accompanied by a gesture that pushes Marisol to the side so that she can have a large space to enact her demonstration of the correct way to execute the move.

In her next moves Carla, acting as the judge, with the account (lines 12–17): "***AY::*** QUE TIENES QUE METERTE EN LA RAYA DE AQUÍ LOS DOS JUN**TI**TOS. AL OTRO PIE NI**Ñ**A." (*Hey you have to place yourself on this line with both feet very close together to the other foot Girl!*), describes in no uncertain terms what the move should have been and what the violation consisted of. The verbal statement is accompanied by enactments of how precisely to place one's feet one behind the other in small steps on the grid. A final feature to note is the judge's use of the diminutive categorization "girl."

Example 2.30

		((Marisol, a newcomer, has just been instructed in how to take baby steps in ABC, putting her heel to the toe of her shoe. She is now trying to take larger steps than permitted.))
1	Marisol:	A(hh), B, C(h) *((smiling))*
2	Carla:	**NO** ⌈::
3	Gloria:	⌊***AY:::*** *((spanking Marisol))*
4	Gloria:	**NO** Chiri**O**⌈na!
5	Marisol:	⌊Okay.
6	Marisol:	⌈A
7	Carla:	⌊Cheater!
8	Marisol:	B, C=*((taking big steps))*
9	Gloria:	**NO:::** *((body lowers dramatically))*
10	Marisol:	*((smiles widely))*
11	Carla:	***AY::*** *((pushing Marisol out of the way so she can demonstrate the correct foot patterns.))*
12	Carla:	⌈QUE TIENES QUE METERTE
		⌊*You have to put yourself*
13	Marisol:	⌊Hih hih!
14	Carla:	EN LA RAYA ⌈DE AQUÍ
		on ⌊*this line*
15	Marisol:	⌊Okay!

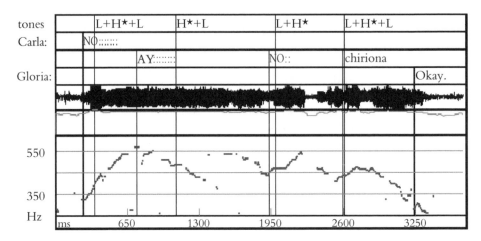

Figure 2.14   No! cry and response cry as used in Example 2.30

16   Carla: LOS DOS JUN*TI*TOS
                 with both feet very close together
17   AL OTRO PIE *NIÑA*!!
                 to the other ⌈*foot Girl!*
18   Marisol: ⌊A.

Here immediately after Marisol takes larger steps than are permitted and keys her talk with laughter (line 1), Gloria and Carla mark that a violation has occurred with oppositional moves: a polarity marker "*NO::*" (line 2) and a response cry "*AY:::*" (line 3). Both of these words are produced with loud volume and with dynamic pitch contours. Such forms of pitch prominence can be considered more broadly instances of "highlighting" (Goodwin 1994) – or making especially salient for recipients features of an exchange. The prosody used in the pitch track for Example 2.30, shown in Figure 2.14, provides a particularly vivid example; in Example 2.30, both the vowel length and the intonation contour are critical to the construction of oppositional talk.

The duration of the vowels in the "*NO:: AY::: NO chiriOna*" sequence is quite prolonged. While 200 milliseconds is considered an extended vowel length for adult speakers, here the vowel length over the first "*NO::*" is 1460 milliseconds. Carla's "*NO::*", joined by "*AY:::*", is sustained for 1140 + 225 milliseconds, producing a total length of 1365 milliseconds, and "*chiriona's*" voiced segment is 1030 milliseconds. The pitch of these utterances is quite dramatic as well. While the typical pitch range for this group of Latina grade girls is from 250–350 hertz, here the pitch reaches from 485 hertz to 580 hertz on "*NO::*" and from 327 to 559 on Gloria's "*NO*" of "*NO chiriOna*".

Over the words "*NO:: AY:::*" (lines 2 and 3), as well as the vowel "o" of "chiri*O*na", a distinctive LHL contour is produced. Although the first speaker with the polarity marker "*NO::*" starts at 306 hertz and the second speaker with her expletive "*AY:::*" starts from 444 hertz, what is remarkable is that both speakers produce similar contours; they join in ascending to over 550 hertz on their accented talk and subsequently produce a falling contour in unison. That they are able to jointly produce this gradually ascending and then falling contour demonstrates the familiarity of this LHL intonational contour for members of this speech community. While the shape of this turn resembles that of other turns for Latina speakers, a comparison of working class Latina and African American girls of comparable age showed that the contours of African Americans were less contoured and vowels were of shorter duration.[36]

Through the intersection of multiple semiotic resources the player is instructed in the appropriate way to move her feet through the grid. While the judges produce the counter and the explanation they lean over at the waist – their bodies intensifying the force of the action. While the girls say "*AY:::*" (line 3) they spank Marisol, and during "*NO:::*" (line 9) Carla lowers her body dramatically at the waist and then subsequently (line 11) pushes Marisol out of the way in order to demonstrate the correct foot patterns, placing one foot closely behind another. With each of Marisol's new attempts to further probe the boundaries of acceptable behavior come increased sanctions. What emerges in this example is a fully embodied opposition move produced through gestural, intonational, and verbal admonishment. Not only is Marisol told about the inappropriateness of her actions, but also the girls physically move her body, instructing her in the appropriate size of steps to take. Such forms of multimodal turns occur throughout girls' adversarial moves as girls provide accounts making explicit their positions of opposition.

In the midst of play the referees take up a very complicated stance toward the rule. While they counter the player's large steps with response cries (lines 3 and 11) and subsequently accounts and a demonstration about how one's feet should be placed (lines 12–16), their action is keyed with laughter by the jumper, who laughs about her own thwarted probes of the rules in the midst of her turn (lines 1, 10). By playing with the possibilities provided by the game in this way, girls are developing the ability to resist the rules that are simultaneously providing structure for the events that they are engaged in.

What happens here raises another issue as well. Social scientists[37] have argued that conflict is so disruptive to girls that they are incapable of continuing to play when it emerges. However, as Examples 2.27 and 2.30 (as well as many other examples in this chapter) show these girls do not treat conflict and play as mutually exclusive alternatives. Conflict about rules and fouls is embedded within a larger participation framework visibly constituted through playfulness and laughter. Instead of breaching relationships the disputes engendered by the game are a central part of the fun of playing it. Rather than treating conflict and cooperation as a bipolar dichotomy, the girls build complex participation frameworks in which disputes, with their rich possibilities for cognitive organization and display of powerful stances, are embedded within a larger ethos of playfulness.

Playing with the Structure of Attentiveness

Such probing of the structures organizing the game can be applied not only to its rules, but also to the frameworks of attentiveness that sustain it. Not only do referees monitor players, but players for their part can monitor the watchfulness of their referees; when they can discern that referees are less than fully engaged in scrutinizing the game, they can try to advance their tokens without referees knowing it – thus playing with the participation frameworks within which the game is conducted.

    In the following example Marisol tricks the other players who are involved in their own side conversation about boyfriends. While invisible to the referees Marisol's movements (as well as a collusive eyeball roll) display

Figure 2.15   Advancing beanbag while onlookers are talking

to the ethnographers the trick she is attempting. She sneaks across the grid and advances her beanbag to the next square, and then dances back to her place with a Charlie Chaplinesque walk. The frame grabs in Figure 2.15 show the sequence of moves she makes to advance her token before returning home to her place.

Of course, the trick would not be any fun were the referees not to eventually discover that they had been tricked. After Marisol has moved her beanbag while Gloria and Carla have been talking, she states "Perdí. Sigues *tú*" (*I lost. Your turn*), pointing to the square where her token has been moved. She then (line 4) chants "Eh YEI!" as she claps her hands. Marisol's posture with hands on hips, and slight bouncing up and down, visibly keys the possibility that something special is going on. In the midst of jumping, as Carla comes to realize that all is not okay, she moves through a sequence of embodied stances. She first puts her hands on hips, in a challenge position (Figure 2.16).

Then Carla uses her extended arm to make an accusatory point as she states "Tú no has pasado *es*te número." (*You haven't even advanced to* **this** *number!*) (See Figures 2.17 and 2.18.)

During "*es*te número" she advances to the square in question, and leans towards Marisol (in another challenge posture) as she stomps on the square she is referring to. Example 2.31 provides a complete transcript of the interaction in question.

Figure 2.16   Slow take on grid (line 5 of Example 2.31)

Figure 2.17   Tú no has pasado (line 6 of Example 2.31)

Figure 2.18   *es*te número (line 7 of Example 2.31)

Example 2.31

		((While Gloria and Carla have been talking about boyfriends Marisol sneaks to advance her token.))
1	Marisol:	Perdí. ⌈Sigues **tú**.
		I lost. ⊦*Your turn.*
2	Gloria:	⌊Whew:::!!! *((twirling around))*
3		Esto es (.) **o**tro problema.
		⌈*This is another problem.*
4	Marisol:	⌊Ey **YEI!** *((clapping hands))*
5	Carla	*((jumps and discovers Marisol has cheated, assumes challenge pose with arms akimbo))*
6	Carla:	Tú no has pasado *((finger point))*
7		**es**te número *((stomps on square))*
		You haven't gotten past this number.
8	Marisol:	*hhhh hih-hih-hih! *((wringing hands))*
		hih-hih-hih-hih! *((kicks bag to lower square))*
		eh hih-hih-hih-hih-hih-hih

In this sequence stance is displayed through both language and the vocal and nonvocal organization of the body. The party who has been tricked uses her pointing finger and leaning body to display her outrage at the wrong done her. In contrast, Marisol, who has successfully exploited a lapse in monitoring to play with the participation structures that frame the game, punctuates the entire exchange with gleeful, playful laughter (line 8). Keyings of many different forms occur, as coparticipants transform their affective alignment towards the game in different ways throughout its course. Within hopscotch stances are displayed, through language choices, intensified intonation contours, gestures, and embodied performances, within the built social world of the game grid as a framework for the interpretation of action.

Girls' Argumentative Stances in Games

The unit of analysis, the situated activity system, provides ways of examining how, turn by turn, participants co-construct their social universe. Local identities of the game are built as participants move through the hopscotch grid and players acting as judges carefully scrutinize the movements of the players. Rules for playing the game are self-administered, and are articulated in the midst of play rather than being predetermined. In subsequent chapters we will consider situated activities as the unit of analysis for examining how girls monitor other aspects of their social landscape outside of the game environment.

Contrary to the notion that females attempt to avoid conflict, the ways in which elementary school girls, of a diverse range of ethnicities and social classes (including white Euro American middle class girls), construct opposition show they are actively seeking it out. Positions are highlighted through particular multimodal practices: utilizing turn shapes initiated by forms of polarity and response cries, using negative person descriptors that provide particular categorizations of the target, employing heightened volume and intensified intonation contours, as well as embodied performances – touching the player and marking the spaces stepped on with physical tapping and jumping – all within the built social world of the game grid.

Feminist sociolinguists argue that we need to move the diverse experience of women from different backgrounds from the periphery to the center of social theory.[38] Ethnographic examination of how girls of various groups play the game produces compelling portraits of girls' interactive competencies. When we analyze the interactions of the Spanish/English bilingual speakers, for example, we also find that girls actively construct themselves as agents who are not passive, but rather responsible for monitoring the social order. The examples we have examined defy the essentialized stereotypes of Latinas as the hapless victims of a patriarchical culture;[39] their voices are not muted. Like the Chicanas studied by Galindo (1992, 1994, 1999), Farr (1994), and Mendoza-Denton (1996, 1999, forthcoming), the second generation bilingual Mexican-American and Central American girls from downtown Los Angeles, as well as the Mexican and Puerto Rican girls living in Columbia, South Carolina, use language creatively and make salient their positions. The multi-ethnic ESL South Carolina group as well as the mixed ethnicity Los Angeles clique (which includes Euro American middle class girls) likewise defy images of females as using powerless language in this context.

Girls intently scrutinize players' actions to produce judgments about the jumpers' moves. As these girls play, they do not simply rotate through various positions, but animatedly and playfully dispute, resist and probe the boundaries of rules as referees and players, in the company of their friends; together they build the game event – without the development of physical fighting. Though research[40] has used hopscotch to build a deficit picture of girls who lack the ability to use and contest rules, ethnographic study of how the game is actually played reveals just the opposite.

3

Social Dimensions of a Popular Girls' Clique

At many public schools in downtown Los Angeles, the space where children eat lunch and play is highly circumscribed; children must walk silently in single file from one school area to another, escorted by their teacher. Children eat in close proximity to one hundred other children on long benches, and can barely hear one another talk because of the din created by the number of children talking under a tin roof. Recreational areas for play at recess on a two-square-block blacktop are pre-specified for each classroom by a weekly rotation chart.

The situation at Hanley School is quite different. The school population is a quarter that of downtown schools. Two expansive playgrounds with multiple shady areas afford alternative types of spaces for activities.[1] During their 50-minute lunch break, children are free to move about across various grassy and cement spaces, sitting at picnic tables or on a curbside, and eat with whomever they choose, though usually they cluster in small groups of six to ten.

Regardless of one's school location, recess constitutes an important time of the day for children, and the playground is an important space in the lives of all children's groups. In the particular downtown school where I conducted my research, the playground provides a safe space where children can play hopscotch, ball games, jump rope, or meet for secret clubs (i.e., the Girl Power Club). The school made a treaty with the local gangs that no violence would be committed in the school area before or after school until dark. If the children did not stay after school, their alternative was to walk home quickly and stay inside their locked apartments. Because the neighborhood was perceived as dangerous, children were not permitted to play on the streets outside their homes. The principal of the school reported to me that when in the evening he visited families in apartments located on the first floor, he would often have to lie on the floor, given the family's fear of stray bullets piercing their windows. If an apartment complex had a common area, children were frequently prohibited from playing in that space because apartment dwellers did not want to have to listen to noisy children.

Middle class children at Hanley School also had limited time to play with friends. After school they were chauffeured to tennis or dance class or to play dates with a friend. Teachers commented that the playground was the closest thing to the neighborhood, where children could wander from one activity to the next, rather than having their lives carefully scheduled and monitored by their parents. In my work with the Sloan Center on Everyday Lives of Families at UCLA I have observed very few occasions when middle class children play with friends after school, given the tight scheduling of various activities for children. In one middle class family, for example, immediately after school a mom will pick up children, and take them to karate lessons. After karate on the way to softball practice the child does her homework on a white board in the back of the car. Children who are being prepared for an upper middle class life style move rapidly from one activity to the next after school, until they arrive home, and are obliged to finish their homework before undertaking other activities.[2] Quite unlike the situation I observed in on Maple Street in 1970–71 for a working class community in Philadelphia, children had very little time to play after school. Moreover, especially for upper middle class children in Los Angeles, it is not the norm to be able to walk out of one's front door and locate a group of friends to play with. Though most Maple Street parents were away at work during the day, mothers with young children, or grandmothers who were not working, monitored play on the street during the day from their screened or glassed-in porches. They ensured that the street was safe for children to play.

In my three years of fieldwork in the progressive southern California elementary school I observed a number of different third through sixth grade children's groups at recess and in various classes (Spanish, biology, math, language, arts, and sex education). Though I was initially present for two different lunch periods (children in grades one to three and grades four to six ate in different shifts), after two months I regularly observed the interactions of about fifty children who had frequent contact with one another. In order to understand the ebb and flow of children's activities in some depth, such as how talk at one point of time influenced subsequent social processes, I focused on a core group of same-sex friends who shared similar interests, a clique[3] of six girls of various ethnicities, and classmates who interacted with them. These girls regularly ate lunch and played together and had known each other for six years, since they started going to the school. I observed the group over a three-year period as they passed from fourth to sixth grade, videotaping and audiotaping their interaction with one another; 80 hours of videotape and 20 hours of audiotape form the corpus of the study. While most of the tape was shot outdoors, the corpus includes six hours of classroom interaction.

The Hanley Elementary School children differ both in age and social class from children who are the subjects of other studies of preadolescent and adolescent children, primarily working class peer groups who actively resist the official school culture of middle class norms and beliefs.[4] Children at Hanley School span a large range of income groups as well as ethnicities. In the late 1990s, of the families of third through fifth grade children, 9.2 percent of the children's families had an income between $7,500 and $14,999; 13.8 percent made between $15,000 and $34,999; 26.4 percent made between $35,000 and $59,999; 28 percent made between $60,000 and $249,999; while 22 percent made over $250,000. The children at Hanley displayed positive attitudes towards school, were high achievers, and actively engaged in interaction with their teachers, often making time to talk with them after class and to confide in them about personal problems. The teachers treated their students respectfully, and created an exciting learning environment for them (dissecting frogs in fifth grade science, learning about neuroscience from a parent who was a physician in his lab), and with a range of different participation frameworks (small work groups as well as whole group discussions). On one occasion a group of fifth graders became so involved in figuring out a math solution at the board as a group that they continued on-task when the teacher was called away for ten minutes; the entire math session stayed on-task over an hour. When a science discussion lesson on the water cycle went especially well, discussing how temperature affected the states of water as liquids, gas, and solids, Ms Harper, a fifth grade teacher, praised her students with statements such as "I think we have a class of graduate physics students here. Absolutely brilliant!" During a class in which students were asked to chart their life course, she encouraged them to think of professional career goals and other milestones they envisioned for their futures. At the end of sixth grade many got into prestigious private and public middle schools.

The Popular Girls' Clique

During recess several groups of girls with different orientations towards play were evident in the schoolyard. The first year of the three-year study when fourth through sixth graders had recess the following groups were observed: (1) A group of five fourth grade girls and one fifth grade girl (most of whom[5] had known each other since pre-kindergarten) and were regarded by many, including themselves, as the most popular group in the school. These girls played games such as jump rope, softball, and volleyball,[6] sat on the swings or jungle gyms and talked among themselves and occasionally with boys. The girls were from diverse cultural and religious backgrounds, and all but one (Sarah, whose family was working class) was from a family of middle or upper middle class background. (2) A group of six fourth and sixth grade second generation Central and Mexican American girls who were bilingual English/Spanish speakers (two of whom were sisters, four of whom were neighbors); these girls participated in jump rope, joke and storytelling, or swinging on tires with a bilingual speaking boy from their neighborhood; their parents were adamantly against their being in any bilingual classes, since they did not want their children to waste time on subjects they already knew about from their home experiences. (3) A group of three fifth and one fourth grade blonde Euro American girls, nick-named the "Blondies" by the popular group (all of whom happened to be brunettes); these girls played ball games with boys (supposedly because they liked to be near enough to be able to "flirt" with them), and walked around the playground. (4) A group of socially marginal fourth grade girls who sat on swings, hung out near the jungle gym, walked around the playground but seldom participated in games. (5) Two super-star (intellectually and athletically) sixth grade girls who organized games of basketball with boys. (6) A group of sixth grade girls who spent most of their time talking (and bothering the fourth graders).

The focus in this chapter and throughout the rest of this book is on the first group, a clique of popular girls, though I will discuss interaction of this clique with other groups (including boys in their age cohort). Adler and Adler (1998:56) describe cliques as "friendship circles whose members tend to identify each other as mutually connected." They argue that cliques maintain a hierarchical structure, are dominated by leaders, and are exclusive. According to Eder and Parker (1987) cliques include the most popular children, who are most respected by those of their age grade. Adler and Adler (1998:145) argue that cliques in peer groups constitute "a culture that is unique in its own right, and yet at the same time is a staging ground for future adult behavior." These descriptions and definitions of a clique are quite appropriate for the clique of girls I studied.

The composition of the group was somewhat fluid, depending on who was available for lunch on any particular day. During the fourth grade, members of the popular clique included an African American middle class girl (Aretha), two Euro American girls (Janis and Sarah, the only working class girl in the clique), and three Asian American middle class girls (Emi, Melissa, and Lisa, a fifth grader and best friend of Janis). I feel it is important to discuss ethnicity not because it was a feature the girls themselves treated as relevant, but because, remarkably, this feature of the girls' identity (in contrast to their access to experience indexing activities of the upper middle class) was seldom discussed in their talk. Janis, Sarah, Aretha, and Emi had known each other since pre-kindergarten; Melissa had only been in the school for one year, but her teacher said she had adjusted quickly and was very popular.

Sarah, the only girl in the clique from a household headed by a single mom, was also the only child in the group who had to recycle part of her lunch for the next day. Girls would on occasion comment on her clothes with statements such as Melissa's "Sarah your t-shirt faded. Yellow" (to which she responded, "I know.") On another occasion Aretha looked in disgust at the sandwich Sarah had brought saying "Ewu::: a cheese sandwich that's not melted? With butter? Ewuu::."

In fifth grade a Euro American girl named Brittany (best friend and classmate of Janis) replaced Lisa, who preferred to play with girls her age. Several of the girls (Sarah, Melissa, Emi, Aretha) were in the same classroom, making possible observations within the classroom as well as on the playground. Kathy (a precocious, athletic, and academically gifted girl a year younger than the other girls in the clique) became an active playmate of the clique the second year of the study; she was in the same classroom as Sarah, Melissa, Emi, and Aretha, as fourth and fifth graders shared the same space.

Table 3.1   The principal group studied

Name	Age	Classroom	
Sarah	10	Classroom A	Working class girl, good organizer of activities
Emi	10	Classroom A	Group leader, who positioned herself above others, and wanted others to follow her lead
Melissa	10	Classroom A	"The whiz" at math, considered very popular
Aretha	10	Classroom A	"The homework person," well liked by all
Janis	10	Classroom B	Group leader, prone to brag and gossip
Angela	11	Classroom A	Tag-along girl, African American Vernacular English speaker
Lisa	11	Classroom C	Friend of Janis
Brittany	10	Classroom B	Friend of Janis and tangential clique member in fifth grade
Kathy	9	Classroom D	Precocious, athletically and academically gifted tangential clique member in fifth grade; classroom A in fifth grade

Table 3.1 provides a chart of the names of the girls in the clique, their classrooms, and ages in fourth grade. This chart is intended for readers who may want to easily reference the principal girls being discussed in subsequent chapters.[7]

Children were permitted to work together on class science projects. Frequently Sarah, Aretha, and Melissa worked together; Sarah also worked with Emi and Melissa, who often formed a group. In fifth grade during small group work at the computer, as well as in whole group discussions, Aretha, Emi, Melissa, and Kathy were quite articulate and eager; their participation in science class demonstrated their ability to grasp with ease concepts that the teacher presented. Aretha provided a dynamic and embodied explanation of features of the water cycle during a science class and had no difficulty in explaining the meaning of evaporation. She quickly mastered the programs needed to complete a computer animation assignment on natural and built water cycles, while Sarah experienced difficulty learning the terms in the assignment. As Sarah read her "Captain Hydro" comic she mispronounced the word conservation. This is quickly met with corrections from a boy seated nearby her, as well as Aretha:

Example 3.1

Sarah:	Because of the- what's the word? con-
Ed:	Conservation.
Sarah:	Conster- consterb- ((clears throat))
Aretha:	Conser*va*tion! ((annoyed, giving eyeball rolls))
Sarah:	Consterbation.
Ed:	**Con**servation. Not con**ster**bation.

Angela, an African American working class girl, frequently followed members of the clique during lunchtime and tried to participate in their play. Her status was marginal in the group; the group members referred to her as a "tag-along." Angela, a speaker of African American Vernacular English as well as Standard English, was physically more developed than the other girls (she was the only girl in fourth grade who wore a bra), was a year older, and had only been in the school for one year. Because Angela's mother wanted her and her brother to receive a good education, she spent more than two hours a day driving her children to two different schools, ones considerably better than the public schools in her downtown neighborhood. Angela's teacher, Miss Harper, told me that Angela's father had died a year ago. In the classroom as they undertook science projects (computer animations of a water cycle, for example) Angela was often treated respectfully by the girls. In fact, Sarah sat on Angela's lap during one phase of computer work activity; on some occasions Angela went to Sarah's house to play after school. On the playground, however, she was frequently the subject of abuse when she initiated inappropriate behavior, such as sitting on tables rather than benches, kicking someone's chair, eating without a utensil, or making fun of Sarah having to recycle her lunch. Often girls mocked her pronunciation of words as well.

While girls never made any explicit mention of her race, they made numerous references to her social status; she was often told she was poor or had "cooties." When Angela insulted someone loudly in retaliation to what had been done to her, Brittany accused her of "being on heroin." The girls who participated in ridiculing Angela included other African American girls (Aretha and Dionne). Boys also made fun of Angela; on one occasion during recess I observed a boy pointing to her and making gorilla-like movements.

Griffiths (1995:32) in her study of multi-ethnic (white, black Caribbean, Indian and Pakistani) adolescent girls' friendships groups in years eight and nine of secondary school in West Yorkshire argues that, "friendships are based on factors such as appearance, ability and interests, class and ethnicity. A combination of these factors usually exists within a pair or group of girlfriends without any one necessarily predominating." The girls in the clique shared a similar form of joie de vivre, were relatively petite, were in the same Girl Scout troop, and had athletic skills. Aretha, Melissa, Emi, and Kathy were excellent students. Sarah was the only girl in the clique from a working class background; she had been friends with girls in the clique since pre-kindergarten and was well liked.

Children's culture

One approach to understanding children's lives focuses on "children as cultural producers" (Caputo 1995). Iona and Peter Opie (1959, 1969) provided explicit documentation of how British children across social classes and communities maintain their oral tradition by passing along songs, games, and folklore from one generation of children to the next without the intervention of adults. The fourth grade girls in the popular clique I studied had a repertoire of jump rope rhymes that they had learned from other children, many of which sported themes of heterosexual relations and middle class preoccupations. Popular rhymes recited included "Ice Cream Soda, Vanilla Berry Punch. Tell me the name of your Honey Bunch,"[8] and "Cinderella, dressed in yella, went upstairs to kiss a fella." A refrain (M-A-S-H) recited at the end of one round of jumping cycled the words of different possibilities for a dwelling in an imagined future: "Mansion, apartment, shack, house."

In addition to jump rope rhymes the girls sang songs learned from older siblings that dealt with hetero-normative themes. The "Bedroom Song" was sung surreptitiously on the playground during games; scenes related to romance and intercourse were replaced with themes of interaction on the playground when it was sung more openly. The text of the "bedroom" version is provided below:

Example 3.2

> One by one, the fun has just begun.
> In the bedroom, dah dah, dah-dah dah-dah
> Two by two, he took off her shoe. [Refrain]
> Three by three, he kissed her knee. [Refrain]
> Four by four we knocked on the door. [Refrain]
> Five by five, we saw a beehive. [Refrain]
> Six by six, we picked up sticks. [Refrain]
> Seven by seven, it felt like heaven. [Refrain]
> Eight by eight we closed the gate. [Refrain]
> Nine by nine, the twins were fine. [Refrain]
> Ten by ten, let's do it again. [Refrain]

Though generally the girls in the clique had lunch and afterwards played games or talked together, they did not exclude others from the lunch table. However, when the girls told stories and evaluated different aspects of their experience at lunch, those who were not in the core group participated only minimally. At lunch, girls who were not members of the clique would not even make a bid to join in games of jump rope, for example, by calling out a position. When someone outside the inner clique attempted to join a game such as jump rope she might be told that a game was already in progress, or that the order had already been decided, with utterances such as "This is sort of like a contest." Food exchanges were also ways that girls defined the boundaries of the group. While clique members would permit girls in the inner circle to munch potato chips from their bags, Angela, the girl who followed the group but did not belong to it, was not granted even a single chip, despite plaintive repeated requests that she made in extremely mitigated forms. (Frequently her mom did not pack lunch for her to bring to school.) At lunch Angela's position was visible spatially as well; she sat on the periphery of the girls' group, was not permitted space in the inner circle, and was actively ignored.

In general the girls of the popular clique played in a group of six. While all the girls in fourth and fifth grade were in the same Girl Scout troop, not all the girls had access to the same activities. Emi, Melissa, Janis, and Aretha

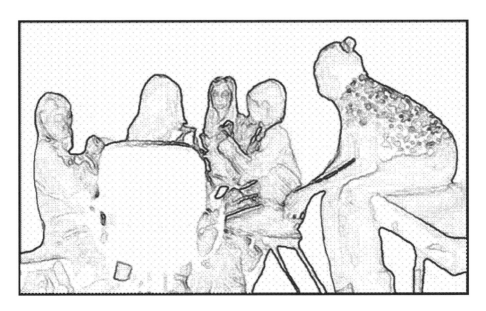

Figure 3.1   Angela's position while girls eat lunch inside classroom

frequently were involved in similar after-school and weekend activities, for example attending private sports, dance, or music lessons, while the working class girl, Sarah, was not.

Griffiths (1995), studying multi-ethnic adolescent girls' friendship groups in years eight and nine of secondary school in West Yorkshire, argued that while there are differentiated friendship groups, and these groups are the main unit of interaction for most of the girls, if the groups split up, girls form interaction sets with other girls (Griffiths 1995:100). This occurred in Hanley School as well; when in fourth grade core members of the popular clique were absent on a fieldtrip, they recruited other fourth and fifth graders to play with them (for example, when playing "house.") When the girls of the clique needed more players to constitute a quorum for sports activities, they recruited girls they seldom communicated with otherwise (younger girls who liked athletics) to play with them. This occurred in the fifth grade when the girls made an attempt to lay claim to a soccer playing field.

My primary concern in this book is with how girls articulate social organization in the midst of their interaction. However, a brief look at how the girls talk about their social organization to the outsider ethnographer and each other is informative. The girls described themselves as a core group of girls whose membership would expand or contract, depending on local circumstances. Girls had "best friends" in dyadic groups, though they noted that groups of three or six would also play together. Girls were conscious of the shifting coalitions in their group, and discussed these while explaining their group's social dynamics. When I asked the girls in fifth grade who their friends were, Aretha responded: "Well, we're kind of split up. Brittany and Janis. Me and Melissa kind of make up a pair." Brittany's version was, "No. Melissa and Emi. You [Aretha] and Sarah." (Brittany did not contest that she and Janis made a pair.) A second later Aretha explained yet another configuration:

Example 3.3

>Aretha: I don't follow Emi but a lot of people follow Emi.
>Me, Janis, and Brittany, we kind of stick together?
>'Cause Sarah and Melissa kind of follow Emi?
>'Cause there's six of us.
>And we split up into twos – twos or threes.

The girls explained different characteristics of girls in the group. Emi tried to assume a position of leadership by having girls follow her into specific parts of the playground. Aretha explained that she (Aretha) was the "homework person" that everyone called to get the assignment straight, though she reported that Melissa was really the "whiz," who they should be calling. (Both Aretha and Melissa were accepted at the top private middle school in the city during sixth grade.) Janis was considered the "gossip," someone who, even according to Janis's best friend Brittany, "always exaggerates." Janis herself provides a portrait of her ideal persona as an actress who is "always mean and grumpy" (lines 8, 14):

Example 3.4

1	Janis:	If you could be one actor. Your personality.
2		I'm most like what's her name
3		The girl in ( ) Class Reunion?
4		***To**by. Fuck off eh heh heh!!*
5		Yeah. ***Love*** her. She's like my favorite actress
6		in the whole world.
7	Sarah:	You ***look*** like her.
8	Janis:	She's always ***mean*** and ***grum**py eh heh heh!!*
9	Brittany:	She's like this ((*smoking dramatically*))
10		Toby. She blows the smoke in her face.
11	Sarah:	Janis you do ***look*** like her.
12	Janis:	I ***lo:ve*** her. She's that- I'm most like her.
13	Sarah:	She was in that cat and dog movie.
14	Janis:	Yeah and she's always grumpy and like-
15		"You're prettier than me.
16		You do this for me." or you're-
17	Aretha:	"You ***suck***. Go do ***this*** for me." eh heh!
18	Janis:	No like um, You like make people ***feel*** bad.

In response to a question I posed to the group in fifth grade about who was in the popular group at the school, Brittany, the girl who replaced Lisa as Janis's best friend in fifth grade, explained that Aretha, Janis, Emi, Melissa, and Sarah, the core group of five, were the "popular girls" at the school (lines 1–2 in Example 3.5).[9] In deflecting the compliment that she was popular, Aretha stated that one of the reasons why the core group had the popularity they did was because they had been at the school for seven years, ever since they were in nursery school (lines 8–9):

Example 3.5

1	Brittany:	No you, Janis, Emi, Melissa, Sarah
2		Are the popular girls in the school.
3	Aretha:	Emi thinks that **she's** the most popular in the world.
4	Brittany:	Well **what**ever. **You** are really popular.
5		Everyone knows you Aretha. So friendly.
6	Aretha:	'Cause I've been around. Anyway, I'm older.
7		Me and Sarah have been here the longest.
8		That's one reason because everyone at the school practically
9		knows us from when we were in pre-kindergarten.
10		Next year is our **eighth year**.
11	Brittany:	This is my seventh year.
12		So I've known these people for-
13		I was with the itty bitty kids.

When I asked them what makes girls popular they responded that popular girls are girls who are well known, who boys like, and who people feel are "cool." Brittany explained that being "cool" means that "Kind of like – when the fashions change, they change. They are kind of like – updated." During the late 1990s in the spring this meant that girls wore t-shirts (in the hot weather with spaghetti straps) that did not expose the belly button but were "not very long," "skorts" (shorts that look like a skirt), big high platform shoes or tennis shoes, and lots of silver bangle bracelets made from guitar strings. During winter months girls wore sweatshirts with logos or sweaters and pants.

When during recess in fifth grade I asked why Lisa, a girl a year older than others in the clique, who had been part of the clique in fourth grade, no longer played with the girls, other definitions of being "cool" were elaborated:

Example 3.6

MHG:	How come Lisa doesn't play with you.
Aretha:	Lisa, she likes to hang out with the sixth graders,
	The boys. And girls. Well **sixth** grader boys.
	She's too **old** for us. She starts acting **weird** now.
	She tries to act like she's **cool**,
	But there is no **real** cool.
	Just what you **think** is cool.

Girls' alliances with boys were treated as signs of their social status. Aretha stated that one of the things that triggered the fifth grade girls' dislike of Lisa was the fact that she claimed to be the girlfriend of a boy Aretha liked. The girls attributed motives of wanting to make another girl feel "jealous" (line 10 in Example 3.7) as the reason for making displays of relationships with boys. The following assessments made about Lisa occurred in talk between Brittany and Aretha.

Example 3.7

1	Brittany:	But Lisa says *ev*ery boy likes him- her.
2	Aretha:	Alan and Denzel like her. They're like kind of a pair.
3		Alan Banks.
4		I personally think that she likes Denzel.
5		'Cause like when she likes me- comes over like-
6		"I guess you're tryin'a make me jealous?"
7		Because she comes over saying
8		"Oh Denzel gave me a ring in second grade.
9		"'Cause I lost one." I was like- "Who *cares*."
10		And she was tryin'a make me *jeal*ous.
11		She was like "Denzel used to like me in second grade."
12		I was like "If you don't shut *up* I will wring your *neck*."
13		I mean she was getting *rea*lly annoying.
14	Brittany:	I don't *like* Lisa.
15	Aretha:	Lisa's an*noy*ing.

Much of the girls' time is spent in commenting on others' behavior. In Example 3.7 we find girls negatively evaluating the behavior of someone who had been a former member of their group, but left the group to play with other children. Arguments about alliances with boys are invoked as symbols of a girl's popularity or status (lines 8 and 11 of Example 3.7 above). Through the use of the adjective "annoying" (lines 13 and 15) categorizing actions of Lisa and the past quote Aretha gave to Lisa (line 12), girls assess the way Lisa attempts to make Aretha feel jealous. Through such assessments we come to see what aspects of the girls' experience are treated as significant enough so as to be commented upon and what type of stances they generate.

As the discussion continues Aretha critiques the way that Lisa makes fun of other girls, mocking them, and insulting them because of their weight.

Example 3.8

1	Aretha:	Lisa and Alicia used to be friends?
2		But Lisa started making fun of her weight
3		Because I guess she thinks that's cool.
4		'Cause she's been trying to be cool.
5		She makes fun of her. She goes-
6		"Alicia you're so fat. How much do you weigh.
7		Like an elephant?" She goes like that.
8		And then she's like-
9		"Well Alicia keeps on calling me a B and uh- uh-"
10		And I go up to Alicia and say, "What's going on."
11		And she said
12		"Well she keeps on doing bad jokes on me."
13		And I was like "Someone spread a rumor?"

The girls provide negative assessments about Lisa: (1) thinking she is "cool" (in lines 3–4 in Example 3.8) and (2) by commenting on the way she makes "fun of" Alicia, a girl who is overweight (line 5). In addition Aretha replays a quotation Lisa made, characterizing Alicia as "so fat" and "like an elephant?" (lines 6–7) to demonstrate her past objectionable behavior. Lisa's talk about Alicia is said to have been interpreted by Alicia, the victim, as "doing bad jokes on me" (line 12). Because assessments (discussed in chapter 6) provide judgmental commentaries on events, through adjectives as well as quotations, they allow ways of uncovering the underlying criteria that animate the ways girls compare group members and sanction untoward behavior.

Descriptions of social roles provide one way of understanding the girls' social group. By examining conversational practices across a range of interactions we can better understand the dynamics of the group. When we examine the structuring of games and activities, we will see Janis, Emi, Melissa, Sarah, and Aretha all participating in decision-making processes. Recurrently, however, Janis and Emi call the shots, often over-riding others' ideas about the orchestration of the activity. The two girls who perform leadership roles are also the most subject to criticism and commentary.

The structuring of relations in the clique and among agemates: Orchestrating playing house

The following instance of playing house provides an example of how roles were negotiated among members of the clique and between the clique and their same-sex classmates. It also is instructive for how activity emerges as girls are walking around the playground. From the interaction we also learn how conflict provides a defining feature of close relationships.

The game of playing house arose spontaneously in fourth grade as three core members of the group (Janis, Sarah, and Lisa) were jumping rope with friends and classmates, Sharie, Ruth (a fifth grader), Gloria, and Nichole; other members of the clique (Melissa, Emi, and Aretha) had gone on a field trip. At a break in the game, Nichole and Ruth began to pick up smoldering cigarette butts from the ground and smoke them. Shortly afterwards Sarah initiated the idea of playing house, with a proposal: "Let's get a game over there. Let's – Guys – Let's play a game. Who's the Mommy." As the drama progressed, girls began selecting roles they deemed appropriate in the frame of playing house. Not unlike in jump rope, where members of the group call out their positions, girls chose their own identities. The family membership categories they elaborated were Mom and teenagers; although the baby category was mentioned once during the 12 minutes of play it was never actualized.

Example 3.9

1	Sarah:	Let's play a game over there.
2		Let's – Guys – Let's play a game.

```
 3   Nichole:   Just grab ⌈one there. ((about cigarette butts))
 4   Sarah:              ⌊Who's the Mommy,
 5   Lisa:      Friends!
 6   Sarah:     I'm not the Mommy!
 7   Janis:     We need a mom.
 8   Ruth:      I will.
 9   Sharie:    Who's the child.
10              That's what I wanna know.
11   Sarah:     I'm a teenager totally.
12              Oh my God!
13              O:::kay.
```

The first order of business, as Sarah saw it, was to select a Mom (line 4). She (lines 1–2) initiated the process through the use of the inclusive "Let's" – an action that signals a proposal rather than either a command or a request, and does not claim special rights over the other as a command does (Goodwin 1990:110–111). Rather than delegating roles, Sarah left open the possibility of each girl making her own selection through her question: "Who's the Mommy" (line 4). She immediately discounted herself as wanting to occupy that category (line 6) with "I'm not the Mommy" and then said, "I'm a teenager *to*tally" (line 11). Not only the use of the adverb "*to*tally" but also the response cry "Oh my **God**!" (line 12) cast Sarah in a Valley girl character role not unlike that of Cher, played by Alicia Silverstone in the 1995 comedy *Clueless*, a favorite film of the group. Ruth, a fifth grader, and the oldest member of the group, volunteered to play Mom (line 8). In contrast to other groups of preadolescent girls playing house[10] the role of Mom was not particularly valued or eagerly sought.[11]

Unlike the game of house observed by Griswold (in press) among Russian girls, no single girl emerged as the ultimate authority or decision maker in the early stages of the play frame. Girls announce their ages and partnerships rather than being told these aspects of their play identity by a mom acting as stage director. The principal parties organizing the play are members of the popular clique. Later on in the midst of play, when Sharie (a peripheral member of the group) argues that she wants to be 16, Lisa, a member of the clique, informs her that she cannot be that age because both she and Janis, who are twins in the fantasy world, have already picked that age.

Example 3.10

```
 1   Sharie:    I wanna be sixteen?
 2   Lisa:      Well you're not.
 3   Sharie:    Why not.
 4   Lisa:      Because we're twins and we're sixteen.
 5              You have to be fifteen.
 6   Sharie:    Fine.
```

While among the African American group I studied in the 1970s a major topic of dispute consisted of who occupied a specific relationship vis-à-vis girls playing mother, and what rights and duties consisted of, among the popular clique disputes concerned relationships in the playworld. Best friends Lisa and Janis wanted to be married to the same boy, Jason, a fourth grade classmate (who was not present during play). In Example 3.11 below both of the girls argue that they had legitimate claims to Jason as their husband; both yelled (lines 4 and 5) the utterance "called it" (a practice that is also used in jump rope when there is a tie). Lisa upgrades the declaration of her entitlement by noting the order of the call: "I called it first" (line 8). Janis and Lisa produce continuous moves of opposition, until Lisa (line 20) proposes that Jason has a twin, and the twin is Janis's boyfriend. This idea is not treated as a viable solution and the dispute continues for several more turns (lines 21–26).

Example 3.11

1	Lisa:	*I'm* married.
2	Janis:	*NO::. I* AM.
3	Lisa:	*NO!* ((*multiple people talk*))
4	Lisa:	I *called* it.
5	Janis:	*I* called it.
6	Nichole:	Ruth is the teenage mother.
7		She had us when she was young.
8	Lisa:	I called it *first*.
9	Janis:	I'm *mar*ried to him.
10	Sarah:	How little were you.
11	Lisa:	Yeah. *I'm* married to him.
12		You're married to his *broth*er.
13	Janis:	They're ex*actly* the *same*.
14	Nichole:	YOU *GUYS!*
15	Janis:	Jason's my boyfriend. ((*chanting*))
16		Jason 's my ⌈boyfriend!
17	Lisa:	⌊*NO:::!*
18	Janis:	Jason's my boyfriend.
19	Ruth:	Jason's right behind you.
20	Lisa:	That- his- his twin *broth*er's your boyfriend.
21	Janis:	*No.* He's *my* boyfriend.
22	Lisa:	*No.* He *is.* I *called* it.
23	Nichole:	You guys. Time out.
24	Lisa:	*I* called it.
25	Janis:	*No.* He *is* my boyfriend.
26	Lisa:	All *right.* ((*stomping feet*))

When Sarah introduces a possible compromise, with the notion of there being two twins (line 27 in Example 3.12 below, the immediate continuation of this dispute), Janis does not settle for this; she states that she has the "real one" (line 29). Lisa disputes this position of Janis as well (lines 31–32). Despite Sarah's attempted intervention arguing that they are both equally "real", the dispute continues for several more turns of opposition (lines 33–38).

Rather than attempting to close off debate, the girls animatedly pursue it with turns that openly mark disagreement and opposition for extended turns (not unlike the disputes of the Maple Street children of Philadelphia I observed).

Example 3.12

```
27  Sarah:    There's two (.) twins. okay?
28            And there's–
29  Janis:    I got the real one.
30            I got the real one.
31  Lisa:     No I do Janis.
32            I called it before.
33  Sarah:    They're both real.
34            They both have everything on their body,
35            okay? that's real.
36  Janis:    But I want the one that goes to this school!
37  Lisa:     No!
38  Janis:    Yeah!
```

In order to resolve the dilemma Janis proposes a procedure invoking a principle of fairness – picking numbers (line 2 in Example 3.13 below). This practice is similar to arbitration that occurs in jump rope when two girls call the same number indicating their order in the lineup. Sarah arbitrates the dispute by asking Lisa and Janis to each pick numbers between one and twenty (lines 7, 12–13). As in jump rope ties, she whispers the number she has selected into someone's ear (line 15) and the person who is closest to the number she picks will be selected as the person who has Jason as a boyfriend. Janis's number comes closest to the number Sarah was thinking of. On winning, Janis (lines 27–28) lifts up her arms to the level of her shoulders in a celebratory gesture, puts her palm into Lisa's face and states triumphantly, "In your face" (line 28). The dispute does not end there, in that Lisa continuously argues that she should get to have Jason as her boyfriend because she "called it first" (line 32).

Example 3.13

```
 1  Janis:    Okay.
 2            Pick a number.
 3            ((sticks out tongue at Lisa))
 4  Janis:    ⌈Uhm,
 5  Sarah:    ⌊Okay. They're twins though? twins?
 6  Janis:    All right. There's two.
 7  Sarah:    Pick a number through:: one and //twenty.
 8  Nichole:  Tell me 'cause I'm not–
 9  Lisa:     SIX! ((jumping up and down))
10  Sarah:    I didn't pick it yet.
11  Nichole:  Tell me::. I'm ⌈fifteen. =I don't–
12  Sarah:               ⌊Pick a number through::
```

13		one and twenty.
14	Nichole:	My lucky number.
15	Sarah:	*((whispers number to Nichole))*
16	Janis:	So Lisa:::.
17	Nichole:	Okay.
18	Gloria:	So what is it.
19	Lisa:	Six!
20	Sarah:	Six and, *((points to Janis))*
21	Janis:	Uh::::::,
22	Sarah:	It's one and twenty.
23	Nichole:	That's **my** lucky number. *((jumping up and down))*
24	Janis:	Ten.
25	Sarah:	Ten? You're the closest. *((pointing to Janis))*
26		It was fifteen.
27	Janis:	Uhm! *((gesture of triumph, arms spread to the side bent up at the elbows))*
28		In your face! *((puts palm into Lisa's face))*
29		I got Jason. *((chanting))*
30	Sarah:	You got the **real** one and she has
31		⌈the fake one.
32	Lisa:	⌊No but I called it way before you Janis.
33	Janis:	So:: it doesn't matter.
34	Sarah:	It doesn't matter. They're **both** real.
35		They both have everything in
36		their bodies *((singing))*
37	Janis:	eh heh heh!!
38	Lisa:	Yeah and mine has a big smile.
39		Not an ugly junky one that looks like
40		a jack'o' lantern.

In the episode examined here, Sarah had done the initial work of calling the game into existence (with "Let's play a game" Example 3.9, line 1), and even choreographed the initial staging of the game by asking the girls to "stand in line" and positioning them in space (Example 3.14, line 1 below); in addition she arbitrated the dispute between Janis and Lisa regarding who was married to Jason (Examples 3.12 and 3.13).

However, with "No. No. I'll point to you" (line 6 of Example 3.14 below), Janis quickly usurped the role of director, objecting to Sarah's instructions, and telling the girls what they must say. Janis makes use of assertive control acts, giving direct commands, setting the frame of play and allocating roles to others, granting themselves higher status roles, and opposing other children.[12] The silence of other girls at this point legitimated Janis's role as stage manager; no objections to her taking over Sarah's role were made. Janis prescribed the explicit script for playing house; she told the girls that they had to "say your life," which was defined as mentioning age, car, and boyfriend (lines 8–10), and sister (line 15) (though this was seldom actualized), and job (see Example 3.15, line 19).

Example 3.14

```
 1   Sarah:   Stand in line. ((positions people in line))
 2            Are you playing? ((to Sharie))
 3   Janis:   Who wants the old Volvo.
 4   Sarah:   Are you playing Gloria? Gloria!
 5            Okay. That- ((lining up herself))
 6   Janis:   No. No. I'll point to you,
 7            And you guys have to walk out,
 8            Say your life, how old you are,
 9            What kind of car you have,
10            Your boyfriend's name,
11            Don't worry,
12            And,
13   Lisa:    What if ⌈they're both the same name.
14   Janis:            ⌊That's it.
15            Who's your sister, blah blah
16            And everything like that.
17            Okay. Go. ((points to Nichole))
```

The ordering of girls giving speeches is instructive with respect to the local social organization of the group. Nichole, Ruth (a fifth grader), Sarah, and Janis (in that order) got a chance to make speeches before the bell called the kids in from recess. Neither Gloria nor Sharie, girls who are peripheral to the core clique and who had not been eating with the popular clique at lunch, had an opportunity to enact their roles.

The following provides an example of how Ruth played her role with Janis serving as acting coach and director of the play (lines 1–3, 12, 18–21). Ruth (line 5) questions Janis about what her name should be, thus ratifying Janis as the authority figure capable of making the major decisions of the play. Janis provides the instructions (lines 1–2) as well as repair moves (lines 12, 18–21), which allow Ruth to develop her role.

Example 3.15

```
 1   Janis:   Okay. I point to you, you guys have to say your name,
 2            Your life, your future, and junk like that.
 3            Okay. **Ruth**. Go. Shh. Silence. **Go** Ruth.
 4   Ruth:    My name's Monique,
 5            No actually- what's my name.
 6   Janis:   Just use Monique.
 7            Just use Monique.
 8   Ruth:    Okay fine. My name's Monique,
 9            And I have a black Corvet,
10            A::nd, my boyfriend is you know who.
11   Sharie:  And how old are you.
12   Janis:   Wait. Say it.
13   Ruth:    ⌈And I'm twenty seven.
14   Janis:   ⌊I forgot.
```

15	Sharie:	You forgot?
16	Ruth:	Yes. Hello Kesha. *((to a girl who walks by, but never makes an attempt to join))*
17	Sarah:	Okay. I– My name ⌈is–
18	Janis:	⌊**Wait. Wait. Wait. Wait.**
19		What's your **job**. What's your **job**.
20		What's your **job**. What's your **job**.
21		What's your job.
22	Ruth:	I'm a model.

Lisa and Janis, who fought long to have the same desired boyfriend as their partner, eventually embrace each other. Lisa and Janis laugh uproariously as they celebrate their play identities, proclaiming: "We're both twins and we have boyfriends who are twins" (lines 1–2 in Example 3.16), and "We're twins and- our boyfriends are twins" (lines 7–8). The girls do a celebratory handclap to affirm, and make publicly visible to all present their alliance and special relationship as best friends (line 10).

Example 3.16

		((Lisa and Janis embrace each other at the waist))
1	Lisa:	We're both twins and we have boyfriends
2		who are twins.
3	Sarah:	I'm seventeen and she had me when I was ten.
4		That does not make me–
5	Lisa:	We are six! She had us when she was eleven.
6	Sarah:	You're sixteen?
7	Janis:	Yeah. And– and– we're twins,
8		And– our boyfriends are twins.
9	Sharie:	Yeah I'm sixteen,
10	Janis:	And she's my twin! *((does hand clap with Lisa))*

In the organization of play, concerns of the girls about same-sex friendships as well as heterosexual partners enter into the talk they produce about their characters. The symbolism of twins married to twins within the play world heightens the display of the most highly valued relationship in the girls' group: best friends. Looking at the overall organization of the allocation of roles in this dramatic play episode we find that though Sharie, Ruth, Gloria, and Nichole can initiate talk about their roles, the major negotiations are between the core clique members (Lisa, Janis, and Sarah). Sharie, Ruth, Gloria, and Nichole participate far less in decision making throughout the play encounter; indeed, Lisa successfully overturns Sharie's selection of her play age (Example 3.10).

While girls spent more time discussing relationships within their same-sex group than friendships with males, nonetheless, relationships with boys often provide the medium through which status is displayed. For example, in the fifth grade Janis accrued special status by frequently being invited by the most popular boy in her grade to play softball and other team sports.

Girls closely aligned with Janis were also invited to play sports with boys. To understand some of the concerns that animate a comparable age group of boys, we now turn to a discussion among some of the boys who regularly played with the clique.

Fourth Grade Boys' Social Organization

Children in first, second, and third grade ate during the first hour-long lunch period, while fourth through sixth graders ate in the second shift. This arrangement separated children with different interests by age. During recess while girls and boys chose to participate in a number of activities in their same-sex groups, they were not physically separated. Girls and boys ate lunch on different picnic tables, but were located close enough for children to yell back and forth to one another and throw things at each other. The model "with then apart" described by Thorne (1986, 1993) characterizes much of children's play at Hanley School.

Generally boys were occupied with playing games such as softball, soccer, football, basketball, or jump rope during recess. One group of boys who frequently played with the clique in fourth grade, however, alternated between entering into games, such as jump rope or soccer, and walking around the playground playing pranks on male classmates – for example, locking them in sheds. Several of these boys regularly played with the popular clique of girls. The following discussion is presented, as it captures the spirit of adventure, play, and involvement with creating disorder that animates the life-worlds of fourth grade boys.

Example 3.17

		((Dan, Alan, and Denzel are sitting on a curb of the playground. Bruce is located nearby.))
1	Alan:	**This** *((pointing to Bruce))* is our midget.
2	MHG:	What types of games do you like to play.
3	Alan:	Oh we just play walk around.
4	Dan:	We like- walk around and annoy people.
5	Denzel:	⌈Yep.
6	Dan:	⌊We get in trouble.
7	Alan:	eh heh! That's our job.
8	Dan:	Eh heh-heh heh-heh!
9	Alan:	Uh::: we play rugby,
10	Dan:	Uh, Then we- till we get in trouble.
11	Alan:	And then, and then,
12	Dan:	Ho-ho ho-ho.
13	Alan:	We walk some more?
14		Then we go to the principal's office,
15	Dan:	eh heh-heh heh!
16	Alan:	And then we get suspen-

```
17  MHG:     How do you get in trouble. What happened.
18  Dan:     We just get in trouble.
19           Like- in rugby I- I sit on people.
20           ⌈Eh heh heh heh!
21  Alan:    ⊢eh heh heh!
22  Denzel:  ⌊ heh heh!
23  Dan:     I sit on people.
24  Alan:    uh- Just stuff. Like- doesn't make any sense. Like-
25  Dan:     Here's somebody getting in trouble right now.
26           ((points to boy being reprimanded))
27  Alan:    Here's a sample- of what happened.
28  Alan:    Uh:, what else do we do. We like- interfere with games?
29  Dan:     Eh eh-heh! yeah!
30  MHG:     What games:
31  Alan:    Like- eh heh!
32  Dan:     Basketball.
33  Alan:    Basketball.
34  Denzel:  Handball.
```

When I asked them to describe further their activities they began elaborating the forms of relationships they maintain with girls in the clique:

Example 3.18

```
1   Alan:    Eh. What else.
2   Dan:     Oh Denzel- Denzel flirts with Aretha,
3            ((pats Denzel on back))
4   Denzel:  ((play hits Dan))
5   Dan:     Okay. I flirt with Emi, ((puts arm around Denzel's
6            shoulder))
7   Denzel:  Here comes Melissa.
8   Dan:     And Alan flirts- I mean Bruce flirts with Melissa.
9            And we usually like-
10           Walk around, sayin like- funny stuff.
```

In talk that develops they discuss various roles they have for members of their group:

Example 3.19

```
1   Alan:  eh heh !! ((points to Edward)) And walk our dog,
2   Dan:   Oh yeah::. We have a doggie here.
3   Alan:  We have a doggie, we have a Chihuahua,
4          ⌈over there, ((pointing to Bruce))
5   Dan:   ⌊Yeap. That's a Chihuahua,
6          And uh, Edward's our doggie.
7          We have a leash for him.
8   Alan:  And then also we have a eagle?
```

```
 9   Dan:    Oh yeah. ⌈Ron's our eagle.
10   Alan:            ⌊Retarded eagle,
11   Dan:    We annoy Ron all day,
12   Alan:   And we have rock- rock fights with
13           Whatever his name is,
14   Dan:    We make fun of Coach Gable because he thinks
15           He's so good,
```

There was an emergent hierarchy in this group. Some of the boys, those positioned as dogs (lines 3–6), eagles (line 9), or monkeys, are obliged to follow the orders of those who were in control. As the boys explain a minute later:

Example 3.20

```
     Dan:    Ron is our hawk (.) and stuff.
             We send him to go and kill people.
             We send him to attack people.
             We say "Attack" to him and he goes and attacks people.
             Like one time he attacked- (0.2) Nathan? Uh:::,
     Alan:   And we use him in emergencies.
             Like when we wanna attack out vermin?
```

Danby and Baker (2001) discuss ways that young preschool boys construct group membership through "escalating terror" during disputes in a block area; the fourth grade boys interviewed here outline ways in which they "get in trouble" and create disorder, by sitting on people, disrupting games, having rock fights, and ridiculing authority figures on the playground. They view their social order as a group of friends, with those of a lower status positioned in different animal roles. They assume a heteronormative sexual orientation when they discuss flirting with particular girls. This orientation towards flirting contrasts with the playful banter in cross-sex relationships that occurred in third grade. In order to understand the transformation in cross-sex friendships from third to fourth grade, we will briefly look at some fragments of talk among third graders.

Playful Cross-Sex Friendships in Third Grade

In the third grade boys at Hanley School were frequently engaged in same-sex activities such as arm wrestling to establish their relative rank.[13] In addition, however, it was not at all uncommon for girls and boys not only to enjoy each other's company playing basketball or handball, but also to engage in playful ritual insult. Third grade girls viewed gender as one of the ways of sorting out groups of classmates, as evidenced from their conversations during lunch prior to games.[14] By way of example, in the following Sandra asks Vanessa, who generally functions as a captain of groups of third graders playing basketball, who is going to be on her team. Vanessa replies that divisions in the game will be based on gender: "girls against boys."

Example 3.21

1	Sandra:	Am I gonna be on **your** team? *((to Vanessa))*
2	Vanessa:	And **Ka**thy and **Mad**ison. In other words it's girls a-
3	Vanessa:	**Girls** against **boys**.
4	Sandra:	Oh great. We **smoosh** boys.
5		Girls **smoosh** boys.
6	Kathy:	Yeah. We normally win.
7	Sandra:	What? You can't win?
8	Kathy:	We **nor**mally win.
9	Sandra:	Be smooshed a**gain**.

Often, as Schofield (1981:72) argues, "Boys' and girls' awareness of each other as possible romantic and sexual partners, concern about rejection in such relationships, and strong sex-typing of interests and activities can result in a great deal of informal segregation of the sexes." In third grade a form of flirting occurred during recess, for example with boys putting ice cubes down the shirts of third grade girls. However, for the most part through the third grade, girls and boys maintained relaxed friendships with one another; boys and girls traded athletic cards, ate lunch together, and even got together after school to play, sharing interests in sports.

Easeful interaction characterized talk during classroom time as well as recess. When third grade children were assigned to small groups and given the task of cutting up pieces of fruit and composing a recipe of the fractions of fruit used, girls had no problem in correcting members of their male cohort when they made mistakes. The following occurred after Carlos said that he was going to keep half of a cantaloupe for himself:

Example 3.22

	((While cutting up fruit for a math exercise))
Sandra:	You can't use a who:le **half** Carlos.
	(0.8)
Carlos:	***I'm*** a cut 'em in ***fourths***.
	(0.5)
Don:	But then ***I*** ⌈can't use any::::.
Sandra:	⌊***That's*** **eighths**.
Sandra:	You need to cut a **half** into **eighths**.

Playful banter was also characteristic of their interaction. At the end of the basketball game as the third grade children were getting ready to line up to come in from recess, a modified form of ritual insult (Labov 1972) developed from conversation between boys and girls when Ken (a boy who was distinguished by having a long blond pony tail) objected to the notion that the girls fouled the boys and were not penalized for it. Ritual insult classically involves pejorative statements about an attribute of the target known not to be literally true. The recipient of an initial ritual insult should make use of the scene depicted in a prior speaker's talk to produce a second description that turns the initial insult on its head and is even more outrageous. A successful return insult leaves the other party with nothing more to say. The following provides an example:

Example 3.23

```
                    ((on basketball court))
 1   Ken:      I got fouled by Kathy, almost ten or eleven times
 2               in this one game.
 3   Sandra:   You know what Ken?
 4               ⌈It's-
 5   Ken:      ⌊Just shut up please.
 6   Donna:    Heh heh heh.
 7   Paul:     ⌈Oh girl you-
 8   Ken:      ⌊Girl you-
 9   Ken:      Just shut up.=
10   Paul:     Big talker.
11   Paul:     What mouth do you wear.
12   Ken:      Is it any of your business? No. I wasn't-
13   Ken:      Was I talking to you?
14   Ken:      Is this any of your business? No:::.
15               I ⌈wasn't-
16   Sandra:     ⌊I wasn't saying no.
17   Paul:     Come on Sandra. What size mouth do you wear.
18   Sandra:   You know- You don't have a size mouth.
19               You come with-
20               What you (.) were born with.
21               ((dramatic hand movements))
22   Paul:     Battery not included- eh heh heh!
23   Vanessa:  Oh. Please! Come on Paul,
24   Ken:      Can I take your batteries out (of this thing)?
25   Vanessa:  What kind of- what size- NOSE do you wear.
26   Ken:      Nose?
27   Vanessa:  You have a big nose.
28   Ken:      Do I have a big nose? ((said turning to Paul))
29   Paul:     (kind of)
30   Vanessa:  eh heh-heh hah-hah hah-heh!
31   Isaac:    You were shooting that three per cent nose.
32   Vanessa:  Do you buy your ponytail at Thrifty? ((to Ken))
33   Paul:     You should see her Mom's nose boy.
34               ((does large motion)) Dnh dnh!
35   Vanessa:  My mom's nose,
36   Paul:     Looks like a sow's nose to me.
37   Vanessa:  No it's YOUR nose that's the mouth
38               (mouse) was just stickin out of the sky on the siren.
```

Variations on the form of classical ritual insult, or "mock impoliteness,"[15] occur here. Ritual insult creates a relaxed atmosphere, where it "cannot be endangered even by seemingly rude utterances" (Kienpointner 1997:262).

Ken complains that Kathy fouled him several times (lines 1–2). As Sandra begins to lodge a counter complaint back to him (line 3), Ken provides a bald imperative with "Shut up," (line 9) and Paul introduces a negative person descriptor "Big talker" (line 10) and a question with an imbedded pejorative description: "What size *mouth* do you wear" (line 11). Sandra returns with a retort to the question Paul posed: "You don't *have* a size mouth. You come with what you were *born* with" (lines 18–21). Rather than respond to this statement, Paul remarks "Battery not included" (line 22) – tying to her talk, and invoking the notion of a mouth as something that is mechanical, as well as bought and sold. A friend of Sandra's, Vanessa, comes to Sandra's assistance in the conflict and questions Ken: "What size- **NOSE** do you wear" (line 25). The topic then switches to discussion of noses. When he responds with a question, "Do I have a big nose?" (line 28), treating the insult seriously, Vanessa provides a second ritualized insult, by commenting on his long pony tail: "Do you buy your pony tail at Thrifty?" (line 32).[16]

Ritual insult typically functions to transform a potentially dangerous contest or conflict into a bout of wit, where the contest involves statements that are known by the players not to be true. Here a complaint about the way a girl allegedly fouled a boy is transformed into a contest of insults about hypothetical commodities that are bought and sold: mouths that run on batteries and cheap attachable ponytails available at a thrift store. Forms of mock impoliteness[17] key the interaction as playful, with each participant building upon the prior speaker's action. The ethos of playfulness resulting from cross-sex disputes is quite different from forms of argumentation that result when girls attempt to make claims for equal access to the soccer field.

Disputes in Cross-Sex Relations

A dramatic shift occurred between the third and fourth grade. The banter and play between co-equal team-mates, with boys and girls playing handball and basketball together quite frequently, came to a screeching halt as the children went into the fourth grade. For the most part, girls who had been athletic and were best friends with boys, stopped playing basketball with them – stating that they did not want to get all sweaty during recess. Studies of elementary school children among the white middle class have found that gender segregation is frequently associated with perceiving the opposite gender as possible romantic and sexual partners.[18]

Playful insult battles were replaced with inter-group contests in volleyball and jump rope in fourth grade and epic fights for the soccer field in fifth grade. The popular clique enjoyed sports and were active in after-school soccer leagues. Though boys and girls did not play basketball together in fourth grade, girls enjoyed playing some games (jump rope and volleyball) with or near boys because they permitted interaction and flirting with otherwise gender-segregated groups.[19] Because jump rope was taught in physical education classes, for a month in the fourth grade gender-segregated groups of girls and boys played jump rope quite near one another on the playground. In fifth grade, when girls wished to play soccer exclusively with girls in the location generally colonized by boys, girls challenged the boys to their exclusive rights to dominate the playing field.

In order to understand the striking shift in play patterns, it is important to consider not only the patterns of interactions which characterize interacting individuals, but also the kinds of social organizations which are structuring "arrangements between the sexes" (Goffman 1977). Thorne (2002:10) has argued that if we want to comprehend the "coercive force of gender arrangements," then we need to look not only at interaction and discourse, but also consider "the dynamics of institutions and social structure."[20] Studies of situated interaction should, in Thorne's opinion, be coupled with studies of "the range of forces that help shape human action" (Thorne 2002:11). Such an account of the social organization of a group is much in line with Giddens' (1984) call for a study of how larger social structures are reproduced or negotiated through the practices of social actors who are both constrained and enabled by social structure.[21]

The popular group of girls had to contend with two major groups who acted as if they had authority over them. The first group was fourth through sixth grade boys who were allowed by playground aides and coaches almost exclusive rights to the soccer, football, and baseball playing fields. As the clique members expressed it, they disliked playing with the boys because "They think that they're professional players. They throw the ball so high. They invade and they never pass to you." "They never let any girls play. Unless you get there first."

The second group that exerted authority over the fourth grade girls was a group of sixth grade girls who often, unbeknownst to the aides or teachers, bullied the fourth graders. Interactions with each of these groups will be discussed to describe the structural arrangements that impact the clique's play activities.

Interactions with boys in play and games in fourth and fifth grade

In fourth grade (as in younger grades as well) girls would on occasion express strong romantic feelings towards particular boys. In one case in fourth grade this resulted in an extended contest between two best friends over who could be "married" to a particular boy while playing "house." Girls were generally much more concerned with how they were viewed by other girls than with how they were viewed by boys or how they sorted themselves into heterosexual pairs.[22] One reason fourth grade girls opted to play jump rope rather than basketball or other sports was that they felt that during the activity of playing rope it was less likely that someone would accuse them of doing something wrong, such as slapping someone with a sweatshirt.

Only in the fifth grade did girls attempt to make use of their friendships with particular boys to gain access to participation in a game of softball when a team was picked. The girls were concerned with how fairly boys treated them in sports; they did not like boys who were "selfish in sports" or "ball hogs," boys who refused to pass the ball to girls during soccer. Neither did they appreciate the way boys hurled the balls when they did pass them to the girls. The deportment of the boys was quite different from the way members of girls' after-school leagues behaved. For their part during softball and soccer, boys complained that girls were more concerned about the dynamics of their peer relations and clothing than with the game on the playing field.

When girls played ball games with boys, girls would complain that the boys played too aggressively.[23] For example, in fourth grade while playing volleyball a boy slammed the ball right at the edge of the net into Aretha's chest. She screamed and demanded that the group talk to the coach. The coach tried to resolve the dispute saying that boys are stronger and need to watch their strength.

Example 3.24

Coach:	Listen. Listen. You're playing with girls. Okay?
Janis:	Oh:: (hhh)!
Coach:	Alright now. *Lis*ten! Listen. ***No*** no no listen!
	Alright see you guys are stronger. Much stronger.
	Is he not much stronger than you? to do that? Is he not?
Alan:	Yes I'm stronger.
Aretha:	eh heh!
Coach:	Well you gotta be careful, with your strength! okay?

Accounts stressing gender differences in the physical strength of girls and boys (and positively evaluating male strength) emerge within accounts the coach gives to boys for why they need to be "careful of their strength."

Cross-gender negotiation of soccer space in fifth grade

Forms of hierarchy have been documented in Thorne's (1993) investigations of how playgrounds are utilized by elementary school children. Boys control as much as ten times more playground space than girls, operating with respect to a "pattern of claimed entitlement" (Thorne 1993:83). Girls are generally relegated to cemented spaces closer to the school building, where, for example, hopscotch grids are painted. Boys at Hanley School controlled not only the soccer and football field, but the baseball diamond as well. If girls were selected to play softball, it was because they were girlfriends of the captain of a team, or her very closest friends. This meant that the chief areas where girls could play were on the jungle gyms, the swing sets, and on the sidewalks leading to the fields. When in the sixth grade a tetherball pole was established, this was accessible by both girls as well as boys. Although girls could also play on the basketball and handball courts, members of the popular clique did not like to play these games.

During fourth grade the clique girls' interaction in sports with boys was restricted to volleyball and jump rope. However, during the fifth grade girls (who often played soccer in after-school sports groups) became interested in playing softball in the baseball mound and soccer on the grassy field of the playground. Usually at lunchtime boys wolfed down their lunch quickly and ran to get the appropriate equipment to play, while girls took often 10–15 minutes longer to eat their lunches and talk. Thus boys took over the soccer field, and it was virtually impossible for the girls to get an opportunity to play. The male aides, men in their late teens and early twenties who earn a minimum wage watching children during lunchtime, assisted the boys in allowing them to have the field to themselves.

One day in May during the fifth grade the girls decided that they no longer wanted to be constrained by the male-dominated rules dictating who could occupy the soccer field. They had talked with their fifth grade teacher, Miss Harper, who sided with them in their position that they had legitimate rights to play soccer. The girls rushed through lunch in order to beat the boys to the soccer field with the ball. Once they had secured the space, they began to organize their teams. Soon, however, two boys arrived and demanded their right to the field. Emi, who was accompanied by two of her friends, Melissa and Kathy (a precocious girl and the only fourth grader who played routinely with the clique in fifth grade), announced to a fifth grader (Ron) and two fourth grade boys, Carlos and Miguel, that the girls had the field that day (line 1), and an argument about rights to the field ensued (see Examples 1.1–1.2).

When the boys leave I ask what happened. The girls narrate their version of the past events as well as their plan for alternating days of occupying the field (a plan earlier discussed with their teacher) with the boys (lines 11–14).

Example 3.25

1	MHG:	So- hey- Melissa. Tell me what **hap**pened.
2	Melissa:	What do you mean.
3	MHG:	Like, the boys got up here first?
4	Melissa:	No. **Em**i- **Em**i got up here first. And they-
5		Then Miguel came and Ron came,
6		And then-
7		After they came they say- it's their field.
8		Which it's **not**. Because they- the whole **school** pays-
9	Emi:	And so we ⌈made-
10	Melissa:	⌊**All** the kids pay for this that goes here.
11	Emi:	So I **told** him- that- if they were there tomorrow,
12		If we got it today,
13		Then we switch off **ev**ery day.
14		So, happy to work.

The boys tell the female aide about what the girls have said, and she approaches them. As the girls begin to provide rationales for their scheme of switching off days and provide complaints against the boys (lines 4–5), a group of five boys join them:

Example 3.26

	((*Boys join the girls' group*))
Emi:	No we- we made a deal?
	And they just hadda accept that.
	They get it- tomorrow?
	And we switch off every day.
FemaleAide:	(°)
Melissa:	All- all their friends ( )
Kathy:	We would let fewer people,
	We would let two people, but not **all** of them.
Melissa:	Only maybe **one** passes the ball to the girls.
Kathy:	Yeah.=**And** they push us **over**
	They're- they're rough. (1.0)
	They're **rough!**
	We don't want to ⌈play with em.
Ron:	⌊They can't ex**clude**.
Melissa:	**No**. We're not ex**clu**ding
Emi:	**No we're**- we're not ex**clu**ding.
	You guys get it tomorrow.
Ron:	But they're just cutting us **off**.
Melissa:	It's not your **field**. ((*pointing, body leaning towards*))
Kathy:	It's not your **field** ((*leaning towards boys*))
Emi:	Last time you guys said "**We** were here **first**."
Miguel:	I **know**. But then we let you **play**.
Emi:	I **know**. So- why- why you w-
	What's the **fight** right now.
	⌈What are you **talk**ing about.
Carlos:	⌊You're not letting us play.
Miguel:	And we let **you** guys play.
Emi:	Well we do **too**.
Melissa:	You guys always **hog** the **ball**,
	When we play you **hog** the **ball**,
Kathy:	And they don't play it right. ((*to Aide, shaking head*))
	They don't play soccer right.
Melissa:	⌈Maybe one of you passes to a girl during the game.
Kathy:	⌊((*demonstrates boys' kicking movements*)) (on the field)
Kathy:	And then they don't even do it **right**.
Melissa:	Not your **field** Ron.

The female aide sided with the girls, agreeing that the girls will play today and the boys the next day. The boys walk off.

Emi, Melissa, and Kathy realize that they need more than three players to occupy the field. Their friends Sarah and Aretha decline playing. Aretha says she doesn't want to play unless the boys do, and also because she feels three people do not constitute a team. Sarah says that she would prefer swinging on the jungle gym that day. Emi and Melissa then recruit three more girls, girls they generally ignore – two fourth grade girls (Sandra and Madison) and a fifth grade girl (Clarita), to play. As they are heading off to play a male aide is heard yelling loudly to them:

Example 3.27

Male Aide:	***GIRLS!*** LET THE BOYS HAVE THEIR ***FIELD!***
	SORRY.
	BO::::YS?
	TOO MU:CH- ***TOO- SOR***RY!
	THEY'RE THERE ***NOW***!

This statement infuriates Emi, who then leads the girls to the far end of the field while taking a strong stance towards the Aide's directive.

Example 3.28

Emi:	°Okay. Okay. This is the final thing.
	I'm sorry. We're sorry. Okay? We're sorry.
	No problem. There's nothing.
Boy:	We get it tomorrow.
Emi:	You guys get it to***mor***row. We're sorry.
Boy:	NO:::. WE WANT IT ***NOW::***!
	WE AIN'T ***FAKE*** DUSTING.
Melissa:	We said you could have it tomorrow.
Emi:	WE'RE ***VER***Y ***VER***Y ***VER***Y ***VER***Y ***VER***Y ***VER***Y SORRY.
	YOU GUYS GET IT TO***MOR***ROW.
	YOU GUYS GET- YOU HAVE TO PLAY TOMORROW.
Melissa:	*((with ball)* Okay rea:dy?
	We're splitting up into teams.
	Three and three.
	There's team captains,
	I'll be a team captain,
	And ***Em***i- Clarita will be one.
Clarita:	*((shakes head))*
Melissa:	***Ka***thy will be a team captain.

The following day as the same girls (Emi, Melissa, Kathy, Sandra, Clarita, and Madison) as well as their friends and classmates Sarah, Janis, Brittany, Stephany, and Angela were playing, the male playground aide (see Example 1.2, pp. 30–1) confronted the girls. With his utterance "***GIRLS!*** Go somewhere ***else***", he produced a bald imperative, the most aggravated or explicitly stated directive form possible (Labov and Fanshel 1977:85). He defined the field as "their [the boys'] field" (line 3), as he said "You took over their field." The rationale he provided with "The boys are ***al***ways here playing soccer" was that the boys habitually play soccer (line 25). He provided alternatives for the girls: either playing by themselves on the jungle gym (lines 15–16) or playing soccer with the boys (line 17).

In his talk the aide takes for granted an asymmetrical allocation of spaces for play (lines 9–10). Boys who have by tradition occupied the soccer field require specific areas whereas "girls can go **any**where" (line 23). The girls do not agree to the plan and provide a counter proposal: "Why can't **they** go anywhere" (line 26). The girls (line 30) challenge the aide's authority mandating that boys need a special space, "They **can't** go anywhere" (line 26) with "Well **neith**er can **we**!" (line 30).

One minute later the aide tells the girls that if the girls play, the boys should be permitted to play as well (Example 3.29, lines 1–2) and characterizes the girls' interactions as "rude" (line 15).

Example 3.29

1	Male Aide:	If you guys wanna play soccer
2		the boys are gonna play **too**, o**kay**?
3	Janis:	Fine.
4	Male Aide:	**Make** (.) even (.) tea:ms,
5	Janis:	Fine.
6	Male Aide:	You **can't just** kick them **out**.
7	Janis:	Okay. ⌈People?
8	Male Aide:	⌊The girls will play today.
9	Janis:	Who wants–?
10		I'll make ⌈**them** play with **you** today.
11	Sarah:	⌊**Sto::p!** ((Miguel is kicking Sarah))
12	Angela:	**Stop it MIGUEL!**
13	Janis:	O**KAY**. **Who** wants to be a team **cap**tain.
14	Male Aide:	Who– who played yesterday. Did they?
15		You guys are **rude** to them.
16		And I'm not gonna **take** it anymore.

As the girls then organize the play with boys, they mention one of the perennial problems – not passing to the girls:

Example 3.30

Melissa:	You guys have to pa:::ss,
	to the g⌈i::rls,
Boys:	⌊We will we will, we will.
Janis:	You can have first pick.

A moment later the male aide continues:

Example 3.31

Male Aide:	**Lis**ten to me. And stop giving me an **at**titude.
	Do you understand? (0.4) Do **you** understand?
	Listen. I'm not gonna **take** this **at**titude.
	You girls came out here on Monday and left the field.
	The boys couldn't play soccer.

Janis subsequently reports to a female aide what happened; she comments that the reason the girls do not like to play with the boys is that the boys do not pass the ball to them, and are "so rough they like kick us." Sandra, a fourth grader complains about the sexism of the boys as well as the aide: "Boys- boys **a:nd** Justin [the aide] are being sexist against the girls." Five minutes later, responding to the call of the male aide, the Vice Principal comes out to arbitrate the dispute. As she approaches what is now a group of nine girls she comments, "I hear there's a big problem out here." Janis answers, saying, "Yeah, Justin's being mean." The following transcript provides the dialogue between the girls and the Vice Principal about the dispute. The Vice Principal permits the girls to express their grievance and then argues that the main issue on the table is that there should not be any type of exclusion on the field (line 18).

Example 3.32

```
 1  VP:        Okay. Hold on. I can listen to one person
 2             at a time.
                        (0.4)
 3  VP:        Okay. Start ⌈now.
 4  Brittany:              ⌊The first thing he said- was that-
 5             The girls aren't- as good as the boys
 6  VP:        Now who said this?
 7  Janis:     No. He didn't say it but it sounded like that.
 8  Brittany:  And then he said- he said- (0.5)
 9             He said- "Well you guys should play on the blacktop?
10             And you can play anywhere? but the boys can't?"
11             and then,
                        (0.4)
12             We said "Why can't the boys play on the blacktop,
13             (0.4) and, or- we (.) all (.) share."
14             =And then he was just like-
15             "Well beca::use, (0.2) kind of, (0.5) the girls can play
16             anywhere b- but the boys- (need it)
17             ⌈(° cuz they have to play there.)
18  VP:        ⌊Okay, but. First of all, should we be excluding.
19  Sarah:     No::.
20  Brittany:  But we're not!
```

The girls explain (in their next utterance) that one of their fifth grade teachers (Miss Harper) helped them devise a plan for alternating boys and girls on the field (lines 1–6).

Example 3.33

```
 1  Janis:     We made a deal in uhm,
 2             The people in Miss Harper's class made a deal
 3             With her that- we get like on uhm, Mondays,
 4             Or Wednesdays,
```

5		Or something like that.
6		And they get it the other days?
7		And on Fri ⌈day?
8	VP:	⌊***They*** being the boys.
9	Kathy:	Y⌈eah.
10	Janis:	⌊Yeah. And then **we**:
11	Clarita:	See ⌈we ***do it*** like ***this*** Miss Noble.
12		⌊And then we share it on Friday
13		Miss **No**ble. We do it like ***this***.
14	Janis:	⌈And–
15		⌊See– the boys get **one** day?
16		And then the next day we get a day?
17		But–
18	VP:	Alternate. *((nodding, twirling hands))*

As the girls offer their reasons for this plan they explain their gripes about the ways that the boys play (lines 7–11). Two girls in Emi's fifth grade class, Thelma and Madison, join in the discussion.

Example 3.34

1	Emi:	Only reason for that was–
2		We did boys and girls?
3		Because we thought the boys
4		were getting kinda **rough**?
5		And unfair?
6	Thelma:	⌈They never throw us the ***ba::ll***.
7	Emi:	⌊They take the ball away.
8	Janis:	They don't pass it to us very much.
9		And they say that only the boys can be captain.
10		And they always pick the boys first
11		when they (umpire).

The girls explain that what bothers the girls the most is the boys' attitude that girls are inferior to boys (lines 1–4, 7–8, 12).

Example 3.35

1	Madison:	And yesterday they said something really mean.
2		They said like–
3		They said– they said that girls are better than,
4		Or– um– boys are better than gi::rls?
5	VP:	And how did you respond to that.
6	Sandra:	I– I asked the person who said that.
7		I– I asked Mi**guel–** that– that
8		boys are always better than girls?
9		And he said "yes."
10		And I– and I said, "***That's*** not ***true***."
11		And when we asked him what else?

12   He answered, "Because we think that you're **weak**."
13   Madison: And then we just left it. A::nd w:e told-
14   Sandra: I ignored it.

The Vice Principal does not pass judgment, but says that everyone will discuss the issue as a group and states that the boys are needed as part of the discussion:

Example 3.36
1   VP: Well I can understand why you're upset.
2   And we can resolve- (0.4) the **prob**lem
3   But we need to ha:ve, the **bo::ys** present.
4   And, (0.5) u::m,
5   Sandra: They're **right** over there ((*pointing*)).

The Vice Principal gathers both boys and girls in a circle and proceeds to discuss very democratically what the problem is:

Example 3.37
1   VP: We **seem** to be having a **prob**lem here.
2   We **need** to resolve it. I need **ev**eryone's attention.
3   And I need **ev**eryone to **lis**ten.
4   And if you have something to **say::**,
5   you will need to raise your hand
6   and **wait** to be **call**ed upon.
7   Otherwise we- We have a short amount of time
8   And we have a lot to discuss.
9   But **first** of all.
10   I was brought out here
11   because I heard there was a **prob**lem
12   That only boys were playing on certain days
13   And **girls** were playing on the **oth**er days.
14   **Now-** at **school** do we exclude **a**nyone
15   From the **game**.

After her opening speech about how exclusion is not permitted at the school she asks each gender group to explain what they perceive as the problems.

The boys say that girls kick them, and that when too many people are playing, there are problems. Girls complain that the boys hog the ball and never pass it to girls. When boys serve as team captains they pick boys first and girls last.

Example 3.38
1   Emi: When we play with the boys sometimes
2   when it comes to picking teams
3   it's usually that boys are always team captains?
4   and they always pick boys first and then girls last?
5   And I think that's what gets us the most.

The male aide counters, and says that it really depends on who arrives first on the field. The VP mentions that there could be another way of organizing play. She asks for ideas and Janis responds, "We could alternate." The VP suggests that they need rules for how many people could play at a time, and ideally would have a rotating list of players. Limiting the numbers who are actually on the field at one time it is decided might diminish problems on the field.

The girls succeeded in staging a micro-revolution, challenging the status quo. During the fall term of the year after this incident the school implemented a policy permitting rotation of football and soccer for those children of either gender who signed up wanting to play that allowed equal access. In addition simultaneously a "safe schools" curriculum was put into play. This was a heightened effort to teach children about tolerance in many different venues, involving students in lessons about social difference not only during lessons about puberty and sexuality, but throughout the curriculum.

The girls' fight for their space to play led to dramatic changes with respect to participation in sports the next year. At first during fall term the girls eagerly participated in soccer, excited to be able to interact at close range to the boys. However, problems with the boys not passing the ball to them so that they could participate, or hitting them with the ball, persisted. A few sixth grade boys sexually harassed the girls, pinching their nipples on the playing field. Some playground aides supervising the children's activities overlooked such behaviors, considering them part of a natural order. The athletics coach, supporting the male aides, told me that the appropriate place for females was as spectators; assuming a passive role now, the coach said, would aid in the girls' socialization to gender-appropriate female adult roles in the future – as spectators rather than participants. Girls' interest in co-ed soccer waned as the year progressed given the way girls were treated during their time on the field (including harassment). In addition the introduction of a tetherball court provided a new arena for negotiating status among the group.

Despite problems, the girls did succeed in initiating a new moral order on their own terms. The overtly political activity of the girls countering the boys challenges the view of girls as non-competitive and displays quite dramatically their engagement in issues of justice and fairness; it also provides a view of girls as wielders of authority and instruments of change.

Asymmetrical Relations among Girls

Not only did the popular girls' group at Hanley School have to contend with boys dominating the play space of the soccer field; in addition struggles for relative positions were evident in the ways that older girls (sixth graders) invaded their space while they were eating lunch during fourth grade. For over three decades the work of feminist researchers of language and gender has demonstrated concern with issues of power asymmetries in interaction and with developing political commentary about them. For example, studies of language and gender have documented relations of dominance[24] in male-female interaction and how patriarchy is constituted in moment-to-moment cross-sex interaction.[25] Henley and Kramarae (1991:19), for example, argue that gender-related language differences must necessarily be "viewed in the context of male power and female subordination." As yet, however, few studies examine how asymmetrical relationships are constituted in all female interaction.[26]

In accomplishing children's social organization directive/response sequences constitute the primary way that children organize their play with one another (discussed in some detail in chapter 4, in "Regulating Activity through Directives"). Directives have been defined as "an utterance intended to indicate the speaker's desire to regulate the behavior of the listener – that is, to get the listener to do something (e.g., provide information, give permission, perform an action" – Becker 1982:1). In their discussions of directives in adult conversations, Labov and Fanshel (1977:84) argue that "in all discussions of discourse, analysts take into account the subject's desire to mitigate or modify his expression to avoid creating offense." Goodwin (1990:75–108), however, has analyzed how children can build either symmetrical or asymmetrical relationships in their play.[27]

Examining children aged 9–14 engaged in a task activity, certain patterns are salient. The turns of those who position themselves above others are not built through mitigated action (asking permission, providing warrants for action, etc.). Instead turns are constructed making use of bald imperatives, pejorative address terms, insults, accounts that index arbitrary needs and desires of the speaker rather than requirements of the group, and explanations that allude to the speaker's ultimate control.[28] Children who position themselves as leaders issue directives formulated as direct commands, while receiving indirect requests from others. They contradict proposals and requests of others while expecting and getting compliance to their own. Finally, children who seek to establish themselves in positions above others can usurp the turn space of others without sanction. Directives and responses to them thus affirm and ratify who has the right to make decisions about various optional ways that the game can be played or how the activity should proceed.

The sequences reported on in this chapter will examine how asymmetrical relationships that endure over time are built in moment-to-moment interaction.

Asymmetry in interaction between fourth and sixth grade girls

Important work in conversation analysis has been concerned with preference organization in agreement and disagreement sequences. Silverman (1998:160) has argued, "Sacks' early interest in 'agreements' was in showing how they were basic to sociality." Conversation analysts have found that in polite adult conversation disagreement is a dispreferred activity.[29] For example, Pomerantz (1984) notes that when disagreement is constructed as a dispreferred action its occurrence is minimized through a number of phenomena such as (1) delays before the production of a disagreement, and (2) prefaces that soften the disagreement. Sometimes prefaces take the form of agreements that are then followed by the disagreement. The following provides a case in point:

Example 3.39

A: She doesn't uh usually come in on Friday, does she.
B: Well, yes she does, sometimes.

The dispreferred status of B's turn is marked through such practices as delay of an action within a turn or across a sequence of turns or prefaces of the action ("Well" precedes disagreement in this example), the qualification (exemplified through "sometimes") or other forms of mitigation, and accounts. Such forms of delays, softened turn prefaces, and mitigations, I found were noticeably absent in the conversations of working class African American Maple Street children in Philadelphia,[30] who more typically displayed a preference for disagreement than agreement. Rather than orienting towards agreement, children created miniature versions of "character contests" (Goffman 1967:254). In brief, rather than organizing their talk to display deference to others, children often seek opportunities to display character and realign the social organization of the moment through opposition. In interactions among sixth grade girls and fourth grade girls in the popular clique in Hanley School, character contests similar to those of the Maple Street group were quite common.

Fourth grade girls viewed sixth graders' concerns about bodily appearance exaggerated and affected.[31] Fourth grade girls in the clique delighted in mimicking sixth graders' alignment towards personal grooming and enjoyed evaluating their demeanor. In the following example (3.40) a portrait of a girl named Vickie is provided by first quoting her talk, showing her distress at having broken a fingernail and second, through use of negative assessments:[32] describing her as "a showoff" while also "not that popular."

Example 3.40

Sarah: Look at Vickie!
Emi: "Oh No! I broke a (.) fingernail!"
Sarah: "What am I going to do *now*."
Emi: She's *such* a show off.
Janis: She's actually not that popular.

Fourth grade girls were frequently taunted by some of the sixth graders, the highest grade in the school, and the group that "ruled." Sixth graders felt free to jump into a game of rope that fourth grade girls had organized without asking. At lunch they often insulted members of the fourth grade girls' group by calling them names and tried to entangle them in he-said-she-said disputes with agemates.

In the following (Example 3.41) we see how three sixth grade girls, Dionne, Julia, and Nancy, through instigating and transforming the history of a past event,[33] entangled fourth grade girls in ridicule of Angela. In Example 3.41 after Julia insults Angela by calling her "an armpit" (line 4), Dionne recounts what Angela told her (lines 6–8) (that all of her friends had left her) and the categorization that the fourth grade clique had used to depict Angela in their talk to Dionne about Angela (lines 9–12) – that Angela was "stupid," a "whore," and a "bitch." In response Angela (line 13) and Aretha (line 16) emphatically deny that that was what was said. Their actions clearly deny the charges made. Angela states, "Sorry. They did not say that." Aretha's denial states "I **NEV**ER EVEN SAID (it) WHORE."

In response to Angela's moves Dionne retorts with a warning to Angela: that she needs to "get herself grounded" (line 19) because she is now being friendly with (line 22) and "being used" (lines 26, 28) by girls who insult her by calling her "stupid" (line 10), a "whore" (line 11, and a "bitch" (lines 12 and 21).

Example 3.41

1	Dionne:	*((adopts a theatrical mode as if in the midst of the play))*
2		Oh looky. uh- well Wait! Wait!
3		Is that- Angela I see?
4	Julia:	uhm- Dripping? Probably just an armpit.
5	Angela:	⌈UH: UH::: UH:::::::::::::::::::::::::::::::::::::, *((undulating sound))*
6	Dionne:	⌊I could **SWEAR!**
7		I don't have any ***friends***.
8		They all ***left*** me.
9		Oh no. We don't ***like*** Angela.
10		We think she's so stupid
11		and nothing but a ***whore***.
12		and a ***bitch***.=
13	Angela:	Sorry. They ⌈did not ***say*** that.
14	Dionne:	⌊Is that the words I // wrote-
15	Janis:	Is that the ***on***ly words // you say?
16	Aretha:	I **NEV**ER EVEN ***SAID*** (it) WHORE.
17	Nancy:	⌈°I knew (you had it in you.)
18	Julia:	⌊I'm ***sor***ry Angela but- like
19		You need to get yourself ***ground***ed
20		Like Miss Smith- Miss Smith calls it anchoring?
21		Because they just called you fat ***bitch***.
22		And then you're back ***friends*** with them?
23		I'm not trying to be mean to you.
24		But I didn't-
25		⌈but you're (*all* along-)
26	Dionne:	⌊BUT YOURE BEING ***USED***.=
27	Aretha:	WE DID ***NOT*** ⌈(just call her whore.)
28	Dionne:	⌊(You know) you're being ***u::sed*** Angela.

In reporting what was said in the past about Angela, Dionne both insults Angela, telling her she is "being used" and involves the fourth grade clique by accusing them of hurling insults at Angela.

The forms of evaluative commentary made with respect to offensive actions that occur provide ways of understanding native categories of inappropriate or immoral behavior. For example, the girls gloss the sixth graders' activity of grabbing hold of them by their clothing against their will as "bothering" them (line 1) and being "really rude" (line 4).

Example 3.42

1	Janis:	She doesn't have the **right** to **both**er us.
2		If we said "Let go" she should have let go of us.
3	Melissa:	Who.
4	Janis:	Dionne. I think that's really **rude**.[34]

In response to the sixth graders' taunting of the fourth graders, the girls begin to hurl insults, in particular at Dionne, who is constantly invading their space and insulting them. In the sequence below Janis calls Dionne "half wit" (line 3). In response Dionne calls Janis a "whore" (line 4). The fourth graders who are positioned as spectators take up different alignments. Aretha provides a meta-commentary (line 7) on Dionne's talk, asking her if "whore" is her favorite word, while (line 8) Sarah bids out of the discussion with, "I'm **out**ie" before leaving. This phrase, used by Valley Girls in the film *Clueless*, means she's not taking part in the argument, that she is "out" of it. The girls frequently made use of gestures and phrases (such as "Whatever!") from the movie *Clueless*. Dionne explicitly warns the girls that she is not someone to be "messed with" (lines 14–15). Later on in the sequence Dionne comments pejoratively on Janis's stomach showing (lines 20–21) and her short shorts (line 22).

Example 3.43

1	Sarah:	Somebody can you turn my rope.
2	Janis:	Dionne I found out that your **new** name is **half** wit.
3	Dionne:	°I just found out that your new name is **whore**.
4	Janis:	((hands up, shaking head))
5		((folding hands))
6		Where'd you find **that** out.
7	Aretha:	Is that your **fav**orite word or something?
8	Sarah:	I'm **out**ie. I'm **out**ie. ((leaves))
9	Janis:	((dancing)) I mean
10		I'm a whore.
11	Emi:	((play fights with Dionne))
12	Aretha:	((play fights with Dionne))
13	Dionne:	No! ((hitting Aretha))
14		Let me tell you guys something.
15		**No**body messes with me.
16	Emi:	Oh oka(hh)y.

17	Dionne:	**No**body. **No**body in the world.
18	Aretha:	Nobody messes with me *((mimicking))*
19	Janis:	(no care) *((does gesture))*
20	Dionne:	I dress the way people are sup**pos**ed to dress.
21		Without their stomachs showing
22		and their shorts going all the way up to their ass.
23	Janis:	**Where.** Where is my stomach showing Dionne,
24		Oh. Stick your butt!
25		Shake your **boo**ty.
26		Shake your **boo**ty.
27	Aretha:	Shake your **boo**ty.

Explicit reference to age ("younger girls") and animosity between sixth and fourth graders is made in the next sequence, occurring prior to the he-said-she-said event involving Angela. The fourth grade girls describe the activities of the sixth graders as "making fun of" younger girls (lines 1–2). Dionne (line 11) provides an insult to the fourth grade girls, claiming that they need to "fake" having breasts. In response Aretha states that she is not the person who "sticks [her] tits out" (line 15). While having breasts to fill a bra is a major concern of sixth graders, with the exception of Angela, in the fourth grade none of the girls in the clique were physically developed or wore a bra, or even talked about wearing one.

Example 3.44

1	Janis:	You guys prove a lot of things to make fun of-
2		kids who are **young**er than you.
3	Sue:	**Young**er?
4	Janis:	Yeah.
5	Sue:	I'm- ⌈Well what grade are you in.
6	Meghan:	⌊Well it's because of the way you **act**=
7	Janis:	Fourth.=
8	Meghan:	Are, and we don't **like** you.
9	Janis:	You guys **prove** so **much**.
10	Meghan:	Exactly.
11	Dionne:	Yes well we don't **fake** as much as **you** like to.
12	Sue:	Yeah.
13	Janis:	About ⌈what.
14	Sarah:	⌊HI: I'm **out**ie. *((leaving the group))*
15	Aretha:	**I'm** not the one who sticks my **tits** out.
16	Sue:	Yeah you **are** and your bra's **o**ver there.
17	Aretha:	**I** don't **wear** a bra.
18	Angela:	Aretha doesn't wear a bra.
19	Angela:	Aretha hallelujah.

The next year in school, as fifth graders, members of the popular clique talked about how members of another clique, the "Blondies" (three blond sixth graders and one fifth grader) imposed their sense of beauty[35] on Sarah and insulted her openly, saying she was ugly (lines 5, 7, 9), and later lied to the principal (lines 17–18), denying that they had insulted her.

Example 3.45

1	MHG:	So Aretha, why- what is with Chloe and stuff.
2		What do they do or something.
3	Aretha:	They're *stu*pid.
4		They think they're really pretty. They're really *cool*.
5	Sarah:	They think I'm ugly and everything.
6	MHG:	***WHAT?***
7	Aretha:	They think Sarah's really ugly.
8	MHG:	Do they go around and say stuff like that?
9	Aretha:	Yeah. They say "Sarah's ugly."
10	Sarah:	And then they deny it
11		when you go to the principal's office.
12	Aretha:	eh heh heh!
13	MHG:	Really? Does it get to the principal's office?
14	Sarah:	Yeah I went there and told him ( ) last week.
15	MHG:	You told that they were ⌈saying?
16	Sarah:	⌊Yeah and then like-
17		"Well we were just joking."
18		She *((referring to Chloe))*
19		made up every single lie that we said.

In the following I ask the girls in the popular clique why a group of girls would do such things. I was told that the "Blondies" assumed that because they were the oldest age group they could "rule the school" and had free reign telling other people off, insulting other girls, because of their "cool."

Example 3.46

MHG:	Well why do they try to do that to you.
	Why do the older kids- Are they older?
	A little bit older?
Sarah:	Well they're gonna be gone
	⌈in one year.
Aretha:	⌊They think they're *cool*.
	And they think that they can do whatever they want.
	That they rule the school and stuff like that.
MHG:	Huh.
Aretha:	So they wanna like-
Sarah:	*((high pitch or loud imitating voices))*
	I'M IN SIXTH GRADE AND I CAN **RULE** THE **SCHOO**L.
	I CAN TELL PEOPLE THAT YOU'RE **UGLY**.

As the conversation continues, the girls explain that the sixth graders are competing with their fifth grade clique for popularity:

Example 3.47

1	Aretha:	Yeah 'Cause they don't wanna say that we're pop-
2		more popular than they are.
3	Sarah:	AND I AM **COOL**! eh heh!
4		AND THAT MAKES ME EVEN **MORE** STUPID.
5		Eh heh heh!
6	Brittany:	Eh heh!
7	Aretha:	'Cause we **are** more popular than they are.
8	Sarah:	I know. We **are** more popular.
9	Aretha:	We are more popular with the (0.4) grades one and
10		two **and** grades three and four than they are.
11	Sarah:	'CAUSE WE ARE **FIRST**. WE ARE **FAM**ILY!

One realm in which there is competition between older and younger groups is with respect to popularity. For Aretha it is important that their clique is well liked by all age groups in the school (lines 9–10), including the younger grades. Sarah likewise feels that ranking first in popularity is important for the members of her clique, identified as "family" (line 11).

Within the competition between groups girls articulate those features of their social universe that matter for them. Older girls attempt to stir up trouble by creating gossip dramas. They report insults (using pejorative adjectives such as "stupid" and negative person descriptors "whore" and "bitch") said about someone in her absence in the presence of both the target of the insults as well as the putative offending parties. Older girls also insult younger girls directly to their face, using descriptors such as "ugly," "whore" and "fake" (referring to their breast sizes). Younger girls retaliate with their own glosses of the behavior of the older girls, considering them "rude," "half wits," and "show offs." The dynamics of a longer exchange will further illustrate the resources that younger girls bring to bear in countering the offensive actions of older girls towards them.

An extended dispute between fourth and sixth grade girls

Struggles over who could insult whom were quite evident in the interactions between older and younger groups of girls. A particular instance entails moves initiated by Dionne, a girl two years older than the fourth grade girls in the popular clique, and the counter responses of younger girls to Dionne's moves, will be considered in some detail.

Not only did Dionne stir up trouble among the fourth graders and invade the younger girls' play and eating space; in addition she frequently attempted to confiscate the fourth grade girls' food from their lunch boxes. On one occasion they offered her carrots and soda when she appeared at their lunch table. In the following sequence, however, the girls resist giving in to her. In this sequence we can see repetitive attempts by Dionne to place herself in a position of relative superiority and the responses of younger girls to such moves. The fourth graders treat Dionne's insults ("You smell")

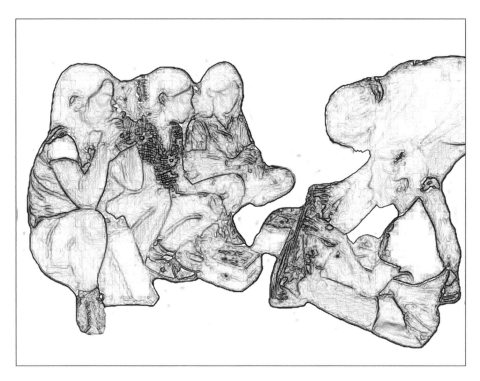

Figure 3.2　Dionne's invasion of the girls' lunchbags

and territorial intrusions as violations. In Figure 3.2 Dionne is the figure positioned on the extreme right, reaching into Lisa's lunch box. Janis, Sarah, Melissa, Sharie (not visible), and Lisa are positioned left to right.

Example 3.48

((Dionne approaches a group of five fourth graders who are seated eating lunch. She asks where one of their group members is.))

1	Dionne:	***Where's*** Aretha.
2	Janis:	She's–
3	Melissa:	In the ⌈***art*** room.
4	Janis:	⌊***At–***
5	Janis:	the art room.
6	Lisa:	⌈***Why:.***
7	Dionne:	⌊Don't talk to me Janis.
8	Dionne:	Can I see what you have in your lunch?
9		(0.6) *((reaching into Lisa's lunch bag))*
10	Lisa:	°Mm hm.°
11	Dionne:	We ***need*** to resolve it.
		Oh my ***go:sh***.
12		⌈Can I have this? *((taking drink bottle from Lisa))*
13	Sarah:	⌊*((collusive mouth wrinkle toward Janis))*
14	Lisa:	***No.*** *((taking bottle back))*
15	Dionne:	***You*** smell.

16	Dionne:	Okay.=**What** do you have in your lunch.
17		*((looking in Melissa's empty lunch box))*
18	Sarah:	Dionne you're **such** a big bully.
19	Dionne:	Did you see us-
20		that milk commercial last night?
21		(1.5)
22	Dionne:	⌈Do you watch tv?
23	Sarah:	⌊*((eyes look down))*
24		**Yes**. I **do**. *((raising eyes))*
25		°But I couldn't leave it on for the milk commercial.
26	Dionne:	°I'm sorry Sarah. *((bends putting hands on knees))*
27	Sarah:	°Hmph. *((nodding two small nods))* Now **go!**
28		*((points towards another part of playground))*
29	Sharie:	eh heh ⌈heh heh!
30	Lisa:	⌊hnh hnh hnh hnh!
31	Janis:	GO **BACK** TO YOUR-
		((palm opens, points to Dionne))
32	Janis:	*((extends arm, points towards where*
		Sarah had previously))
33	Dionne:	SHUT **UP** ⌈**JAN**IS.
34	Janis:	⌊(°over there.)
35	Dionne:	I don't like **talk**ing to you any more.
36	Sarah:	⌈Eh uhm *((throat clear))*
37	Janis:	⌊(°)
38	Dionne:	After what you said lastertime when y-
39		yesterday-
40		⌈last week.
41	Sarah:	⌊EH **UHM!** *((stands up, facing Dionne, spreading*
		arms out as if a road block))
42	Dionne:	**Sar**ah, *((stands up, extending arms with palms up))*
43		⌈eh heh heh heh
44	Sharie:	⌊eh heh heh!
45	Dionne:	⌈And **no**body here has a good lunch. *((hands on hips))*
46	Melissa:	⌊*((stands up spreading hands imitating Sarah's roadblock))*
47	Dionne:	And **where's** Aretha.
48	Melissa:	In the artroom.
49	Melissa:	She's doing that treasure chest now.
50	Janis:	At the art room.
51	Dionne:	Kay.
52	Dionne:	That's **Li**sa, I have no idea *((pointing to Sharie))*,
53		Melissa? *((pointing))*
54	Melissa:	*((nods head))*
55	Dionne:	Sarah,
56	Sarah:	Yeah her's name's // No Idea.
57	Lisa:	That's.
58	Janis:	⌈°Sharie.
59	Dionne:	⌊What's your name?

```
60   Melissa:   ⌈Sharie.
61   Sharie:    ⌊Sharie.
62   Dionne:    Sharie, Lisa, Sharie, Melissa, Sarah.
                ((shoulder shrug))
63              Nice to meet you guys. ((walks away))
64   Sarah:     ⌈((makes face to Dionne's back))
65   Janis:     ⌊((makes face to Dionne's back))
66   Lisa:      eh heh!
67   Janis:     (°           dresses nice              )
68   Melissa:   Well Dionne's nice to me. Dionne's nice to me.
69   Sarah:     ((continues to make face at Dionne))
70   Melissa:   Dionne's really nice to me.
71   Janis:     'Cause she thinks that you're- (like her      )
72   Sarah:     Arrr:::: ((growling)) Ar ar eh // heh heh!
73   Janis:     eh heh heh!
74   Lisa:      eh heh! heh heh heh!
75   Janis:     She goes- ((does imitation))
76   Melissa:   Dionne's nice // to Sarah, me, and Lisa.
77   Sarah:     Arr arr arr
78   Melissa:   Isn't Dionne nice to us Sarah and Lisa?
79   Sarah:     Yeah.
80   Lisa:      That's Valerie.
81   Sarah:     Let's go play- ((gets up))
```

Struggles for relative position are observable in the ways that girls respond to Dionne physically intruding into the girls' space, attempting to take their food, delivering a personalized insult (line 15), and initiating topic shifts that index her status (lines 19–20) when she is refused food. The girls treat these actions as objectionable in several ways: (1) They address Dionne with a negative person descriptor,[36] "big bully" in line 18. (2) They speak to her with bald imperatives (lines 27, 31–32), ("Now *go*!" and "GO *BACK* TO YOUR-") the most face-threatening type of directive possible,[37] with growls (lines 72 and 77) and with gestures signaling their opposition in response to her moves by pointing the way to leave (line 28), blocking her advance with outstretched arms at shoulders (lines 41–46), and making faces to her back (lines 64, 65, and 69).

Sacks (1995b:159) compares the opening sequence of an encounter to moves in a chess game. Commonly when someone initiates interaction they provide a first pair part in a greeting which initiates a "supportive interchange" (Goffman 1971). Through such conventionalized acts an individual "portrays his respect and regard for some object of ultimate value" (Goffman 1971:62). However, alternatively, as argued by Sacks (1995b:159), "one can think of the tactics in the greeting sequence as possible ways to, e.g., control who gets a first chance to raise a 'first topic.'" When Dionne initially approaches the girls, she avoids any of the conventional ways of bracketing entry into an interaction and goes straight to a "first topic." Dionne begins the interaction with "*Where's* Aretha." She uses a highly aggravated question form, demanding rather than requesting information about one of the group members. More-over, she provides no warrant for why she is asking this information.

In a discussion of "warnings, challenges, and corrections" Sacks (1995b:354) argues that people might be systematically differentiated by the apparatuses they use to make argumentative actions and that those who hear a threat as a challenge could themselves be just those sorts of persons who themselves make argumentative types of actions in the first place. Indeed in response to the demand for food differentiated responses are forthcoming. Two of the girls respond immediately to Dionne's question with an answer, overlapping one another (lines 3–4), while Lisa, a girl who herself challenges others' argumentative moves, responds to Dionne's question with her own question: "*Why:.*" Providing an answer to a question is one possible trajectory in Question/Answer adjacency pair sequences, while another is the initiation of an insertion sequence (Schegloff 1972) following the question. Insertion questions treat a question as something requiring more information before it can be addressed. Lisa makes explicit that the initial question posed to the group is one requiring some explanation.

A next series of questions and moves are constructed as oppositional as well. Dionne asks Lisa "Can I see what you have in your lunch?" as she reaches into Lisa's lunch bag (lines 8–9; see Figure 3.2). The fact that the question is accompanied by reaching makes it more than a simple request for information. The action that occurs here is visibly an intrusion into someone's "territory of the self" (Goffman 1971:28–61).[38] Lisa's first re-sponse to Dionne's invasive action is a whispered "°Mm mm°" (line 10). However, when Dionne takes Lisa's drink bottle as she states "Can I have this?" Lisa responds with a more emphatic negation: "*No.*" and reclaims the bottle (line 14). Sarah, an onlooker to the scene, responds silently and nonvocally, with a collusive wrinkle of her mouth towards Janis (line 13).

Dionne has attempted to build within the interaction a specific slot (Sacks 1995a:308) where the issue of whether or not Lisa will acquiesce to demands from her can be publicly witnessed. When Dionne is unsuccessful in this attempt, in a subsequent move she initiates a dramatic topic shift. Dionne's next move to Lisa (line 15) is a personal insult: "*You* smell." Though Dionne's move shifts topic, it does not shift addressee: it is sequentially relevant in that it sustains the pattern of moves of opposition towards Lisa, moves which position her as subordinate to Dionne. Such types of shifts in frame are useful strategies in children's arguments following refusals.[39]

Dionne's next move is to shift recipient, moving to a next addressee (Melissa) in her "round" of questioning and invasions of lunch boxes. Sacks (1995a:292–295) has discussed a "round" as the machinery that makes possible a series of introductions in a setting as "ordered events on single occasions." In a round of greetings, after an identification of participants and a greeting, a next sequence of contingently relevant events are produced in a similar fashion. In Example 3.48 Dionne brackets her move from a prior to a new recipient with the word "Okay:" "Okay. *What* do you have in your lunch" (line 16). As we saw with the last request for food, recipients have available various responses, various ways of expressing "no" or commenting through a collusive facial gesture. Here, however, the next move following these intrusive moves by Dionne is an explicit commentary on Dionne's behavior. Sarah categorizes the activity as a form of intrusion – and more explicitly, as a form of domination by using a negative person descriptor, "big bully," in her statement "Dionne you're **such** a big bully" (line 18).

Accusations generally make relevant a denial or some type of counter move by their recipients (Goodwin 1990:240–241). However, rather than addressing this charge, Dionne responds to her addressee by once again radically shifting topic while keeping the floor alive for putdowns and implicit comparisons between herself and the other girls. She asks a question that indexes her identity as an actress in commercials: "Did you see us- that milk commercial last night?" As none of the other girls are actresses (though some aspire to be them) her question serves to make topically relevant her status vis-à-vis the younger girls. In response to Dionne's question Sarah remains silent and refuses to enter into this new topic. Several moves later Sarah delivers a bald imperative which emphatically affirms her position with respect to Dionne's moves: she states "Now **go**!" (line 27) extending her arm and pointing to a far area of the playground. Other girls evaluate Sarah's bold moves with laughter; Janis, piggybacking[40] on Sarah's action, states "GO **BACK** TO YOUR-" and points to where Dionne should go (line 31). Directives that instruct an interlocutor to leave are perhaps the baldest or most "aggravated"[41] of all possible directives issued among girls. Dionne clearly treats Janis's imperative move as oppositional; she responds to her with a bald insult: "SHUT **UP JAN**IS. I don't like talking to you any more. After what you said lastertime when yesterday- last week" (in lines 33–40). For her next move Sarah stands up, spreads her arms out to her side constructing with her body a roadblock (line 41). Melissa mimics her action, and the fourth grade girls laugh at these baldly produced actions.

Relations between older and younger girls are negotiated in this sequence. The younger girls provide several moves which are responsive to Dionne's physical invasion of their space and personal insult: the negative person descriptor "big bully," the bald imperatives "GO **BACK** TO YOUR-" and "Now **go**!" as well as the physical actions of pointing to where Dionne should go and making one's body into a roadblock. Such moves clearly display that the younger girls treat Dionne's actions as moves of attempted invasion of their lunch space. Faces made by both Janis and Sarah to Dionne's back as she leaves, as well as Sarah's growling noises, clearly display their stance, their displeasure with her. These more private commentaries constitute younger girls' forms of resistance, their "weapons of the weak,"[42] which can be used backstage, behind Dionne's back, as a form of commentary on someone who positions herself as a member of the ruling elite.

Alliances within the group are publicly delineated in this sequence. Dionne points to all of the girls except Janis; she then repeats their names and comments, "Nice to meet you guys." Melissa, who a moment earlier had produced arm gestures which blocked Dionne's access to the group (as well as a throat clear commentary), comments that Dionne is friendly with herself, Lisa, and Sarah (all of the girls at lunch in the clique except Janis). Despite their displayed dislike of Dionne, being on friendly terms with her is one index of a form of status that accrues from knowing a pre-teen actress. Dionne's choice of who to greet and Melissa's (line 76) listing of who is included in friendship relationships with Dionne proclaims a vernacular "Who's Who" and demarcates boundaries and alliances with older girls.

Concluding Thoughts on Asymmetrical Relations on the Playground

In this chapter we have examined forms of asymmetrical relations on the playground based on categories of gender and age. Quite explicit orientations towards the membership categories of girl and boy, as well as older and younger girl, are observable in the talk of the children, in both their complaints and accounts.

Girls exhibit a great deal of agency in their ability to structure and restructure social relations. They demonstrate their ability to dispute the claims of those who assume authority over them across various contexts. When negotiating the use of the soccer field, girls confront the boys and male playground aides who act as defenders of the boys. Girls bring their grievances to the representative of authority in the school, the Vice Principal, who listens to the complaints of the girls and calls a meeting between girls and boys to evolve a new plan for usage of the field. The girls thus demonstrate their ability to effect transformations in the most entrenched ideologies of the school – boys' control of the playing fields. Girls also contend with older girls, sixth graders who "rule the school" and assert their superiority over the younger girls in various ways – through insults, putdowns, and spreading rumors. Sixth grade girls also make territorial claims to the play space, as well as the contents of the lunch boxes, of younger girls. The younger girls defend their rights to not be treated in an insulting manner. Across both contexts girls in the clique make use of bald imperatives, accusatory statements invoking age and gender, pejorative person descriptors, and generally demonstrate their ability to artfully collaborate to present a position and debate it through clever, appropriate, and forceful comebacks.

Appendix 3.1

Other children with whom the clique interact:

Name	Age	Classroom
Girls		
Dionne	12	Classroom G
Julia	12	Classroom G

(Continued)

Appendix 3.1 (*Continued*)

Nancy	12	Classroom G
Sharie	10	Classroom B
Ruth	11	Classroom C
Gloria	10	Classroom A
Clarita	10	Classroom A
Nichole	10	Classroom E
Wendy	10	Classroom E
Sandra	9	Classroom D
Vanessa	9	Classroom D
Madison	9	Classroom D
Thelma	9	Classroom D
Stephany	9	Classroom B
Kimberly	10	Classroom A
Prestina	10	Classroom B
Kesha	11	Classroom F
Alicia	11	Classroom C

Boys

Carlos	9	Classroom D
Sean	10	Classroom E
Brian	10	Classroom F
Dan	9	Classroom H
Edward	10	Classroom A
Bruce	9	Classroom A
Denzel	10	Classroom F
Brian	10	Classroom A
Tom	10	Classroom F
Ken	9	Classroom D
Jack	10	Classroom F
Lyle	10	Classroom F
Jason	10	Classroom F
Paul	9	Classroom E
Miguel	9	Classroom D
Nate	10	Classroom E
Alex A	10	Classroom F
Ron	10	Classroom F
Alan	10	Classroom A
Dan	10	Classroom A
Malcolm	10	Classroom F
Sean	10	Classroom E
Stephen	10	Classroom H

4

Social Organization, Opposition, and Directives in the Game of Jump Rope

Previous work on children's play has found that girls' and boys games are quite different in their role structure.[1] For example, boys' games are said to generally have larger numbers of players, a more intricate division of labor and be more competitive. During my fieldwork in Philadelphia on Maple Street, boys did turn many activities that could be pursued as individual pastimes, such as building model airplanes, into contests, and boys frequently discussed ranking in terms of skill displayed in games.[2] However, neither strategic interaction nor competition was absent from girls' activities. For example, in pretend play elaborate extended family networks were constructed with groups of eight or more girls, featuring an intricate division of labor and articulation of social roles.[3]

Across all of the girls' groups among whom I have done fieldwork, competition occurs in the midst of the activity of jumping rope, although girls seldom brag about their skills. Ranking was implicit in the favorite jump rope game among the Maple Street girls of Philadelphia: "One, Two, three, Footsies." In this game each slapping of the rope on the ground co-occurred with counting by tens, so participants knew who was the best jumper. In the past decade Double Dutch has been featured in international athletic competitions shown on Wide World of Sports. In fieldwork I conducted in Columbia, South Carolina, in the mid-1990s with a world champion Double Dutch team, the Double Dutch Forces, elementary school girls on the team were highly competitive. At Hanley School the fourth grade popular clique challenged both a fifth grade group they called "the Blondies" as well as fourth grade boys who played jump rope at recess to participate in a contest to see who could jump the longest.

While frequently regarded as a girls' game, during spring of the first year I did fieldwork in the mid-1990s, jump rope at Hanley School was an activity that was promoted by the coaches and played during Physical Education classes by both fourth grade boys and girls. In that jump rope was played by both genders at Hanley it provides an opportune activity to investigate with respect to how it was structured by boys as well as girls.

Jump Rope as a Situated Activity System

The game of jump rope can be viewed as a form of situated activity system.[4] For the participants this involves such things as "a single visual and cognitive focus of attention, a heightened mutual relevance of acts, and an eye-to-eye ecological huddle that maximizes each participant's opportunity to perceive the other participants' monitoring of him." In the game of jump rope, there is an expected pattern of orientation of players toward one another. In the game of Double Dutch two "enders" turn two ropes in opposite directions in "eggbeater fashion" while a third person jumps within. African American girls I observed in Philadelphia,[5] in urban and rural South Carolina (in school programs for children of migrant laborers), as well as in south Los Angeles (for example, at a 68th Street school) played Double Dutch. According to David Walker, president of the National Double Dutch League, the game was probably brought to the United States by Dutch settlers and has had an especially strong tradition in African American neighborhoods of large cities.[6]

Among the Latino girls and mixed ethnic group I observed in southern California, however, a single rope was much more common. Two parties hold opposite ends of a single rope and turn it for a third player, who jumps when the rope hits the ground. The rope is usually turned to a jump rope rhyme with four beats per line that is similar in its metrics to rhymes used for counting out or clapping games.[7] When the rope hits the pavement, to a major beat of the rhyme, the jumper should jump over the rope. Movements requiring athletic agility take place in the midst of some of the rhymes of jump rope. For example, in the game entitled "Texaco Mexico"[8] players must jump in the air while doing kicks, splits, turning around, touching the ground, "paying their taxes" (by slapping the hand of a turner), and "getting out a town" (jumping out of the rope) while the rope is in motion. This was the favorite rhyme of the popular clique in Los Angeles.

Within the game of hopscotch (as discussed in chapter 2) the frame used for evaluating the appropriateness of moves consists of the lines on the hopscotch grid painted or drawn on a flat surface. Girls who are the referees position their bodies huddled around the edges of the grid to inspect whether or not someone's feet can be seen as touching, which indicates that the jumper landed on the lines of the grid and they replay the movement of someone's feet in terms of the grid's architecture. Cries such as "out" argue that someone's turn is over and clear accounts follow as girls enact the past movements of a player. Within jump rope, however, there is no permanent grid against which players can check a player's moves. In jump rope, what can be seen at any one moment is the position of the rope on the ground, and where the jumper's feet are located with respect to it. The "field" in terms of which the movements of another are evaluated include (1) the turning rope, (2) the players and (3) their interaction. The rope can be argued to be turned too fast, too slow, or too high. In jump rope, in comparison to hopscotch, blame for mistakes can be attributed to the turners or bystanders as well as the player, leading, at points, to multiple disputes simultaneously. This makes scrutiny of moves even more involved and consequential for judges of the plays in jump rope.

Turn Taking in Jump Rope

The system for taking turns at jumping over a rope can be described in terms of (1) a series of units making up one turn at jumping, and (2) a set of rules for rotating the position of jumper. A player is entitled to continue jumping over a rope until she fails to complete a jump successfully; this failure must be the fault of the jumper herself. If upon a miss both jumper and turners agree that the error was the fault of the turner rather than the jumper, a jumper is entitled to continue jumping. The number of continuous jump opportunities per turn is generally not specified until the first player of the game makes a miss. There is, however, a general practice of allowing two units of jumping per turn; if a player is a latecomer in the game, she may be granted more turns to make up for her late entry.

After girls decide they will play jump rope, the first person to yell "first" gets the most valued position of first jumper; girls call out the order of who will jump second, third, fourth, fifth, etc. The order of taking turns is decided by the players in the midst of the game, and not decided in advance. Certain priorities regarding turn order accrue to the party who retrieves the rope and makes it available for play. As disputes often occur regarding order for jumping, procedures for arbitrating turn order are available. The two people who call out the same number pick a number between one and another number (usually 5, 15, or 20). The dispute arbitrator whispers a number in the ear of a noninvolved party. The people in a tie are then asked to state the number they selected and the number closest to the arbitrator's number wins.

The following, which occurred among fourth graders at Hanley School, provides an example of such a procedure. As girls are eating lunch on the curb of the playground Janis sees Sarah at a distance with the jump rope on the pavement walkway, where girls play. She yells to Sarah that she is coming, and immediately players begin to negotiate for their turn order in jumping. Melissa calls out "I'M *SE*COND!" However, both Janis (line 3) and Lisa (line 7) counter Melissa's call.

Example 4.1

		((Sarah is standing in a distant play area with the rope))
1	Janis:	**COM**ING! ((to Sarah))
2	Melissa:	I'M **SE**COND!
3	Janis:	Nope. Sorry. ((countering Melissa as she runs to Sarah))
4	Lisa:	Yummy peanut butter and jelly.

```
5              I'M THIRD!!
6  Sharie:     Fourth.
7  Lisa:       You're fifth. ((pointing to Melissa))
```

In interaction that immediately follows, in Example 4.2, Melissa, Janis, and Lisa gather around Sarah, who has one end of the rope; Sharie, who is not a regular with the group, goes elsewhere. By jumping across a still rope, and yelling out "I wanna be first" (line 7), Janis makes her bid to be first jumper. Both Melissa, who had yelled, "I'M *SECOND*!" while eating on the curb (in Example 4.1, line 2), and Sarah, who had retrieved the rope and was holding it, argue that they want to be second (Example 4.2, lines 2–3). In line 11 Melissa concedes the second place spot to Sarah, but states that it is "only fair" for her to take a place behind Sarah. With both Lisa (line 5) and Melissa (line 11) claiming the third position in the game ("one behind second"), Lisa suggests a way to decide who can have that spot by yelling, "*PICK* (.) *A* (.) *NUM* (.) BER!" Lisa's bid to arbitrate, however, is not picked up by any of the players. The girls continue to dispute who will occupy what position until Sarah (line 25) claims that she had yelled "second" when she got the rope. Melissa concedes second place to Sarah, but continues to argue with Lisa about who is in third position for several turns.

Example 4.2

```
1  Janis:      ((jumping over the still rope claiming the role
                  of first jumper))
2  Melissa:    I said I'm second.
3  Sarah:      Oh I'll be second then.
4  Melissa:    ⌈No.
5  Lisa:       ⌊I wanna be third.
6  Sarah:      ⌈All right.
7  Janis:      ⌊I wanna be first. ((jumping into the air))
8  Sarah:      ⌈I'm-
9  Melissa:    ⌊No.
10 Sarah:      ⌈Second.
11 Melissa:    ⌊Then I'm one behind if I'm-
12             if I'm not second.=
13 Lisa:       Nen! ((pointing above her head))
14 Melissa:    It's only ⌈fair.
15 Lisa                 ⌊PICK (.) A (.) NUM (.) BER!
16             ((jumping up and down and pointing to Sarah))
17 Sarah:      ⌈I-
18 Janis:      ⌊Oh
19 Sarah:      I'M THIRD. OKAY?
20 Lisa:       ⌈I'M THIRD. ((slaps hand on hips))
21 Melissa:   ⌊I'M SECOND! ((jumps in place to accentuate))
21 Melissa:   ⌈I'm second.
22 Sarah:     ⌊No.
```

23   Lisa: I already called ⌈it Sarah.
24   Melissa: ⌊I'm second.
25   Sarah: I ⌈called second when I got the rope.
26   Janis: ⌊Hold on.
27   Lisa: Just pick a number between one and fifteen.
28   Sarah: I called second. I did Melissa.
29   Lisa: ⌈One and–
30   Melissa: ⌊One
31   Lisa: One and ⌈fifteen. Pick a number.
32   Sarah   ⌊You're third. *((looking at Melissa))*
33   Melissa: I'm third.
34   Sarah: Okay I'm second.
35   Lisa: *((stomps foot))*
36   Melissa: *((looking to Lisa))* You're fourth.
37   Lisa: I called third before you *((shakes head no))*
             ⌈Melissa.
38   Sarah: ⌊Please. ⌈Just let me be third.
39   Melissa: ⌊(   )
40   Sarah: Let me be ***third***.
41   I don't ***wan***na be ***fourth***.
42   I'm not even fourth. I'm ***se***cond.
43   Janis: Sarah's second.
44   Lisa: I wanna be ***third***.
45   Melissa: ***I*** wanna be ***third***. *((lowers body emphatically))*
46   Sarah: Pick a number–
47   Pick a number between one and five.
48   Janis: I got it.
49   *((begins to position herself as*
50   *whisperer in Sarah's ear))*
51   Sarah: No.= Wait. Wait. *((pushes Janis away))*
52   Janis: Okay fine.
53   Sarah: *((whispers in Janis's ear))*

This example demonstrates the considerable *desire* that players express with respect to negotiating their place in taking turns jumping. In addition the sequence shows that game order, as in conversational interaction, is not decided in advance, but rather locally administered, negotiated turn by turn by participants themselves. Janis's calling out "***COM***ING" and actually placing herself in the midst of the rope (which Sarah was holding) were the moves she executed to become the first jumper. Sarah's having retrieved the rope, her own statement (line 42) and Janis's affirmation (line 43) that she should be second, gave her rights to be ahead of others in the turn order. When both Melissa and Lisa wanted to become the third player to jump, Sarah carried through with Lisa's initial suggestion (line 15) of picking a number to resolve turn order. Sarah whispered to another girl (Janis) whose position was already decided, to resolve the dispute for third place.

In addition to negotiating turn order, rotation of players must be decided. When a comparatively large group of jumpers (above six) are jumping, as frequently occurs on the playground, the two "enders" do not rotate until one of the enders tires of turning. Following a complete round of rotation of participants, the jumper with the highest number of jumps, jumps first, followed by the second highest jumper, and so on. Deciding who is best jumper is easiest when the rhyme involves counting the number of success-fully executed jumps, as in "One, Two, Three, Footsies," played in Phila-delphia. However, participants may just as well know who "beats" another when traditional rhymes are used, in that for each party's turn the same sequence of rhymes in a particular round is used.[9] The number of successful jumps is also obvious when letters of the alphabet are used. For example, after recitation of the rhyme "Ice cream soda, Vanilla berry punch, Tell me the name of your honeybunch" turners recite letters of the alphabet until someone misses. When the jumper misses, girls call out the name of a male classmate whose name starts with the letter that was missed; boys call out female classmates' names. Often commentaries (primarily response cries) on the children whose names are selected follow. Girls giggle and shriek if the name of a boy they particularly like is called (and they may intentionally miss a jump on the initial letter of a boyfriend's name).

When a jumper misses she exits the rope. Unlike in hopscotch, spectators do not generally scream "*Out!*" (unless there is a tie for largest number of jumps executed, as occurred for African American players in Philadelphia during "One, Two, Three, Footies"). The jumper might make a comment on her own jumping (with a response cry expressing disappointment, such as "Ow" or "Ugh") or, alternatively, say something about the turning of the enders. Spectators can comment that the enders are at fault with utterances such as, "That was *Jan*is's fault" or "*My* turn" or "You get one more turn." Occasionally spectators congratulate the jumpers with "Good girlfriend!" and a "high five," a hand slap, or "Oh you got so far! She's *at tax*es."

After a jumper has failed a unit of continuous jumping, the turner speaks the last words of the rhymes jumped to in one of two types of intonations. If the words are produced with slight rising intonation, this indicates that the jumper is entitled to a second part of her turn. Repetition of the last phrase allows the jumper to warm up for entry into the next part of her jump. By way of contrast, the completion of a party's turn is signaled by falling intonation on the last two words recited as a miss occurs. The completion of a jump, the end of a turn, or an interference provide natural junctures in the activity, places where verbal interaction is likely to occur.

In general the fixed pattern of the activity designates rotation of particip-ants. However, as with the turn taking system in conversation (Sacks et al. 1974:727), participants themselves make local decisions about the flow of rhymes. Generally, the ordering of rhymes is decided during the course of the game by the parties reciting the rhymes. The first party who begins reciting a rhyme as the rope is turned generally decides what rhyme will be recited. The person who jumps first can call the rhyme she wants as in "I want Teddy Bear, Teddy Bear.=Okay you guys? And sing it slow."

There is a built-in motivation to turn the rope fairly. If one turns too fast or not in synchrony with the beat, there is a chance that when the jumper next "gets the ends" she will do the same for the previous offender. Although one might assume that the role of the jumper is the more important role, in training for professional games of Double Dutch that I observed in Columbia, South Carolina, the turners are considered equally as important for their role is to keep a steady beat. Onlookers do not passively watch as someone takes her turn. Rather, they watch intently, hoping to detect mistakes so that they can get a turn.

Variations on the Game

Both female and male groups at Hanley School played three variations on the game. The most common way the game was played involved jumping to a rhyme, such as "Teddy Bear," "Texaco Mexico," "Ice Cream Soda," or "Cinderella."[10] In another game called "Clock," children lined up behind each other; each player in turn would jump into the moving rope and jump progressively higher numbers of jumps (1–12). If a person missed a jump in the rotation of numbers, that person was eliminated. A third version of the game was "speed jumping" – jumping as the rope was turned at a very fast pace. "Red Hot Peppers," a form of speed jumping, involved multiple children jumping inside the rope simultaneously; when someone missed, they were eliminated from the game. Though the popular girls' clique preferred to jump to rhymes and have individual players excel at jumping in intricate patterns, among a friendship group of second generation Mexican American and Central American girls, as well as with the fourth grade boys at Hanley School, the most popular game was jumping together in the rope while speed jumping (where number of turns are counted, rather than rhymes recited). Though generally the popular girls at Hanley School jumped with members of their own clique, during one recess period fourth grade girls challenged fifth grade girls to a contest to see who could jump rope to one hundred first, and on another occasion challenged fourth grade boys.

Negotiation in Girls' and Boys' Games of Rope

Although jump rope is not an inherently competitive game and requires the cooperation of all participants to function smoothly, proposals for action regarding particular features of the game made during its course may engender disagreement. On each occasion of play the game of jump rope provides an arena for extensive negotiation of rules: who can jump and what the turn order will be; who can be a turner; what role a newcomer will take; how fast (or slow) the rope is to be turned and in which direction; how high the rope will be turned so that it will not twist or hit someone's head while the jumper is jumping; what rhyme will be used; what moves are required by a jumper in keeping with the rhyme selected; how many chances at jumping a player receives during her turn; how many players can get into the rope at the same time; whether or not someone gets another turn if the partner jumping in misses; the number of times a jumper can make a mistake without forfeiting her turn; or how the interference of a passerby or an ender's inappropriate turning will affect a jumper's turn. Negotiations about how many jumpers were allowed in the rope at one time during speed jumping frequently occurred when groups of eight to ten boys would play together. A rule such as "Let's say the max is four with this rope" would be improvised in the midst of the game. Each time they jumped participants would try to beat their own former record.

Many features of the activity cannot easily be decided in terms of clearly objective criteria and therefore lead to more extended sequences. In contrast to many children's disputes that can terminate without a resolution being reached,[11] argument relating to the playing of jump rope, like hopscotch, *is treated as* requiring some form of settlement so that players may proceed to a next stage of the activity.

Turn Shapes of Opposition and Accounts in Girls' Jump Rope

In jump rope, as in hopscotch, considerable negotiation takes place regarding every aspect of the game. Many disputes center around who is to blame for the miss, the turner or the jumper. Girls in the third through sixth grade (ages 8–12) who I observed were expert at providing reasoned accounts for the calls they made or positions they took up with respect to the move in progress.

Opposition turns took one of two possible shapes: (1) Disagreement with a prior move expressed with a **polarity marker**,[12] (No or Yes) + an Account, or (2) **return and exchange** moves,[13] in which a move equivalent to the one being opposed is returned. Both types of moves are buttressed by justifications that have sequential consequences of their own. Disagreement turns provide a polarity marker right at the start of the turn; as in hopscotch, little work is done to disguise the position of the opposition, in marked contrast to what occurs in polite adult conversation where a preference for agreement constitutes the most prevalent stance.

Polarity markers

The following provides a simple example of such disagreement turns in the midst of jump rope. In the first disagreement turn, during this round of jump rope Janis has taken four turns. Following a statement "I get one more", Lisa provides a counter: "**No** you don't. You had four already."

"**No**" is positioned as an opposition marker at the start of the turn, so that opposition is highlighted rather than modulated. Following the polarity marker the accuser provides an account justifying the opposition. In her next move, Janis, whose problematic move in the game is the topic, agrees with the position that her turn is up, and exits the game. The sequence thus has the character of a "remedial interchange,"[14] in that Janis accepts that her initial offensive act was out of line.

Example 4.3

	((Janis has taken four turns))	
Janis:	I get one more.	**Problematic event**
Lisa:	**No** you don't.	**Polarity marker**
	You had four already.	**Account**
Janis:	Okay.	**Acceptance**

The following provides a brief example of a sequence in which denials and polarity markers occur until accounts are provided and accepted by the jumper. In this example, when Janis misses her jump she argues that she as jumper is not to blame for making the rope stop (line 2). Players coordinate their united opposition to the jumper's denial of fault (lines 3–4). Two different accounts are offered for why she is out. Aretha (line 5) points to the physical evidence with "See where it touched your leg?" and (line 6) locates Janis's position relative to the rope as a proof of the jumper rather than the turner being blamable.

Example 4.4

1	Janis:	*((Janis misses as she touches the rope and makes it stop))*	**Problematic event**
2	Janis:	That wasn't me.	**Denial**
3	Melissa:	Yeah. That was.	**Polarity**
4		Yes it was Janis.	
5	Aretha:	See where it touched your leg? *((points))*	**Account**
6	Melissa:	No **YOU** were on the wrong side.	**Account**
7	Janis:	*((moves out of the rope))*	**Acceptance**

In this example the girls attempt to locate physical evidence (a point where Janis's leg was touched in order to allocate blame). Disputes may be expanded or contracted depending upon the move of the player who misses; in Example 4.4 (as in Example 4.3 above) the sequence is not elaborated, as Janis accepts the verdict of onlookers, as well as the two different accounts for her miss.

Accusation/counter accusation sequences

Alternatively, in return and exchange moves,[15] a move that preserves much of the former move being opposed is returned, and redirected at the prior speaker. The second speaker's action is reciprocal, rather than a disagreement with the previous action. Features of the return and exchange move, such as who is referred to by the pronouns in it, change as the participation framework changes. However, the relationship of action, current speaker, and current recipient is preserved.

Within jump rope reciprocal accusations or threats occur. In the following[16] Janis misses her jump, while doing splits when Melissa turns the rope fast. When Melissa accuses Janis of blaming her own jumping error on Melissa, the turner, Janis does not respond with a denial, but instead retorts that a similar process occurred earlier, with Melissa blaming Janis.

Example 4.5

	((Janis misses while doing the splits as Melissa and Lisa are turning the rope))	
Melissa:	Janis [you] [**blame** it on me.]	**Accusation**
Lisa:	Yeah.	
Janis:	Like [you] [blamed it on **me**!]	**Counter accusation**

Much like other sequences built out of format tying,[17] the framing of Melissa's first action is used for a retort in Janis's subsequent second action. This short exchange in Example 4.5 is taken from a more extended dispute composed out of reciprocal pairs of return and exchange moves, Example 4.6, below. The accusation/counter accusation sequence above (located in lines 8–10 in Example 4.6 below) becomes the new set of moves following a set of complaints and denials (lines 2–4) and demonstrations and counter demonstrations (lines 5–6).

Example 4.6

1	Janis:	*((misses doing splits))*.	**Problematic move**
2	Janis:	Not *fa:st*.	**Complaint**
3	Lisa:	I'm **not**.	**Denial**
4	Melissa:	I wasn't *ei*ther.	**Denial**
5	Janis:	Melissa! You're like-	**Demonstration**
		((does a fast turning motion))	
6	Melissa:	I was just doing it.	
		((demonstrates her version of how she was turning the rope, which is rhythmic and slower))	
			Counter demonstration
7	Janis:	*((Janis jumps again, misses in her jump doing the splits))*	
8	Melissa:	And Janis [you] [**blame** it on me.]	**Accusation**
9	Janis:	Yeah.	
10	Janis:	Like [you] [blamed it on **me**!]	**Counter Accusation**
11	Angela:	**Duh**::, *((eyeball roll))*	**Metacommentary**
12	Lisa:	**Oh: An**gela.	**Return comment**
13		⌈You weren't even **here!**	
14	Melissa:	⌊You weren't even **here!**	
15	Angela:	Neh neh neh!	
16	Janis:	Go! *((resumes jumping))*	

In this interaction we find a mixture of disagreements and return and exchange moves. When Janis first misses she says, "Not fast" (line 2), indicating that she feels her miss was the result of the fast turning, rather than her own move. Both turners in response provide denials that turning was at issue in Janis's missed turn (lines 3–4). As in the hopscotch sequences we examined in chapter 2, in order to lend credibility to her position, Janis can provide a **demonstration** (line 5). She enacts a gesture indicating how the turner, Melissa, was turning the rope. In response to this argument in her defense, Melissa provides a counter version of how she had been turning (line 6).

Janis's next move is to take another turn at jumping. When she misses, Melissa takes the initiative and provides a new meta–accusation to Janis (line 8): "Janis [you] [*blame* it on me."]. This gets a reciprocal meta-accusation in response (line 10): "Like [you] [blamed it on *me!*"]. The return and response moves are brought to a close with the introduction of a new topic that reconfigures the participation framework. In line 11, Angela provides a meta-commentary on the event and says "*Duh::*," marking that this is a ridiculous dispute. The next commentary (line 12) is about Angela's comment rather than the game itself, and the dispute dissipates. The girls state, "You weren't even here." The game resumes with Janis saying, "Go!" Players who are not jumpers have a built-in motivation for settling the dispute so that they may proceed to a next stage of the activity where they get a turn.

Allocating blame in more extended disputes

While the game of hopscotch centers almost exclusively on the player's moves, the game of jump rope is inherently one that depends as much on the actions of the turners as it does on the jumps of the jumper. The fate of the jumper is (literally) in the hands of the turners. At issue in many jump rope sequences is who is to blame for a jumper's miss. Because of the nature of jump rope as a co-constructed activity, return and exchange actions occur frequently in the midst of jump rope disputes about whether the turners or the jumper is to blame.

In Example 4.7 Lisa and Aretha are turning. Sarah is jumping while Emi and Janis are looking on. Sarah steps on the rope and misses. A series of accusations and counter accusations regarding responsibilities in the game ensue. At issue is not only what constitutes appropriate rope turning speed, but also whether or not it is the responsibility of the jumper to signal the turners (with phrases such as "Faster!") so that the rope gets turned at an appropriate speed.

Example 4.7

1	Girls:	*((chanting while Sarah jumps))*
2		Teddy Bear, Teddy Bear, turn around.
3		Teddy Bear, Teddy Bear, touch

4		⌈the ground.	
5	Sarah:	⌊*((steps on the rope))*	**Problematic move**
6	Sarah:	Guys you're going too **slow**:!	
7		*((hands extended))*	**Complaint**
8	Melissa:	⌈Sarah it's not their **fault**!	**Disagreement**
9	Emi:	⌊No they **aren't** Sarah.	**Disagreement**
10		⌈It's-	
11	Sarah:	⌊Well to **me** it's slow!	**Complaint repeat**
12	Aretha:	Then say **fast**er Sarah.	**Counter**
13	Melissa:	When you're **jump**	
		roping you say **fast**er.	**Counter**
14	Sarah:	O**kay**.	**Acceptance token**
15	Melissa:	Last turn.	
16	Sarah:	Okay.	

In this example alternative accounts for the miss are provided. The jumper claims that the turners are not turning fast enough: "Guys you're going too **slow**:!" (line 6). Two onlookers yell that it is not the fault of the turners (lines 8–9). When Sarah disagrees and repeats that it is the fault of the turners with "Well to **me** it's slow!" (line 11), Aretha, one of the turners, argues that it is the obligation of the jumper to tell the turners that they are going too slow: "Then say **fast**er Sarah" (line 12). Melissa echoes this with her statement "When you're **jump** roping you say **fast**er" (line 13). The actions of Melissa, Emi, and Aretha provide a consensus of opposition against the jumper. When the jumper (line 11) refutes the onlookers' cry that the rope is not being turned too slowly, multiple parties counter her complaint. This leads to the jumper acquiescing with "O**kay**" (line 14), closing the complaint sequence before the turners begin turning once again. Clearly in this sequence girls are negotiating issues of blame and responsibility, and dealing litigiously with issues of rights, responsibilities, and fairness.

Repetitively when the jumper misses, she will attempt to blame the turners for faulty turning. In the following, as Emi is jumping she misses; one of her feet does not clear the rope. While Aretha has continued one more turn of the rope, Janis stops turning. The first thing she attempts to do is allocate blame. In Example 4.8, Emi, the jumper, accuses the turners, saying, "No it's your **fault**" (line 2). And "You guys **stopped**" (line 10). Aretha provides an alternative explanation for her miss: "No. It was because it was **stuck** on you" (lines 11–12). In both cases polarity markers (lines 6, 7, 9, 11) are used to preface the turns of opposition. Emi (line 13) eventually accepts the position of the turners and spectators and exits from the rope.

Example 4.8

((Emi is jumping and she misses during her jump;
one of her feet does not clear the rope. The rope ends up between
her legs. Following the miss, she looks at Aretha.
She sees that Aretha has continued one more turn of the rope
while Janis has not.))

1	Emi:	((Emi misses while jumping))	**Problematic move**
2	Emi:	No it's your *fault*.	**Accusation +**
3		You guys didn't-	**Account**
4		((does action with hand mimicking jerky turning))	
5		⌈Go on.	
6	Janis:	⊦*NO*. No. No. No it isn't.	**Polarity marker**
7	Aretha:	⌊*No*.	
8	Emi:	No they didn't- go on.	
		((shaking head))	**Polarity marker**
9	Janis:	⌈No.	**Polarity marker +**
10	Emi:	⌊You guys *stopped*.	**Account**
11	Aretha:	No. It was because	**Polarity marker +**
12		it was *stuck* on you.	**Account**
13	Emi:	Oh(hhhh). ((moves to sidelines))	**Acceptance token**

Such types of sequences negotiating blame occur across a range of the girls' jump rope episodes. These sequences involve each of the clique members in equivalent positions of blame as they rotate through the game. What differs across examples are the types of opposition that are invoked, using either (1) polarity markers (Example 4.8) or negations and denials (Example 4.6) to mark disagreement or (2) return and exchange moves (Examples 4.6 and 4.7).

An extended example with multiple negotiations

One final fragment provides an example of the multiple types of accounts that are negotiated during play. This time (Example 4.9) an onlooker, rather than a turner, is blamed for the miss. As Aretha prepares to jump, Melissa makes moves to jump into the rope with Aretha (though she never actually executes such moves), and Aretha produces a response cry expressing exasperation, "Ugh." Later Aretha claims Melissa's attempted jump into the rope is the reason for her miss when told that she (Aretha) gets "one more turn" (a statement indicating that her last turn was counted as a "miss").

Example 4.9

1	Aretha:	((Aretha steps on the rope)) Ugh!
2	Lisa:	(okay)
3	Melissa:	⌈ONE MORE *TURN*!
4	Lisa:	⌊One more turn left.
5	Melissa:	One more// *turn*!
6	Aretha:	That was-
7		That was *not* a *turn*! ((she leans into Lisa))
8	Lisa:	*Yes* it //was.
9	Janis:	Yes it was.=
10	Melissa:	Yes it *was* Aretha.

11		You're mess//ing up for yourself.
12	Janis:	They counted **me** out as a turn Aretha like this!
13		*((demo of rope was turned for her))*
14	Aretha:	**You:** were in my **way**!
15		*((does finger point at Melissa, leaning into her))*
16	Lisa:	No Janis // you jumped in!
17		*((does demo of Janis's past jump))*
18	Melissa:	I **did** get outa the way.
19	Lisa:	And jumped **on** the rope.
20	Janis:	They count turns like that. *((does motion))*
21		⌈You have to.
22		⌊You get another–
23	Janis:	⌈You have to turn like that.
24	Melissa:	⌊It's your last turn.
25	Aretha:	Okay.

In this example as Aretha started her jump, the girls had decided that she was entitled to multiple turns since she had only recently joined the group. Aretha jumps on top of the rope and misses during the rope turning, and the group says that she has one more turn left (lines 3–4). However, Aretha disputes this because she feels that blame should be attributed to an external cause, a spectator, whose preparatory moves sidetracked the jumper, rather than to herself. She states, "That was **not** a **turn**!" (line 7). While she produces her talk, she provides a gesture that intensifies the utterance by leaning into one of the turners, Lisa. The dispute about whether Aretha should be considered out or not continues for several turns, with Janis and Melissa siding with Lisa (lines 8–10).

Melissa then provides a more direct accusation, stating that it is Aretha who is to blame: "You're messing up for yourself" (line 11). The phrase "for yourself" is an optional part of the utterance that intensifies the accusation by placing blame squarely on Aretha. Aretha, herself provides an upgraded accusatory statement: "**You:** were in my **way**!" (line 14). Making use of a finger point as well as a posture that leans into Melissa (line 15), Aretha argues that Melissa was in her way (line 14) as she was preparing to move into the rope. Melissa denies this (line 18), but in her next turn says that Aretha is entitled to another turn (line 22).

While Aretha and Melissa dispute, a side disagreement involves Janis and Lisa (lines 12–21). In providing her account for why Aretha should be considered out, Janis addresses Aretha, stating that she herself was called out before when it was really the turners who were at fault: "They counted me out as a turn Aretha like this" (line 12). She argues from "precedent" (an event that occurred in the past) and produces a demonstration of how the rope had been turned jerkily before. Lisa disputes that the case that Janis brings to bear was equivalent, saying that when Janis jumped in, she landed on the rope, so that she herself was at fault (lines 16–19). (The dispute between Janis and Lisa, however, is ignored, as Aretha chooses to address Melissa rather than Janis.)

In this example, multiple perspectives are brought to bear on the dispute. Negotiations that take place in jump rope negate the notion that girls' games lack complexity or possibility for extensive dispute without the game breaking up, a perspective argued by Lever (1976:482). Here we find evidence for the ability of girls to present their cases through sophisticated forms of argument (juxtaposing past decisions and arguing from precedent) as well as demonstrations making use of embodied actions.

Turn Shapes and Accounts in a Boys' Jump Rope Game

Boys' games contain similar types of disputes about who is blamable. For example, in the next fragment (Example 4.10) when Ron misses he provides an account for the miss, that the turners stopped turning: "I didn't mess up. You stopped! I was on the other side of the rope" (line 10). In this example while thinking nobody is looking Ron then moves his feet to the far side of the rope, making it look like he had cleared the rope.

The rhyme used in the following is "Ice Cream Soda." In this rhyme, which ends "Tell me the name of your honey bunch," participants yell out the name of someone in the jumper's classroom whose first name begins with the letter associated with the jumper's miss. Here Malcolm marks Ron's turn is over by repeating "C", the letter on which Ron missed a jump and saying "Carrie."

Example 4.10

1	Brian:	Come *in* Ron.	
2	Ron:	I'm comin.	
3	B, M:	A, B, C ((*chanting*))	
4	Ron:	((*As Ron is jumping he misses as the rope hits*	
5		*the ground on the letter "C"*	**Problematic move**
6		*in the rhyme Ice Cream Soda.*))	
7	Malcolm:	C. Carrie.	**Marking turn over**
8	Ron:	((*hands up as if innocent*))	
9	Brian:	Carrie.	
10	Ron:	I didn't mess up. You *stop*ped!	**Denial**
11		((*keeps body straight, though moves feet*))	**Counter**
12		⌈I was on the other side of the rope.	
13	Malcolm:	⌊*No::*. You messed up Ron.	**Accusation**
14		⌈*Face* it.	
15	Ron:	⌊Okay. Fine	**Acceptance**
16	Brian:	*Car*rie. You marry *Car*rie.	

Here after an onlooker, Malcolm, yells, "C Carrie" (line 7), pronouncing that the turn is over, Ron (line 8) produces first a nonvocal gesture which claims innocence with his hands up and then in his next turn produces a denial – "I didn't mess up" – as well as a counter accusation: "You *stop*ped" (line 10). Ron's move attributes blame to the turner. The jumper next does some fancy footwork, quickly placing his feet to the side of the turned rope to make it look like the turners were at fault. After moving his feet, he produces another account: "I was on the other side of the rope" (line 12). Malcolm, however, rejects his account and re-introduces the accusation: "*No::*. You messed up Ron. *Face* it" (line 13). Afterwards Ron accepts the decision with "Okay. Fine" (line 14) and the sequence is closed.

A second example of how moves of opposition in jump rope among boys parallel those of girls (similar to those in Examples 4.6 and 4.7 in particular) occurs in Example 4.11. In the following Malcolm misses his jump and blames the turners, saying they made the rope hit his leg. The judges, Ron and Bruce, however, disagree (lines 3, 5–9). Malcolm (line 10) accepts the turners' verdict and exits the rope.

Example 4.11

1	Malcolm:	*((Malcolm misses during his jump))*	**Problematic move**
2	Malcolm:	That was the fault of the *turn*er.	**Accusation**
3	Ron:	*((shakes head no))*	**Denial**
4	Malcolm:	YOU *DID*. IT HIT MY *LEG*!	**Accusation**
5	Bruce:	That wasn't *turn*ers.	**Denial**
6	Ron:	⌈Nope.	**Denial**
7	Bruce:	⌊That wasn't the *turn*ers.	**Denial**
8		That was because it was doing	**Account**
9		like this *((does circling motion))*	
10	Malcolm:	Okay fine. *((moves out of the rope))*	**Acceptance**

This example, as the girls' examples (Examples 4.6–4.7), shows the way multiple players rather than one single party designating himself as arbitrator dispute a jumper's complaint about the way the rope is being turned. Both return and exchange moves (Example 4.10) as well as opposition expressed through polarity and disagreement (Example 4.11) are found in boys' jump rope disputes.

Both girls and boys played jump rope with enthusiasm; the game provides a perspicuous context for analyzing how different gender groups organize a similar activity and make use of directives in both same- and cross-sex interaction. Lever (1978:479) has argued that "Girls' turn-taking games progress in identical order from one situation to the next. Given the structure of these games, disputes are not likely to occur." Although it is commonly considered a game lacking in complexity[18] as the examples we have seen testify, in fact a great deal of negotiation occurs regarding every aspect of the game.

Regulating Activity through Directives

Directives, actions that are designed to get someone else to do something, are used to make bids regarding how the activity should proceed. The grammatical shape of directives varies during different phases of the activity. In keeping with Ervin-Tripp's (1976: 60) perspective it is important to note that directive forms in no way "lie along a scale of increasing politeness for all social conditions." Bald imperatives such as "Faster. Come on!", "Not too early!", "Okay. Turn it!" or "Get in more!" help regulate the activity. They are the expected or the unmarked types of actions in the midst of the activity of rope, as they promote the game's onward development or critique the style in which it is being played.[19] The situation of the moment itself may warrant the use of a directive format that in other circumstances would be seen as aggravated.[20] At junctures in play activity, however, direct-ives may take a more indirect form;[21] rather than making demands, children make proposals about possible courses of action using "Let's" as in "Let's see how many people can get in at one time" (said by a boy during same-sex jump rope) or "Let's play a game of snake" (a girl's utterance, referring to a game of jumping over a rope that is wiggled on the ground).

Directives may take alternative forms, and make different claims about how the recipient is positioned with respect to them. Some directive formats suggest that the addressee has complete control over whether the requested action will in fact be performed (e.g., "Can I turn the rope?" or "Can we do snake?). As Gordon and Ervin-Tripp (1984:308) argue, such "conventional polite requests, with few exceptions, are interrogatives that appear to offer the hearer options in responding . . . Conventional polite forms . . . avoid the appearance of trying to control or impose on another." Alternative to such "mitigated" types of requests directives may be formulated in a more aggravated fashion, becoming more demanding while increasing directness[22] – as in imperatives ("Give me the rope!"). While Labov and Fanshell (1977:84) argue that participants routinely attempt to mitigate or modify their expression to avoid creating offense, I do not find this to be the case with children's directives.

The embodied ways in which directives are formulated and responded to can create contrastive forms of social organization.[23] While many studies of directives ignore responses of recipients, ethologically oriented researchers of children's dominance hierarchies have argued that a crucial feature of social conflict is its interactional nature which "requires that equal attention be given to the activity of both participants in the aggressive social exchange" (Strayer and Strayer 1980:154). Directives and responses to them affirm and ratify who has the right to make decisions about various optional ways that the game can be played. They are especially powerful types of moves in deciding the scope of participation in the game.

Although the Hanley School children enjoyed playing with their friends in groups of four to six or more, the larger the size of the group, the more time it took for someone to get their next turn at jumping. Children attempted to exclude children who were not core members of their friend-ship group. Boys had more inclusive groups than girls, but limited the participation of those who did not have the same skills as the other members of the playgroup – for example, by making them turners. Thus a critical site for the examination of directive use is in decision making about roles in the game and the organization of jump rope. In this part of chapter 4 I explore the accomplishment of such tasks in mixed-sex groups where first girls and later boys are dominant. An important dimension of this study is that it investigates changing social roles for defining rules over time; as children become more skilled in the activity, the forms of speech actions they invoke to construct social identities shift as well. Two jump rope sessions held a month apart will be investigated with respect to how directives are used and provide alternative forms of participation frameworks. First, however, I will briefly sketch how the game is played in same-sex groups.

The Orchestration of Boys' Same-Sex Jump Rope

Boys construct a range of types of social orders in the midst of jump rope. Analyzing a particular session of jump rope among members of a fourth grade group of boys at Hanley, boys who played with the popular group, Wingard (1997) found that a hierarchical structure emerged in which a particular boy's directives were treated as binding, while others' were not. Malcolm had the power to orchestrate participation in the activity while others exercised relatively little control over their own participation. In the boys' group Malcolm's directives were frequently followed. His abilities to jump rope were superior to the other boys'; he could jump continuously for longer periods of time than any other boy. His superior jumping skill led to his authority to control the activity with respect to (1) commenting on the players' performances ("Everyone's messing up!") and (2) determining who could take which roles in the activity – who could play and who could turn the rope. Malcolm denied the opportunity to turn the rope to a particular player the group wanted to exclude (on this and other occasions[24]) in utterances such as "***NO:: TOM!*** Tom you can't do it!" *((grabbing the rope from Tom and pushing him out of the way))* or "Tom you're not gonna spin it. Just get it into your head."

Malcolm delivered directives in the imperative form: "Make it touch the ground! And turn it right!" or "Slow it down Tom!" It was his directives regarding who should turn the rope, what the speed of the rope should be, or who could take the next turn at jumping that were ratified by others in the group; generally Malcolm's directives were accepted with minimal contestation. In fact, other boys frequently echoed the directives he gave, as they attempted to affiliate with him.

Tom, the least coordinated boy of the group, had great difficulty jumping over the rope, and was initially denied his request to participate as a turner. Eventually he got to play when Malcolm overturned the other boys' mandate that Tom not be permitted to participate. As Tom ran to pick up the rope when someone dropped it, Malcolm stated "Let Tom ***DO*** it." Malcolm reallocated participant roles at his own whim. He later reversed the group's characterization of Tom as a bad turner and defended him. When a boy said "Tom's doing it way up here" *((holding rope high))*, Malcolm responded, "Watch. Tom's doing it right! Look! See. Tom's doing it right!"

Whereas Malcolm's directives were formulated as imperatives, Tom's directives took the form of statements of future action such as "I'll turn." Tom offered to take the ends of the rope rather than demanding that others give it to him. His relative powerlessness was evident in the fact that in nine out of ten attempts, the boys refused to give him the ends of the rope. Thus, while Malcolm's directives were either ratified or echoed by other boys, Tom's requests received no uptake and in fact were refuted. The boys also felt at liberty to critique his turning style. Dramatic differences in status were thus made evident through interaction in directive/response sequences.

A quite different type of arrangement occurred three days later that month. Rather than refusing Tom a role, Ron, a friend of Malcolm's and along with Malcolm one of the most respected players in jump rope, aligned with Tom through several moves: (1) he coached him in his jumping, saying, "Tom you're jumping too late"; (2) he gave him a second chance when he failed: "You can go again"; and (3) he offered him the role of turner: "Let's let Tom be an all time turner!" In a form of "twinning ritual" Ron said that Tom's jumping was similar to his own: "I'm jumping too early too. Tom, I don't blame you." When Tom said, "I'd rather spin than jump." Ron replied, "That's like me Tom." Rather than excluding Tom, he gave him a role and told him that his performance in the game was no different from one of the other principal players'; for this play session others did not complain about Tom's performance. Boys thus can create types of social arrangements that exclude or include others through their language choices.

Social Organization in Girls' Same-Sex Jump Rope

Within the fourth grade girls' clique leadership was more diffuse. Power to orchestrate the activity (naming the rhyme that would be chanted, deciding who played what roles, determining how many jumps were permitted before someone forfeited a turn, etc.) or challenge turners' style of moving the rope, or a jumper's moves was more equally distributed among group members than in the boys' group. (Example 4.20 below shows four girls of a five-girl group calling out rules in cross–sex interaction.) Example 4.7, for example, shows the way that multiple players rather than a single party designating herself as leader, dispute a jumper's complaint about the way the rope is being turned: only on one occasion did jumping ability determine status or roles in the activity.

Although Janis was the worst jumper in the group, in same-sex play she was as assertive as any other player in the game and she took on the role of spokesperson for the group when boys were onlookers to the game wanting to play (see Examples 4.12–4.14; 4.16–4.17 below). However, in the seri-ous contest between girls and boys (Example 4.30) she was asked by the girls not to play, as she was considered the least skilled jumper. During the cross-sex competition Emi provided the rules that others had to abide by. (See Emi's directives in Examples 4.12, 4.16, 4.18, 4.35 and 4.37 below.) Dispute among members of the girls' group was quite common and not restricted to particular girls.

While authority to direct, critique and counter was not restricted to particular individuals in the girls' group (as in many sessions of boys' jump rope), forms of exclusion occurred more frequently, across a range of activities. Angela, the working class "tag-along" girl would on occasion attempt to play with the clique despite the fact that she was frequently ridiculed and ostracized by them. Because she was often prohibited from playing with the others (usually by the girls rather than the boys), she generally jumped in a single rope by herself. While jumping rope alone several feet from the group, she was targeted as the cause of a player's missing a turn. When she was briefly permitted by the girls to turn the rope, she was told to quit because of her poor turning style. On several occasions she decided that jumping with the boys was a preferable alternative and also more fun, and the boys permitted her to join their group; members of the girls' clique labeled her activity of playing with the boys "flirting." Thus while some features of the girls' group showed less hierarchical social organization than the boys', girls' practices of exclusion towards out-group members were more pronounced and provided a way of defining the boundaries of their playgroup.

Directives and Participation in a Female–Controlled Mixed–Sex Game

At the end of April during my first year of fieldwork the fourth grade boys in this study had little experience with jump rope and generally participated as onlookers to the girls' game, commenting on their activity. In the first series of examples I examine from April, five girls – Emi, Melissa, Janis, Sarah, and Aretha – jump while three boys – Denzel, Stephen, and Ron – are standing on the periphery looking on at the game. When observing the girls, one of the onlookers states that it had been three years since he had jumped rope. Another complimented the girls on the extraordinary skill required for the intricate moves of the girls occurring during the "Texaco Mexico" rhyme. After Aretha executed acrobatic movements in space, Denzel, who was exceptional in the boys' group for his jump rope skills, stated, "I Aretha, I can**not** do that." At the same time that boys provided positive assessments of the girls' jump roping, they distanced themselves from the activity. In initial sessions watching the girls, the boys ridiculed the chant-like quality of the rhymes using exaggerated singsong intonation, and mimicked the dance-like movements of the jumpers preparing to jump into a turning rope with exaggerated up and down head and arm movements. This activity, however, was ignored by the girls, and treated as of no concern to them.

Asymmetry in directive use

At Hanley School in spring of my first year of fieldwork, fourth grade boys generally controlled who played on softball or soccer teams. Boys frequently declared themselves the captains of the teams. When they picked players girls were usually the last to be selected, and usually only a small number of girls, generally those who were friends with the captains, were selected to play.

Jump rope provided a quite different story because the girls were the ones with the expertise in this activity. In orchestrating participation in jump rope during the April session the girls used directives and responded to boys' requests to play in ways that demonstrated their control of the activity. Repetitively the girls told the boys what the ground rules were when asked if they could play. Originally Denzel, among the best jumpers of the boys, was scheduled to be the fourth jumper in the game. However, (line 7 of Example 4.12 below) when he stated that he did not want to have to jump into the rope while it was turning and that he did not want to have to execute the complicated movements involved in "Texaco Mexico" (turning around, touching the ground, doing kicks and splits, and slapping the palm of a turner while "paying taxes"), three of the girls (lines 3–5) in the four-person girls' group tell him that he can't play unless he does so:

Example 4.12

1	Denzel:	*You're* jumping in.
2	Stephen:	No *I ain't* jumpin in.
3	Janis:	You guys will *have* to jump with it.
4	Emi:	You guys will have to jump in.
5	Melissa:	Yeah.
6	Melissa:	And *Now! Now*! ((*preparing for Sarah to jump in*))
7	Denzel:	⌈I don't wanna do that- Mexico Texaco.
8	Mel/Em:	⌊*Now! Now! Now! Now!*
9	Janis:	You *have* to.
10	Mel/Em:	Texaco ⌈Mexico
11	Denzel:	⌊*No* I don't.
12	Janis:	Yes you *do*.
13	Mel/Em:	Where far away where they do some ((*singing chant*))

In response to Denzel's proposals (line 1) that he does not have to jump into the rope while it is turning – or jump to a difficult rhyme – the girls counter that the move is obligatory with "You *have* to" (lines 3, 4, 5, 9) and a retort to Denzel's objection (line 12) "Yes you *do*." The girls state in no uncertain terms that particular moves have to be made by the boys if they are to play with the girls.

In Example 4.13 Stephen displays his subordinate position vis-à-vis the girls by making a bid to enter the game through a mitigated request – "Can I try it?" (line 4):

Example 4.13

   1 Stephen: *((makes a nonverbal bid to join the group))*
   2 Janis: Stephen we're having a contest.
   3   ⌈We're having a contest.
   4 Stephen: ⌊Can I try it?
   5 Janis: Well not ***really*** because-
   6 Melissa: Because there's three against- one.

Inquiries by boys to the girls about joining the game are responded to with refusals. In Example 4.13 opposition first occurs in response to a nonvocal bid with the account from Janis: "Stephen we're having a contest." Next in response to "Can I try it?" Janis states in line 5 "Well not ***really*** because-"; her utterance is completed by an account from Melissa: "Because there's three against one" (line 6).

In Example 4.14 (the continuation of Example 4.13) two boys, Denzel and Stephen, make a second bid to enter the game through a request again phrased in a mitigated form: "Can you guys just- turn the rope?" Though initially Janis (line 3) grants permission, she quickly retracts it when one of her teammates argues that the game should be exclusively for the girls "No:: ***us***" (line 7).

Example 4.14

   1 Denzel: Can you guys just- turn the rope?
   2   eh heh-heh!
   3 Janis: Okay ***fine***. You can ***play***.
   4   You can play.
   5   ⌈You can ***play***.
   6 Stephen: ⌊(Hey. Can I play if I-?).
   7 Emi: No:: ***us***. *((shaking head))*
   8 Denzel: I don't want to do that
   9   Mexi⌈co thing
 10 Janis: ⌊Oh ***yeah***. =You're not part of our gang.
 11   So you can't.

In response to her teammate Emi's objection, Janis revises her prior granting of permission to play with first a change of state token – "Oh ***yeah***." – followed by an account which expands on Emi's turn (line 7), arguing for the exclusivity rather than inclusiveness of the game: "You're not part of our gang so you can't" (line 10). The girls agree to prohibit boys from playing in the game.

A form of asymmetry exists with respect to the obligatory nature of rules. In Example 4.15, two and a half minutes after Janis insisted that the boys had to jump into the moving rope to execute the acrobatic moves of "Texaco Mexico" (Example 4.13), she herself encounters difficulty in executing the moves. While the boys are watching the girls jump Janis argues that she herself is not bound by the rule and can jump to whatever rhyme she wants to. In Example 4.15, when she misses after one jump to "Texaco

Mexico" she states, "I don't want Texaco Mexico" (line 3). Although at first a turner argues that Janis's turn is over ("Okay, Emi's turn" – line 4) Janis rejects the statement that it is someone else's turn and stands on the rope so that it cannot be moved (line 5). Another player then proposes an easier rhyme that does not entail turning around or performing acrobatic moves while the rope is in motion: "Ice Cream Soda then" (line 6). When Emi next proposes that it is Denzel's turn (line 7), Janis holds out for getting another turn; she provides a dramatically executed counter with her polarity marker "No" and repeats Sarah's proposed replacement rhyme "Ice Cream Soda" (line 8) in a pleading gesture with her hands extended.

Example 4.15

		((Janis misses her jump as she begins
		to jump into the rope during Texaco Mexico))
1	Turners:	Texaco Mexico
2	Janis:	Yeuw! *((Janis misses – unsuccessfully*
		jumping after her first jump))
3		I don't want Texaco Mexico.
4	Melissa:	Okay. Emi's turn. Emi's turn.
		((looking toward Emi))
5	Janis:	No. I don't want Texaco Mexico.
		((stands on the rope so that they
		cannot start turning for a new person))
6	Sarah:	Ice Cream Soda then.
7	Melissa:	It's Denzel's turn. Denzel's turn.
8	Janis:	**No**. Ice Cream Soda *((does a pleading gesture with*
		hands extended intensifying her action))
9		Ice Cream **So**da guys.
10		Not loud 'cause–
		((Girls turn for Janis as she jumps))

An asymmetrical situation of power develops; the rules invoked by girls for boys as mandatory are ignored by the very girls who articulate their obligatory nature.

The girls display their control of the game not only by rejecting the boys' bids to play with them; in addition the girls make decisions about an activity the following day, a volleyball game, which would involve the participation of the boys, without even consulting them. With an inclusive "Let's" Emi addresses the girls: "Hey you guys. Let's still have a contest with them."

Example 4.16

1	Emi:	Hey you guys. Let's still have a contest
2		with them. *((looking at her teammates))*
3	Denzel:	(I would never ever let you call me)
4	Alan:	( )
5	Emi:	We're having a contest with you tomorrow for
6		volleyball.

7		Okay. Bye. *((waves them away))*
8	Janis:	Bye. We don't **want** you any more.
9	Sarah:	How many turns do we get. *((boys move away))*

In Example 4.16 in line 5 without any input whatsoever from the boys Emi informs them that the girls and boys are having a volleyball contest together the next day. Following the giving of this directive, the girls tell the boys to leave, through initiating the ritual closing move of an encounter in line 7; they wave while stating "Okay. Bye." Janis provides an explicit account for why the boys should leave: "We don't **want** you any more" (line 8). This account depicts the girls' desires rather than the requirements of the current activity[25] and thus constitutes among the most aggravated ways of formulating a directive.[26]

The account that Janis provides argues quite forcefully that on this occasion girls control who can play. When the boys return 15 seconds later, now agreeing to the girls' conditions for being a part of the activity – stating that they will execute the difficult moves of "Texaco Mexico" – Janis once more rejects their bid to join the game:

Example 4.17

	((Boys return arguing that they want to play))
Alan:	Alright. We (will) have to do that Texaco Mexico.
	Eh heh heh
Janis:	Well we don't **want** you to.
Emi:	**Go::. Go:::.**
	((The girls continue to jump, ignoring the boys.))

Through their actions the girls (in particular Janis and Emi) define when they will play with the boys and patrol the borders and boundaries of their play space through "borderwork" (Thorne 1993:64–88).

Controlling a peripheral girl's entry into the game

Continuously girls respond with denials to the boys' requests to play. Bids to join the game are made not only by boys; they are also made by girls who are peripheral to the play group. In Example 4.18 girls also reject a bid to join the activity made by Kesha, a fifth grade girl who sometimes has lunch with Janis's group but does not regularly play with them. She makes the bid to join by asking who is the last person in line to jump:

Example 4.18

1	Kesha:	Who's- last.
2	Emi:	Uh- one of them is last *((does a large*
		handwave in direction of boys on the sidelines))
3	Emi:	Nobody's- **No**body's last.
4	Emi:	⌈**No**body's last.
5	Janis:	⌊Nobody's last.

6   Kesha: *((body deflates))*
7   (Boy):   (Denzel Go.)
8   Janis: This is kind of like a **con**test.
9   Kesha: Oh. Okay. *((walks away))*

Here Kesha's inquiry "Who's last" is interpreted as a bid to play with the girls; asking about the appropriate turn order is only relevant for those who might be participating in the game. The girls forestall Kesha's positioning herself in the lineup by responding that there is no "last" position. While the girls do not state overtly that Kesha cannot play, they effectively imply it through their "Nobody's last" response (lines 3–5). Because the person who is last is not known, it is impossible to find a place for Kesha in the game. By way of a second account, the girls state that they are having a contest (effectively one that excludes her.) The account the girls give to Kesha is more indirect than the explanations given to the boys; nevertheless, it functions in a similar way to exclude her and is treated as a rejection by Kesha, as evidenced by the deflation of her body (line 6) following the girls' refusal to let her play and by her walking away from the game shortly afterwards.

Shifting participation framework while maintaining control

For six minutes the game was played exclusively by girls. Then in the midst of the girls' jump rope session the participation structure suddenly shifts from one excluding the boys to one that includes them. In the midst of a dispute between the turners and (the jumper) about the direction the rope is to be turned (toward or away from the jumper), Sarah (a turner) suddenly drops the rope to the ground and begins wiggling it (line 9). The dispute stops. Subsequently, through the use of requests and inclusive directives using the modal verb[27] "can" (line 11) and the inclusive "Let's" (line 16), the girls decide to play a game called "snake." In this game children must jump across the rope as it is wiggling close to the ground. The participation framework suddenly shifts from one in which girls alone were participants to one that is open for anyone to play:

Example 4.19

              ((The girls have been turning the rope
              towards the jumper making it difficult
              for Melissa to jump in.))
1   Melissa: Other **way** Sarah!
2   Janis: You **guys**.
3   Melissa: Emi, I don't do that to **you**.
4   Sarah: Emi-. That's what you did to **me**
5   ⌈And I didn't like it **ei**ther.
6   Emi: ⌊I know.
7   Melissa: I know but then, *((sigh))*

8		I never did it on Emi's turn.
9	Sarah:	((Sarah begins to wiggle the rope on the ground. and then Emi sits down and joins her in wiggling the rope))
10	Sarah:	La de dah de
11	Emi:	Now. Can we do snake?
12	Sarah:	Yeah.
13	Melissa:	But this does not count as one of my turns.
14		Anyone could do this.
15		((Boys go across wiggling rope))
16	Sarah:	Let's play a game of snake.
17		No wait! Till we play a game of snake!
18	Emi:	A game of snake. *Any*one could play.

The new activity initiated by Sarah with her wiggling movement of the rope on the ground (line 9) and Emi's subsequent request (line 11) "Can we do snake?" is ratified by others, through Melissa's "Anyone could do this" (line 14) and Sarah's "Let's play a game of snake" (line 16). The course of the game now shifts and the participation framework becomes more open, allowing the boys to play. Directives using modals and "Let's" are used at major junctures in an activity to suggest new alignments of participants and seek ratification from others. They propose rather than order.

Girls make the decisions about how the activity should be organized. In Example 4.20, a continuation of Example 4.19, Emi suggests what a new course of action could consist of through her request "Can we try like limbo or something?" (line 7). Girls specify which side of the rope girls and boys should be on as they divide up into teams (line 1, 2, 6) and tell the boys to hold the ends of the rope (lines 5, 23, 25):

Example 4.20

1	Sarah:	KAY! ***GIRLS*** ON ***THIS*** SIDE,
2		Girls on *this* side,
3	Janis:	Here. Get it! ((referring to the end of the rope))
4	Denzel:	What the heck *is* it.
5	Janis:	ONE BOY! // HERE! Hold the end.
6		Hold it! ((throwing rope to Denzel and pointing))
7	Melissa:	BOYS ON ***THAT*** SIDE!
8		Get on the other *side*.
9	Emi:	⌈Can we try like limbo or something.
10	Sarah:	⌊((kicks Alan, then pushes him))
11	Melissa:	Okay! // (Can we get)
12	Janis:	Only- no only // the girls!
13	Melissa:	*Lim*bo!
14	Melissa:	⌈We're playing ***Lim***bo!
15	Alan:	⌊((begins to do wiggling of rope as grabs it))

16	Janis:	Oh ⌈LIM**BO::**!.
17	Denzel:	⌊Limbo!
18	Alan:	De op! de wat! de wat! *((sings and does dance turning around, changing framework))*
19	Melissa:	We're playing Limbo!
20	Emi:	get out!
21	Melissa:	Okay! You saw- Tie! Limbo!
22	Emi:	I'm not holding the other end.
23		I kept on holding it.
24	Me/Ja:	DENZEL. HOLD IT!
25		*((several people talk simultaneously))*
26	Emi	It has to be one girl one boy hold
27		the ends of this. Each for a snake.

In organizing the activity the girls make use of the most aggravated form of directives, bald imperatives: "Here! Get it!" "ONE BOY! HERE! Hold the end. Hold it!" (lines 3, 5–6); "DENZEL. HOLD IT!" (line 24); "It has to be one girl one boy hold the ends of this." (line 26–27). For the most part, girls agree with each others' directives, affirming a particular version of the game. Differences of opinion regarding what the next stage of the game should consist of are short-lived. Sarah, Melissa and Emi affirm that the game of snake is open to anyone who wants to play, and Janis's (line 12) proposal that only the girls play is not upheld. When Melissa subsequently invokes an alternative game, limbo (lines 13–14), Janis immediately accepts this suggestion (line 16).

With the switch to the limbo game, boys (Ron, Alan, Malcolm, Stephen, Denzel, Bruce, and Tom) become participants rather than mere onlookers. The girls eagerly embrace their participation; in this game turns are exchanged rapidly as players move across the rope and boys initiate playful song and dance movements, adding to the fun. Despite the boys' change in participation status, nevertheless it is the girls who shape the event through their directives. While girls exclude, counter, and command boys, boys ratify the girls' position of authority by posing requests to them. Moreover, when the girls are displeased with the way that a move is being executed, they push boys who are turners, swing the beaded ends of the rope like a lasso in their direction, and chase them while everyone laughs; boys, however, do not initiate similar physical moves towards girls. The girls' superior position with respect to knowing the game entitles them to dictate how it will be played.

Directive Use in a Mixed-Group Contest

During the weeks following the initial session the boys had with the girls, the boys practiced during recess and eventually became quite skilled in jump rope, with the exception of jumping to the rhyme "Texaco Mexico," a rhyme that involves fancy footwork in the rope (see Appendix B). At lunchtime the girls talked excitedly about the fact that the boys were also interested in playing rope, and made guesses about which boy would be first to run for the rope after lunch. For the most part the boys pursued their own game apart from the girls. On occasion, however, Angela, treated as an outcast by the girls' clique, would join the boys. When this occurred, the girls said Angela was "flirting."

Boys' decision making

In May, a month after the initial session of boys attempting to join the girls' group in jump rope, as seven boys and seven girls are jumping in separate groups, but near each other, the idea for a tournament arises. Angela approaches Ron and Malcolm and says, "We'll racing against you two." The suggestion is quickly ratified by one the boys, Malcolm, a boy who, with Ron, is the most experienced jumper; Malcolm subsequently provides his definition of the shape of the tournament – one in which only two of the boys (the best jumpers) rather than the entire group of seven will be competing.

Example 4.21

Angela:	Okay, We'll racing against you two.
Malcolm:	Okay. Me and Ron versus two- (.) girls.
	Two girls versus two of the boys.

While in the April encounter between girls and boys, girls made most of the decisions and boys made requests to the boys, on this occasion the boys have considerably more say in what takes place. The two best jumpers, Malcolm and Ron, initiate many of the decision-making moves. They assert their position of authority through issuing directives (Examples 4.22–4.23) and statements that the event is a "contest" (Example 4.23). The boys explicitly construct the event as one that is gendered through statements that the girls should leave (Example 4.22, line 1) so that the boys get to practice on their "home field." (Example 4.22, lines 3–4). The principal players are Malcolm, Ron, Jack, and Dan, the jumpers, and Brian, Jack, and Bruce, who alternate turning the rope.

Example 4.22

		((After the girls have practiced several minutes the following occurs))
1	Malcolm:	All the girls go bye bye.
2	Girls:	*((Girls start to move to another area))*
3	Malcolm:	Okay. Now the boys get to practice.
4	Ron:	This is our home field.

Example 4.23

1	Malcolm:	The contest is going nowhere fast.
2		Start the event.

Asking someone to make decisions ratifies them as having certain authority or power. Both girls and boys ratify Malcolm and Ron's position of authority by posing questions to them:

Example 4.24
Aretha:	Malcolm are we gonna use one rope?
Malcolm:	*((nods))*
Aretha:	We're using one rope.

Example 4.25
Dan:	Ron. I'm the manager and the- and the- the judge. Okay?
Brian:	Screw you. Go away *((play-kicks Dan))*

While Malcolm and Ron make the more important decisions of the game, two boys, Brian and Jack, boys with considerably less skill in jumping rope who frequently end up turning the rope, play the role of gate-keepers regarding the group boundaries. They tell those who are not ratified participants to leave or where to locate themselves in space. In addition they define their addressees as "problems."

Example 4.26
Brian:	IF YOU'RE NOT IN THE TOURNAMENT GO OVER **THERE** SOMEWHERE!

Example 4.27
Jack:	If you are not-
Brian:	IF YOU'RE NOT IN THE COMPETITION GO OVER THERE!

Example 4.28
Jack:	Come on! You and Ed are the **bigg**est problem. Too many people around here.
Malcolm:	Jack. Leave him alone. What's he doing wrong.

Example 4.29
Jack:	Edward, Stephen, Tom. Is it **such** a hard decision. Stay behind the tree. Now you can watch. But stay behind the way of the tree.

Example 4.30
Jack:	Tom. Where you are right now is perfect. Okay?
Tom:	Jack. Does it really matter where I am?

Example 4.31

Jack:	You guys wanna jump rope.
	There's too many people in this rope.
Tom:	Jack. If there's too many people
	why don't you **leave**.

Negotiation while specifying group boundaries

Malcolm and Ron initially specify that the game will be played with four girls and four boys: "Okay we need a cot- the four goils." Six girls (Emi, Melissa, Aretha, Janis, Sarah, and Lisa) then all state that they want to be the four girls in a highly competitive exchange. The intensity with which the girls raise their hands, pleading to be among the contestants, is mimicked by Malcolm (line 12) below in Example 4.32. Because only a limited number of girls are going to be permitted to play, extensive bidding for the positions among the girls ensues, and one player, Janis (the girl in Examples 4.12–4.14 who had been the person responsible a month earlier for the boys' initial dismissal from the game) leaves in tears after she is asked by her girlfriends if she thinks she could actually beat the boys.

Example 4.32

1	Malcolm:	Okay we need a cot- the four goils.
2	Ron:	We need the four girls.
3	Aretha:	Me, Emi,
4	Emi:	Okay. ***I'm*** one of the four girls.
5	Malcolm:	It's an authentic way.
6	Emi:	***I'M*** ONE OF THE
		⌈FOUR ***GIRLS***.
7	Lisa:	⌊Melissa-
8	Melissa:	I'm ⌈one.
9	Lisa:	⌊I'm one.
10	Aretha:	I'm one of the four ***girls***.
11	Janis:	⌈***I'm*** one.
12	Malcolm:	⌊***I'm*** one of em.
		((raising hands and mimicking gestures))
13	Emi:	Then get i(hh)n. *((looking at Lisa))*
14	Janis:	⌈I'm one of-
15	Lisa:	⌊You said four.
16	Emi:	I know. I told-
17		I'm one of the four girls
		⌈who's gonna come in.
18	Lisa:	⌊Oh.
19		Oh. I am too!
20	Janis:	⌈***I*** want to.*((hands up))*
21	Melissa:	⌊I am. *((hands up))*
22	Aretha:	Janis. Do you think you could beat one of the boys?
23	Janis:	*((goes away crying))*

While the boys ask the girls to specify who is on their team, the girls do not initiate a reciprocal action with the boys. However, boys join the girls in ridiculing Angela (recall Example 1.4 in chapter 1). In contrast to Janis, who leaves crying when she's told she can't be on the team, Angela holds her own, coming back with counters to each imperative and exclusionary statement made by Lisa (Example 1.4, lines 13, 16). Further imperatives are delivered to her a minute later by boys as well as girls (lines 1, 4, 5), although this time she stands silently ignoring them.

Example 4.33

		((throughout the following Angela stands motionless))
1	Lisa:	Move Angela.
2	Brian:	Are you in the competition Angela?
3	Lisa:	*No*. She's *not*.
4	Brian:	Then *MOVE*! It's a competition.
5		Go get another rope to jump.
6	Malcolm:	Look. There's one
		⌈right there!
7	Lisa:	⌊*REG*GIE! I'm gonna go tell on her.

In numerous ways they degrade her. Later when she does get a chance to jump, they tell her to get to the end of the line:

Example 4.34

Angela:	I'll jump with Raymond.
Ron:	*NO!*
Melissa:	NO! You gotta go to the back of the line. Angela.
Angela:	Well don't yell at me okay?

Girls' decision making

While the boys make many of the decisions, power is not completely in the hands of the boys. The girls decide two critical features of the game: (1) how girls will compete with boys; and (2) what rhyme will be used. At the onset multiple people are jumping simultaneously. Malcolm argues that teams of two boys and two girls should compete in the rope simultaneously (line 3).

Example 4.35

		((Multiple players are jumping at once and having a problem jumping more than one time.))
1	Malcolm:	Then there're too many people.
2		It should be two-
3		It should be like two of the boys
4		versus two of the girls.
5	Emi:	Hey Aretha do you wanna be- in one- one-
6		um of the events?
7	Malcolm:	Me and Ron together.

```
 8   Emi:       The other side.
 9   Emi:       No.
10   Emi:       ⌈Okay.= We're four girls. Whoever has
11   ( )        ⌊I wanted(              )
12   Emi:       *We're* four girls.
13   Emi:       ⌈Whoever's last–
14   Aretha:    ⌊Because he just told me to get in
15              and I didn't know we were
16              ⌈jumpin yet.
17   Emi:       ⌊GET OUT!
18   Emi:       OKAY. LI**S:::TE:::N!**
19   Jack:      Bye, bye bye. *((pushing Ed))*
20   Emi:       We're (.) four (.) gi(hh)rls.
21   Sarah:     ⌈The other four girls *((dancing, chanting))*
22   Emi:       ⌊Whoever
23   Emi:       WHOEVER (.) GOES (.) **LAST** (.)
24              VERSUS whoever's
25              best on your **team::.**
26   Ron:       We **have-**
27   Aretha:    It should be one at a time.
28   Malcolm:   It should be **two–**
                it could be one boy, one **girl**.
```

Malcolm's proposal that two boys should compete against two girls is countered by Emi (lines 10, 12–13, 17–18, 20, 22–25), who yells loudly over the others' talk her vision of the contest as one between teams of one boy and one girl rather than two against two as Malcolm had suggested. After Aretha ratifies this proposal ("It should be one at a time" – line 27), Malcolm (line 28) revises his original designation of two against two (lines 2–4) to "one boy, one girl." The phrasing that Emi uses in lines 20 and 23, with micro pauses after each word (so as to emphasize them), adds to the directness of her statement.

As four girls are jumping simultaneously during a practice session before the official tournament, the boys start turning the rope fast, as if the event were speed jumping. Aretha yells at the boys for going too fast and tells them the rhyme that will be used. This is important in that the "Texaco Mexico" rhyme the girls select is one they are expert in.

Example 4.36

```
             ((Boys turn rope rapidly))
     Aretha:  GO SLOWLY.
              WE'RE DOING TEXACO MEXICO.
              DON'T GO SO FAST!
```

During the first real event in the contest, Malcolm asks the girls to confirm his idea that the event is speed jumping. However, Emi (lines 3, 6) and Aretha (line 5) counter his proposal that the event is speed jumping by saying that the event is "Texaco Mexico."

Example 4.37

1   Raymond: Malcolm. Go in with Emi.
2   Malcolm: What's this one. It's speed jumping?
3   Emi: ⌈NO:::,
4   Lisa: ⌊What is this.
5   Aretha: [It's Texaco Mexico.
6   Emi: *No* who could- who could get-
7   Texaco Mexico the longer.

Thus while boys organize the game through imperatives throughout the jump rope session, girls define who will jump against whom and what form of jumping will take place. They win against every contest between a girl and boy when "Texaco Mexico" is the rhyme being jumped to and celebrate their victories with hand slaps, victory signs, and loud score-keeping, shouting "Yeah the girls are winning." After several rounds of jumping to the rhyme "Texaco Mexico" the game becomes more chaotic as the contest shifts to speed jumping with several people in the rope simultaneously (the boys' favorite event) and new female players who are not expert jumpers join the contest, without any particular attention to skill. Even Angela joins in jumping.[28] Eventually the boys gain ground. As the first recess bell rings, Alan (as manager) declares that the score is sixteen to twelve. As the final bell rings the girls, feeling that they have the higher score jubilantly chant, "We won. We Won. Uh huh. Uh huh!" while boys claim victory as well. When I informally asked the boys about the contest as they were standing in line waiting to go to their classroom, their comments were on the organization of the contest rather than who had won. They considered that it was a good event but they wanted it better organized the next time, with more people on the sidelines rather than entering into the contest.

Separate Worlds or Special Skills? A Plea for Longitudinal Studies

The separate worlds hypothesis proposes that because males and females grow up in different subcultures, males and females learn to "do different things with words in a conversation" (Maltz and Borker 1982:200) as a result of "the very different social contexts" in which they interact in segregated sex/gender arrangements. Alternative styles of communication are said to be related to subcultural differences based on gender and to lead to miscommunication. My own research among African American children revealed little miscommunication among girls and boys and relatively little gender separation. As Cameron (1998b:444) has argued, the separate worlds theory "lacks robust empirical support, since few researchers on male-female talk have carried out the kinds of explicit tests for miscommunication that Gumperz and others have done for different ethnic groups."

In the analysis presented here, boys and girls participating in the similar activity, organizing participation in a game, have no difficulty in understanding the moves of one another. Girls' dominance in the game was observed to change over time. In mixed-sex groups while boys were learning how to jump, girls frequently set the agenda regarding how the game was to be played. However, as boys gained proficiency in the game over a month's time period they became equal partners in calling plays and making decisions.

Both boys and girls make use of similar types of speech acts. The middle class ten-year-old girls in this study demonstrated their ability to use bald imperatives – acts which are similar for organizing game activity across sex/gender groups – and speech forms I earlier (Goodwin 1980a) characterized as a masculine organizational style. What differentiates the present study from my earlier work is that the context[29] is not the organization of task activity in a neighborhood playgroup, but rather the coordination of activity in a game on the playground. In the organization of girls' task activity such as making rings from glass bottles there was little role specialization, and tasks could be completed individually. In games such as jump rope, by way of contrast, there was more role differentiation and a premium on limiting the turn of a player and the number of players; the more limited the number of participants or the turn of a jumper, the more frequently one gets to jump.

The way in which jump rope is played demonstrates that the relative skill level of participants is important in determining who has the authority to define the rules of the game. In the earlier play session boys initially displayed their subordinate status vis-à-vis the girls by making requests to join the activity. Refusing their requests, girls, by way of contrast, issued imperatives and directed counter moves to the boys. The girls told them they couldn't play, using accounts such as "We don't want you any more." When the girls shifted the game to "snake" and "limbo" and included the boys in their play, they still maintained control of the play activity, defining who had to hold the ends of the rope and where teams of boys and girls would stand.

In the mixed-group situation a month later after they had gained skill in the game, boys had considerably more voice in the organization of the activity. Two boys who were expert in jumping emerged as leaders and were ratified as having control over many features of the activity – organizing practice before the event, determining the timing of the event, deciding how many ropes were to be used, selecting players. Other less skilled (yet in-group) players assumed the role of gate-keeper – telling boys who were unratified participants with bald imperatives where to go and what to do. The decisions the girls (primarily Emi) made – determining how many players from different teams would jump simultaneously and what type of jumping would be used in the contest – were important (in that they favored the girls' jumping style) but more limited.

In both the cross-sex jump rope session examined here, excluding out-group members – an activity commonly associated with female social organization[30] – constitutes a feature of the interaction (Examples 4.26, 4.27, 4.29, 4.33). In the initial phase of the April jump rope session girls (primarily Janis) refused permission to boys (Example 4.13, 4.14, 4.16, 4.17) and a girl who was not a member of their clique (Example 4.18). The account they provided to Kesha (Example 4.18) – that they were in the midst of a contest – was less direct than the account they gave the boys: "We don't want you any more" (Example 4.16). In the May jump rope contest, boys created a clear separation between participants and onlookers through utterances (primarily directed at boys) such as "IF YOU'RE NOT IN THE TOURNAMENT GO OVER THERE SOMEWHERE!" (Example 4.26). Janis was excluded on this occasion because only a limited number of jumpers were participating and her female teammates felt she was the weakest jumper. Although both boys and girls used aggravated, face-threatening directives to an outcast girl, they did not direct such actions to boys.

In other work (Goodwin 1990) I have argued for the relevance of studying speech activities longitudinally. Ethnographically based studies that provide a form of time depth permit us to examine how the social orchestration of an activity can change over time.[31] With practice boys became more skilled and were no longer in a position of subordination with respect to girls. Boys began to use the aggravated directive style of girls when they become more proficient in the game. Both girls and boys can make use of a variety of directive forms; the use of imperative forms and aggravated counter moves is related to acquired skill. This is dramatically demonstrated by the way Janis, the party who initially had prevented others from playing, is herself ousted from the game.

Rather than being sex-linked, features of language use may be closely related to one's achieved position in a specific context, a finding resonate with that made by O'Barr and Atkins (1980) in their analysis of language in a US trial courtroom and Evaldsson (2004) regarding interaction in the midst of the game of foursquare among low-income and ethnically mixed (Syrian, Kurdish, Chilean) children in an elementary school in Sweden. Evaldsson (2004) found that the same preadolescent athletic girls who downplayed their skills in interaction with less skilled girls, participated in extended disputes with boys. Dunn (2001) in longitudinal studies of US and UK preschool children found no gender differences in conflict behaviors with close friends, siblings, and mothers. While girls might utilize more mitigated strategies with their peers in play groups, they do not differ in how they deal with conflict in close relationships. Perhaps the dramatic differences that the Two Cultures theorists have proposed are an artifact of the way that studies are conceived and conducted. As argued by Underwood (2003:48), methodological choices driven too strongly by Two Cultures theory may make it less likely that the theory will fail to be supported; what happens, as Thorne (1993:96) warns, is that, "the wheels of description and analysis slide into the contrastive themes and move right along."[32]

5

Language Practices for Indexing Social Status: Stories, Descriptions, Brags, and Comparisons

Social scientists concerned with process and identity formation in children's lives have examined gender, ethnicity, race, and childhood itself as social constructions,[1] as features of the social world that are built through interactive practice. As yet, however, we have few studies of how children index difference or inequality among group members with respect to symbols of social class[2] in the midst of their everyday talk.[3] Despite the importance of social class as a feature of identity, social science researchers tend to underplay its relevance in ethnographic analysis of culture. Ortner (1991:166)[4] has argued persuasively that anthropologists for the most part "do not bring class into analytic focus" in their ethnographies, due to a bias by anthropologists to emphasize ethnicity,[5] and also because the concept of class does not constitute a central category of cultural discourse in the United States (Ortner 1991:169–171).[6] Presenting a similar argument, Liechty (2003:9), states that anthropologists shy away from the study of class not only because of their bias towards examining more "traditional" societies, but also because Americans prefer to believe they live in a classless society[7] and tend to consider the notion of class both "antisocial and unpatriotic."[8]

Liechty (2003) maintains that the production of class-cultural space is accomplished through two conceptually distinct forms of cultural practice: discursive, narrative, or linguistic practice on the one hand, and embodied, physical or material practice (including the use of goods) on the other. Similarly, Bettie (2003:44) argues that, "the expression of self through one's relationship to and creative use of commodities (both artifacts and the discourses of popular culture) is a central practice in capitalist society. In this chapter I investigate "the hidden life of class" (Ortner 1998) by examining how, in the midst of crafting their social relations through talk during play, girls index social status with reference to events and objects in bids to both assert their position in the group and circumscribe the boundaries of their group.

Indexing Social Status at Hanley School

In interviews with me, teachers at Hanley School commented that they felt that socio-economic status was a more salient factor used by students to make comparisons than race or ethnicity. A fifth grade teacher, Miss Harper, described that a major problem teachers encountered was when students returned from vacations and children began to recount their leisure-time experiences. While some students reported on their vacations skiing in Telluride, para-sailing in Hawaii, visiting museums in Paris, or playing tennis in the Caribbean, others who had stayed at home and lacked money for vacations, had nothing to report. Hearing the stories of the fabulous vacations of their classmates made the homeless and less privileged kids feel poor by comparison.

At Hanley, children as young as four played power games based on social status. Johnson (2004), in a study of nursery school children at Hanley School, reports that in a pretend game using super heroes to fight evil, four-year-old children made distinctions in terms of relative power based on cost. Leadership was decided initially by who had a (pretend) power ring. At the start of the game someone argued for her position as leader, saying "I have a gold power ring so that's better than you. Follow me." Later, another girl interceded saying "Wait guys, I have the diamond power ring and that is more money than her ring so I am the leader" (Johnson 2004:19). At other points in contests over who had the best power ranger or action figure, children invoked their parents' ability to enable them to *meet* real actors playing super heroes as the ultimate squelch to their peers' attempts at one-upmanship. Notions of class among nursery school children at Hanley School were often linked to ethnicity in the talk of four-year-olds as well. While playing house, when a Latino boy said he wanted to play "dad" he was told that he could not be dad because "You guys don't have families. You will be the worker. Yeah that is a good job or you. Now go upstairs and start working" (Johnson 2004:20). K. Scott (2002, 2003, 2004) describes forms of "racial positioning" among black and white first graders at two mixed elementary schools she studied in the Eastern United States, and examines intersections between gender and racialized identity. Among the fourth to sixth grade children I studied, race or ethnicity was seldom made an explicit feature of social differentiation, perhaps because teachers displayed an ongoing concern with interweaving themes of racial and ethnic tolerance throughout their classroom activities and discussions.

Boys I observed in the third grade differentiated themselves with respect to rank in contests of physical strength (as exhibited in arm wrestling games), their skill in sports and at computers, European trips they had taken, and also their knowledge of films, sports, characters in role-playing computer games, and brand name clothing and shoes.[9] The following discussion about shopping for the latest fads in clothing and skateboards occurred among fourth grade boys at lunch. Dan excitedly reports that he is going to purchase a "Zero" jacket, similar to one that a famous professional skate boarder wears, as well as a new skate board. With each object that he mentions, he identifies an important person who is linked to the object he will purchase (either as user or endorser of the product). He makes use of multiple identifications of the person (through "try markers").[10] In response his recipient either provides an acknowledgement token or an evaluative response to his description (in the present case "Dope", meaning "cool," in lines 5, 10, and 26).

Example 5.1

1	Dan:	I'm going to Hot Rod[11] after school!
2	Alex:	What are you getting.
3	Dan:	They're having a sale.
4		I'm gonna get a Zero jacket?[12]
5	Alex:	Dope.[13]
6	Dan:	The one like Jamie Thomas[14] has?
7		What else am I gonna get.
8	Alex:	Oh.=a sweat shirt?
9	Dan:	((nods))
10	Alex:	Dope!
11	Dan:	I'm gonna get-
12		I'm gonna get a new skate-
13		I'm gonna get a new skate board.
14		A Tom Betty.=You know the guy
15		Who's smoking in Cigar City[15]
16		And then he does a back side board side?
17	Alex:	((shakes head))
18	Dan:	I just noticed that.
19		Me and my brother were putting it in slow mo
20		And he's holding a cigarette.
21		While he's doing that. Dope.
22		You know the real short guy in the jacket?
23	Alex:	Mm. ((nods))
24	Dan:	That guy?
25		I'm getting his board.
26	Alex:	Dope.
27	Dan:	That guy is **dope**.
28		He does all his tricks with cigarettes in his mouth.
29		He's like doing his backside
30		And he has a cigarette in his mouth.

A minute later the following occurs:

Example 5.2

1	Dan:	((taps Alex))
2		They're having a sale. They're own-
3		The shoes? All the shoes are only
4		Twenty five bucks.

5   Alex: Get as many a(hh)s you can!
6   Dan: I know. I'm gonna buy like- **all** the crappy shoes,
7   **All** the good shoes,
8   Alex: Get the twenty threes!

In Example 5.1 positive assessments ("dope") occur following Dan's descriptions of what he will buy on a shopping expedition; they are produced by Dan (lines 21, 27), as well as his recipient Alex (lines 5, 10, 26). Through the use of the assessment term "dope" (meaning cool) we are afforded a procedure for understanding what objects are formulated as valuable in these children's social worlds.

The adverbial "only" is important as well in commonsense calculation of relative value. Through the use of "only" Dan formulates the price of the shoes as outside the norm (as less than would be expected). In response his recipient Alex once again orients towards the shoes as valuable commodities, saying, "Get as many a(hh)s you can!" Alex's action to Dan is structured grammatically as a directive, though it is answered by Dan with an agreement token, "I know." Alex's statement encouraging Dan to purchase lots of shoes is ratified, indeed enthusiastically embraced, by Dan's comment; Dan states that he's going to buy "**all** the crappy shoes, **all** the good shoes."

While the boys in Example 5.2 display agreement in response to the depiction of an assessable event, another option is a response of "So what?" (Example 5.3, line 3) or ironic positive assessment (lines 4–5), followed by descriptions that run counter to the formulation of the initial description. Next utterances need not deal with the description put on the floor, but can instead provide alternative ways of reading the topic at hand. For example, among fourth graders when one of the boys described his brother's having been to Amish country, the following occurred:

Example 5.3

		((Malcolm is joking with Brian about the Amish)).
1	Edward:	My brother went on a- went to Amish country
2		in Pennsylvania.
3	Nathan:	**So** [**:?**
4	Brian:	└Good for **him**.
5	Malcolm:	Wow::::! ((*gesture of mock astonishment*))
6	Fred:	I have a friend who beat **up** an Amish guy in Pennsylvania.
7	Denzel:	I have a **bro**ther who's Amish.
8	Malcolm:	I've been inside stupid country before.
9	Brian:	Shut up with the **Am**ish already.

Edward's description of his brother's exploits are greeted with actions that treat the description as an attempt to one-up other participants, to display in some way the uniqueness of an experience. Next actions to descriptions, through either positive assessments or put-downs, can thus formulate the sense of that action. Bragging was characteristic of boys' groups in my Philadelphia study,[16] as well as at Hanley School, and has been observed by researchers studying boys in Norway,[17] and in Australia[18] as well. By way of contrast, in my work in the early 1970s among working class African American girls in Philadelphia, I did not find that girls bragged among one another. In fact, attempts to position oneself above others in terms of possessions or privileges were met with critiques, largely through gossip, and on occasion, ostracism.

Both female and male children in the Hanley School clique, however, openly discussed consumer objects (clothing and shoes), sports skills (in utterances such as in Janis's "I bet I'm a better kayaker than you. My two best sports are skiing and kayaking."), and leisure activities, as a way of indexing their social status during lunchtime conversation. In fourth grade Emi became the proud owner of a Japanese toy, a *Tamagotchi* (loveable egg), an egg-shaped electronic bird creature that resembled a digital pet chicken.[19] This pocket-sized gadget had a cartoon pet that appeared on a screen; owners reared it by punching buttons at regular intervals. The pet had to be nurtured, fed, put to bed, and taken care of at scheduled times. The digital pet was so novel and desirable that girls in the clique competed to be able to care for the "chickie;" Emi put into place a rotation for caring for it. Emi used the fact that she had this relatively rare commodity to differentiate herself from others. When she was asked where she got the digital pet, she explained to her friends that she got it on Sawtelle Avenue, a main street in a Japanese American area of the west side of Los Angeles. Emi quizzed her friends, asking them if they knew where the street was. She indexed ethnic affiliation with Melissa by stating that at least Melissa knew where the street was located.

Example 5.4

```
 1  Janis:    Emi. Where did you get it.
 2  Sarah:    Who's after ⌈Aretha.
 3  Emi:                 ⌊Sawtelle.
 4  Girls:    ((blank faces))
 5  Emi:      Nobody knows where Sawtelle is?
 6  Janis:    No.
 7  Emi:      ((looking at Angela))
 8            Do you ⌈know where Sawtelle is? ((incredulous look))
 9  Sarah:            ⌊They may have it at my uhm-
10  Aretha:   No. No. No.
11  Emi:      Melissa knows it because-
```

The digital toy thus provided an artifact that, being a highly desirable object whose possession depended on her granting access to it, constituted a resource, a form of cultural capital, that Emi used to position herself above others, as well as to index ethnic identity. In his book *Distinction* Bourdieu (1984) defines cultural capital as a form of knowledge, an internalized code or a cognitive acquisition that equips the social agent with empathy towards, appreciation for, or competence in deciphering cultural relations and cultural artifacts. Such judgments of taste are the product of practices of socialization.

As Bourdieu (1984:57) argues, "Objectively and subjectively aesthetic stances adopted in matters such as cosmetics, clothing or home decoration are opportunities to experience or assert one's position in social space, as a rank to be upheld or a distance to be kept." Yet while Bourdieu outlined a brilliant program for research, he never actually came to terms with investigating what the practices entailed in the socialization of class values looked like on the ground and in the flesh; nor did he investigate how people negotiate and give meaning to their objects of value in particular local contexts of use.

Liechty (2003:30), in his ethnography of the making of middle class culture in Kathmandu, argues that social class and consumption are "mutually constitutive." He views commodities as the primary currency of middle class life. (Liechty 2003:31). In the course of making an assessment or evaluative commentary about some object or experience, girls at Hanley School negotiate what constitutes value, patrol the borders of their group, and put people who do not have access to the activities and artifacts that animate their world in their place. In addition, they critique girls who affiliate with current fads that members of the clique deem to have become passé.

Participation and Positioning in Storytelling

Games provide visible portraits of the alignments of ratified players and those who are excluded. Generally all girls in the in-clique participate in regulating the course of the game. At points they actively police participation so that nonmembers cannot play. The alignment of participants within the frame of pretend play provides another medium for looking at processes of relative ranking and the expression of friendships (as best friends can take on the role of sisters, married to twins, as we saw in chapter 3). In the course of storytelling, perhaps the most ubiquitous of all speech events, we are also afforded a way of examining the structuring of social relations. Social status in a small group can be investigated by examining the ways that descriptions are put forward and are taken up. Both through (1) the way in which speakers select topics and either invite or close off participation in them, or (2) positively or negatively assess contributions of others into the story, speakers and hearers make visible different types of social order and ratify different types of participation.[20] In order to investigate the ways in which participation in stories can take alternative forms, we will first examine a story that eventually provides for participation of all girls present, with little differentiation among them.

Participation in storytelling about a news event

The following storytelling example provides an instance of how all girls who are present can engage as participants in the story. The girls have been talking about how Melissa's younger sister does Power Ranger motions

while seated within a laundry basket. This triggers a story Aretha heard over
the news about a boy who got his arm caught in a laundromat dryer. All the
girls who are recipients to her talk about the news event attend to the story
in ways that construct themselves as able to participate in the topic at hand;
they ask questions, provide commentary on the ongoing line of the story,
or assist in activities of the speaker, such as searching for a word.

The scene takes place as Aretha, Sarah, Melissa, Lisa, and Angela are
sitting eating lunch. The group is sitting in a circle, and Angela, a member
of the group who is not always granted the right to participate, is seated at
the periphery of the group.

Example 5.5

		((Girls are seated on a curb of the playground eating lunch))
1	Aretha:	There was this boy- this boy?
2		He was like a–
3		You know like the foreign laundries-
4		⌈places?
5	Angela:	⌊Uh **huh**!
6	Sarah:	Hm ⌈m.
7	Aretha:	⌊He opened up the laundry?
		(0.5)
8	Aretha:	The laundry- the uhm dryer?
		(0.6)
9		He s–
10		And the- the dryer is supposed to stop.=Right?
11		It didn't stop?
12		He stuck his **hand** in? *h And–
13	Melissa:	Uh::::.
14	Aretha:	And the dryer uhm, like–
15	Lisa:	°Took his- *((with motion to arm))*
16	Angela:	Cut it off?
17	Aretha:	Pulled his **hand** off.
18		It pulled his whole **arm** off.
19	Angela:	**OH** ⌈::::
20	Melissa:	⌊**UH::::.**
21	Angela:	**UHH!**
22	Aretha:	And so he had to go to the hospital
23		And they- like–
24		Put- they had to–
25	Aretha:	⌈Retape–
26	Sarah:	⌊Reattach it?
27	Aretha:	Yeah.
28	Sarah:	*((eyeball roll))*
		(1.0)
29	Melissa:	You mean they take the arm with them?
		(1.2)

30	Aretha:	**DU::H**, eh hih!
31	Sarah:	eh heh!
32	Melissa:	⌈Do you–
33	Aretha:	⌊They like– he like– *((massages arm))*
34	Angela:	Oh **YEAH**.
35		That's– what happened to that boy?
36	Aretha:	*((nods))*
		(1.0)
37	Aretha:	⌈(See that?)– And they're–
38	Sarah:	⌊Is he dead?) *((to Lisa))*
39	Aretha:	And they gonna **sue** the laundrymat
40		for ⌈not making it shut.
41	Angela:	⌊Do you know Bernice,

In the midst of Aretha's story, three story recipients, Sarah (line 26), Melissa (line 29), and Angela (line 16), enter into the discussion by posing questions or providing commentaries (lines 13, 19–21, 28, 31) that contribute to the ongoing progression of the story. Aretha's telling includes several word searches[21] as well: "He stuck his **hand** in? *h And– And the dryer uhm, like–" (lines 12–14). Here, in response to a word search, both Lisa and Angela enter to collaborate in attempts to complete Aretha's utterance.[22] Lisa quietly produces "°Took his– *((with motion to arm))*" (line 15) and afterwards Angela states, "Cut it off?" (line 16). There is no objection to Angela's completion of her utterance; in fact, Aretha next makes use of Angela's contribution and completes her story with "Pulled his hand off."

When Aretha repairs her utterance with "It pulled his whole arm off" (line 18), Angela (line 19), and shortly afterwards Melissa (line 20), provide response cries, appropriately appreciating the gist of the story. Aretha next initiates yet another word search as she states, "And they– like– put– they had to–" (lines 23–24). This time Sarah comes in with her own version of a possible re-completion of the word search with "Reattach it?" (line 26) as Aretha states "Retape" (line 25). In response Melissa's next move is a query about the events depicted in the story: "You mean they take the arm with them?" (line 29). This Aretha responds to with "**DU::H**, eh hih!" (line 30), an expression interpretable as "of course."

The kind of participation afforded Angela in this sequence is equivalent to that of other story recipients. Angela is not only able to come in and complete a word search that the teller initiates; in addition, her interjections in line 19 are ratified by another participant, Melissa, who enters with a response cry (Goffman 1978) that mirrors that of Angela. Moreover, Angela (lines 34–35) responds to the story by introducing a topically tied demonstration of understanding, a possible initiation of a second story (Sacks 1995b:249–268), which is acknowledged with a head nod by Aretha (line 36).

However, if we examine the interaction that led up to the story immediately previously (while the girls were talking about Melissa's sister "*Booboo*") we find that, in response to Angela's "*Booboo* head" alliteration on "*Booboo*," the girls started calling Angela pejorative names[23] (lines 7, 13–14, 16), and made faces at her (line 17).

Example 5.6

1	Aretha:	This is a-
2		This is **sad** and disgusting.
		(0.6)
3		And r::eally=
4	Sarah:	I call her Boo**boo**.=
5	Aretha:	Boo**boo**.=That's really funny.
6	Sarah:	I call her Boo**boo**.=
7	Angela:	**Boo**boo head.
8	Sarah:	⌈And I was like- ((to Melissa))
9	Aretha:	⌊Okay. Okay.
10	Sarah:	I'm not even // (listening to her).
11	Aretha:	**HEY**! ((puts arms up dramatically))=
12	Sarah:	((looks towards Aretha))
13	Melissa:	How would you like it
14		⌈if someone called you Angela Audi.
15	Aretha:	⌊I heard this on the news?
16	Lisa:	Angela Bootie.[24] ((glances at Melissa))
17	Melissa:	((makes faces at Angela))
18	Sarah:	eh heh heh! eh heh heh!! ((to Aretha))
19		⌈((mumbles))
20	Aretha:	⌊This- this little boy?
21		He opened up the dry//er=
22	Angela:	Was there any light in there? ( )
23	Sarah:	**HEY**!=We're listening to **HER**! ((to Melissa))
		(1.0)
24	Angela:	Now.
25	Aretha:	There was this boy- this boy?

Girls treat comments that Angela makes as asides or self-comments (line 7) quite seriously and they sanction her. Angela's utterance "**Boo**boo-head," no doubt intended as a playful rendering of "Boo**boo**," is responded to with a reprimand (line 13): "How would you like it if someone called you Angela Audi." Lisa then provides an insult to her with "Angela Bootie" (line 16). Lisa and Melissa trade knowing glances in response to Angela's talk, and Melissa makes faces directly at Angela.

Differentiated participation in the midst of storytelling: chained stories

Storytelling provides opportunities for each member of the group to present a particular version of events; in response recipients can ask for elaboration of the story, ratify or challenge one another's contributions, and display their similar or disparate views on a particular topic. In a storytelling session that occurred moments before the laundromat story, the topic initially on the floor was first words the girls remembered saying as babies in relation to labeling objects. Potentially everyone who was present could have said something about her experiences regarding strange pronunciations of new words, as this is not something that is dependent upon special access or membership.

In fact, to demonstrate understanding of the initial telling about first words, each of the members of the in-clique (Lisa, Aretha, Sarah, and Melissa), in turn, upon completion of a story, related a new story of a strange first word she had used as a baby. This produced a series of chained "second stories" (Sacks 1995a:764–772). Thus, following a first story in which the teller located herself as a protagonist in a scene in which she produced a new word with a strange pronunciation, a second teller related a similar incident in which the new teller was the protagonist. Next speakers made bids (and often in elaborate competitions) to tell a linked story.

The rounds of stories were triggered by Lisa's introduction of the word "snickerdoodle"[25] in talk with Aretha (see Example 5.7a–e): "If you go- to my house we'll make snickerdoodles" (lines 3–4) – talk that occurred while Sarah and Angela formed another conversational grouping. Aretha responded to this strange word by providing a second strange word "poppydoo" (line 12).[26] The introduction of this word triggered a telling by Aretha and Lisa about their past discussion of first words. On a previous occasion together, while Lisa and Aretha were talking about some of their memories of their first words, Lisa told Aretha about how as a baby she used the word "poppydoo" for popsicle. In response to Lisa's mention of the word "poppydoo," Aretha commented, "At least mine was a table" (line 21). This triggers the short version of Aretha's story by Lisa, who says, "*Ta*boo" (line 22). Lisa makes explicit for the rest of the group the general topic: "We're talking about what we called things when we were a baby" (lines 29–31). Both Lisa and Aretha subsequently competed for the telling of Aretha's story about how she had tried to inform her dad of her new word "Taboo" (lines 57–64).

With this general topic on the table, Sarah enters into the talk by discussing how the term she used as a child for freckles was "fuckles" (lines 38–44). After multiple attempts to enter with her own story, Melissa tells about how she had called milk "moy" (lines 123–128).

While each of the tellers provides a story about the pronunciation of new word in a strange way as a baby, Angela makes no bids to enter the conversation in this way, and no one asks her about her experiences. When she does enter into the storytelling by providing a short commentary, her contribution is sanctioned; she is told in no uncertain terms to "shut up" (line 144). Participants in the midst of storytelling thus can make evident their local social order.

Girls align with the teller of each segment of the story by (1) asking questions that advance her telling (lines 47, 95, 130, 132), (2) providing appropriate affect through laughter[27] (lines 22, 26–27, 55, 67, 81–83, 104, 127), (3) animating a voice (lines 52–53; 117–118), or alternatively, (4) critiquing someone's (here Angela's) participation (lines 138, 144 146–147).

By examining an extensive sequence of turn at talk one can examine how, turn by turn, participants themselves demonstrate their co-alignment, while simultaneously policing their local social order, so that only those with legitimate standing can enter with comments (thus providing for differentiated status of the participants).

Talk begins during lunch while girls are seated on a curb eating sandwiches; Lisa invites Aretha over to her house to make snickerdoodles.

Example 5.7a

		((Girls are eating lunch))
1	Lisa:	**Re**tha.
2	Aretha:	Yeap. *((looks up from lunch to Lisa))*
3	Lisa:	If you go- to my house we'll make
4		snickerdoodles. Okay?
5	Aretha:	Okay. Okay.
6	Aretha:	*((looking up to mike))* Snickerdoodles.
7		eh heh ⌈ha ha
8	Lisa:	⌊Ha ha ha!
9	Aretha:	**No. Oo**:::. That's dis**gus**ting. Snickery **doo**dles.
10		(2.5) *((Melissa begins to move))*
11	Angela:	Doodles. Doodle-lees.
		(1.0)
12	Aretha:	**Pop**pydoo! *((Melissa sits down next to Sarah))*
13	Lisa:	Shut up! *((to Aretha))*
14	Aretha:	Ah:::::::
15	Angela:	⌈*((begins to suck a lemon))*
16	Aretha:	⌊It's so **cute** ⌈though! *((to Lisa))*
17	Sarah:	⌊Is **that** a lemon, *((to Angela, said*
18		*with furrowed brows and disgust face))*
19	Angela:	*((shakes head))*
20	Aretha:	Well at **least** I didn't say it all the time.
21		At least **mine** was a **ta**ble.
22	Lisa:	**Ta**boo. eh heh heh ⌈hah hah!
23	Aretha:	⌊*((smiles, puts head in lunchbag))*
24	Aretha:	That was one of my first words.
		(1.0)
25		"Daddy! Tab**oo**:::::!!" *((falsetto, pointing downwards))*
26		Eh ⌈heh heh heh!
27	Lisa:	⌊hah hah hah!
28	Sarah:	*((looks toward Aretha and Lisa))*
29	Lisa:	⌈*h We're talking about what we called things
30	Aretha:	⌊Um,
31	Lisa:	when we were a baby.
32	Lisa:	⌈*h Like I used to call popsicle ⌈poppydoo.
33	Aretha:	⌊See my mom- ⌊No no we wo we wo
34		I wanna tewa tewa tewa *((talking baby talk))*
35		*((puts hand on Lisa's head over her mouth as if trying to*

```
36              stop her from talking))
37   Aretha:  (                        )
```

In this example we see the ways in which Aretha, Sarah, Lisa and Melissa in turn bring up their stories about learning a new word. All of the participants who are present potentially have access to similar experiences (memories of the first strange words they mispronounced as a baby) and could provide a story linked to a prior one. Initially Lisa and Aretha are talking, while Sarah is engaged in talking with Angela; Melissa was occupied with changing the place where she was sitting. In lines 24–25 Aretha provides a shortened version of her story with "That was one of my first words. 'Daddy! Tab*oo*:::::!!' ((*pointing downwards*))." Aretha and Lisa indicate their shared view on the story by providing a positive assessment of this story through their conjoined laughter (lines 26–27).

In her next move, Lisa addresses the entire group with "We're talking about what we called things when we were a baby" (lines 29–31). This opens up the story to others who are present. At the completion of Lisa's preface, both Lisa and Aretha compete for next speakership. Lisa provides the encapsulated short version of her story with "Like I used to call popsicle 'poppydoo'" (line 32). At the same time Aretha starts to launch her own story with "See my mom" (line 33). Finding herself in overlap with Lisa, she next switches to talking baby talk and dramatizes herself as a child, while putting her hand on Lisa's head and over her mouth and chin, attempting to stop her from talking (lines 33–36).

Upon termination of a story by one participant, a new participant can make a bid for a turn by initiating a story preface. That is what happens next here; on completion of Lisa's story about "poppydoo" Sarah initiates an elaborate pointing gesture as she states, "When I was little?" (Example 5.7b, line 38). Despite the fact that Lisa slaps Sarah on the leg and Aretha continues talking baby talk to Sarah and even taps her on the head, Sarah continues with her own chained story: "I used to call freckles 'fuckles?'" (lines 43–44).

Example 5.7b

```
38   Sarah:    When I was little? When I was little?
39             ((making extensive pointing movements))
40   Lisa:     ((slaps Sarah on the leg)) Wait!
41   Aretha:   Ah we wo we wo ((baby talk to Sarah))
42             ((taps Sarah on the head))
43   Sarah:    I used to call- freckles? (1.0) '°fuckles'? eh heh!
44             ⌈°for freckles eh heh!
45   Aretha:   ⌊((smiles))
46   Lisa:     ⌈When I was-
47   Aretha:   ⌊Did you know what it means?
48   Lisa:     When I was little
49   Lisa:     ⌈I used to call popsicles]        "poppydoo".
50   Sarah:    ⌊I didn't know what it means.]
```

```
51   Melissa:   Poppydoo! I want a poppydoo!
52   Aretha:    No! She was like- "Poppydoos!" ((high baby voice))
53              "Mommy! Poppydoos!"
54              ((lifting hands rapidly up and down by sides))
55              eh heh heh!! ((looks to Sarah)
```

In this sequence girls compete to take the floor. Here on completion of
Sarah's stories, commentary in the shape of laughter by Sarah and smiles
from Aretha (lines 44–45) occur, affirming the end of one story. Two
speakers then provide next moves. Lisa (lines 46–48) begins to relaunch her
story, by tying her own talk to some of Sarah's talk (line 38) through use
of a similar frame: "When I was little I used to call popsicles 'poppydoo'"
(lines 48–49). The unusual word "poppydoo" becomes a resource for
multiple speakers in their own next moves. Meanwhile, as Lisa tells her
story, Aretha simultaneously asks a question of Sarah: "Did you know what
it ['fuckles'] means?" (line 47) which Sarah answers (line 50).

Aside from asking a question, another possible next move at the completion of one of these stories is a re-enactment of one of the characters. Upon
completion of Lisa's story, Melissa, who had been silent, animates a small
child saying "Poppydoo! I want a poppydoo!" (line 51). Aretha next makes
a correction of the quotation with "No! She was like, 'Poppydoos'!" with a
high pitched baby voice (line 52) animating Lisa as an infant. Aretha adds
yet more to the animation by lifting her hands rapidly up and down by her
sides as she screams "Mommy! Poppydoos!" (lines 53–54).

As she laughs and looks at Sarah at this possible story ending, we find
that Melissa begins to launch her own story with "When I was-" (line 56),
though she is interrupted by Lisa, who now wants to tell Aretha's story
(line 57). Aretha, as rightful teller of her own story, intervenes with "Let me
say it. Let me say it Lisa" (lines 58–60). This then launches Aretha's next
expansive turn discussing how she had recalled using the word "taboo" for
"table" when she had been at a restaurant with her family (Example 5.7c,
lines 64–79).

Example 5.7c
```
56   Melissa:   When I was-
57   Lisa:      No you called- Oh listen to this! ((pointing))
58   Aretha:    ⌈Let me say it. Let me ⌈say it. ((pushes Lisa))
59   Lisa:      ⌊(              )      ⌊Taboo.
60   Aretha:    Let me say it. Let me say it Lisa.
61              Let me tell you. (      ) it goes.
62              Okay.
63   Lisa:      ((hits own leg several times in excitement))
64   Aretha:    My daddy? we were-
65              We were at a restaurant? (0.2) for um (0.2)
66              Mother's Day? (0.2) And um
67   Lisa:      Heh heh heh!
68   Aretha:    My dad said-
```

69		We were- I don't know **what** we were talking about-
70		⌈they were-
71	Lisa:	⌊We were talking about what we said
72		when we were little.
73	Aretha:	**No** before that. They were talking about something
74		when we were=
75	Lisa:	Children.=
76	Aretha:	They were talking about **some**thing about children.
77		★ hh And- my dad brung up this thing when he- I-
78		(0.4) And he was babysitting me once?
79		(0.2) And I said "**Da**ddy! (0.4) **Ta**boo!!"
80		((looks at Sarah))
81	Aretha:	⌈eh heh!
82	Sarah:	⊢eh-heh!
83	Lisa:	⌊eh heh!eh-heh!
84		A(hh)nd he was // like "huh?"
85	Melissa:	You said what-?
86		You said daddy what?
87	Aretha:	⌈Taboo.
88	Lisa:	⌊Taboo.
89	Aretha:	And then- and then, he said, an he was like "Huh?"
90		And I said "Daddy. Ta**boo**!" ((hitting her leg))
91		and I was pointing to the table.
92		And he's like, "Oh:::. **Ta**::ble."
93		(5.0)
93	Aretha:	Well Taboo sounds mo:re like table than, poppydoos.
94		(2.5) ((Aretha and Sarah gaze at each other))
95	Sarah:	That's a table?
96	Lisa:	Ta ⌈boo.
97	Aretha:	⌊Taboo.
98	Sarah:	⌈Oh.
99	Lisa:	⌊Not poppsidoos.
100		No. I called poppydoos popsicle.

As talk about Aretha's story (linked to Sarah's) winds down, Melissa prepares to launch her own story, with a preface that resembles that of previous turns introducing the remembrance of events of childhood: "When I was little? Since milk is one of my favorite drinks, And you know I like it and stuff?" (Example 5.7d, lines 101–103). She secures the involvement of her coparticipants with the sentence "And you know I like it and stuff?" (line 103), produced with rising intonation; the utterance offers them slots to talk ("You **love** milk!" – line 105) before she launches into a major part of what she wants to say.

Example 5.7d

100	Lisa:	No. ⌈I called poppydoos popsicle.
101	Melissa:	⌊When I was little? (2.0)

102		Since milk is one of my favorite drinks,
103		And you know I like it and stuff?
104	Lisa:	eh heh heh!
105	Aretha:	You **love** milk!
106	Melissa:	Oka(hh)y.=
107	Lisa:	Nicole does. =
108	Melissa:	I love it more than-=
109	Aretha:	Melissa does.
110	Melissa:	My dad said I could be on- (0.4) um- (0.3)
111		on ad- advertising milk.
112	Aretha:	What?
113	Melissa:	My dad said I could be on-
114		advertising //milk.
115	Sarah:	Yeah you'll think it was for the- commercials.
116	Melissa:	eh heh heh! Okay.=
117	Aretha:	You'd be like- (1.5) ((*gestures drinking from bottle*))
118		Ah:: (0.4) goo::d! ((*puts up index finger*)) eh heh!
119	Melissa:	eh hheh-heh! ((*smiles*))
120		°Milk does the body good. ((*holds out hand as if*
121		*embracing a bottle*))
122	Sarah:	Very good,
123	Melissa:	I called milk when I was little?
124		(1.4) uh,
125	Aretha:	Milky.
126	Melissa:	No.
127	Aretha:	eh heh heh!
128	Melissa:	⌈Moy.
129	Aretha:	⌊Milky.
130	Aretha:	Huh (0.5) What?
131	Aretha:	Moy.
132	Aretha:	Moy(hhh)?
133	Melissa:	I WANT MOY!
134		That's what-

As Melissa launches her own story, she makes use of hesitation in her talk: "I called milk when I was little? Moy" (lines 123–128). The rising intonation over "I called milk when I was little?" as well as the hesitation "uh," in her talk here solicit co-participation; in response, Aretha (lines 125, 129) can come in with her candidate guesses about what Melissa called milk. By introducing the figure of her dad in a story about first words, reporting he had said she could advertise milk (lines 110–111), Melissa links her story to a past one; Aretha's story involved telling her Dad her word (*Taboo*) for table.

Angela, in contrast to the other girls, remains silent throughout most of the tellings. When she does offer up a commentary, punning on something said by Aretha ("dud" with "dud milk"), she is very severely sanctioned. Lisa makes a face as she says "EEuw" (Example 5.7e, line 138) while Aretha yells "**STOP** IT!" (line 142) Lisa next states "Shut up Angela" (line 144) and Melissa loudly addresses her with "SHHHH!!!" (line 147). Aretha makes explicit Angela's need to be silent through "We're just telling you to stop it" (line 149).

Example 5.7e

135	Aretha:	No. Okay. My: my uhm,
136		whatever it's called? My (.) dud,
137	Angela:	Dud milk. *((raspy voice))*
138	Lisa:	*((makes face))* EEuw.
139	Aretha:	You know. My uhm,
140	Angela:	⌈Got milk.
141	Aretha:	⌊My-
142		***STOP*** IT! My uhm,
143	Angela:	God.
144	Lisa:	Shut up Angela.
145	Aretha:	Uhm my,
146	Sarah;	Errhh!
147	Melissa:	***SHHHH!!!*** *((to Angela))*
148	Angela:	Why::,
149	Aretha:	We're just telling you to stop it.
150	Aretha:	Okay. (0.5) My g- godniece? She said "I wanna haa daa." (hot dog)

By observing differential forms of alignment in the midst of stories we can understand the practices through which girls can (1) display that they have carefully attended what other parties have said and make visible their congruent version of events, or (2) demonstrate how someone has no standing to participate in providing comments into the ongoing storyline.

Topic selection and the alignment of participants

The kinds of topics that speakers invoke in the telling of stories can position those who are co-present differentially. In previous work[28] Charles Goodwin and I described how in the midst of a sling shot making contest when a speaker switched from giving commands within the realm of a sling shot fight to giving commands within a realm of household duties, the shift in topic signaled a shift in participation structure, making relevant responses from only a particular set of individuals (those who inhabited the same house). Recipients to stories are positioned actors. They are aligned in one of two ways: (1) as parties who were participants in the past scene being recounted, and thus have rights to comment on that which is at issue, or (2) as actors who by virtue of their exposure to particular types of experiences (congruent with those of the speaker) have the standing to participate.[29] Across a range of settings among the girls in the popular clique, speakers can treat topics as ones about which their recipients have limited access or knowledge – either because they have not co-experienced an activity

(Goodwin 1981), or because they have not been exposed to particular domains of knowledge or "fields of cultural production" (Bourdieu 1993). By examining the ways that speakers invoke different types of topics, making relevant particular forms of participation, and participants to an interaction engage in a co-telling, we can examine important social processes at work. It is not always the case that all participants exhibit similar possibilities for coparticipation. The observable practices, and emergent structure of interaction, are the products of participants' own actions.[30]

Girls in the popular clique differentiate themselves in terms of their access to activities and privileges of the upper middle class.[31] Among the topics that girls discussed at lunch were activities which indexed their social ranking, such as after-school soccer leagues, drama class, singing class, Japanese class, piano lessons, and recreational activities – weekends skiing in Canada, Colorado, or at a family ranch in southern California, as well as summer camp activities, and concerts.

Differentiation with respect to leisure activities associated with wealth was a frequent topic among the girls. The following occurred in the sixth grade after Janis's mom, who is visiting during lunch, has just told Melissa that she would be happy to take her to play tennis in Palm Desert (an exclusive resort community in southern California) while Melissa's mom was away. Parents also participate in the process of openly providing displays of wealth and status that differentiate participants. Though beyond the scope of this book clearly parents' values appear to be intimately related to the types of comparisons that the girls themselves deem important.

Example 5.8

		((Several girls are eating together))
1	Janis:	You can play tennis every day in the Dominican.
2		Melissa, I was starting to play-
3		Playing tennis in one of my friend's house?
4		And they had all these rackets.
5		And they were like- "Choose."
6		And they said "No you can't use that one.
7		It's Jimmy's."
8		And I said "Who's **Jim**my."
9		And they said "Jimmy Conner."
10		No it' s -was somebody else.
11	Melissa:	Andre?
12	Janis:	Yeah it was Andre Agassi.
13		Then she said "Andre Agassi."
14		I said "Okay. I won't use it.
15	Aretha:	And you always take something without asking.

Janis directs her story about almost using Andre Agassi's tennis racket to Melissa, another girl who shares her tennis club experience. The explicit address term, as well as this topic-invoked participant framework, provides relevant identities for particular participants. It is not uncommon (see

Example 5.10, 5.14) to index specific relationships of duos that set girls apart from others through talking about shared experiences.

The implicit attempts at bragging in such stories, however, can be challenged. One possible reply to Janis's story about almost using Andre Agassi's racket could have been response tokens displaying positive affect or amazement. However, Aretha refuses to ratify the exalted status that Janis is proposing for herself through this description. Instead of responding to the news that Janis had used Andre Agassi's racket, Aretha (line 15) makes a comment about the fact that Janis had taken something without asking for it, and provides a negative evaluation: "And you always take something without asking." Evaluations or assessments of stories thus make possible a range of readings in response to the proffered description. While evaluations or assessments may make relevant a stance displaying desire or envy (see Example 5.3), Aretha expresses disdain toward the events in the teller's story, and undercuts it.[32]

Similar types of undercutting or challenging attempted brags occurred in the following instance where girls are discussing junior high. In the sixth grade lunchtime consisted of endless comparisons of who had been accepted at which private junior high school, who was on the waiting list for one, or who would be attending a public school.[33] Each mention of a school provides the possibility for assessments to be made. In the following Melissa, who was accepted at the most prestigious private school in the city, comments that Brentwood (deemed the "Hyannis Port West" by *Los Angeles Times* reporter Mary McNamara in 2003, and known for its comparatively good middle school) is deemed low in status ("bad") by comparison with Harvard Westlake. Melissa provides an explicit comparison assessment with her statement "Harvard Westlake is better." She thus positions herself as someone entitled to assess the relative ranking of middle schools.

Example 5.9

```
1  Janis:    What school is Joan going to.
2  Regina:   Brentwood. With Donna.
3  Melissa:  Brentwood's bad man.
4            Stay away from there.
5            Harvard Westlake is better.
6  Regina:   Well we didn't get into Harvard Westlake.
```

Once a topic, such as a local middle school, is on the floor, participants may provide their commentary on it. One's evaluation positions him or her relative to a particular topic. These assessments can be used in displaying alliances with other participants. Through her comparison "Harvard Westlake is *bet*ter," Melissa displays that she has unique epistemic authority[34] and knowledge about the relative ranking of the middle schools in the Los Angeles area. She positions Harvard Westlake above Brentwood Middle School. Regina's commentary "Well we didn't get *in*to Harvard Westlake," displays opposition with Melissa. In her counter move, Regina provides an explicit gloss for the implicit meaning of Melissa's statement – a brag about the school Melissa would be attending. While Melissa may have had the authority to make such a statement, in so doing she is marked as having violated an implicit norm.

In the midst of lunchtime conversations about their after-school and weekend activities, conversations make relevant participation of those who have access to similar experiences; the activity of talking about ballroom dancing makes relevant next moves which attend to the details of such an activity by actors who are positioned to be able to talk about it. Such comparisons are accomplished through descriptions in the midst of stories, brags, and assessments. On one occasion when eight fourth grade girls were eating lunch together, discussion between Melissa and Emi took place about Cotillion (ballroom dance classes that are preparation for debutante balls and "coming out" parties). These two girls, who were sitting next to each other, had both participated in such a Cotillion dance class. Though Janis knew about Cotillion classes, she had not yet participated in them. The telling of a story sets up the relevance of a topic-invoked participant framework;[35] the topic of Cotillions makes relevant the participation of those who have **access to** such events. Melissa, making obvious displays of her familiarity with the dance moves, began to demonstrate with Emi, who had also attended the Cotillion event, how dancing partners were expected to position their arms with respect to each other's bodies. Girls make use of "kernel stories," in Kalčik's (1975) sense, each in turn adding one element to the developing storyline in next moves.

Example 5.10

		((Several girls are eating lunch together. Emi has her arms positioned as if involved in a ballroom waltz))
1	Emi:	But you have to be like that.
2		⌈((demonstrating ballroom dance position of arms
3		⌊ with elbows bent aligned to shoulder))
4	Melissa:	[You gotta be like this. ((arms with elbows bent))
5		Straight. You gotta be like-
6	Emi:	He was going like this.
7		((beating rhythmically on lunch table))
8	Sarah:	I wanna do Cotillion! ((longingly))
9	Melissa:	Nope. You do not. ((shakes head))
10	Emi:	((smiles))
11	Sarah:	I wanna dance (dirty) eh heh!
12	Janis:	Oh my god Melissa. Melissa! Melissa! ((yelling from far end of the table))
13		Melissa, Andrew's doing Coti(hh)llion.
14	Melissa:	Emi's doing the Cotillion with me *too*.
15	Janis:	Andrew *wants* to though.
16	Emi:	I do too!
17	Janis:	What do you *do* though.

Because girls express affiliation with upper middle class culture through mention of access to elite types of activity such as attending a ballroom dance class, those who do not possess such access are left out of the talk, and are vulnerable to experiencing gender-specific forms of "hidden injuries of class" – feelings of inadequacy when one contrasts oneself to others. Sarah, who was working class and was not attending the dance class, could not participate in the discussion by explicating types of dance positions. Instead she responded to the description with a whining, "I wanna do Cotillion!" (line 8). Such plaintive cries demonstrate the stance girls take up towards certain activities, constituting them as valuable, as well as inaccessible, for certain people.

The description of attending Cotillion dance classes does not in itself require a next move. However, with Sarah's utterance (line 8) we can see that one possible emotion that describing such an experience calls forth is the expression of desire.[36] In addition, we can note how the description itself operates to partition the clique into different subgroups (those who know and those who do not know about ballroom dancing).

The telling of this story by Emi and Melissa is achieved through utilizing utterances that have sentence structures parallel to the immediately previous utterance, a practice identifiable as format tying (Goodwin 1990:177–185).

```
(1)   You   have to be   like that.
(4)   You   gotta be     like this
(6)   He    was going    like this
```

Parallel forms of structures also occur in the sequences that follow when Janis joins the discussion:

```
(13)  [Andrew's]  [doing Cotillion.]
(14)  [Emi's ]    [doing the Cotillion] with me too.
```

```
(15)  [Andrew]  [wants to]  [though.]
(16)  [I ]      [do]        [ too. ]
```

In these sets of paired utterances several parallel structures are observable. First, in line 14 Emi replaces "Andrew" in Melissa's next utterances to Janis with "Emi." In the next set of utterances, close format tying occurs as well. In Emi's utterance (line 16) "I" replaces the subject "Andrew" and the pro-verb "do" replaces "wants to." Thus Emi, Janis, and Melissa produce utterances that are closely tied in format to one another. While Janis attempts to argue that she is allied with a boy who wants to do Cotillion, Melissa argues that their mutual friend, Emi, is going with her. With the moves that both Janis and Melissa make we can witness how a description of an event becomes the occasion for a contest between two girls.

The discussion of the dance class partitions participation, and results in the act of making explicit differential access to ballroom dance classes among clique members. It provides a forum for a limited number of people to elaborate details of the activity, as only three participants have first hand experience of the event. Another girl, Sarah, who had no experience with ballroom dancing made explicit her differentiated status through her expression of "longing." Talking about Cotillion dance classes provides an opportunity not only to index social status, but also to signal special friendships in the group, as well as alliances with boys (line 13 of Example 5.10), which themselves may provide indices of social class.[37]

Topic and Participation: A Critical Concern in Clique Interaction

As the previous example demonstrated, a topic may be invoked that is constructed as relevant only to a circumscribed number of participants – for example, those who participated in a past activity. This occurs in the midst of the next example, a storytelling about a trip to the Santa Monica Pier, a boardwalk that houses an amusement park. Only three of the four members of the clique who are talking together in the present interaction (Sarah, Melissa, and Lisa) were present at the scene being depicted. In this example we can observe that among the inner circle of friends, mentioning prior encounters when one of the girls in the present encounter did not participate in it is treated as a delicate matter.

A major issue in the lives of these girls, in fact one of the most important for defining their local social organization, concerns who participates in social outings. Across any number of encounters of story telling, girls display intense concern with knowing who went where with whom on weekend or after-school afternoon excursions – to Halloween parties, concerts, play dates, or birthday parties at each other's houses. For example, in the following there is discussion about the birthday party of Kathy (a fourth grader who sporadically hangs out with the clique). Janis expresses intense interest in who was invited and in the fact that Emi was invited but she was not.

Example 5.11

MHG:	So Kathy is this your birthday or is it coming up or what.
Kathy:	Yes. This afternoon.
Janis:	I wasn't invited.
Kathy:	Yes you were going to be but then my mom said I could only have small number 'cause my dad wasn't gonna be there.
MHG:	How many girls are going.
Kathy:	Twelve. Um, Emi, Melissa,
Janis:	You invited Emi? And not me?
Kathy:	Aretha (was sick). Emi wasn't gone. I knew Emi was gonna be here.

Kathy: Emi, Melissa, Aretha.
Janis: You invited Sarah?
Kathy: *Uh* uh.
Kathy: There was a limit. I was only allowed to invite a
            certain amount because my mom wasn't gonna be
            there. June and Rachel are invited. And then Rachel's
            cousin Alicia is invited.
Brittany: I would go but I made plans before with Janis.

The example we will now investigate (Example 5.12) took place while
the girls (Melissa, Sarah, Lisa, and Janis) were seated eating lunch. One of
the core group members, Melissa, began to reminisce about a trip that some
members of the group took together. Melissa, Sarah, and Lisa had attended
the event, while Janis had not. The story begins as Melissa poses explicit
questions to her interlocutor seated immediately to her left, Sarah, asking
her if she remembers an event that both of the girls participated in: "Oh
remember Sarah? At the Santa Monica Pier?" (lines 1–3). In the next turn
to Melissa's requests to remember, however, Sarah provides non-lexical
utterances that display non-recognition, and could be interpreted as subtle
messages to Melissa to stop this line of inquiry: "Hmmm?" (lines 2, 4, 7, 9).
She takes a turn without providing any recognizable appropriate next move
or second pair part to the questions that her interlocutor poses to her. Such
a strategy continues over several turns, in lines 10–12, with Sarah passing
the opportunity to participate in the invitation to co-tell the story:

Example 5.12
```
 1   Melissa:   Mm-? Oh remember Sarah?
 2   Sarah:     ⌈(Hmmmm?)
 3   Melissa:   ⌊At the Santa Monica Pier?
 4   Sarah:     Hmmm? ((tilts head toward Janis))
 5   Lisa:      ⌈eh huh-huh!
 6   Melissa:   ⌊Come on. ((slaps Sarah on the arm))
 7   Sarah:     Hmmm?
 8   Melissa:   Sarah!
 9   Sarah:     ((shoulder shrug in direction of Janis mumbling))(°us two)
10   Melissa:   uhm Remember at the Santa Monica Pier?
11   Sarah:     ((nods slightly looking at Melissa))
12   Melissa:   I mean- at Pat's birthday party.=
13   Lisa:      Stop! ((to Sarah))
14   Sarah:     ((looks towards Janis))
15   Melissa:   Oh sorry sorry sorry. ((puts hand over mouth, smiles))
16   Janis:     That's all right. I don't care. ((makes face))
17   Melissa:   Never mind.
18   Janis:     I don't ⌈care.
19   Sarah:            ⌊(              whurly ⌈bird)
20   Janis:                                   ⌊I don't care.
```

What accounts for Sarah's lack of uptake to Melissa's requests to involve herself in the story? The participation structure of the present group in relation to the participation structure of the events being recounted is quite relevant when we consider that exclusion from participating in past events is among the important concerns of the girls' group. The structure of nonvocal as well as vocal moves is important for understanding how the story progresses. In response to Melissa's questions, Sarah opts not to respond with an on-record reply. Rather she states "Hmmm?" and tilts her head in the direction of Janis (line 4), a present participant who was not at the outing being described. Sarah does not, however, reposition her body so that her facing formation (Kendon 1977) is changed; instead, she retains a position seated next to Melissa, the speaker, with her gaze focused outward toward the center of the circle of friends. In response to this non-response, Melissa makes more explicit her request for a response from Sarah with "Come on" and physically slaps Sarah on the arm (line 6). Once again Sarah responds solely with "Hmmm?" (line 7).

Melissa's next attempt to get a response from her recipient is to use an address term "*Sar*ah" (line 8). This time Sarah passes the opportunity to respond by producing a shoulder shrug in the direction of Janis (line 9), as if using it to point to Janis in order to cue her recipient that she should in some way attend to this third party in constructing her talk. Melissa, however, does not attend to the gesture. Melissa recycles her request to remember with "Remember at the Santa Monica Pier?" (line 10). Sarah's response this time is to look at Melissa and produce a small head nod (line 11). In the midst of doing a repair on her utterance "I mean – at Pat's birthday party" (line 12), Lisa, a girl who had been present at the Santa Monica Pier adventure, enters the conversation with an abruptly spoken "*Stop!*" (line 13). This utterance makes verbally explicit what the gestures of Sarah were implicating – namely that this line of inquiry should cease. At this point Sarah looks explicitly towards Janis and Melissa provides an apology to Janis: "Oh *Sor*ry *sor*ry *sor*ry." (line 15). She intensifies the apology nonvocally by putting her hand over her mouth (a gesture which can indicate that a mistake has been made, often used in contexts where embarrassment is at issue). These remedial actions (the apology and the gesture of hand over mouth) clearly construct the activity of mentioning an event that a present in-group member did not attend as an act that should not have occurred. In Janis's next utterance she makes explicit that bringing up the story about the Santa Monica Pier is something that one would be concerned or "care" about, with "That's all right. I don't care" (lines 16, 18, 20).

As the story develops further, the girls describe various adventures of other participants on the outing, some of whom were not even part of the inner circle of six who regularly play together. This results in an explicit query from Janis about past participants in the activity: "You and Sharieay were together?" (line 15). In the following Sarah is describing a ride that she went on at the amusement park. She is describing the activity of asking the attendants at the amusement park to push her. Janis initially attends to the story with commentary not dealing with the excitement of the rides, Sarah's story-line, but rather talking about how they make her "barf" or "vomit" (line 4).

Example 5.13

1	Sarah:	Me and Emi asked them
2		to push us before we went? eh heh!
3		Just to push our thing?
4	Janis:	I would barf.
5		⌈I mean probably.
6	Lisa:	⌊They did that–
7		To me and Sharieay.
8		We were sitting there?
9	Janis:	⌈Sharieay went too?
10	Lisa:	⌊And she went "Ooooo!!"
11	Lisa:	⌈'Cause me and Sharie
12	Melissa:	⌊*Shari*e, Sharie *AY!*
13	Lisa:	Sharie*AY*. I have *food* in my mouth.
14		(3.0)
15	Janis:	You and Sharieay were together?
16	Lisa:	Mm *hm*.
17	Sarah:	°Sharieay?
18	Lisa:	'Cause Aretha wouldn't *go*.

Among the multiple and diverse features of the description of the amusement park that which Janis selects to inquire about is who Lisa was with (line 15), as this is for her among the most significant features of the description that Melissa has provided. She states: "Sharieay went too?" (line 9) and "You and Sharieay were together?" (line 15).

Thus throughout this example we see girls orienting towards the activity of doing things together as important for defining the inner circle of friends. Participation in events is an explicit concern that they care intensely about. Stories[38] provide ways of organizing political organization in a group for future plans; they provide ways of mobilizing participants in particular ways in terms of future projects (such as ostracizing someone). Stories of this sort thus provide one way that girls may indirectly yet powerfully sanction the behavior of those, like Janis, who attempt to show themselves superior to others. By evoking a reminiscence about a past event in which one of the current participants was not present, girls can sketch a portrait of their social organization which positions someone as an outsider both in the past (when she was excluded) as well as in the present, in that she has little standing to collaborate in the telling of a story. Janis, for her part, can show how she positions herself with respect to the event at issue, distancing herself from it, through portraying it as something which is distasteful rather than pleasurable.

Participation, Access, and Status Differentiation during Storytelling

The organization of participation in the midst of stories provides ways of subtly distinguishing or categorizing group members. In the midst of eating lunch one topic that comes up that differentiates members is after-school activities. Talk about tennis, for example, provides one way in which certain girls can display their unique access to a particular sport, one often associated with upper middle class status. In the next example two of the girls who regularly play in tennis tournaments, Emi and Melissa, discuss various features of the game. As the sequence begins, Kathy poses a question to Emi.

Example 5.14

```
 1   Kathy:      Emi did you win your tournament?
 2   Emi:        ((horizontal head shake))
 3                        (1.2)
 4   Aretha:     Melissa didn't win 'cause-
 5   Sarah:      ⌈(Can you pass the   )
 6   Emi:        ⌊I lost in the third set ((turning to Kathy))
                        (1.3)
 7   Emi:        You probably have no idea
 8               what *that* mea(hh)ns.= right?
 9   Aretha:     What?
10   Melissa:    Third set,
11   Emi:        I lost in the *third // set*.
12   Sarah:      Is that (    )
13   Kathy:      I don't- remember but I // used to.
14   Aretha:     (I think I knew that before.)
15   Emi:        And um, each // set is six games?
16   Melissa:    I lost in tie-breaker before, (.)
17               in the third // set.
18   Emi:        We played.
                        (0.4)
19   Emi:        We ⌈played um
20   Aretha:        ⌊What?
21   Melissa:    Tie-breaker
                        (0.3)
22   Aretha:     How do you lose a tie-breaker,
23   Melissa:    No, it's where you go into tie-breaker,
24               It's where like- (0.2) you serve- like- one,
25               and then two two?
26               (0.3) And you have to get (.) seven points?
27               And you have to win by two?
28               If it's like seven all you gotta go
29               until you win by two?
30               (              ), I- I won it-=
31   Emi:        =In a real tournament you
32               could play up to eleven ((shakes head))
33                        (2.0)
34   Emi:        ((giggle)) eh heh heh!
35   Melissa:    In satellite you don't do it.
36   Emi:        I know.
37               Oh yeah. I forgot.
```

Talk about tennis provides for differentiated forms of participation in story-telling. In Example 5.14 Kathy (line 1) asks Emi a question about her tennis tournament, displaying that she knows the types of activities that Emi participates in. However, when Emi begins to verbally respond (lines 7–8), she makes evident her belief that Kathy probably has relatively little under-standing concerning the culture of tennis – in particular, what it means to have "lost in the third set." With her statement "You probably have no idea what that mea(hh)ns.= right?" (line 7), Emi makes explicit that her know-ledge about tennis is specialized with respect to others present. Melissa, for her part, acts as part of the "team"[39] assembling the story in progress, by assisting Emi in responding to Aretha's question "What?" (line 20). Melissa answers Aretha's question posed to Emi with "Tie breaker" (line 21). She also responds to Aretha's question "How do you lose a tie breaker" (line 22), with a definition of what a tie breaker consists of (line 23).

In this sequence what we find is that specialized knowledge partitions the group in particular ways; in line with Charles Goodwin's (1981:149–166) definitions of types of "knowing" and "unknowing recipients," and Schegloff's (1972)[40] discussion of membership analysis, we find here that the division of those who have knowledge of an event and those who do not makes a difference for the types of participation in which they engage during the story. Emi and Melissa, the girls who know about tennis, are not only able to exhibit their knowledge, but also to compete in the present interaction with respect to their knowledge. After Melissa (lines 23–30) answers Aretha's question "How do you lose a tie-breaker" (line 22), Emi (lines 31–32) enters the conversation with her correction of the description Melissa provides, stating, "In a real tournament you could play up to eleven." She colors her talk with lateral headshakes, which serve to intensify the negation; upon completion of her talk she also giggles. Melissa, for her part, in line 35 delivers the next volley: "In satellite you don't do it." Melissa's move is effective in that it is interpreted as requiring a response, and Emi provides a repair to her prior talk.

Stories thus provide ways of constituting the local social group through alternative ways of organizing or re-organizing participation with respect to the current talk – either expanding participation to include more members of the group,[41] or segmenting and limiting participation to a specifiable set of persons who are viable, ratified participants.[42] Though jockeying for posi-tion is frequently discussed with respect to all male groups,[43] here in a girls' group we find evidence for competing for status as well. In chapter 6 we will explore, across a range of examples of assessments, how girls' interactions can demonstrate an orientation towards positioning oneself above others in a competitive arena.

Format Tying in Comparison Sequences

In a previous example (5.10) we saw how format tying is used to build a next utterance from a prior one and to demonstrate that the minds of the recipient and prior speaker are together in the collaborative evaluation of the topic at hand. A second speaker makes use of the syntax in the description in a prior utterance and in her next turn provides a mirror utterance with slight changes in meaning, affiliating to prior speaker's talk. Format tying can be used in forms of contests resembling ritual insult (Labov 1972), in which the second speaker attempts to "top" the prior speaker with a more exaggerated depiction, or provide some form of counter discrediting the prior move. Thus, moves that counter as well as moves that affiliate are accomplished through the activity of format tying.

In the next example, we can observe the process of format tying used in sequences in which two upper middle class girls compare their experiences with those of a working class girl. In making comparisons girls work out their relative rankings vis-à-vis one another. After the sixth graders took a class trip in April to San Francisco, at lunch one of the classmates, Wendy, a Euro American working class girl, disclosed that this was the first time she had ever been on an airplane. Janis and Brittany responded by comparing Wendy's one trip on a plane with the ten they had taken that year, commenting, "And, it's only April" (line 8).

Example 5.15

1	Wendy:	I wanna go on the airplane again.
2	Janis:	How many times- how many have you
3		been on.
4	Wendy:	Two. To San Francisco and ⌈back
5	Janis:	⌊*Oh* my god.
6	Janis:	I've been- I go on like- *twen*ty a year.
7	Brittany:	I know. *More* than twenty a year.
		. . . . (several lines of talk omitted)
8	Janis:	I've taken *ten* this year and it's only *A*pril.
9	Wendy:	I know.
10	Brittany:	I've taken like *twelve trips*.
11	Wendy:	I've taken *two* this year, and it's probably all
12		this year.
13	Janis:	You've taken two your whole life.
14	Wendy:	eh huh!
15	Janis:	*((eyeball roll))* eh huh huh huh!
16	Wendy:	Except when I was in my mom's stomach,
17		But I guess that doesn't really count.
18	Brittany:	Why didn't she go away once when you were
19		born?
20	Janis:	Why didn't you go-
21		You've never been out of the United States?

Response cries provide particularly appropriate ways of reacting to descriptions, and producing a first move in an evaluative sequence. The very first reactive commentary that Janis provides in this sequence is negative: "*Oh* my god!" (line 5). This is used to respond to Wendy's statement that she had never taken an airplane before the class trip to San Francisco (line 4).

Here the practice of format tying[44] is used to provide closely linked next utterances to prior moves. In response to Janis's question "How many times–how many have you been on" (lines 2–3), Wendy responds "two" (line 4).

The participants make use of the phrase ["I've taken"] and fill in numbers for how many trips they have taken. Wendy's two a lifetime is compared with "more than twenty a year." Thus, in response to Wendy's "Two. To San Francisco and back" Janis states:

[I've taken]   [*ten* this year]   and it's only April.

Brittany then one-ups Janis:

[I've taken]   like   [*twelve* trips.]

Because the frames used to sequence next utterances are parallel structures, and the changes that are made are the numbers inserted before the word "trips," the comparisons, measured numerically, stand out in bold relief. As talk continues, more tied utterances appear.

[I've taken]   [*two* this year]   and it's probably all this year.
[you've taken]   [two your whole life]

Wendy's utterance "I've taken *two* this year and it's probably all this year" (line 11) clearly positions her below Janis and Brittany in the ranking based on number of plane trips made. In a next comment Janis, collaborating with the position Brittany is putting forth, comments on Wendy's statement with "You've taken two your whole life" (line 13) and laughter (line 15).

Along with the explicit comparisons, assessments of the experience of flying are made throughout this sequence as well. In response to Wendy's positive assessment about an airplane experience (line 1), Janis provides a question about how often she flies (lines 2–3). When Wendy provides the response, "to San Francisco and back" (line 4), Janis utters a response cry, "**Oh** my god" (line 5), and compares Wendy's relative lack of experience flying with her own extensive experience (line 6). When Wendy repeats that she'll probably only go twice that year (lines 11–12), Janis produces a repeat of that talk (line 12); such a repeat provides a form of assessment, a "take" of incredulity, and it is followed by laughter (line 15). Through her repeat "You've taken two your whole life" (line 13), and "You've never been out of the United States?" (line 21), Janis makes explicit the contrast between Wendy's experience of flying and her own. Thus the mention of enjoyment on a recent class expedition is transformed into an elaborate contest of social rank.

Material Girls

Proweller (1998:72) in her ethnography of adolescent girls in Best Academy, a historically elite, private, single-sex high school, states that girls discuss dress, jewelry, and cars as important class indicators. Liechty (2003:126), discussing the role of clothing and other adornment in Kathmandu, Nepal, has argued that rather than marking social categories, clothing provides an indicator of a consumer aesthetic of newness, pleasure, and even progress." Arguing that "adornment is social practice," Liechty (2003:121) cites Simmel (1950:432) who argued that adornment constitutes an important semiotic resource: "The radiations of adornment, the sensuous attention it provokes, supply the personality with such an enlargement or intensification of its sphere."

When I asked clique members what differentiated various girls at the school, they responded immediately that it all boiled down to the stores where girls shopped;[45] some girls were "up to date" and could afford to go to purchase brands such as Gap or the Limited, while others could not. Rather than mentioning personality characteristics, they commented on one's access to consumer objects of value. The girls actively read the important symbols of consumer culture, such as flying on airplanes, shopping at upscale stores, or visiting exclusive resorts as indices of class differences between group members. For example, they distinguished girls in their clique from other girls at the school by the places they buy their clothes, preferring Calvin Klein, Gap or the Limited clothing, and often checked the labels of their friends' t-shirts and sweaters (as well as the ethnographer's). In the science notebook of one of the girls (Emi) was a picture of three friends entitled "The Gap Girls."

Girls in the clique jockey for position making comparisons of ascribed features of their status, for example in terms of property their family owns. Consider the following talk between two close friends, Janis and Brittany, during the fifth grade:

Example 5.16

1	Brittany:	*How* many houses does your family own.
2		'Cause like- I'm going to *one* of your houses.
3		My dad's side of the family they own *two* houses
4		And my *mom*'s side of the family
5		They own *three* houses.
6		But they're all kind of family.
7		We can all kind of go whenever we want.
8		My grandparents have a separate house
9		In Palm Springs too.
10	Janis:	My grandparents have a farm.
11	Brittany:	So do *my* grandparents.
12	Janis:	But it's two hundred *a*cres.
13		It's either one hundred or two hundred acres.
14		Two hundred acres.
15	Brittany:	And I had a hundred fifty. My grandparents-
16		Our grandparents' families are so alike.

As in Example 5.15, after a first participant has provided a description or frame for making a comparison, a next speaker uses the structure of that prior utterance to produce a next related one which positions herself with respect to the prior description. Making use of format tying, and reusing the structure of a prior utterance to produce a next related one that tops the prior description, participants jockey for status. The topics that get developed in the comparisons point to experiences or objects that are culturally relevant features of the children's world, the "stuff" in terms of which comparisons are made. When Janis states that her grandparents have a farm, Brittany responds that her grandparents do as well. Next Janis and Brittany compare the size of their farms in terms of acreage:

```
10   Janis:      [My grandparents]     [have a farm.]
11   Brittany:   [my grandparents.] So [do]
12   Janis:      [it's]           [two hundred acres.]
13               [It's]           [either one hundred or two hundred acres.]
14                                [Two hundred acres.]
15   Brittany:   [I had]          [a hundred fifty.]
```

Working class girls in Philadelphia in the early 1970s seldom made comparisons in terms of access to wealth. Among the Los Angeles girls, quite literally a social geography is used as a taken-for-granted means of comparing social positions within the society.

The girls themselves are conscious of how Hollywood values color their everyday experience. At lunch as several sixth grade girls were talking about where they would ideally want to raise children, Janis offered the following commentary to her friends.

Example 5.17

> Janis: Do you want to stay in California?
> I don't wanna raise my kids here.
> **Bad** place to raise kids.
> People are so caught up with like-
> Caught up with like- stars. And everything.
> Every single child, every single like-
> Little kid wants to be actors or actresses or models.
> A lot more. Like ninety per cent.

Mike Davis (1992:21), in his book *City of Quartz*,[46] comments that European writers and directors living in Hollywood in the 1940s viewed Los Angeles as "the ultimate city of capital, lustrous and superficial, negating every classical value of European urbanity." Here, similarly, Janis reflects on the values that animate her own practice.

Within the middle class girls' group, wealth is invoked not only in comparison sequences, but also to index one's special privileges vis-à-vis others – for example in accounts for not complying with rules of the school. One day on the playground when the bell rang signaling the end of recess, Janis told her friends that in no way was she obligated to go in then because her grandfather had donated thousands of dollars to the school, and she would go in whenever she felt like it. Social position in the group is indexed with respect to such things as how many family houses one can claim and how large the acreage is on one's grandparents' farms, what middle school one will be attending, how many airplane trips one takes a year, and whose tennis racket one plays with. In next moves recipients locate their stance toward such criteria and their implicit assessments.

Such understandings of class privilege and difference with respect to consumer products were evident even in the interactions of four-year-olds in this school. Johnson (2004) found that children as young as four in the school made distinctions about whose lunch box was "cool" (one-of-a-kind decorated boxes purchased at exclusive stores) and whose was not, and argued that identical labels ("cool" or "not cool") could be applied to the owners of the lunch boxes as well. Children whose parents had Hollywood connections argued that their parents could get them anything they wanted or could enable them to meet anyone they wanted.

Making Comparisons within the Frame of Play

Apart from explicit comparisons that girls make in assessment sequences, one important window into understanding the concerns that occupy girls' attention is looking at how they construct worlds of their own making, their fantasy worlds during dramatic play. Goffman (1979), in his work on "footing," has described how we enact an entire theater while storytelling. In the midst of dramatic play girls make evident not only the categories of person which are important to them, and their social positionings vis-à-vis one another, but also their relationship to the larger consumer culture that envelopes them. As Bucholtz (2003) argues, forms of "discernment" in young people's discourses of consumption are thoroughly social rather than individual. By examining how the clique girls choose to structure the activity of pretend play, not only with insiders to the clique, but also with classmates not part of the clique, we can examine how girls organize and orchestrate social roles in a type of play quite different from games, but nonetheless one that allows for differentiated roles.

The types of format tying which occur in activities of making comparisons (Examples 5.17–5.18) are found in other activities, such as playing house, as well. The criteria girls use to describe their identities include name, car, age, and occupation:

Example 5.18
Janis: My name is Becky
         I drive a: a:
         A purp- a silvery purple Mustang.
         And I'm sixteen years old,
         And my job is, I'm a famous actress.

One of the important features of playing house is making assessments about objects that are critical to the construction of identity. We will now turn to a consideration of how this is accomplished. Girls playing house describe the types of cars they own and their age, making use of formats supplied by prior speakers and tying their talk closely to the talk of prior speaker. For example, girls use the format "I got a" or "I have a" and next fill in a car model.[47] For example:

Example 5.19

    Janis: I have a purple silver Porsche.
    Ruth: I have a black Corvette.

The type of car that is mentioned can then be evaluated for its appropriateness within this interactive frame. Through this process of presenting their car brand the girls socialize one another with regard to important symbols in their culture and test each other's knowledge of objects of value. The game has high stakes because within this frame one's taste can be called into question and challenged.[48]

This is what happens with Sarah, a working class white girl, and the person who had called the game to order. Sarah, line 10, identifies her car as a Miata. Immediately Janis critiques Sarah's car choice with "***No*** you don't" (line 11) and laughs. Several turns later, when Sarah once again states that she has a Miata, Lisa critiques her choice with a questioning repeat and a negative assessment. "A Mi*a*ta? You do? That's the ***stink***iest car the Miata"[49] (lines 28, 33–34). This interaction occurs in the midst of the following sequence, in which a number of features of the play, including age as well as car brands, are negotiated simultaneously (lines 15–16, 20–21).

Example 5.20

     1   Sarah: Wait. Everybody who's playing come ***here!***
     2   All right. ***Lis***ten.
     3   ***These*** are the ***two–***
     4   Lisa: I got a Nisan convertible.
     5   No I- I GOT A GREEN ***MUST***ANG!
     6   Janis: I got a silver Mus–
     7   I got purple- silver Mus–
     8   Purple– ⌈glitter Mustang.
     9   Sharie: ⌊I wanna be sixteen?
    10   Sarah: I have a Mi*a*ta.
    11   Janis: ***No*** you don't. ah hah hah! Heh heh!
    12   Lisa: ⌈She has a Miata. ((*pointing to Ruth*))
    13   Sharie: ⌊I wanna be sixteen.
    14   Ruth: Nope. ⌈I have a Corvet.
    15   Sharie: ⌊I wanna be sixteen.
    16   Lisa: Well you're ⌈***not***.
    17   Sarah: ⌊I have a Miata.
    18   Sharie: Why not.

19	Janis:	⌈I have a- I have a purple silver Porsche.
20	Lisa:	⌊Because we're twins and **we're** sixteen.
21		You have to be *fif*teen.
22	Ruth:	⌈I have a black Corvet.
23	Sharie:	⌊Fine
24	Sarah:	I have a purple and silver- No wait. No- I-
25	Janis:	I have ⌈a- I have a sparkly- purple-
25	Sarah:	⌊It's- (.) purple and blue Miata.
27	Janis:	I have a sparkly purple Mus ⌈tang.
28	Ruth:	⌊A Miata?
29	Sarah:	Miata,
30	Janis:	Sparkly purple Mustang.
31	Belicia:	⌈And I have a- And I have a Ghia.
32	Ruth:	⌊And I have a- I have a- sparkly blue-
33	Gloria:	⌈You guys? This's all I'm sayin.=
33	Ruth:	⌊You **do**? That's the ***stink***iest car.
34		⌈The Miata. ((*tapping Sarah's shoulder*))
35	Lisa:	⌊Oh! I-
36		I have the newest Mustang.
37		It has like a snake in front of it?
38		And has like a cobra sort of?
39		And then- it change-
40		And then- from different angles
41		It looks like different colors.
42		And it's blue?

Here the girls define themselves in terms of what luxury items they own in the play realm. Through interactive games of this sort girls construct a shared vision of the world. They establish what objects and events in the world are to be considered of value, and display who has access to them. When Sarah makes her bid in this game (lines 17, 25, 29), she is ridiculed for her selection of a Miata as her car of choice. As in other more quotidian conversation they are involved in, comparisons made with respect to cars provide a way of subtly ranking one another. With each turn judgments can be made about someone's taste and ability to make appropriate discriminations.

Practices for Indexing Status

In this chapter we have examined practices of categorization of persons that occur in the midst of a range of speech activities. Members of the clique construct formulations about events in the world as a way of positioning themselves in relation to other group members. Rather than examining specific terms that are used to classify members, we have instead looked at the practices through which participants index social status, with their references to and formulations[50] about wealth (estates, private schools, trendy clothing and sports equipment, and expensive automobiles), famous people, and elite activities (cotillion dance classes, tennis lessons, plane trips, etc.). As was evident with Example 5.12, mention of a group excursion provides a way of delineating current group membership by reporting previous group composition. Format tying provides a way of building one utterance upon a prior one and delineating points of difference or contrast. With Example 5.16 we saw that in response to a first description, a new speaker makes use of a previous formulation to provide a new move that can attempt to top the prior speaker or discredit her. Group members constitute their alignment with others through the ways they participate in description sequences, with positive or negative assessment, questions that elaborate a speaker's description, attempts to close it down, reluctance to speak, or rebuke.

While a number of scholars have noted that the practice of openly bragging is not as common among girls as boys, there has been little discussion of the ways in which girls talk about status differentiation.[51] Berentzen (1984:108) has argued that "The girls' cultural premises and criteria of rank lead to their constantly denying each other's rank, whilst those of the boys lead to their allowing each other's rank and acting with reference to it." The African American working class girls of Maple Street I studied[52] actively disparaged girls who attempted to show that they were better or superior because of their access to particular adults or friendships with boys. While some of the girls at Hanley School openly flaunt their symbols of wealth and class, their attempts at one-upmanship can also be subject to sanction, a topic we will address in the next chapter.

6

Stance and Structure in Assessment and Gossip Activity

While by no means the exclusive terrain of females,[1] one of the favorite pastimes of girls is providing commentary on features of their social landscape by evaluating people and events.[2] This type of talk can occur among friendship groups either in the presence of the party talked about[3] or in her absence.[4] When talk is about another person who is physically or symbolically non-present or absent,[5] it is considered a form of gossip. Gossip is a highly collaborative activity, usually constructed of comments that support an initial evaluation.[6] Consensus,[7] leading to positively oriented involvement[8] is expected; disagreeing with a negative evaluation entails considerable more work than agreement.[9] Through talk about others, girls form coalitions against a targeted party,[10] and delineate local social organization. While it can function to maintain good social relations within a group,[11] increase group cohesion, and establish normative boundaries,[12] gossip can also provide ways of sanctioning inappropriate behavior,[13] creating social differentiation and intragroup conflict.[14] Eder (1995:53) found in her study of adolescent girls that social isolates were criticized behind their backs rather than being openly ridiculed. In contrast, Kalčik (1975:5) found that in personal narratives containing evaluative commentary told in women's consciousness-raising sessions about male relations, women avoided direct criticism of each other and tried to keep others from criticizing themselves. Coates (2000) finds that gossip provides opportunities for the presentations of alternative deviant selves through the expression of negative emotions in a backstage arena.

While much discussion of evaluative commentary about others in their absence has been described as a form of gossip, assessment activity (Goodwin and Goodwin 1987, 1992) can occur either in the presence or absence of the target. During assessment sequences a speaker provides a short description of something and evaluates it (either positively or negatively). Moral categorizations of individuals and their activities provide forms of social control (Sacks 1995a:639) in the girls' group. As Fine (1986:419) argues with respect to his work on teenage gossip, adolescents are not guided by an objective set of standards; rather in the midst of talk they actively seek standards of action and rules of morality, and establish such moral codes according to their own local culture. Moral rules are emergent from local sequential contingencies of action.[15]

In response to an assessment several next moves are possible: (1) agreement or disagreement can occur or (2) sequences can be structured as "return and exchange moves,"[16] sequences in which an initial move is responded to with a reciprocal action. Moves are linked through forms of "tying techniques"[17] or "format tying."[18] Using parallel forms, a second move makes use of the grammatical structure of the prior with minimal semantic shifts that either replicate or change the meaning of the prior talk. C. Goodwin (in press, b) demonstrates how in the midst of argument the reuse of elements of prior talk of one's opponent can have the character of a karate move, by using one's opponent's own actions against them.

These language resources provide ways that girls accomplish a number of tasks important to their social organization. Assessment descriptions provide a principal way in which girls come to terms with how they understand their world, how to make sense out of experience and objects in it. Through assessments girls continuously comment on the types of actions others take up towards them. A first speaker offers an assessment, which establishes a field for agreement, disagreement, or adjustment[19] in next utterances. Participants take up positions with respect to a description, and weigh in with their particular point of view relative to it. In other words, through taking up stances with respect to talk, girls make visible their current alignment with regard to others who are present or talked about. In addition to disagreements, return and exchange moves (Pomerantz 1984) – sequences where a speaker becomes the principal character in a reciprocal description – in response to assessment descriptions provide ways in which participants can compare their understanding of actions and events and contest another's position, as a second speaker attempts to match or top the prior speaker in a reciprocal move.

Evaluation in Assessment Sequences

The following provides a clear example of assessments performed by speakers in the midst of their talk. The person being assessed (Melissa) is described as having formerly been "geeky."

Example 6.1

		((Girls are eating lunch as Sharie addresses Melissa.))
1	Sharie:	Monique said you used to be **geek**y.
2	Melissa:	((stops eating, raises eyebrows))
3	Janis:	**Not** geeky,
4		⌈But not- (.) **hip**.
5	Sharie:	⌊°Not **geek** geeky.
6	Janis:	**Not** like she is **now**.
7		**Well neit**her was I:. I mean-
8		⌈I had no **clue** about bell bottoms.
9	Melissa:	⌊Monique was-

| 10 | | really the biggest teacher's pet in the world there. |
| 11 | | *((shakes head from side to side))* |

In next moves to first assessments Pomerantz (1984) argues that second assessments may either upgrade or downgrade the evaluation provided by the first speaker. In response to Sharie's report of what Monique said about Melissa, Janis counters the negative assessment with a less pejorative one. Janis replaces the adjective "geeky" with "not hip" (line 4). In her next move Janis changes the participant structure of the activity, and makes herself, rather than Melissa, the principal character in a similar assessment activity: "*Well nei*ther was I:. I mean, I had no *clue* about bell bottoms" (lines 7–8). In providing a gloss[20] for the term "hip," Janis describes knowing about a particular style of clothing "bell bottoms" (a kind of baggy pants flaring at the ankle popular in the United States during the 1970s, and returning to style in the late 1990s) as one index of being "hip." We thus learn about various aspects of the girls' experiences they deem of value through the kinds of descriptions and evaluations that they make.

While Example 6.1 showed a careful calibration of second speaker's position with regard to the initial assessment, so as not to offend the face of the party depicted who was copresent, quite vivid disagreements can be made as well, as in the following, which occurs during a lunchtime conversation.

Example 6.2

		((Girls are eating lunch as Hannah walks by))
1	Janis:	Hannah's pretty.
2		(1.5)
3		Don't you think?
4	Aretha:	No. I think she's *butt ug*ly.

In this example Janis provides a description of an older girl who is walking on the playground. A delayed reaction to the initial assessment from her interlocutor occurs in the next move. Not only is there is a 1.5 second pause (line 2); Janis has to explicitly solicit a second assessment from her interlocutor (line 3). In conversation, minimization of disagreement can occur through delays before the production of a disagreement.[21] This feature of the sequence in Example 6.2 displays an orientation towards a preference for agreement (Pomerantz 1984). However, following the solicit, rather than mitigating her disagreement through some form of qualified statement, Aretha responds by positioning her disagreement right in the initial part of the turn: "No. I think she's *butt ug*ly" (line 4). Aretha's second assessment selects a descriptive adjective that is the opposite of pretty; in addition, she modifies her assessment with "butt," using a compound collocation[22] meaning "as ugly as a butt." This further intensifies the negative assessment she provides. In contrast to forms of positive assessments in female talk, which display agreement,[23] "connectedness,"[24] and "cooperative talk,"[25] among the Hanley School clique possibilities for next moves include disagreements as well.

As I have discussed elsewhere,[26] the activity of assessment itself constitutes what Goffman (1961:96) has defined as a form of "situated activity system:" a "somewhat closed, self-compensating, self-terminating circuit of interdependent actions." After the speaker offers her version of the event, recipients provide their take on the same event. The activity of assessment affords for recipients resources for displaying to each other a congruent or divergent view of the events they encounter in their phenomenal world, and provides one way we can attempt to understand how participants negotiate a particular vision of experience.

As girls provide their commentary on an object under discussion, either divergent or congruent perspectives may be offered. In Example 6.3 the girls are seated around a small table in a classroom eating lunch. During lunch Sarah has been discussing *Girls' Life*, a magazine billed on the "Looksmart website" as the #1 magazine for teenage girls: "Real stories about real girls facing the challenges of growing up." Sarah asks Melissa if she has sent in for a free trial subscription, which was offered through the Girl Scouts. Sarah provides an evaluative description of the magazine by first saying "it's really cool" (line 2) and then (lines 3–5), comparing it with another pre-teen magazine, *American Girl*. She states that she likes *Girls' Life* "more than" *American Girl*, and asks the group if they have ever read the magazine (line 5). Using the intensifier "*to*tally" as an adverbial modifier for the adjective "different," she then makes a declarative statement that assesses it: "It's *to*tally different than that."

Example 6.3

```
 1   Sarah:      There's "Help" and all these stuff in there
 2               like- what you are. And it's really cool.
 3               I like it more than-.
 4               It's different tha:n-
 5               Have you ever read American Girl?
 6   Melissa:    Yeah,
 7   Emi:        Mm hm.
 8   Sarah:      It's totally different ⌈than that.
 9   Kathy:                             ⊢I like American Girl.
10   Aretha:                            ⌊I hate-
11               I hate American Girl.
12   Sarah:      It's sorta the same con⌈cept?
13   Kathy:                             ⌊I get American Girl.
14   Sarah:      But it's really- it's like different,
```

With her statement "I like it *more* than-" Sarah launches an evaluative description or assessment. She then states "It's *to*tally different" (lines 3, 8). Sarah receives two divergent responses from recipients. Immediately after the word "different," two speakers provide their alignment towards the assessment with verbs that present contrasting positions: Kathy states, "I *like* American Girl" (line 9), while Aretha states, "I *hate* American Girl" (line 11).

Format tying is used to build one utterance upon a prior one. Aretha's statement aligns with Sarah, while Kathy's utterance provides a positive statement about the magazine that disagrees with how Sarah has positioned herself with respect to the magazine. As Sarah continues with her evaluation of the magazine, "It's more like-", Angela (who herself has not offered a position), enters and asks for an explicit tally of the girls who receive the *American Girl* magazine (Example 6.4, line 2). In asking this question through use of a valley girl voice, she makes evident her own position of disdain towards the magazine. While frequently Angela's talk is ridiculed, here her question, positioned in agreement with the stance taken by the principal members of the clique, is treated as worthy of response:

Example 6.4

```
 1   Sarah:    ⌈It's more like-
 2   Angela    ⌊Who gets like- American
 3             ⌈Girl. ((spoken in a valley girl voice))²⁷
 4   Sarah:    ⌊It's more like-
 5   Melissa:  ⌈((holds hand up answering Angela's question)).
 6   Sarah:    ⌊American Girl is more like-
 7   Aretha:   American Girl has too much "help" in it.
                    (1.0)
 8   Sarah:    It's like more ⌈girly things because-
 9   Emi:                     ⌊Too much help (and business).
10   Sarah:    An then an then-
11   Sarah:    But Girls' Life is about like- like- like- what your
12             change ⌈is an stuff.
13   Melissa:         ⌊It's more mature.
14   Sarah:    It's more like what you do:
15   Melissa:  ⌈Yeah:.
16   Sarah:    ⌊When you're cha:nging and what should happen.
17   Emi:      ((coughs))
18   Kathy:    They use it for teenagers.
19   Melissa:  Mm mm. ((shaking head))
20   Angela:   No:.
21   Sarah:    Yeah there's people that read it when
22             they're- ⌈fourteen.
23   Aretha:            ⌊So? ((extending face toward Kathy))
24   Melissa:  They can't ⌈(       ) that's what I said
25   Angela:              ⌊Seventeen.
26   Aretha:   Well the ages for teenagers are like
27             sixteen and something.
28   Sarah:    There's this- Have you ever-?
29             I was gonna write to a pen pal.
30             Did you ever write to a pen pal?
```

Forms of alignment are displayed as individual girls provide their assessments of the magazine. Aretha expounds on her position of dislike for the magazine by saying that "*American Girl* has too much **help** in it" (line 7).[28] Sarah elaborates reasons for her dislike of *American Girl* magazine with, "It's like more **girl**y things" (line 8). In her next move, Emi affiliates with both Aretha and Sarah's positions by negatively assessing the magazine with, "Too much **help** (and business)" (line 9).

Other forms of affiliation with Sarah's position follow as the sequence progresses. As Sarah (lines 11–12) discusses what for her is the crucial feature of *Girls' Life* – that it is about "what your change is an stuff" (referring to changes of the body during adolescence, a topic in the group's fifth grade science class at the time of fieldwork), Melissa provides a congruent positive assessment about *Girls' Life* with, "It's more ma**ture**" (line 13). Sarah continues the onward development of her own description with "It's more like what you do: when you're **cha:ng**ing and what should happen" (lines 14–16). The three 11–12-year-old girls who are close friends with Sarah – Melissa, Aretha, and Emi – each align in similar ways. They provide negative assessments about *American Girl* ("too much help") and a positive statement about *Girls' Life* ("It's more ma**ture**"), and thus make apparent through their talk a congruent understanding about the magazine. Kathy, who is a year younger than the other girls in the clique, and a more infrequent participant in their play, makes a comment that addresses the issue of age appropriateness of the magazine, offering a new direction for commentary: "They use it for teenagers" (line 18). Melissa (line 19) and Angela (line 20) disagree with Kathy, and Aretha with her "So?" (line 23) treats Kathy's comment as irrelevant to what's being discussed. Through their responses to Kathy's talk girls position her as outside of the inner circle of girls, who view *Girls' Life* as an age-appropriate magazine. Sarah, principal teller, does locate something to agree with in Kathy's talk, stating, "Yeah there's people that read it when they're- fourteen" (lines 21–22). Following Aretha's comment that teenagers are sixteen and older, Sarah switches topic to a discussion of writing to a pen pal.

The activity of assessing an object thus provides for alternative ways that speakers can either positively or negatively evaluate something through contrastive verbs such as "like" and "hate," and statements containing assessment adverbs and adjectives which position the participant with respect to the object. The adjectives selected provide ways of understanding what issues, popular culture, or material objects are significant for girls. Clearly one way of constituting and displaying alliances is through affirming similar perspectives with respect to an event, here while commenting on the girls' popular culture.

Grammatical Resources for Constructing Stance in Assessment Sequences

In the midst of assessment sequences, as girls express their position with respect to some object of value, they also make statements about their taste in popular culture and style. Such statements can be considered important for constructing oneself as a particular type of person. In the next example participants line up with respect to their positions on particular pop stars, the Spice Girls, and girls who possess Spice Girls' objects. The Spice Girls (Sporty, Baby, Scary, Posh and Ginger) were a British pop culture sensation of the 1990s – in particular among young female children and teens. The group promoted "Girl Power," a 1990s feminism celebrating the independence and strength of women. The Spice Girls' attitude has been said (on the Spice Girls' website) to "have packed more punch than their voices."

In the following instance, occurring during lunch several minutes after the discussion of *Girls' Life* and *American Girl* magazines, Angela makes an observation about an absent party, Sharie, who she has recently been seen with a Spice Girls' folder (lines 1–4). One way in which Angela can attempt to locate herself as a ratified participant in talk is by talking about an absent party whose actions are objectionable. An appropriate next move to Angela's pejorative talk about Sharie is a parallel "second description"[29] – a move providing a description about a similar character, someone in possession of an abundance of Spice Girls' objects. On this occasion the second description (in lines 8–12) is about another absent party, Janis, who is imagined by Aretha and Melissa to possess multiple Spice Girls' paraphernalia: fifteen shirts as well as a wall filled with the posters. In essence, Aretha provides a move that tops the initial one by Angela by describing someone who is even more enamored with the Spice Girls than Sharie.

Example 6.5

		((The girls are seated inside their classroom eating lunch))
1	Angela:	If you guys go outside and see Sharie's folder,
2		(0.2) it's like–
3		filled with Spice Girls pins and all this kind of stuff. =
4		⌈ *h She even // h–
5	Aretha:	⌊*Shar*ie not Sha*rie.*
6	Angela:	°*Shar*ie.
		(5.0)
7	Melissa:	Sarah can I have one more? *((requesting a potato chip))*
8	Aretha:	Janis's– probably has a– (0.2) a Spice Girls–
9	Sarah:	⌈*((coughing))*
10	Aretha:	⌊Fifteen Spice Girls t-shirts–
		(0.8)
11	Aretha:	Spice **Girls**, **all** over her **walls**,
12	Melissa:	She has a Spice Girl wall.
		(0.5)
13	Aretha:	She has **more** than one.

In what continues immediately afterwards, Melissa, Sarah, Aretha, Emi, and Kathy take up stances towards the Spice Girls:

Example 6.6

1	Sarah:	They're *so s*:ickening.
2		*I ne*ver liked *them*.
3	Angela:	*Who* likes the Spice Girls,
4	Melissa:	⌜*Emi did*.
5	Aretha:	⌞*Emi did*!
6	Kathy:	*I* do. *((puts hand up))*
7	Sarah:	Emi- (.) *used* to like // them.
8	Aretha:	I'm not *crazy* about them. *((raises hand))*
9	Emi:	I *ne*ver liked the Spice Girls. *((shaking head))*
		(0.8)
10	Sarah:	I thought you *did*,
11	Emi:	No. *((horizontal head shake))*
12		I *ne*ver liked the Spice Girls.
13	Sarah:	⌜*You* do. *((looks to Kathy))*
14	Angela:	⌞*((taps Melissa on the arm in an attempt*
15		*to solicit food))*
16	Melissa:	⌜No. *((to Angela who is bothering her))*
17	Sarah:	⌞Go girl. *((hand up in air, looking at Kathy,*
18		*nodding at her, though Kathy does not gaze at her))*
		(1.0)
19	Aretha:	*You* like- (0.8) You're kinda like- (1.0)
20		*You're* not a trendy person. *((addressing Emi))*
21	Emi:	I know,
22	Aretha:	You like to- *you* don't like things that are trendy,
23		o:r popular or anything.

Sarah provides two different assessments in her turn (lines 1–2): "They're *so si*:ckening" and "*I ne*ver liked *them*."

Remarkably similar strategies for presenting assessments are provided by examples we have examined thus far in this chapter. The grammar of the emerging utterance provides for local social organization, as participants take up some form of stance with respect to the assessment. As with other assessments (Goodwin and Goodwin 1992:162), there is a division of activity within the utterance. The first part of the utterance is occupied with referencing the assessable; the second part of the utterance, after the copula form of the verb, is occupied with the activity of assessment itself. The adverbial intensifier of the utterance, with enhanced stress, provides a way of marking the assessable nature of the adjective, and moving towards heightened participation. Considering the examples we have looked at so far the following similarities in structure are observable:

(6.1)   You used to be geeky.
(6.2)   She's *butt* ugly.
(6.3)   It's *to*tally different
(6.6)   They're *so si*:ckening.

Pronoun +	Verb	Adverbial intensifer +	Assessment adjective
[You]	[used to be]		[geeky]
[She]	[is] +	[*butt*]	[ugly]
[It] +	[is] +	[*to*tally] +	[different]
[They] +	[are] +	[*so*] +	[si:ckening]

In Examples 6.2 and 6.3, the work of performing the assessment occurs in other utterances of the fragment as well. After the object is mentioned, participants make explicit their stance vis-à-vis the objects, using either the word "like" or "hate" or some qualification of these positions. The speaker, rather than the assessable object, is the subject of the sentence; she is the agent doing the assessing. The assessable object occurs in the third part of the utterance as the direct object. In this way the party performing the assessment makes explicit and publicly accountable her position.

Pronoun	Adverbial intensifier	Verb	Object
I		hate/like +	*American Girl*
I	(never) +	liked +	Spice Girls

Different alignments are taken towards the Spice Girls. Melissa and Aretha (lines 4–5) state that Emi used to like the Spice Girls, though Emi counters this characterization, stating emphatically that she never liked the Spice Girls (line 9). Kathy (a year younger than the other girls) provides a positive assessment (line 6), while Aretha provides her own explicit alignment with "I'm not crazy about them" (line 8). Following a description of one's position vis-à-vis the pop stars, a possible next move in the sequence is a depiction of a type of person who affiliates with them. Aretha provides a meta-commentary about the position taken by Emi with "You're not a trendy person. You like to- *you* don't like things that are trendy, o:r popular or anything" (lines 20–23). Aretha makes explicit what it means to like the Spice Girls and possess objects associated with them. The girls link alignments people take up toward objects and events to categories of person. What began as assessments about absent parties develops into assessment about current participants and their positionings[30] as well.

Differentiated forms of participation occur in Examples 6.4 and 6.6. While Sarah, Melissa, Emi, and Kathy offer their opinions, Angela, the marginalized girl, participates by soliciting an explicit tally of how people feel about the Spice Girls. While it was Angela who brought to the group's attention Sharie's multiple Spice Girls' objects, rather than commenting on the newsworthiness of Angela's report, Angela is told that her pronunciation of Sharie's name is wrong (line 5). One way in which Angela is frequently differentiated from the other girls is through finding fault with the ways she does and says things, including not only her misplaced stress on syllables, but also her voice quality.

The activity of assessing objects provides a way for girls to make evaluations about present as well as non-present participants. In Example 6.6, by taking up a negative position vis-à-vis the Spice Girls, members of the group of the moment align with each other against absent parties (Sharie and Janis). While assessments about absent or present parties are quite similar in shape, the activity of talking about absent parties is always fraught with danger,[31] as someone who has heard the negative assessment may disclose it to the targeted individual (and possibly reframe it). In the following example, immediately after providing an evaluation of an absent party, the speaker, Janis, admonishes her friends not to disclose her assessment:

Example 6.7

		((Girls are eating lunch))
1	Janis:	Emi's getting chubby.
2		⌈***Don't*** tell her I said that.
3	Angela:	⌊Ah ***HA HO***!
4	Janis:	Yeah- ⌈my- my-
5	Aretha:	⌊Why ***would*** I.
6		I think the same ***thing***.
7	Janis:	Angela you ***bet***ter not ***tell*** her.
8	Angela:	I will tell ***ev***erybody.
9		I'm just kidding.

In Example 6.7 when an initial pejorative description is made (line 1), speakers orient to the fact that it very well might be repeated to the party who is the target. The very next utterance after the pejorative assessment (line 2) is an admonition not to repeat the description to the target. Aretha (line 5) states that she is unlikely to do so because she maintains an equivalent opinion. The likelihood of diffusion of pejorative statements is thus cast as tied to one's alignment to the proffered assessment. Angela, for her part, provides an elaborate laugh "Ah ***HA HO***!" registering her position as someone who has heard something that should not have been said. Janis immediately interprets Angela's utterance as indicating something that is implicative and potentially damaging to Janis by saying, "Angela you ***bet***ter not ***tell*** her." Angela playfully taunts Janis with her next utterance "I will tell ***ev***erybody", but quickly backs down with "I'm just kidding." Talk about other people provides for intrigue, as well as high drama with the girls; quite importantly, it also provides powerful ways of sanctioning inappropriate behavior, as will be seen with the next example.

"I Like Sitting Here and Being Mad and Talking about People": Stance and Format Tying in the Context of Righteous Indignation

One environment in which assessments occur quite frequently is in response to an event where someone in the peer group attempts to place herself above others. To sanction the party who does this, girls participate in elaborate gossip sessions in which they collaborate in building evaluative commentary about the targeted absent individual. One such session occurred when several girls (Aretha, Sarah, and Angela) were excluded from a soft ball game, though Janis and her two best friends, Emi and Melissa, were permitted by Janis's boyfriend Sean to play. The event was so upsetting to Aretha that she screamed across the field, yelling to Sean and the others about the injustice of her friends' exclusion:

Example 6.8
```
 1   Aretha:   IF YOU GUYS ARE GONNA BE LIKE THAT
 2             IN THE FIRST PLACE
 3             WE DON'T EVEN WANNA PLAY WITH YOU!
                (9.0)
 4             I don't care!
                ((to Sarah and Angela amidst crying))
 5             If they're gonna act like that in the first place,
 6             Why play with them
 7             If they're gonna be that mean to us.
```

The structure of this commentary, as well as evaluative statements through-out the gossip session, makes extensive use of format tying. Aretha utilizes the structure of her first negative comment to Sean (lines 1–3) to launch a second negative depiction about Sean for her new recipients (lines 5–7). As the participation framework changes, and Aretha addresses her copresent friends, the referent "you guys" (line 1) is changed to "they" (line 5) and "with you" changes to "with them":

```
If   you guys   are gonna be   like that   we don't even wanna   play with you
If   they        are gonna act   like that   why                    play with them
```

While Aretha expresses anger at having been excluded, she exudes pleasure in being able to talk to her girlfriends about having been excluded. Talking about and evaluating other people is one of the activities enjoyed most by the girls.[32] Although Aretha complains and even weeps about having been excluded from the softball game, when Angela and Sarah suggest playing another game rather than sulking, Aretha responds that she doesn't want to play because, as she states, "I like sitting here and being mad and talking about people." At another point in the day when Sarah suggests, "Let's go be a lunatic together!" and Sarah attempts to pull Aretha away from a bench where she has been sulking, Aretha responds vigorously with "*NO! NO!* I wanna sit here and *talk* all day." While gossip can provide a form of female solidarity and way of maintaining "good relations in a group,"[33] it can also provide a way of marking the boundaries of the group,[34] sanctioning offenders, and reacting to forms of exclusion.

Reciprocal format-tied actions occur throughout the discussion of exclusion as participants build on their own as well as others' prior talk to provide pejorative next utterances or descriptions. As the talk continues, the girls develop a theory about why Janis and Sean are so close. Janis protects Sean (who frequently gets in trouble at school) and Sean, who is generally selected as the captain of games such as softball, soccer, or football, in exchange allows Janis (and her two closest friends Emi and Melissa) to play team sports.

Example 6.9

1	Aretha:	Sarah don't you understand,
2		Janis likes Sean because she's always-
3		*h protecting his- **damn** back,
4		And he's like- letting her play.
5		And Sean's **al**ways being nice to her.=
6		And he's always being assholes to **us**.
		(2.5)
7		Whenever we play basketball
8		He always tries to play with- **Jan**is,
9		But he **ne**ver plays with me. *((crying))*
10	Sarah:	Even if **we**'re better than **Jan**// is.
11	Aretha:	**He's** letting Janis play baseball.
12		He's not letting- us- **me** play.

In the complaint that Aretha makes a first utterance is used as a frame for a subsequent utterance that builds upon it. Paired utterances contrasting the way Sean treats Janis with how Sean treats Aretha are built in this way:

(line 5)		Sean's always	being nice	to her.
(line 6)	And	he's **al**ways	being assholes	to us.
(line 8)		He always	tries to play	with **Jan**is
(line 9)	But	he **ne**ver	plays	with me
(line 11)		He's letting Janis		play baseball
(line 12)		He's not letting us- me		play

Because the structure of paired adjacent utterances remains similar with the exception of parts of the utterance which are replaced (being nice → being assholes; to her → to us; with Janis → to me; letting Janis play → not letting us play) the contrast between how Sean treats Janis and how he deals with Aretha is highlighted.

While disagreement with an assessment occurred in several of the examples we have examined thus far in this chapter (6.2, 6.3, 6.6) one context in which participants generally express agreement in second assessments is when they are providing negative next descriptions about an absent offending party. As Eder (1995:110) has argued, in gossip sessions once someone supports a first critical remark, others follow suit and join in the initial criticism. Feelings of righteous indignation towards the offender generate similar types of stances with respect to an absent party. In the midst of providing such descriptions girls make use of format tying to provide utterances that display a congruent view of the party talked about.

Example 6.10

```
 1   Sarah:    And then it's like
 2             Why would you wanna play with somebody
 3             That's all mad at you an everything. (0.4) Right?
 4   Aretha:   Why would you wanna play with somebody,
 5   Sarah:    See! ⌈He let's-
 6   Aretha:      ⌊Who only lets you play because-
 7             ★h his girlfriend ⌈suddenly-
 8   Sarah:                     ⌊His so called- ((small hand movements))
 9             little- honey bunny is- eh heh heh!
10             ⌈eh heh heh!
11   Aretha:   ⌊Eh heh hah hah
12             So called little
13             hon ⌈ey bunny, ((sarcastically, hand movements))
14   Sarah:       ⌊Honey bunny, ((small hand movements))
15             Ooo:::
```

In this sequence utterances in lines 2–3 and 4–6 are built parasitically on prior ones as follows:

Why would you wanna play with somebody   That's all mad at you
Why would you wanna play with somebody   Who only lets you play
                                         because his girlfriend
                                         suddenly-

One common feature of assessments that display congruent understandings is that a second party provides her assessment in talk that is overlapping with the first speaker's; in that way the participants can display that their minds are together.[35] In Example 6.10 as Aretha continues with her utterance, immediately after the phrase "his girlfriend" (line 7), Sarah joins in with her depiction of Janis as "his so called little- **hon**ey bunny" (lines 8–9), talk produced with a sarcastic tone of voice. She simultaneously makes small hand movements at the level of her shoulders; these are seeable either as quotation gestures or hopping movements of a small rabbit.

When Aretha repeats this phrase Sarah (lines 12 and 13) joins her after the first syllable of "honey" so that the two are producing similar assessments concurrently. This time the stance changes; congruent views are evident now through the laughing together[36] that occurs in lines 10 and 11. Note also that when Aretha provides an action imitating that of Sarah (line 8), she not only adopts the words, but also the bunny hop movements (line, 13) of Sarah as well. The hand movements serve as additional commentary on the diminutive "honey bunny" term selected to characterize Janis's relationship to Sean.

Through talking together girls articulate and elaborate their moral positions regarding how members of their age cohort should treat one another. In Example 6.11 they discuss not only events in the present (lines 1–2, 5–6, 10), but also *future possible* events (lines 3–4, 10), involving figures in the present scene under discussion. In utterances that follow, together the girls provide their evaluative commentary about Sean, who has excluded them from the game.

Example 6.11

1	Sarah:	You wanna have fun in the game.
2		You don't like wanna be like yelled at by Sean.
3		I mean, it's like if you're gonna have fun
4		Don't be mad at everybody.
5	Aretha:	*((crying))* I don't want him to boss me around.
6	Angela:	Sean ain't her daddy. Don't you know that?
7	Sarah:	WHADDYA THINK? *((laughs at Angela))*
8	Angela:	He's not yours *ei*ther. He's not // mine.
9	Sarah:	I know. I'm glad he isn't. Trust me. (He's like)-
10	Angela:	Trust me. I will **hurt** Sean. Okay?
11	Aretha:	Think about this. Sean lets him- her play.
12	Sarah:	(Sean lets her play. Boo-hoo.)
13	Angela:	That's not fair. He's just-

In their gossip event girls make use of format tying to produce next moves. In response to Sarah's (line 2) "You don't wanna be like yelled at by Sean," Aretha states (line 5) "I don't want him to boss me around."

You	don't want	by Sean	to be yelled at
I	don't want	him	to boss me around

Angela joins in the discussion providing a reason for why Janis should not permit Sean to boss her around: (line 6) "Sean ain't her daddy." Tying to her own talk, she adds (line 8), "He's not yours either."

Sean	ain't	her daddy	
He	is not	yours	either

Sarah (line 9) responds, "I know. I'm glad he isn't." and then adds "Trust me." Angela uses Sarah's "Trust me" as the preface to her own next move "Trust me. I will **hurt** Sean." Next utterances are repetitively making use of material from prior utterances to build a next evaluation, here a depiction of Sean as an undesirable person. Participants make use of the resources at hand to elaborate their congruent vision.

   Discussion of Sean is linked to negative assessments of his girlfriend, Janis. Aretha describes the criteria that she feels underlie Janis's perception of herself as "popular": "being up to date" or wearing clothing that is currently fashionable. While the working class junior high school girls studied by Eder (1995:113) critiqued girls from lower working class backgrounds who could not afford to buy brand name clothes, among the Hanley School girls, Aretha (a middle class girl), Sarah, and Angela (who are both working class) critique Janis for her obsession with materialism, including clothing that indexes wealth. They can display their difference from Janis with respect to how they position themselves in terms of valuing trendy clothing, as occurs in Example 6.12 below.

Aretha first describes the abundance of Spice Girls photos that Janis has decorating the walls in her bedroom (lines 3–5), and then mentions that Janis wears "the most popular clothes" (line 6). Providing her own commentary on defining oneself in terms of these criteria, Sarah (lines 7–8) states that her own shirt is three years old,[37] and, moreover, she doesn't care. Angela provides a next move that is in alignment with Sarah (lines 9–10); she states that her shirt is a year old and she also could not care less.

Parallel structures involved in these assessments are the following:

(lines 8–9)   I got this **three years** ago   I don't really **care**.
(line 11)   I had this last year.   *I* don't really care about it.

Example 6.12

```
 1  Aretha:   No, you know what?
 2            Janis thinks she's popular
 3            Because she stays up to date.
 4            She likes the Spice Girls,
 5            She has Spice Girls everywhere. *hh
 6            She-⌈wears the most popular clothes-
 7  Sarah:       ⌊Look! You see this shirt?
 8            I GOT THIS THREE YEARS AGO.
 9            I don't really care. ((looking at Angela))
10  Angela:   Neither do I. ((looks down at her shirt))
11            I had this last year. And I don't really care about it.
12  Sarah:    BECAUSE I AM NOT TREN DY:::! ((taps Aretha's knee))
13            People like me for who I am and not how I look.
14            Girlfriend! Gimme some- ((arm around Aretha))
15            ((assumes glamour girl pose, hand behind head))
16            Gimme some sugah.
17            ((drapes arm over Aretha))
18  Aretha:   Gimme some- Gimme some dap!
19            ((Aretha and Sarah execute a 3-beat hand clap game))
20  Sarah:    Here's the sugar.
21            Here's the su⌈gar! eh heh-heh!
22  Angela:      ⌊Woe woe! Woe woe! ((A and A clap))
23            Woe- woe-Ow!
24  Aretha:   eh heh heh!!
25  Sarah:    Neh neh! ⌈ow:::::! ((Angela and Sarah clap))
26  Angela:      ⌊Ow:::⌈:! !
27  Aretha:         ⌊Eh heh-heh! heh-heh!
```

At the conclusion of her evaluative statement Sarah provides a description of the criteria that she herself uses as a guide for her lifestyle. She proclaims in a loud voice that she has no interest in being "trendy" (line 12). In marked contrast to Janis, she is concerned with "**who** I **am** and **not** how I **look**" (line 13). Parallel structures occur here as well:

Who   I am
How   I look

"I am" and "I look" provide contrastive pairs; "who" and "how," words with similar rhythmic structure, frame each of the linked phrases. Ironically Sarah assumes the pose of a model (the image she proclaims she objects to) while she states, "Gimme some **su**gah." She uses African American Vernacular English phonology with the production of the word "sugah" in her alignment with Aretha, and subsequently makes use of an African American celebratory handclap, saying "Give me some dap."

In response to Sarah's "Gimme some **su**gah" Aretha provides in her matching move a slightly different version of the same phrase with "Gimme some dap" (high five). "Sugah" ("sugar") is replaced with "dap," while the rest of the utterance remains the same. Through her action Sarah requests that Aretha collaborate in a celebratory handclap to seal their congruent stance with the negative assessment of Janis (see Figure 6.1). Together Aretha and Sarah then begin a three-beat exchange of poundings with closed fists: a first player hits the partner's rounded fist from above, the players reverse positions, and the second player hits from above; and then both knock fists sideways in the final move of the three-part fist pounding exchange. While the exchange begins with poundings of paired fists between Sarah and Aretha, Angela's joining in (during line 22) is not objected to.

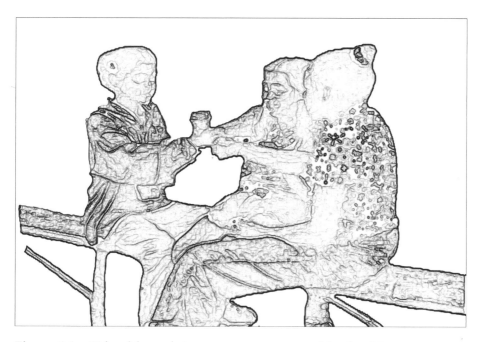

Figure 6.1   Girls celebrate their congruent assessment with a handclap

The hand clap provides a final "seal" on the pact they have just made, celebrating their united stance opposing Janis's way of being in the world.

When the celebratory handclap game began, only Aretha and Sarah participated. At the close of the sequence comparing shirts the three girls produce a fist pounding sequence in which Angela joins with Sarah and Aretha. While generally marginalized, on this occasion Angela collaborates in the construction of negative commentary about an absent party. Angela's embodied participation in the sequence is ratified by the other girls.

Differentiated Participation and Alliances in Assessment

Researchers examining assessments across various contexts – in compliment sequences,[38] forms of "good gossip,"[39] and in pejorative commentary on other people[40] – have argued that such types of talk lead to alliance building. In this chapter we have seen how pejorative commentary about absent parties establishes a joint framework for lively coparticipation with congruent positioning as well as differentiated stance-taking towards offending parties. Once someone has provided an assessment, a new second assessment may be built from this utterance; either agreeing or disagreeing with the prior speaker is possible. In this way group members can build their local social organization. In the *American Girl* example (6.3–6.4) we saw that Kathy, a peripheral member of the group, belonging to a younger age cohort, did not provide the same alignment toward the magazine that Sarah and her friends did. Clear lines of difference between Kathy and the other girls were made evident from the different perspectives taken towards the magazine.

Gossip about absent parties provides other ways of temporarily reconfiguring group dynamics. In Examples 6.5–6.6 Angela, a girl frequently excluded from discussions, could join in the pejorative talk about Sharie and Janis; in fact, she initiated the commentary on Sharie's having a notebook filled with Spice Girls paraphernalia. When excluded from a ball game, Angela joined with Sarah and Aretha in gossip about Janis and her boyfriend.

In the midst of a gossip session, however, differentiated forms of coparticipation occur. Aretha and Sarah (Example 6.10) collaborated in both gesture and talk about Sean as Janis's "little honey bunny." Not only what one says, but also how one positions the body, can display a participant's terms of engagement. In Example 6.12 (line 17) Sarah embraced Aretha, not Angela, as she adopted a glamour pose. While Angela joined in pejorative talk about Janis, she was treated more as a peripheral rather than a fully ratified participant. In the *American Girl* examples, Angela was seated at the periphery of the group of girls gathered around a small table; the girls never made space for her to sit next to them and refused her solicits for potato chips.

A next example will show how though Angela attempts to enter into a gossip session, her talk does not always receive uptake. Differentiated forms of participation are evident not only in the ways that interlocutors choose to sequence their talk, but also with respect to the positioning of participants' bodies.

Example 6.13 occurs on the playground during recess after the lunch when the girls had discussed how both Sharie and Janis were aficionados of the Spice Girls. Angela initiates the talk about Janis with a question "Tell me naturally. Do you really like Janis?" (lines 1–2). As Angela poses her question, Aretha (lines 3–5) launches a description about Janis with "Janis does everything that's trendy. She thinks that she's so popular 'cause she stays up to date."

Example 6.13

```
 1   Angela:   Tell me naturally
 2             ⌈Do you really like Janis?
 3   Aretha:   ⌊Janis does everything that's trendy.
 4             She thinks that she's so popular
 5             ⌈'Cause she stays up to date.
 6   Sarah:    ⌊Look at her now.
                    (2.0)
 7   Sarah:    I don't *like* being trendy.
 8   Angela:   She's not even matching
 9             To tell ⌈you the truth.
10   Sarah:          ⌊I got this three years ago.
11   Sarah:    Trust ⌈me.
12   Aretha:        ⌊I *HATE* THOSE *PANTS*!
                    (0.8)
13             THEY'RE *UG*LY!!
                    (0.8)
14   Sarah:    Ooooo! *Girl*friend!
15   Aretha:   They *are! Look* at 'em!
16             They look like some boys' shorts.
17   Angela:   They look-
18   Angela:   Okay.
19             They ⌈look like- Shaka Zulu.
20   Aretha:        ⌊You know how boys wear their shorts?
21             They look like she's trying to be like-
22             She wants to- *h match Sean! ((eyeball roll))
                    (0.8)
23             So she's wearing some tren⌈dy-
24   Sarah:    ((chanting))                ⌊Sean has a shirt like that!
25             Sean has a shirt like that!
26             ((high fives Aretha)) Girl! Girl! Girl!
                    (0.4)
27             Girl! Girl! (0.3) Girl! eh heh-heh!
28             Gi(hh)rl*friend*!
```

In this example Aretha (lines 3–5) depicts the activity of valuing trendy clothes and objects as objectionable, and links being trendy with a particular attitude about oneself, thinking of oneself as "popular." Sarah summons her interlocutors (line 6) to look at Janis, and distances herself from Janis by stating that she herself does not like being trendy (line 7). Angela, for her part, comes in with a commentary on the topic at hand by stating, "She's not even matching. To tell you the truth" (lines 8–9). Angela's commentary is not, however, treated as deserving a next move by either Aretha or Sarah. Instead, Sarah further develops her line about not caring about trendy clothing by stating that her shirt is three years old (line 10).

Aretha provides additional pejorative commentary that ties to Sarah's directive to look at Janis's pants by yelling "I *HATE* THOSE *PANTS*!" (line 12) and "THEY'RE *UGLY*" (line 13). In return Sarah provides a commentary on Aretha's comment with "Oooooo! Girl*friend*!" (line 14), an expression used among African Americans as a response cry, expressing heightened appreciation for what has just been said. Aretha comments that Janis's pants resemble boys' shorts (line 16).

When Angela attempts to enter with a statement that they look like "Shaka Zulu" (line 19), she is once more ignored. Instead Aretha sequences to her own commentary on Janis with "You know how boys wear their shorts" (line 20), as well as a commentary on why Janis is wearing the clothes she selects: she aspires to look like her boyfriend (she wants to "match Sean!") (line 22). In response to Aretha's disdainful commentary (accompanied by an eyeball roll) Sarah states "Sean has a shirt like that!" (lines 24–25), and raises her arms in preparation for an extended hand clap as she adds the address term "Girl," which acts as an intensifier for her statement (lines 26–27), and repeats it five times as she claps Aretha's hands. What effectively occurs is that Aretha and Sarah, through their celebratory handclap, display to each other their convergent assessment of Janis. Angela, for her part, attempts to join in the hand clap as Sarah states "Gir(hh)rl friend." In the midst of the word Angela reaches over Sarah to attempt to slap Aretha's and Sarah's raised celebratory fists.

If we examine positionings of Angela's body with respect to other girls, as we find that while Angela can join in a celebratory handclap with Aretha and Sarah (as in Figure 6.2), she does so in a manner which is contrastive with the way Aretha and Sarah align their bodies, in a facing formation directly opposite one another. Although Angela joins in, she must extend her arms from behind the body of one of the focal participants, and does not make direct contact with Aretha's hands. Instead her hands land on top of Sarah's hands, which touch Aretha's. As soon as Angela reaches over Sarah's shoulders, both Aretha's and Sarah's arms go down to their laps, as if exiting from any possible reading that their bodies are aligned with Angela. Clearly the use of the body here is critical for displaying stance and alignment.

What we see in this sequence is that although Angela makes multiple bids to be part of the negative commentary on Janis, neither Sarah nor Aretha provide moves that sequence to hers. In addition, when she attempts to join their collaboratively evaluating of what has taken place, both Aretha and Sarah quickly stop providing congruent nonvocal assessments through hand claps.

Figure 6.2   Angela participating in celebratory hand clap at a distance

Concluding Comments

The analysis of assessment sequences provides a way to examine the practices involved in talk about present or absent persons, often glossed as gossip. Negative talk about absent parties provides for vivid and varied forms of involvement. Thus in the midst of aligning against a third party, participants in the present interaction make visible their differentiated forms of participation and engagement with each other, not only through talk, but also through alternative types of access to the bodies of other participants. In the course of assessing something, speakers also display their alignment through the ways that they exhibit their differentiated forms of access to particular types of knowledge and experience. With respect to forms of involvement in narrative descriptions, girls can display their enthusiasm or utter disdain for a particular worldview. Assessments provide ways of sanctioning untoward behavior (permitting only one's girlfriend and her best friends to play softball, being nice only to certain individuals, being overly materialistic or trendy) through ridiculing someone whose behavior is deemed as outside the bounds of acceptability. In addition they provide an important window into the processes through which girls come to construct notions of normative value and articulate their notions of cultural appropriateness and moral personhood.

7

Constructing Social Difference and Exclusion in Girls' Groups

Linguistic anthropologists[1] have for several decades documented forms of confrontational behavior in the female linguistic repertoire. During the 1980s and 1990s, however, it was not uncommon for social scientists investigating language who based their studies on the behavior of white middle class, to argue that male speakers are socialized into a competitive style of discourse, while women are socialized into a more cooperative style of speech,[2] one which emphasizes solidarity and positive politeness,[3] intimacy rather than status.[4] Maltz and Borker (1982) proposed that the gender segregation that girls and boys experience results not only in differing activities which are the focus of their worlds, but also alternative ways of speaking; girls' collaborative talk is said to contrast with boys' competitive talk. These forms of dualisms permeate psychological research on gender differences as well. Leaper (1994), in his work on the psychology of gender segregation, argues that girls' sex typed activities help to foster nurturance and affection, as well as forms of "social sensitivity," whereas boys' physically aggressive forms of play emphasize overt competition and dominance. Such dichotomies persist despite the recent flourishing of best-selling books about "mean girls."[5]

This chapter documents the linguistic and nonverbal resources through which girls practice forms of social exclusion and ridicule in their spontaneous play, focusing on an age group whose practices of exclusion have to date received little attention (10–12 year olds). With respect to a marginalized girl, Angela, I examine forms of bullying, defined as negative actions occurring *repeatedly* over time on the part of one or more persons.[6] Negative actions include many diverse behaviors, including direct verbal aggression (name calling and threats), indirect aggression (spreading rumors),[7] as well as nonverbal aggression (often taking the form of stares).[8] This chapter provides among the first documentations of the embodied language practices children use to perform the activity of peer victimization; the few qualitative studies available rely on focus groups or interviews for data collection.[9]

By examining actual instances of negotiated interaction, we can document the process through which social organization is produced and avoid perpetuating essentialist generalizations[10] about the nature of girls' groups. In addition, documentation of the interactions girls engage in causes us to seriously question the adequacy of current psychological models of gender role behavior. The examples in this book call into question certain taken-for-granted ideas about conversational interaction, for example, the notion that talk is organized to preserve social solidarity; when girls are sanctioning someone or positioning the tag-along girl as an outsider, we find girls highlighting rather than downplaying the display of oppositional and face-threatening moves.

Studying Social Exclusion across Ethnographic Contexts

Within a girls' group, constant negotiation occurs with respect to who will be friends with whom, and who is excluded from such friendships. Girls delineate their social groups through forming alliances against particular individuals, in coalitions of two against one, not unlike those described by social psychologists.[11] Across three children's groups of 10–12 year olds with whom I have conducted long-term fieldwork – (a) African American working class girls in Philadelphia, (b) second generation Spanish/English speaking Central American and Mexican girls in downtown Los Angeles, and (c) a group of children of various ethnicities and social classes in a private, progressive school in southern California – I observed girls' ability to negotiate disputes in the midst of games.[12] Rather than seeking to avoid conflict,[13] or having little concern with legal elaboration,[14] the ways in which girls construct extended opposition sequences demonstrate that they are actively seeking it out.

Other forms of dispute were evident as well. Among African American working class girls in Philadelphia, studied in 1970–71, processes of social exclusion through which girls manage their social relations and delineate the boundaries of their group were quite evident. While the actions of the boys made visible a hierarchy, within girls' groups there were continuous processes of coalition formation. The girls talked extensively about other girls behind their backs,[15] and sanctioned girls who attempted to act like they were superior to other girls (having better clothing, being in an accelerated class, enjoying privileges with other girls' moms, having boyfriends, etc.). Such issues are not explicitly addressed in girls' complaints. Rather, within "he-said-she-said" disputes, girls level formal charges against girls who they claim talk about them in their absence through utterances such as "Kerry said *you* said that I wasn't go around Poplar no more." The disputes that emerged from such accusations were more elaborate and more extended than any of the disputes that occurred among the boys. For example, when a girl was said to act as if she "think she cute" because of the way she walked down the street in new clothes, she was ostracized from a playgroup for a month and a half. The playgroup of girls insulted not only her, but her mother and brother as well; this almost led to the family moving from the street.

Forms of exclusion were also observed during my fieldwork among a group of second-generation Mexican and Central American girls in a downtown Los Angeles school. While studying fifth grade Latinas from 1997–98, I found girls were careful to delineate whom their friendship group consisted of during recess. Artwork (shown in Figure 7.1 with pseudonyms) produced for me during free time read: "Schedule. Hop-Scotch. Priscilla, Sylvia, Ariana, Donna ONLY. No more girls."

Figure 7.1 Artwork of exclusion

The artwork was specifically designed to instruct me not to include a girl named Natalia in my filming of hopscotch. In this girls' group, Natalia – a Salvadoran American girl whose mother was secretary to an important LA dignitary – bragged about the outings and privileges she enjoyed. Natalia made good grades in fifth grade (though she gave lame excuses for tardy homework), touted the fact that she was going to be bussed to a junior high school in an upscale West side neighborhood in sixth grade, was in a special after school club for Gifted and Talented children, and continually reminded the girls of this fact. She wore fashionable clothing, bragged about the stylish outfit and shoes she was wearing for graduation from elementary school, and often ridiculed Jun, a Chinese American girl, who wore second-hand dresses, to the extent of making Jun cry, and steal money from her mom to buy a new dress. In that Natalia frequently acted as if she were better than other girls, her classmates tried to prevent her from playing with them at recess, did not permit her to join an informal girls' after-school Girl Power Club they organized, and avoided talking to her throughout the summer when she worked at the school with them as a teacher's aide.

While crafting their social relations through talk during play children delineate the boundaries of their group. As argued by Fine (1980:316):

> Each friendship group develops its own culture derived from past knowledge of members, norms of legitimate interaction, functional needs of the group, status and power considerations, and is formulated by the particular events in which the group participates.

Among the girls' groups I have studied, girls sanction members of their peer group who act in ways interpreted as putting on airs with respect to other girls. Across the various groups I have studied ethnographically, boys participate in a continuous cycle of sports activities, which permits the opportunity for constructing different rankings.[16] Because girls evaluate themselves with reference to the relationships they maintain with others (other girls, boys, and adults), rather than in terms of how they rank in a hierarchy of sports, social exclusion and ridicule constitute powerful ways of delineating the group and dealing with those who offend the social order.

The view of moral development specifying that males are concerned with equality, reciprocity, justice, and rights, while females are concerned with an ethic of care and response[17] provides a distorted view of gendered behavior. As I have discussed in chapter 2, as well as elsewhere,[18] girls are equally as concerned as boys with issues of rights and rules in the midst of spontaneous play. In this chapter I explore forms of exclusion and ridicule that are clearly not oriented to care and response. I concur that "an inner sense of connection with others is a central organizing feature of women's development" (Brown and Gilligan 1993:3) and that girls evaluate themselves with respect to particular situations, relationships, and people, themes important in the work of Gilligan and her colleagues.[19] However, I do not subscribe to the notion that caring relationships provide the best depiction of how girls treat others. Simmons (2002:9) has argued that while the desire for connection propels children into friendship, "the need for recognition and power ignites competition and conflict."[20]

While some forms of exclusion constitute sanctions to acts interpreted as attempts to position oneself above others, other forms of exclusion and ridicule develop in line with a social group's strong feelings of differentiation of in-group and out-group membership.[21] The offense generating some forms of exclusion is not that someone puts herself above others, but that she attempts to affiliate with the group in the first place. Following a particular group of girls from fourth through sixth grade, I found that within the friendship group practices of exclusion among the girls were accomplished not only in covert ways (for example by exchanging knowing glances) but, in addition, through quite explicit and direct verbal speech activities as well – using resources such as insults, bald imperatives, and stories in which the target is portrayed in a negative way.

Differentiating Forms of Aggressive Behavior

Despite the omnipresence of disputes in children's everyday life, (as seen in chapter 2) such speech activities are often downplayed in the accounts of female social organization. Girls are portrayed as inclusive,[22] collaborative,[23] or "cooperative and reciprocal."[24] In sharp contrast to the paradigm that asserts that females are socialized to be non-confrontational, ethnographic work by Goodwin (1990), sociological studies of girls' friendships,[25] recent studies of girls in psychological literature,[26] as well as recent accounts of girls' aggression for lay audiences[27] have discussed forms of oppositional moves in girls' interactions.

Psychologists have distinguished direct or overt acts of verbal and physical aggression (associated with males) from forms of aggression that are intended to cause harm by making use of gossip and social exclusion (associated with females).[28] In talking about forms of aggression among females psychologists have used the terms indirect aggression,[29] relational aggression,[30] and social aggression.[31] Forms of aggression among females differ from more direct aggression; "instead of directly inflicting harm, their aim is to manipulate the reputation of another or to exclude them from the group" (Archer and Coyne 2005:213). Covert or "behind–the–back" methods are used rather than direct action to achieve social exclusion.

The work of Feshbach (1969) and Feshbach and Sones (1971) argued that what they termed indirect aggression was more prevalent in girls than in boys. Feshbach and Sones (1971:385) state that social exclusion may be "functionally equivalent to a verbal insult or even a physical blow." Their experimental results showed that female friendship pairs displayed a more negative, rejecting attitude towards a same-sex stranger than comparable pairs of male friends. Girls, more than boys, ignored, avoided, refused to help or excluded the newcomer within the first sixteen minutes of the experiment. They also found that gender differences in "direct physical aggression" were not salient under all conditions. Finnish researchers in the 1980s were the first to look carefully at the harmful effects of indirect aggression;[32] indirect aggression was defined as "a type of behavior in which the perpetrator attempts to inflict pain in such a manner that he or she makes it seem as though there is no intention to hurt at all" (Bjorkqvist et al. 1992a:118).

In the 1990s American psychologists replaced the term "relational aggression" for indirect aggression. "Relational aggression" was "purposeful withdrawal of friendship or acceptance in order to hurt or control a child" (Crick and Grotpeter 1995:719). Behaviors associated with an updated definition of relational aggression include "ignoring someone to punish them or get one's own way, excluding someone socially for revenge, using negative body language or facial expressions, sabotaging someone else's relationships, or threatening to end a relationship unless the friend agrees to a request" (Simmons 2002:21).

Cairns et al. (1989:323) proposed the term "social aggression," which they defined as "the manipulation of group acceptance through alienation, ostracism, or character defamation." The longitudinal studies (rare in psychology[33]) of the Cairnses provide for more nuanced interpretations of children's practices of exclusion. The focus of their research was "the ecological perspective of the person in context."[34] Important sex differences in forms of social alienation were found in the longitudinal studies of the Cairnses. These studies followed the pathways of 695 young people growing up over a 14-year period. In their study Cairns and Cairns (1994) made use of semi-structured interviews, which permitted subjects (ages 9–17 from suburban, small town, and rural areas of North Carolina[35]) to give extended answers in their own words, rather than having to respond to explicitly defined categories characteristic of most survey methodology. Cairns and Cairns (1986) found that girls reported more themes of social alienation and ostracism in early adolescence than they did in childhood. While in the fourth grade only 10 percent of the girls studied reported such themes, by the seventh grade, over one third of the same gender conflicts among girls involved the manipulation of group acceptance through alienation, ostracism, or character defamation. By way of contrast, boys rarely reported themes of social aggression, in either the fourth or seventh grade.

Building upon the work of Cairns and Cairns, Galen and Underwood (1997:589) argue that "Social aggression is directed towards damaging another's self-esteem, social status, or both, and may take such direct forms as verbal rejection, negative facial expressions or body movements, or more indirect forms such as slanderous rumors or social exclusion." Such indirect forms are rated more hurtful among girls than boys. Forms of girls' social or relational aggression cannot, however, be seen as completely different from overt aggression, because the act of telling friends they will stop liking them unless they do what they say is itself quite direct and overt, not covert or indirect. My own ethnographic research shows that girls' aggression to other girls can in fact be quite direct in that it involves forms of verbal insults and ridicule.

Through cross-cultural studies conducted largely through questionnaires and surveys, psychologists have analyzed forms of (relational/indirect/social) aggression among preschool and adolescent females in Norway,[36] Finland,[37] the United States,[38] England,[39] and Australia.[40] Built on work by Whiting and Edwards (1988), a cross-cultural study of early and middle childhood in six cultures, in the 1980s the "Two Cultures" or "Separate Worlds Hypothesis"[41] maintained that boys and girls evolve different goals for social interactions and communicative styles as a result of separated peer play in childhood. Studies of the communicative styles of girls and boys[42] found boys more adversarial while girls were more collaborative. Psychologists who link overt aggression forms of direct physical and verbal aggression – hitting, kicking, threatening, commanding, and refusing to comply with another's request – with boys and "relational aggression" or "indirect bullying[43] with girls support a new form of gender dualism.

Problems with such dualisms have been noted by a number of researchers. Countering studies finding gender differences, Pulkkinen and Pitkanen (1993:253) in their longitudinal study of social development in Jyvaskyla, Finland, found no gender differences in aggressiveness when peer nomination[44] rather than teacher rating was employed.[45] Counter to the popular belief that direct physical and verbal aggression are more the province of boys than of girls, recent work[46] argues that few gender differences have been found with regard to direct verbal aggression. In fact Ahmad and Smith (1994) report that English girls are more likely than boys to be the victims of name calling. Despite the association of relational aggression with girls, some studies[47] find no gender differences in its practice. Rarely have researchers analyzed forms of indirect aggression among boys. However, Cadigan (2003) describes incidences of social aggression at a Los Angeles middle school and I observed processes of exclusion among fourth and fifth grade boys at Hanley School that were devastating to the targeted boy.[48] Crick et al. (1997) found that while teachers described girls as more relationally aggressive than boys, and boys as more overtly aggressive than girls, children's own peer nominations did not reflect these differences.[49] Researchers[50] caution against drawing conclusions about gender differences in bullying until more longitudinal studies are conducted.

Processes of Exclusion among Friends within the Clique

Eder and Kinney (1995) have argued that girls can have a high degree of popularity or visibility in a school, and simultaneously experience a decrease in peer status in terms of friendship relations. Specifically, if girls are thought of as snobbish or stuck up, this can lead to a withdrawal of friendship offers. Adler and Adler (1998) argue that there is always fighting among the girls at the very top for competition and once they are there, they are on their way out, because people get jealous of their status. Girls who make attempts to display that they are superior to others are subject to forms of censure, in the form of gossip, by others.[51]

This occurs in the popular clique at Hanley School. Emi and Janis were considered leaders and thought of themselves as the most popular girls of the clique. These two upper middle class, petite girls were skillful at organizing games, good storytellers, good athletes, and were always chosen for teams by the boys. Janis and Emi frequently acted in ways that others felt were displays of considering oneself above the other girls in the group. In games of tetherball in the sixth grade, Janis violated rules that she made others abide by with impunity. When she was called for her cheating, she responded with excuses such as "I just got excited."

Both Janis and Emi frequently made reference to their involvement in extracurricular activities of the upper middle class. Though the six core clique members were close friends, ways that Janis or Emi presented themselves to others often precipitated involvement in collusive commentaries on or ridiculing of these girls by members of the core group. Emi on many occasions would attempt to see if she could get members of the clique to congregate in a particular part of the playground; rather than asking girls if they wanted to play in a new area, she would arbitrarily go to a new spot and see if they would follow. In response, girls would resist her attempts, and talk about her. Janis was prone to brag about her position on Student Council, as well as about her access to famous celebrities; this resulted in mocking Janis's attempts at one-upmanship.

Members of the popular girls' clique sanctioned members of their own group, such as Janis or Emi, when someone attempted to show herself better than other clique members. This could occur in a variety of ways: (1) through cryptic comments and exchanges of collusive "knowing" looks and gestures in the presence of the targeted individual; (2) indirectly, through talk about someone in her absence; (3) or more directly through excluding someone from play; or (4) yelling insults from a distance.

By way of a specific example, at lunchtime one day the girls sanctioned both Janis and Emi for behavior the group interpreted as putting themselves above others in the group. On this particular day Janis approached the group late during lunch break because she had been attending a Student Council meeting. As she joins the group she provides a commentary on her student meeting: "The **worst** student council meeting we have *e:*ver **been** to." While she delivers her commentary as a complaint, the mere mentioning of the meeting serves to differentiate herself from others of the group.[52]

In the following Aretha, Lisa, Melissa, Ruth, and Nemika are eating lunch as Janis joins them.

Example 7.1
```
1  Janis:   The worst Student Council meeting I have- we
2           have ⌈e:ver been to.
3  Lisa:         ⌊Okay. Ruth!
4           ((head movement to Ruth, as if
5           commenting on Janis's announcement))
```

6   Ruth: Hm? *((to Lisa))*
7   Janis: So *bor*ing!
8   Ruth: **OH**::. Okay. *((gazing toward and nodding to Lisa))*

In Example 7.1 Janis's talk is produced as an announcement, a form of story preface and puzzle;[53] the assessment in the preface ("the **wors**t Student Council meeting") invites further talk. However, rather than talking into Janis's talk, instead Lisa (a fifth grader and reputedly one of Janis's best friends) and Ruth (another fifth grader, who is Emi's sister) comment among themselves about it through collusive "byplay."[54] Lisa's talk – "Okay. Ruth!" (line 3) – acts as a summons to Ruth; it is accompanied by a head movement, which also comments on Janis's talk. Lisa's comment is answered quickly by Ruth, who provides a request for clarification: "Hm?" which is then followed quickly by Ruth's "**OH**::. Okay." This action provides an acknowledgement of the prior cryptic commentary, produced with a "change of state token" (Heritage 1984a), and closes down the dyadic exchange.

In the midst of these exchanges between Ruth and Lisa, Janis begins another conversation with Aretha, tapping Aretha's arm to invoke her coparticipation. Ruth questions why Janis is not at her Student Council meeting (lines 4–5). Janis explains that she took off early from the meeting ("I'm done. Well we kind of did a blast off") (line 6). Ruth next launches an explicit negative assessment of Janis's prior activity; she describes her as "**wi:::ld**" (line 9) and jumping on tables and chairs like wild animals (lines 14–15). Lisa for her part also provides fuel to Ruth's negative assessment with "That's very retarded" (lines 10–11):

Example 7.2 (continuation of 7.1)

```
 1   Janis:    ((taps Aretha's shoulder to get her
 2             attention))
 3             Steam room? ⌈Are you ready?
 4   Ruth:                ⌊Janis!
 5             Aren't you supposed to be at Student Council?
 6   Janis:    I'm done. Well we kind of did a blast off.
 7   Aretha:   Is it ready? ((to Janis))
 8   Janis:    ((shrugs shoulders))
 9   Ruth:     You guys are just like ⌈wi:::ld!
10   Lisa:                            ⌊That's very
11             retarded.
12   Ruth:     And you're jumping on tables and chairs?
13   Janis:    ⌈No:.
14   Ruth:     ⌊And it looked- act like lions and tigers
15             in a zoo.
```

In this sequence we find girls who are close friends providing collusive commentaries about the talk of one of their members. In addition they provide assessment adjectives ("wild" and "retarded") and a negative depiction; Lisa compares Janis's activity to that of wild animals. The original comment, one that could launch a story portraying Janis, the teller, as someone who enjoys special privileges is transformed; the story becomes one about children who were out of control.

In the process of sanctioning girls in their friendship group, girls often talk about feeling states, for example, why someone is "mad" or "angry" at someone, or "jealous." In the particular example to be examined, ten seconds after Janis is sanctioned (in Example 7.2 above), the girls talk about how they should deal with Emi, who has (1) attempted to show her power in the group by walking to a distant area of the playground and expecting other girls to follow her, and (2) called Lisa a lesbian. The girls retaliate and concur that they want to make Emi feel "jealous" (lines 18, 33).

In response to having been called a lesbian (line 1),[55] Lisa yells a taunt in Emi's direction: "I HOPE THEY **SLIP**! OFF THE **SWINGS**! AND CRACK THEIR **HEAD** OPEN!" (lines 8–10). The girls categorize the situation brewing between Lisa and Emi as a "fight" (line 14) in which girls take "sides" (line 11).

Example 7.3

1	Lisa:	She called me a **les**bian.
2	Janis:	*Hhhhhh! *((inbreath))*
3		Emi called you a lesbian?
4	Lisa:	Yes. So **fuck**in **la:me**.
5		. . . (21 seconds later)
6		*((Emi and friend swing on the swings at some*
7		*distance from the girls))*
8	Lisa:	I HOPE THEY **SLIP!**
9		OFF THE **SWING!**
10		AND CRACK THEIR **HEAD** OPEN!
11	Janis:	**I'll** be on **your** side.
12		eh heh!
13	Lisa:	Of ⌈**course** you are.
14	Janis:	⌊Hey Ruth! What's the **fight** about.
15		uh since you guys
16		(°have known her for so long).
17	Lisa:	Because um-
18	Aretha:	**I** wanna make Emi **jeal**ous.
19	Janis:	Yeah. Let's j's ⌈ignore her-
20	Ruth:	⌊**No:** you guys. **No. No.**
21	Janis:	You guys and laugh.
22	Ruth:	I don't think that's such a great ⌈idea.
23	Janis:	⌊Let's laugh guys.
24	Lisa:	We can do it if we want to.
25		**You** can't tell us what to do.
26	Aretha:	eh heh!
27	Ruth:	Okay. **Fine**. I'm **out** of this then.=
28	Janis:	You guys let's ⌈go tell her (then).
29	Aretha:	⌊No. but she hasn't got-

30	Janis:	They half laughing.
31	Janis:	Okay. Something **rea**lly bad.
32	Melissa:	⌈(I'm in the middle of it.)
33	Janis:	⌊How can we- **how** can we make her jealous.
		((to ethnographers))
34	Aretha:	Then be in the middle.
35	Janis:	What should we do.
36	Lisa:	Ruth. Ruth. ⌈Ruth.
37	Aretha:	⌊***I*** know something!
38	Janis:	What.
39	Aretha:	When you guys come over my house,
40		and she would have to leave by one thirty four
41		kinder time.
42	Ruth:	eh heh heh heh!
43		And so we could say "**Oh:::** I'm so **sad** that
44		⌈you have to **leave**."
45	Janis:	⌊Yeah but will- you guys won't be in a **fight** by
46		then.= will you?
		(0.5)
47	Janis:	What ⌈did she-
48	Ruth:	⌊You guys it's gonna become a-
49	Janis:	What did she ⌈say.
50	Ruth	⌊A- much (.) worse (.) fight.

In this sequence girls take up different stances towards sanctioning Emi's behavior; past and future possible scenes are enacted in the midst of a developing storyline. Lisa screams taunts to Emi wishing that she crack her head open (lines 8–10). Aretha suggests that they attempt to do something to make her feel "jealous" (line 18). In desperation Janis even asks the ethnographers how to make Emi jealous (line 33). The girls attempt to come up with specific types of activities they can engage in that would generate this emotion state in Emi. Janis's solution is to ignore Emi and laugh at her (lines 19–21). Aretha's idea is to invent a scenario in which after inviting Emi over to her house, she will have to leave earlier than the other girls (lines 39–44). In this way she evokes a hypothetical situation in which exclusion occurs. Aretha enacts the words which she would say in mock sympathy with Emi: "**Oh:::** I'm so **sad** that you have to **leave**" (lines 43–44). Not all the girls present agree with the projected scenario. Ruth, Emi's sister, disagrees with the plan and opts out of sanctioning her (lines 20, 21, 22, 27).

As the story about Emi winds down, the girls go to play hopscotch. Although Janis originally argued that she wants to make Emi feel jealous, she subsequently decides she wants to invite her to play hopscotch. As Janis runs over to Emi, ostensibly to ask her why she is "angry" at the girls, she is quickly summoned back. In choral succession the girls implore Janis to "Think!"

Example 7.4

1	Janis:	**E**mi! Come on! **E**mi! _((yelling to Emi))_
2	Aretha:	_((screams))_ **NO!**
3	Lisa:	_((Shrill scream))_ **What** are you **do**ing!
4	Aretha:	**Jan**is!?
5	Janis:	What?
6	Aretha:	_((points to head))_ **Think!**
7	Janis:	Don't do that-
8	Sarah:	_((sing-song))_ **Think**, think, **think-**
9	Melissa:	**Think**, think, **think**
10	Sarah:	⌈ **Think!**
11	Melissa:	⊢ **Think!**
12	Sarah:	⌊ **Think!**
13	Janis:	I know. But if we're having everyone except
14		Emi that would be very mean.
15	Aretha:	Well it looks like she's having fun with**out** us.

This set of events, in which Janis (Example 7.3) first talks negatively about Emi and then (Example 7.4) runs to ask her to play, illustrates the quick-changing nature of alliances among girls that "fluctuate like a merry-go-round" (Canaan 1987:394).

Interactive Practices for Co-constructing a "Tag-Along" Girl

Recent work by post-structuralist theorists on the interactive construction of social categories has investigated gender and racial identity as the negotiation of discourses and practices (rather than a set of attitudes). Bucholtz (1999a) has examined linguistic practices associated with the performance of a particular marginalized adolescent social identity, the nerd.[56] With respect to other forms of marginalized identities, however, we have few studies of how, in the midst of ongoing interaction, children articulate difference or inequality[57] among group members, in particular with respect to their own understandings of social class.

Much of the work in conversation analysis has argued that talk is organized in ways that preserve social solidarity and inhibit or avoid conflict.[58] However, in the midst of children's conversations among friends in a peer group, participants often create character contests,[59] interactions that display an orientation towards the social construction of rudeness[60] rather than the protection of face.

Actions such as those in Examples 7.1–7.4 above, which sanction inappropriate behavior, are short-lived; they endure only during the time that someone is being chided for having violated norms of comportment. Girls can select ways of interacting that do not treat peers as co-equals,[61] but rather sanction behavior and inflict harm, even in the absence of an initial triggering act. Forms of negative commentary, rude behavior, ridicule, degradation, and exclusion can develop in line with a social group's strong feelings of differentiation of in-group and out-group membership.

Sanctioning through ridicule and exclusion

Forms of exclusion were quite evident in the clique with respect to their interactions with Angela, the "tag-along" girl (defined in terms of her efforts to affiliate to a particular group without being accepted by the group). A tag-along, like a "wannabe"[62] or an "isolate"[63] is a child defined by her marginal relationship to a peer group. The term "social misfit" refers to individuals whose behavior deviates from what is normative for their own group.[64] In the case of the group I studied, Angela played with or near the group, but was treated as a marginalized member of the group. During lunchtime girls explicitly complain about the fact that Angela "follows" them. In the next example, the girls make no attempt to mitigate the description of her as always following the group:

Example 7.5

1	Janis:	Angela do you have to *foll*ow us
2		*Ev*erywhere we go?
3	Angela:	*Why* do people always ask me that.
4	Janis:	Well I mean you're always-
5		You're always **with** us. ((*knits brows, puckers lips while looking at Angela*))

In the following interaction the term "tag-along" is explicitly used to describe Angela. Three girls (Aretha, Sarah, and Angela) are sitting together talking about having been excluded from playing softball. Sarah explicitly targets Angela as someone in the present social group who is herself marginal.

Example 7.6

1	Angela:	*I-* I mean like- **you** guys are like-
2		I don't **judge any**body because you guys know,
3		that like I just, you know, follow you guys.
4		((*shoulder moves in time with words*))
5		⌈wherever you guys go, but um,
6	Sarah:	⌊You're like a **tag**. You tag along. ((*left palm extended with arm bent towards Angela*))
7		*extended with arm bent towards Angela*))
8		Basically- ⌈Angela tags along.=
9	Angela:	⌊So,
10	Sarah:	That's it.=right?
11	Angela:	So li⌈ke- **Yeah**. ((*shoulder shrug*))
12	Sarah:	⌊Right Angela? Admit it. eh heh heh!
13	Angela:	Yeah like-⌈whatever.
14	Sarah:	⌊AD**MIT** IT ANGELA!

```
15   Sarah:      ⌈ADMIT IT! ((extends arms palm up to Angela))
16   Angela:     ⌊OKAY! ((leaning towards Sarah))
17   Sarah:      Say it. "You:: (.) are:: (.) I: am a: (.)"
18               ((using hands as if conducting on each beat,))
19               then extends hands palm up towards Angela
20               as if asking her to complete the utterance))
21   Angela:     I'M A TAG-ALONG °girl! ((jerks body in
22               direction of Sarah))
                          (0.4)
23   Sarah:      Good girl! eh heh!
24   Angela:     °°I'm gonna get you! ((play fight))
25   Sarah:      heh-heh Oka(hh)y.
26               heh-heh ⌈hmh-hmh-hnh-hnh-hnh!
27   Angela:            ⌊Okay!
```

In this encounter Angela (lines 1–5) describes her position as someone who doesn't enter into the group by "judging" others but merely follows other girls. Sarah (lines 6–8) then reformulates Angela's talk with a meta-commentary on Angela's status in the group with her utterance: "You're like a *tag*. You tag along." Rather than accepting Angela's bid for inclusion, Sarah (lines 10, 12, 14–15) next asks Angela to publicly confess her position: "AD*MIT* IT ANGELA!" When Angela agrees with "Yeah" (line 13) and "O*KAY*" (line 16), this is not treated as adequate. Sarah provides the explicit frame Angela needs to repeat (line 17). In this degradation ritual (Garfinkel 1956), Angela is allowed no role distance from the marginalized identity she is asked to assume as she fills in the remainder of Sarah's utterance with "I'M A *TAG*-ALONG °girl!" (line 21). Sarah places herself in the position of evaluating Angela's performance (line 23) with "*Good* Girl!", using an intonation contour similar to one that might be used to praise a dog. In response Angela provides a protest move with a play fight jab towards Sarah and says under her breath "°°I'm gonna *get* you!"

The girls have yet other ways of casting Angela as someone with a soiled identity. The girls feel at liberty to ask questions, the answers to which degrade her. Angela has been a student at Hanley School for one year. In the midst of jump rope, the girls question whether or not people were mean to her at her former school and if she had any friends there. The following occurs after Lisa misses her jump and Angela is turning an end of the rope because Melissa got tired of turning it.

Example 7.7

```
                 ((during jump rope))
1   Aretha:      Angela Booty Butthead ((rhymes with last name))
2                Eh heh!
3   Janis:       Who made that up.
4   Aretha:      From your old school?
5   Janis:       Were they mean to you at your old school?
6   Angela:      Yeah.
```

7	Janis:	Who made that up.
8	Aretha:	Did you have any friends at your old school?
9	Angela:	Yeah.
10	Aretha:	How many.
11	Janis:	Here. ((*throwing the end of the rope to Melissa*))
12		Why'd you leave the old school.
13	Angela:	((*shoulder shrug as she continues to swing the rope she has in her hand without answering*))

While the girls pose several questions that provide negative portraits of Angela, this process is not reciprocal. Though the girls in the clique feel at liberty to address her in this way, she on no occasion asks questions that pose negative descriptions of them.

Angela is frequently targeted as the cause of things gone awry. In the following jump rope session she is jumping at some distance from the other girls by herself (because she was not permitted to play with them). What occurs here is that in the midst of turning the rope Aretha decides to do splits while the jumper is jumping, replicating the action that the jumper must perform (done to make the game more interesting for the turner). Because she is doing splits, she is not attending to turning the rope appropriately and Lisa misses her jump. When Lisa misses Melissa claims that she missed because of her own turning "My turn- My fault." She then credits the mistake as having been caused by Angela jumping into the rope and making her let go, though Angela was not even close to the rope while it was turning.

Example 7.8

		((*Lisa is jumping Aretha turning. In the midst of her jumping she lands on the rope.*))
1	Lisa:	This is my second turn.
2	Turners:	Texaco Mexico went over the hills
3		And far away where they do some splits
4	Aretha:	((*turns around and does split in the midst of doing turning*))
5	Melissa:	My turn- My **fault**.
6		Angela went like **that in**to the rope so I let go.
7	Angela:	**I** did **not**.
8	Lisa:	**Yes** ⌈you did.
9	Melissa:	⌊You did.
10	Aretha:	I went like this= ((*showing movement*))
11	Angela:	Did not.
12	Aretha:	Ah:, ah:,
13	Lisa:	I went round.
14	Angela:	She went like this. Aretha went like this.
15	Aretha:	Stop it Angela.
16	Angela:	((*demonstrates how Aretha turned around in place
17		while turning*))
18	Melissa:	Okay.
19	Lisa:	One more turn.

In this sequence girls collaborate in constructing Angela as deviant. Though Angela was jumping at some distance, Melissa claims that Angela was the cause of her dropping the rope (line 6). Angela is outnumbered as multiple participants ratify Melissa's position, and it stands as the official version of events (lines 8, 9, 12). Such an imbalance of power within the interaction constitutes one of the features of bullying.[65]

In smaller acts of micro-aggression, girls in the group would comment on Angela's pronunciation of words. When Angela reported the news that a girl named Sharie had Spice Girls pins and other objects in her school folder, rather than commenting on the newsworthiness of Angela's report, Aretha responded immediately with, "**Shar**ie not Shar**ie**." During lunch while the girls were discussing lipstick, Angela commented that the color one of the girls had was similar to that of a famous model: "It's like the color that **Ty**ra Banks had on." When Sarah subsequently asked, "What color did Tyra Bank wear." Angela corrected her by shouting, "**TYRA BANKS!**" Animating her version of Angela's voice, Sarah then re-produced Angela's talk with lower volume and pitch, and a breathier quality as she said, "I don't even know who T^{h}aira tey~ŋ Iŋ !" (Tyra Banks is). The last three words of her utterance were produced without fully articulating any of the final consonant clusters, and with nasality. The sounds were velar, but were not completely articulated.[66]

On another occasion the girls mocked Angela's pronunciation of "friend" by using nasality, a "chipmunk" or "helium" voice, and exaggerated diphthongs on "ie" when pronouncing the vowels of the word. In the following the word "friend" is produced without fully articulating any of the final consonant clusters of the word: Fr**ie**nd → Frie::: ŋ. In addition Sarah provided an exaggerated head movement as she pronounced "Frie::: ŋ," and the girls exchanged collusive smiles affirming their mutual orientation of mocking Angela.

Example 7.9

	((Girls are eating lunch and telling stories))
Angela:	She told me- a lie:.
	I know it was a lie.
	'Cause you don't know any of- my friends.
	But her. (0.6) She's not my fr**ie**nd.
Melissa:	Who.
Aretha:	She's not mah fri:e::: ŋ eh heh!
Sarah:	She's not mah fri:e::: ŋ ((cocks head))
Angela:	Lisa said-
	There's this girl name-
Aretha:	((looks and smiles at Sarah))
Sarah:	((smiles at Aretha))
Angela:	You don't even know her name. ·

Angela's identity was not solely the product of others' antagonistic utterances directed toward her. Angela herself initiated behavior that was abnormal or annoying (for example, eating food with her tongue, eating others' rejected food, correcting the pronunciation of words by yelling, and sitting on a table rather than on a bench during lunch) which resulted in pejorative descriptions of her. During lunchtime she would tag girls and claim they then had "cooties." In response Kathy told her "The point is Angela, that you are always touching people and you always say that now they have cooties. So you're kind of saying that **you** always have cooties." On one occasion as the girls were coming in from baseball practice at recess, Angela chased relentlessly and tagged girls. Brittany told Angela, "You're on heroin Angela. I don't want to smell like it." Angela frequently disputed the attributions made of her. In response to the pejorative descriptions of her as being "on heroin", she responded by providing a reciprocal action in kind. Angela responded to the thin and beautiful Brittany, "Elephant. Bumpy eyes."

When her behavior generated negative commentary, she on occasion would agree to the pejorative descriptions made of her:

Example 7.10

		((Angela is eating pudding with her fingers))
1	Nate:	*((yelling from another lunch table))*
2		You are a **weir**do!
3	Angela:	I'm your worst **night**mare!
4	Aretha:	⋆h Ho!
5	Lisa:	*((pointing at Angela and nodding yes))*

In response to others' talk, Angela would often cast the prior talk as irrelevant. For example, in the following (Example 7.11) when Sarah explained that she had to take the uneaten part of her lunch home, rather than providing a move that aligned with Sarah's position, Angela responds, "Who cares" (line 6). Sarah provides a next counter move to Angela's utterance with "Whatever" (line 7) and an explanation. Through this utterance Sarah mirrors the character of Cher, who made the expression "Whatever" famous in *Clueless*, a mid-1990s comedy film about Beverly Hills high school students. Girls at Hanley used slang and speech patterns from this movie frequently in their talk. In addition, Sarah colors her talk with an eyeball roll and a neck jerk, a gesture that ridicules Angela through its exaggerated caricature of a Clueless girl. Angela's response to Sarah is a direct imperative ("Oh be quiet" in line 10). This time, in her response Sarah upgrades her response through a reaction of righteous indication, using a direct imperative: "Don't tell me **any**thing Angela" (line 11). Sarah accompanies this utterance with an exaggerated head gesture and eyeball roll. In response everyone but Angela laughs: instead, she characterizes the demeanor of the girls as "nasty": "You guys are **nas**ty."

Example 7.11

		((During lunchtime at table))
1	Sarah:	Oh stop it! Nobody rip my lunch again!
2		No: I'm- seriously I have to like- you know

3	Emi:	Reuse it.
4	Sarah:	No. No. Seriously I have to like- you know- there's-
5		food in there so I have to like- take it back home.
6	Angela:	Who cares.
7	Sarah:	Whatever! I don't waste my things!
8		((rolls eyes, does neck jerk))
9	Melissa:	Emi! Emi!
10	Angela:	Oh be quiet.
11	Sarah:	Don't tell me **any**thing Angela.
12		Oh my **Go::d**. ((does an exaggerated head action, rolls eyes))
13	Girls:	((Laughter))
14	Angela:	You guys are **nas**ty. You guys are just like- you're just-
15	Sarah:	Like **you're** not nasty?

Forms of directive imperatives, such as "Oh be quiet!" (line 10), were made by Angela on other occasions as well, when, as in Example 7.12 below, she would directly tell someone in an unmitigated way "Shut **up**" (line 4). This utterance is reciprocated with a dismissive remark: "I don't have to- if I don't **want** to" (lines 5–7).

Example 7.12

		((in the midst of hopscotch))
1	Lisa:	I hope you get shot. ((said to Angela))
2	Sarah:	Who's after Janis?= Oh.
3	Janis:	Don't be mean Lisa.
4	Angela:	Shut **up** Lisa.
5	Lisa:	I don't have to- if I don't **want** to.
6		You're not my mama.
7		You don't tell **me** what to do.

When Angela challenged others' talk, in response girls rebuked her, showing how her utterances were inappropriate.

The social construction of Angela's nonperson and polluted status

Across a range of circumstances Angela was treated as a nonperson (Goffman 1963:40), an undesirable member of the group. This was especially evident when games were being played. For example, while the girls were drawing a hopscotch grid, as Angela approached, Lisa commented (line 2) despairingly, "Guess who's here. A::::." (line 2). When Angela asked if she could play, the girls, who had not yet begun to play, excluded her by saying "Angela we already started the game" (line 4).

Example 7.13

		((Angela approaches the group))
1	Lisa:	Guess who's here.

    2 Aretha: Guess who's here. **A:::.**
    3 Angela: Can I play?
    4 Janis: Angela we already started the game.
    5   ((*yelling*)) We already started the game.
    6 Girls: We already started,
    7 Mel, Emi: We already started.

The girls treat Angela and objects she is associated with as polluting.[67] She frequently does not bring a lunch and asks to eat other people's food. On the occasion of Example 7.14 below, Aretha had offered Angela half of her sandwich, while the other half had been thrown in the trash. Angela has put the sandwich down temporarily next to Aretha's desk. When Aretha addresses Angela, she thinks that the sandwich she is currently eating is the half that had been thrown in the trash. Despite the fact that Angela clarifies that she is not eating a part of the sandwich that was thrown in the trash, Sarah (line 9) provides a commentary built on this notion. Her turn includes a response cry displaying disgust in the initial part of the turn ("E::::w"), a derogatory depiction of Angela, and laughter directed at her.

Example 7.14

              ((*during lunch inside the classroom*))
    1 Aretha: ★hhh E::w you got that-
    2   the sandwich back from the **trash** can.
    3 Angela: No::.
    4 Aretha: Is that the one you ate?
    5 Angela: Yeah.
    6 Aretha: Why you put it next to **me**! Throw it **away**!
    7 Angela: Huh?= I'm not **fin**ished, (.) **That's** not the one
    8   that I got outta the **trash** can? **Uh** uh,
                          (1.4)
    9 Sarah: E::::w. Angela eats this garbage outa the trash can,
    10   Eh heh heh

With many of the previous examples we find ways that explicitly target Angela as the agent of ritually defiling acts. Goffman (1971:62) in his discussion of supportive interchanges argues that ritual is a perfunctory, conventionalized act through which an individual portrays his respect and regard for some object of ultimate value. Greetings and farewells provide ritual brackets around a spate of joint activity;[68] greetings mark a transition to a condition of increased access and farewells to a state of decreased access. In the following (Example 7.15) Angela approaches a group of girls seated on the ground eating lunch, as they are discussing a potential fight between two friends. Here a greeting "**Hi** Angela!", produced with a ritualized hand wave, is followed immediately by a farewell: "**Bye** Angela!", with no intervening conversation. The girls are discussing an impending dispute between Emi and Ruth as Angela approaches.

Example 7.15

		((Angela approaches the group))
1	Ruth:	A- much (.) worse (.) fight.
2	Janis:	What did she say.
3	Ruth:	**Hi** Angela! **Bye** Angela! *((waving hand "Bye"))*
4	Lisa:	Shoo shoo **shoo::!**
5		*((Angela does not move))*
6	Janis:	What did she **say**.
7	Ruth:	**HI:.** Eh heh heh! *((to Angela))*
8	Aretha:	Nothing.
9	Melissa:	She was angry at me first.
10	Lisa:	She was?
11		*((Angela goes away running))*

The rituals of greeting and farewell in this example are not intended as ones that bracket activity or affirm the presence of the approaching party, but rather ones that dismiss her. "Shoo shoo **shoo::!**" (line 4) provides a gloss of the farewell "**Bye** Angela!" shooing is used by people in a position of superiority to dismiss younger children, pets, or pests. Here we find a simple access ritual, as powerful as any more elaborated speech event, such as a story, used to define who is excluded from being a ratified member of the social group. The action is comparable to an imperative telling Angela to get lost.

In the midst of games, such as volleyball (Example 7.16 below), others feel free to address Angela with insulting comments about the way she plays (lines 6, 10–11) and directives that are baldly formulated (lines 13, 16) and indicate her degraded status. In the midst of play the girls ventriloquate teachers who admonish her not to plug her ears "when someone's telling you something" (lines 13–14).

Example 7.16

		((Angela hits the ball before it bounces during volleyball))
1	Sarah:	**AN**GELA!!
2	Gabriella:	⌈Don't ( )
3	Sarah:	⌊No you didn't let it bounce,
4		And you're telling **ot**her people how to bounce?
5		Play- till-
6	Melissa:	Angela do you know how to play volleyball?
7	Angela:	Yes. I **do**.
8	Melissa:	**Sure** you do.
9	Angela:	**O**kay o**kay** o**kay** o**kay::**.
10	Melissa:	You're telling **ot**her people how to play
11		And **you** don't even know how to play.
12	Naomi:	Did you hear what Miss Dillon said to you?
13		**Don't** plug your ears when somebody's telling you s-
14		something.

15	Angela:	Well not when they're- when they're yelling in my *ear*! Angela catches the ball
16	Sarah:	NOW ANGELA! LET IT **BOUNCE**!
17	Angela:	STOP **YELL**ING AT ME. *((screaming))*

Angela's position in the group is evident from her differentiated participation in directive sequences as well. While others direct bald imperatives to Angela, she addresses the other girls with requests. While other girls in the group ask each other for food from their lunch (and are granted it) with imperatives such as "Give me some of your potato chips" or accusative statements such as "Sarah, you owe me some chili cheese chips!" and food was shared, Angela's requests for this food frequently fell on dead ears.

Example 7.17

1	Angela:	⌈May I have a Dorito? *((pleading))*
2	Aretha:	⌊(They fell on the ground. Ew::.)
3	Aretha:	Ee::ww, no.
		(1.0)
4	Angela:	Can I have a Dorito,
		(1.3)
5	Emi:	Let me see. Aretha?
		(1.0)
6	Angela:	Melissa can I have a Dorito:,
		(0.4)
7	Melissa:	There's – *((looks in bag, gives chips to Aretha))*
8		(1.2) *((Aretha eats, doesn't offer anything to Angela))*
9	Aretha:	I'll eat this.

In this sequence Angela makes mitigated requests using the modal verbs "may" and "can" with a pleading voice (lines 1, 4, 6), yet no one responds to her. In fact, Melissa (lines 7–8) hands the bag to Aretha, who finishes off the remaining chips. The mitigated directive forms of Angela contrast markedly with the direct imperatives that are continually issued to her (Example 7.16 above).

Negative assessments of Angela's behavior provide yet another way the girls cast her as deviant. At lunch Angela's resistance to complying with traditional norms is frequently sanctioned. For example in the midst of having lunch girls comment on the way she eats chocolate pudding without a utensil. They first ask her to leave and eat at another table. The girls treat the way in which she was eating with her tongue as despicable both (1) through the way in which they gloss her deportment as "disgusting" and (2) position themselves away from her (see Figure 7.2).

Example 7.18

		((Aretha, Janis, Lisa, and Angela are at lunch))
1	Lisa:	If you're gonna have to *eat* that
2		Could you go like-
3		Go to **that** table? *((pointing to the side))*

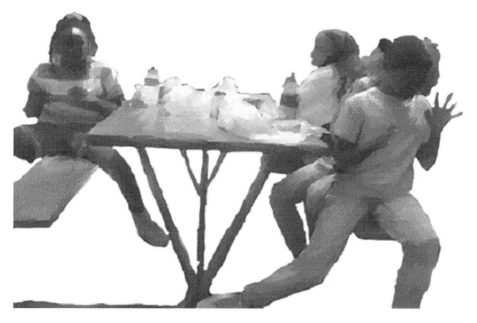

Figure 7.2   Girls react to Angela eating with her tongue

4	Angela:	*((turns away from picnic table while eating))*
5	Aretha:	Janis? *((lifts up Janis' plastic food bag))*
6	Lisa:	Not to be **mean**
7		But we don't **want** to see chocolate with carrots.
8	Janis:	⌈Now **plea::se-**
9	Aretha:	⌊Oh that's dis**gus**ti:::ng! *((closes eyes))*
10		**She** has chocolate pudding on- get-
11	Angela:	*((begins to eat with her tongue))*
12	Aretha:	**OU:::** ⌈:::::::: *((Aretha, Lisa, Janis turn away in disgust))*
13	Janis:	⌊**OH::::!** *((turning away in disgust))*
14	Janis:	Oh!=
15	Aretha:	**AN**GELA!= *((slaps hands to lap))*
16	Janis:	**Oh** my **god**. *((raises hands to head, lowers head with eyes shut))*
17	Aretha:	You just-
18	Lisa:	Can ⌈I-
19	Aretha:	⌊**AH:::::::** *((eyes closed))*
20	Lisa:	I- **I need** to go to the room. *((starts to walk away))*

Here the girls take up a position vis-à-vis Angela's activity of using her tongue rather than a spoon through an explicit assessment statement, "Oh that's dis**gus**ti:::ng!" prefaced with the response cry "oh" (line 9). As she continues to eat, not heeding their requests or listening to their assessment they produce response cries (lines 12–14) that are accompanied by nonvocal movements that convey disgust. The girls put their hands to their closed eyes as they rapidly turn their backs on the table so that they are no longer facing Angela (lines 12–13).

Personal and ritual insult

Insults were other forms of negative assessments directed to Angela. In the following (Example 7.19) format tying is used to redirect an initial statement that Angela provides about the coach's hairy legs into a statement about herself. Aretha (line 7) looks under the table where the girls are eating at Angela's legs and redirects the statement to her (line 8):

Example 7.19

		((Aretha, Lisa, Janis, and Angela are discussing a male coach. Angela turns to look in his direction.))
1	Janis:	Marcus flirts with everyone.
2	Lisa:	Look at them!
3	Angela:	**Da::n**g, That man got some hairy le:(hhhh)gs.
4		(1.0) ((Aretha and Janis look at the coach))
5	Angela:	He doe(hh)s!
6	Aretha:	Like uhm,
7		((looks under the table at Angela's legs)) you?
8		**YOU** you you you you you you yah! ((chanting, points chin in Angela's direction))

Here an initial assessment offered by Angela (line 3) is not responded to with an equivalent assessment about the object that she is referring to. Rather, the next speaker, Aretha (lines 6–8), provides a pejorative description about Angela. Talk that Angela puts on the floor is transformed into pejorative descriptions about her rather than elaborated, agreed to or disagreed with as in other assessment sequences (see chapter 6). By examining the taken-for-granted organization of sequences and their transformations, we are afforded a way of looking at how someone can be constituted as deviant.

Ritual insult provides a way in which readings of the social status of persons are mobilized in interaction to differentiate people in the group. The recipient of an initial ritual insult (Labov 1972), an insult about an attribute of the target known not to be literally true, must utilize the scene described in prior speaker's talk to produce a second description which turns the initial insult on its head and is even more outrageous. At Hanley School among fourth grade boys, ritual insult concerns fictive attributes of the target. Jokes about mamas, in paired utterances, are told in contests; "judges" are asked to evaluate the best jokes. For example "Your mama's so horny she fucks the ground like a dog" is answered with "Your mama's so fat she's got to sleep in the Grand Canyon." "Your family's so poor they only have two channels on the TV. On and Off." is responded to with "Your family's so poor you ask to use the bathroom he say 'Yeah start digging.'" All of these moves make use of the return and exchange structure we have looked at above.

In the fifth grade among the girls insult volleys are not only concerned with fictional aspects of self, but also with attributes of the target known to be true. The assessments and comparisons that the girls make among themselves (chapters 5 and 6) contrast with those that are made with regard to the outcast girl Angela. While middle class girls of the group compare themselves with reference to access to material wealth, they depict Angela as poor and unemployable in insult sequences with her.

The bout of personal/ritual insults opens in Example 7.20 when Angela answers "Who cares!" in response to Sarah, herself a working class girl, who tells the others she will need to take home uneaten lunch food. Playful joking begins when Angela depicts Sarah as working at a discount grocery store, "Pick and Save," when she grows up; in response everyone present joins in laughter. Sarah, Emi, and Brittany then counter with an action that is not playful. Rather than providing a reciprocal action, they state that they are uncertain whether or not Angela will even *be* working (lines 4–9). Melissa chimes in, arguing that Angela will have the low status job of cleaning out the gutters (lines 10–12). While Angela retorts in the frame of play that such a job would be preferable to working at Pick and Save (line 16), others counter with degraded images of her, describing her as rejected by all (line 17) occupying the status of a chimney sweep (line 18), and not even being accepted by the gutters (line 19).

Example 7.20

1	Angela:	When you grow up, you gonna be working
2		at **Pick** and Save.
3	Girls:	ah hah hah ha ⌈HAH HAH HAH HAH!
4	Sarah:	⌊*So?* Are you going to be **work**ing?
5	Emi:	You're not ⌈even **go**ing to be working!
6	Brittany:	⌊At Sears.
7	Sarah:	I know!
8	Angela:	So you gonna be-
9	Brittany:	You can't find a job **any**where.
10	Melissa:	Angela you'll be-
11		Angela you're gonna be
12		You'll be cleaning out ⌈the gutters.
13	Emi:	⌊Everywhere will eh heh
14		heh!
15	Girls:	eh heh hih hih hih!
16	Angela:	Well that's better than working at **Pick** and Save.
17	Emi:	**Ev**erywhere will reject you.
18	Kathy:	**Chim**eny Woman.
19	Melissa:	As **if** the gutters are going to accept her
		((smile voice))

Five minutes later the contest between Sarah and Angela (Example 7.21) turns more explicitly to indexes of economic status through use of the frame of "at least I don't." The phrase "at least" is a language resource that can be used to make comparisons between current speaker and hearer. The speaker makes herself the subject of an utterance initiated with "at least" which compares herself with the degraded situation of the target or hearer. These frames project the addressee (the target) as an actor in a scene in which economic poverty is depicted. The insults concern where girls purchase clothing – at Payless (line 1), the Good Will (line 4) or the Thrift Store (line 7) and whether they are supported by county assistance, Food Stamps or Welfare (lines 15–21). In line 3 with the framing "Let's not go there," Angela ties back to the prior utterance before she depicts Sarah through using an address term "Miss" coupled with a quotation by Sarah: "Miss 'I Shop at the Good Will.'"

Example 7.21

1	Sarah:	At least I don't get my shoes at Payless.
2	Girls:	Eh heh hih hih hih!
3	Angela:	**OH:** Let's not go there
4		Miss "I Shop at the Good Will!"
5	Sarah:	Huh? *((opens mouth wide, drops bottle to table))*
6	Girls:	eh heh heh!
7	Brittany:	At the Thrif(hh)t Sto(hhh)re.
8	Sarah:	At *least I* don't-
9	Angela:	At *least-* ⌈At *least I'm* not on the county.
10	Sarah:	⌊At least I don't say that-
11	Angela:	At least *I'm* not on the *coun*ty.
12	Sarah:	At least- at least-
13	Angela:	At least I'm not on the *coun*ty.
14	Sarah:	Ok*ay*::::::::⌈::
15	Angela:	⌊At *least* I don't have to-
16		At *least* I don't have to- have-
17		food tamp- food stamps to pay with my
18		money.
19	Brittany:	eh heh!
20	Angela:	At least I ⌈don't-
21	Sarah:	⌊*You* have the *Wel*fare!

The comment "*You* have the *Wel*fare!" (line 21) makes an explicit comment on Angela's degraded status of being poor. In subsequent pairs of insults an initial "at least" prefaced turn embodying a ritualized statement is returned with a statement of fact.

Example 7.22

Angela:	Well at least when I sit on the tree
	The branch doesn't break.
Kathy:	Well at least all our teeth are gonna be straight
	When we grow up because we *all* had braces.
Melissa:	Yeah. *Or* we have them now.

Angela continues on with the insult, though in another domain, explicitly commented upon by a member of the audience as "funny." She next takes up the topic of bra sizes (Example 7.23). Sarah and Angela make comparisons in a playful realm by comparing bra sizes that do not exist. Each party in turn provides a more exaggerated size, first dealing with numbers (size 85 in line 1), then letters (a "Z" in line 4), corrected to a "double Z" (line 5), and finally "size triple X" corrected to triple XZ (lines 7–9). Sarah then exits the sequence disputing Angela's ability to know her size when she (Sarah) in fact does not even wear a bra.

Example 7.23
```
 1   Angela:    At least I don't wear a size eighty five.
 2   Sarah:     ((makes quizzical look at Kathy))
 3   Melissa:   Rrrr! This is funny.
 4   Sarah:     At least I don't wear a Z.
 5              A double Z.
 6   Girls:     eh heh heh!
 7   Angela:    Well at least I don't wear a size triple (.) ⌈X.
 8   (    ):                                                 ⌊((screach))
 9   Br/J:      ah heh heh heh ha ha!
10   Angela:    You wear a triple // X Z.
11   Emi:       Angela! You guys!
12   Sarah:     How do you know what I wear.
13              I don't even wear.
14   Angela:    Yeah. You need to.
```

In her subsequent volley Angela provides a description of Sarah as someone who aspires to be a girl who wears a bra with "At least I don't have to be like- a little- wanna be- top bra person." Sarah immediately returns a commentary with "Who said I was. Who said I was."

A subsequent round of interactions (Example 7.24) finds Angela initiating a playful hit towards Sarah. Sarah gives a warning in response – "Don't touch me" – in addition to the admonishment that she will get Emi's dad, a lawyer, to sue Angela (lines 3–4). This results in a cascade of other girls mentioning that their moms are also lawyers (lines 6, 10). Angela (line 11) next attempts to counter these actions, saying she will get an even more powerful attorney, Johnny Cochran (the African American attorney who defended O. J. Simpson) to defend her. Emi provides a summary statement about the fact that others have volunteered their parents to assist Sarah's case against Angela with "Sarah will have all the lawyers she wants!" (line 12). In her next move Angela switches frame and depicts a possible scene involving Sarah with "At least I don't go out with ten year old boys."

Example 7.24
```
 1   Angela:    ((play hits Sarah))
 2   Sarah:     Don't touch me Angela.
 3              Don't even touch me.
```

```
 4                    If you do I'll get Emi's father to sue you.
 5   Brittany:        eh heh heh!
 6   Brittany:        ⌈My mom's a lawyer too.
 7   Angela:          ⌊Yeah.
 8   Kathy:           My ⌈mom-
 9   Sarah:              ⌊Yeah:. Ah:: ((waves hands between girls))
10   Kathy:           Mine's ⌈a lawyer too! eh heh heh!
11   Angela:                 ⌊And I'll get Johnny Cochran.
12   Emi:             Sarah will have all ⌈the lawyers she wants.
13   Angela:                             ⌊At least I don't-
14                    At least -at least I-
15                    ⌈At least I don't go out with ten year old boys.
16   Brittany:        ⌊Where's Johnny Cochran.
17   Sarah:           Who said I go out with ten-year old boys.
```

Toward the end of ritual insulting, the following more personal ritual insult is delivered to Angela:

Example 7.25
```
     Angela:      At least I don't wear holey underwear.
     Kathy:       At least- at least we have friends.
```

Here in Example 7.25 we see a ritualized insult returned with a personal insult. The episode ends after a game of cooties with Angela. Kathy argues that Angela herself is polluting with the following logic: "The point is Angela that you- always- are touching people, and you always say that now they have cooties. So you're telling me- yourself- that you always start out with cooties?"

Two fundamentally distinctive language games are in play simultaneously. Personal insult provides ways of framing events that are depicted in fictional present and future scenes with a negative valence. Here, while Angela is an initiator of many of the playful ritual insult sequences, she figures as the target of return comments portraying being poor as a degraded status. She is defined as not being able to find a job when she grows up, working as a cleaning woman, unable to afford braces, needing to be on Welfare, and without friends.

Stories about exclusion

In addition to being explicitly excluded from games and ridiculed in the midst of them, in the fifth grade she is the subject of stories by girls in the clique about her tag-along behavior. The following occurs as the girls are eating lunch. Beforehand, members of the clique ran into a restroom and hid until Angela came outside because they did not want her to know where they were eating. After Emi comments on Angela's attempts to follow them (lines 1–3), Janis launches into a story about a girl without friends (lines 4–8), who Janis feels should "go find another friend" (lines 9–10).

Example 7.26

1	Emi:	***Why*** do you always follow us.
2		I saw you just a few ***mo***ments ago
3		Walk into that ***oth***er yard.
4	Janis:	I was gonna tell you a story about a little girl
5		Who followed a bunch of other girls,
6		And ***did***n't make friends,
7		And was ***no*** fun at all.
8		They had already established their friends.
9		So why doesn't the girl
10		Who ***foll***owed the friend
11		Go find a***noth***er friend.
12	Angela:	Why don't ***you*** shut up!
13	Janis:	eh heh-heh -eh!
14	Angela:	Janis that's really not- ***so*** not fair.
15		*((shaking head, speaking softly))*
16	Janis:	I just said it as a ***joke***.
17	Angela:	I don't ***care***.
18	Janis:	***So:?***
19		*((Angela walks away))*
20	Melissa:	Angela, come back! *((walks off))*

Angela leaves the group and three minutes later Kimberly, a sixth grader, accompanies her as she returns to speak with Janis. Apprehensively, Janis wonders if she will have to go to the vice principal's office (line 1). When Angela and Kimberly return, Janis attempts to redefine what she said as a joke (line 3) and claims that this is her way of trying to tell people that they should try to make friends (lines 12–13). Kimberly challenges the status of Janis's prior talk as a joke (line 4) and Angela categorizes Janis's strategies as a "bad way" to deal with her (line 14).

Example 7.27

		((as girls are seated eating lunch))
1	Janis:	Oh no. Am I going to Miss Murphy's office?
		((looking towards Kimberly accompanying
		Angela back to lunch table))
2	Kimberly:	Janis ***why*** did you ***do*** that.
3	Janis:	I was just ***jok***ing with her.
4	Kimberly:	Janis I don't think it's a ***joke***.
5	Kathy:	***Jan***is it wasn't ***you***.
6	Janis:	I'm ***sorry***.
7	Emi:	°Yeah somebody's gonna have to be
8		⌈( ).
9		⌊( ). I bet it ***was Jan***is.

10	Kathy:	Yeah I know.= But I mean it's not her
11		business to ride Janis.
12	Janis:	That's actually **my** way of saying to someone,
13		"You **should** try to make friends."
14	Angela:	Janis. It was a **bad** way Janis.
15		It really was.
16	Janis:	I'm sorry. Okay? It was my mistake.
17		I'm not gonna do it again.
18		Angela sits down and Kimberly walks away
19	Kathy:	Listen. **Some**times people just **don't** get along.
20		Okay? And I **think** this is one of those times.
21		Janis and Angela just aren't getting along.
22	Janis:	You're hard to get along with Angela.

Across a range of different speech activities, including assessments, ritualized bracketing activities such as greetings and farewells, bald imperatives delivered in the midst of play, storytelling, and ritual insult, girls sanction the behavior of the tag-along girl Angela. For the most part Angela is positioned as the lowest ranked girl in the group, and even at times an invisible member of the group that she wants so much to be a part of. Though on some occasions she participates in storytelling with the girls (Example 5.5), she frequently sits on the margins of the group when they eat lunch. She more often than not jumps rope by herself at the periphery of the group rather than in the rope with the core group of girls. She is charged with making someone miss in rope, even when she is playing rope solo at some distance (Example 7.8). Though she is known as one of the best jumpers, when she suggests a co-ed contest of jump rope she is told that she cannot play (Example 1.4). When she is permitted to play hopscotch, she is told that she will be last to jump and that her name will not be inscribed in chalk on the list of players. In the midst of a game of volleyball the girls yell bald imperatives to her and treat her as a social inferior: "Did you hear what Miss Murphy told you? Don't plug your ears when somebody's telling you something!" (Example 7.15).

In fourth and fifth grade Angela was on occasion a ratified participant in storytelling. At points during fifth grade she played on a volleyball team with the clique members. She was asked to play soccer when the girls are told that they need a quorum in order to occupy the field without the boys. She even participated in a gossip session with Sarah and Aretha about Janis when they are excluded from playing baseball, because the team leader selected only Janis and her friends Emi and Melissa to be on the team (chapter 6). Her slightly greater involvement in the fifth grade led to more stigmatizing behavior by the clique. In the fifth grade she was made to confess her role as a "tag-along," was the recipient of personal insults in what she constructed as a playful genre, with ritual insults, was the target of stories that cast her as an outsider, and as the source of cooties. For the most part Angela remained a peripheral figure of the girls' group throughout fourth, fifth, and sixth grade.

Directness and Social Positioning in Girls' Groups

Many theories of politeness have proposed that white middle class females are more polite than other social groups.[69] Representations of working class people, by way of contrast, have tended "to stress the directness and loudness of their language" (Mills 2003:149). As the examples in this chapter make abundantly clear, however, among middle class girls when the target is someone deemed deserving of ridicule, girls interact in ways that convey insult quite openly.

Often I encountered among the middle class girls an attitude of entitlement to being confrontational. This was particularly evident during recess in sixth grade, when an aide read a policy of Zero Tolerance for aggressive behavior at lunch. Despite the seriousness of the message in the speech, the response of Kathy (lines 16–17 of Example 7.28 below) was that she had been mouthing off her entire life and she was not going to stop doing so; furthermore her mother condoned the behavior because she considered it was in her nature (lines 14–15):

Example 7.28

		((on the playground))
1	Aide:	Can I have your attention.
2		Teachers and administrators are really concerned
3		about the frequency of physical contact, wrestling,
4		play fighting, joking around.
5		So if you continue to do this you're going to be cited.
6		And also, there's a lack of respect.
7		And if teachers and administrators approach you
8		about something, display your best manners.
9		Speak in your most polite language.
10	Janis:	They're talking about Sean.
11	Aide:	Your conduct. Is a reflection on yourself and your family.
12		It's in your interests to behave in your most polite fashion.
13	Kathy:	I don't really care.
14		My mom says "This is how you are."
15		So I don't really care.
16		I've been mouthing off my entire life
17		and she can't really control it.

Across both working class and middle class groups I have observed for the past 35 years, girls who attempted to present themselves as superior to others are subject to extensive gossip. Members of the Los Angeles clique sanctioned Emi and Janis when they put on airs or acted as if they were better than other girls. In the working class Philadelphia neighborhood I studied, exclusion provided a way of sanctioning girls who "think they cute" (better than others) or talk about others in their absence.[70] Exclusion is part of a political process. On other occasions, however, exclusion may occur with minimal provocation. Kim Scott (2002:193) observing relations between white middle class girls and poor and working class African American girls found that the "out" girls were frequently girls of color who had not committed any noticeable offense. At Hanley School group girls in the in-clique devoted considerable attention to positioning themselves above others. They put in their place girls who through their talk displayed their lack of access to experience or knowledge of the symbols of upper middle class culture, and in particular with respect to Angela, a social misfit, who tagged along with the group.

Recently there has been considerable attention in the popular media about features of girls' social aggression or bullying. Psychologists debate the nature of girls' aggressive behavior, in particular what forms of behavior are associated with it, and how to classify it. With some exceptions[71] psychologists have tended to associate direct or overt aggression with boys, while girls have been associated with indirect, relational, and social forms of aggression, for example harming others through purposeful manipulation and damage of their peer relationships.[72] This chapter has demonstrated multiple ways in which girls practice forms of exclusion from games and activities.

The investigation of actual sequences of interaction in this chapter has shown that episodes of social aggression include forms of nonvocal behavior,[73] as well as direct name calling, insults, verbal abuses, pejorative evaluations (direct forms often associated primarily with males). My earlier work among working class African American girls[74] showed that girls use indirect language practices to reconfigure alliances though storytelling behind someone's back, while accusation statements in a he-said-she-said confrontation may be presented directly to someone's face. Videotaped interaction of the girls' clique group at Hanley School makes visible the fact that nonvocal collusive displays (eyeball rolls, pointing done with moves of the head, knowing glances, etc.) may accompany utterances that are intendedly direct.[75] The examples presented in this chapter support the notion that direct and indirect forms of aggression among girls are by no means mutually exclusive.[76]

8

Conclusion

Recess marks an important time in the day, as this is one of the only opportunities when Hanley children can play with agemates, unless their parents chauffer them to special play dates after school. Since the children who attend Hanley School are scattered in all parts of megalopolis Los Angeles, recess provides an opportunity for children to elaborate forms of social organization of their own making, apart from adult supervision. Psychologists[1] consider recess, and play in particular, critical for the development of social skills. Pellegrini and Bohn (2005:16) argue that "Mastering the skills important for membership in a peer group should provide a basis for the successful interactions with peers and teachers that are necessary for adjustment to school." The finding that children's social competence develops when they interact with peers is important given the recent trends in both the United States[2] and the United Kingdom[3] toward limiting recess time in schools. In this book I have demonstrated how children's agency was indeed demonstrated through the ability to orchestrate rule-governed play in hopscotch, cross-sex contests in volleyball, and jump rope, and to enact theatrical roles in playing house. At the same time, recess provides opportunities for children to articulate difference in lines of gender,[4] ethnicity,[5] race,[6] intersections of race and gender,[7] as well as social class, as discussed in this book.

At Hanley School the actions of fifth grade girls, calling the boys' colonizing of the playground into question, resulted in a massive change in the structuring of team sports that occupied large areas of the playground during sixth grade. Soccer and football were reorganized on a rotational basis, so that anyone, female or male, who wanted to participate could sign up to play. Sixth grade also ushered in a new social justice program. Teachers attempted to introduce notions of respect for diversity throughout the curriculum. During classes students talked openly about prejudicial practices towards people of various ethnicities (including Japanese American internment in Manzanar), differences in body sizes and shapes of similar-age children, gender discrimination in sports. There were exercises that made children confront what it felt like to be a member of an excluded group (blue-eyed vs. brown eyed).

In sixth grade the social structure of the Hanley clique had changed very little. Emi, one of the girls who frequently took on the role of organizer of girls' games, and, with Janis, was considered one of the ringleaders of the girls' clique[8] transferred to another school (to prepare herself for a highly ranked middle school). This left Janis in the position of principal spokesperson for the girls in various public disputes. One early October day the sixth graders gathered for a game of tetherball. In this game, the first person to make a rope with a ball on the end of it circle the pole the rope is attached to with no rope hanging, wins the game. Players must hit the ball, rather than directing it with one's hands.

A dispute developed because one of the boys (Marcus) who had clearly lost the game (because his opponent's ball tethered first) would not move off the court or admit defeat. When the Vice Principal came to ask what the argument was about, Janis took on the role of spokesperson for the group. She proposed the rules that should be in play, which others, including the Vice Principal, agreed to. As the game ensued, Angela was equally as vocal as the other players in calling Marcus on his violation of the game rules (line 7 in Example 8.1). She positioned herself as one of the principal players commenting on Marcus's inappropriate behavior (lines 4, 7–9), his refusal to leave when, from Angela's perspective, his turn was over.

Example 8.1

((Marcus had touched the ball multiple times before the ball tethered))

1   Aretha: MARCUS GET OUT OF THE **WAY!**
2   ((bends at waist towards Marcus))
3   Marcus: ((Marcus talks with other player; stays in court))
4   Angela: OK! OK! MARCUS YOU'RE **OUT!**
5   Tray: Take it over. Take it over.
6   Marcus: ((refuses to get off the court))
7   Angela: No Marcus you are **out!** You can't keep playin.
8   Marcus- **No! No!**
9   You just wanna- ((pushes him with left hand))
10 Marcus: Don't touch me Angela! **Damn!** ((walks away))

When Aretha yelled out her imperatives to Marcus, she thrust the upper part of her body towards Marcus (line 2), intensifying the action. Angela, however, selected an alternative nonvocal accompaniment to her imperative. When Marcus insisted on staying next to the tetherball pole instead of allowing another player to step up, Angela pushed Marcus with her hand (line 9). Immediately this led to a corrective action – "Don't touch me Angela! **Damn!**" from Marcus (line 10). Though Marcus was clearly the party whose actions were offensive, the way in which Marcus chose to respond to Angela constructed her, rather than Marcus, as the accused, and, moreover, as someone who was polluting.

When it was Angela's turn to play tether, Janis whispered secrets in the ears of Angela's opponent, Melissa. She then said to both Sarah and Aretha, on the sidelines, "I want Angela to win so that I can kick her ass." Sarah subsequently gave a high five sign to Janis and told her, "You go girl!" while Angela was looking on.

As the game progressed, both Janis with her statement "Come on you guys. Let's play this game fair and square" and Aretha's "Let the best win" made claims that they wanted the game to be fair. However, during a contest between Angela and Melissa, when Melissa took her turn, rather than hitting the ball and waiting for it to wind as far as it might, she instead grabbed the ball in her hand and with it slowly guided the rope around the pole (line 1 of Example 8.2). The kids present yelled (lines 5, 7, 14), proclaiming that Melissa had won the game, and ignored Angela's protests (lines 4, 6, 11).

Example 8.2

1	Melissa:	*((Melissa slowly wraps ball around pole))*
2	Janis:	**She** won.
3	Sarah:	Tether.
4	Angela:	No. You can't **do** that.
5	Alan:	She won! She **beat** you!
6	Angela:	She can't do that. That's not **fair**.
7	Sarah:	She **beat** you! She **won**!
8	Janis:	No. No. No.
9	Sarah:	*((points up))* It's **hooked**. It's **hooked**.
10	Janis:	*((Janis walks out to Melissa and high fives her))*
11	Angela:	You can't **do** that.
12	Melissa:	*((to Angela))* ( ).
13	Angela:	Yeah, but you had it like **this**. You **touched** the rope.
14	Alan:	*((runs onto court))* You lost.
15	Janis:	*((tries to take ball, but Angela won't let her))*
16		Angela, you lost.
17		*((takes ball))*
18	Tray:	Angela, just get in the line.
19	Angela:	*((remains standing for a few seconds and then gets in line.))*

The actions which children use with Angela repetitively cast her as someone occupying a degraded status; they whispered about her in her presence and denied her rightful claim as the winner. Despite these multiple forms of abuse, however, Angela did not withdraw from interaction with the group members; she stood her ground and displayed her ability to endure the insulting comments delivered to her.

Throughout the game Angela, for her part, repetitively attempted to show solidarity toward various players, as in her cheers, "Go Melissa! Go Melissa!" In response, however, the girls in the clique treated Angela in a demeaning way. As Angela was standing in line cheering for Melissa, she started dancing in rhythm with the chanted cheer. Janis then told the girls "Angela's shaking her butt in my face!" Angela quickly denied this with "**No** I'm not" as she playfully punched Janis and laughed. The following then occurred:

Example 8.3

>   *((Angela is dancing in place apart from other girls))*
> Janis: *((to Angela))* You guys.
>   Angela's shaking her butt in my face.
> Angela: *No* I'm not.
> Janis: *((dancing))* Angela's going-
> Melissa: Be *equ*itable Angela.
> Angela: What a***bout*** equity and integrity.
>   Remember. You can always ask me.

By stating "What a***bout*** equity and integrity" Angela demonstrated her competence in the use of phrases taught by the school psychologist in the school's social justice curriculum. Repetitively Angela stood up for her rights, and showed her ability to endure the multiple derisive actions hurled towards her, while speaking out for her rights. Her work in school did improve steadily during the time she was in fifth grade. Her teacher, Ms. Harper, commented that in fifth grade she was the only student who knew her multiplication tables by heart. Ms. Harper also told me that by fifth grade Angela had ceased using the shuffling motions she had used in the fourth grade to walk around the playground.

Despite these positive changes in Angela's life from fourth to fifth grade, on multiple occasions members of the girls' clique would play tricks on Angela. For example, they would not leave any space at the lunch table for her to eat, forcing her to eat alone. Perhaps she persisted in playing with the clique because it was considered to be the group with the highest status on the playground. Scott (2002) discusses an exclusive first grade clique at an Eastern US middle class school in which white girls were leaders of a club, the "in" group to be associated with. White girls created the rules of the game of Monster Chase; African American girls gained social acceptance by publicly (though not backstage) following the club's rules.[9] Angela gained some status by playing with the girls in the popular clique, though she endured much abusive talk. Though Angela maintained a strong friendship with Elena, a Latina girl who was similar in body build to Angela, she frequently ate alone, and had no alternative group to seek refuge in. In sixth grade she turned from playing exclusively with sixth grade girls to playing more with fourth grade girls, and was successful in orchestrating games of handball with them, and teaching them various moves.

Contributions to Studies of Children's Peer Socialization

This study has examined the language practices through which children, in social groups apart from adults, build the meaningful events of their lives. Traditional views in psychological anthropology[10] assume that socialization is unidirectional; norms and values are transmitted to the child through parents. In this view childhood consists "primarily as a passage towards the skills and accomplishment and distortions of adults."[11] While families do provide important contexts for socialization (for example, for the learning of class values), such views give little credit to the child's ability to shape interaction apart from adults.[12] Once we understand that the everyday interactions of the child express children's agency, documenting the social character of these interactions becomes an important task.[13]

In this book I have considered how children interact with other children to negotiate the form their social order takes by providing transcripts of children's conflict interactions. Developmental psychologists consider forms of interaction during conflict situations "an essential impetus to change, adaptation, and development."[14] Piaget (1965:397) states that argument among peers permits the development of "mutual understanding;" through processes of comparison, contrast, and confrontation, individuals must learn "to 'place' themselves in reciprocal relationship with each other without letting the laws of perspective . . . destroy their individual points of view." Psychologists propose that communication between parents and children tends to be more unilateral than interaction among peers.[15] While adults may well constitute the source of the overall framework of rules, it is through a process which has been called "cooperation," "mutual engagement,"[16] or "consensual validation"[17] that children learn to *understand* important rules of their society through interaction with their peers. Piaget's work on morality of cooperation provided a framework for our understanding of late childhood as a time of negotiated reality in which children begin to turn from adult-based social rules to a social code built out of negotiation with peers.[18]

Understanding this negotiation of moral reality and children's social rules requires investigations of language in use.[19] The methodology of conversation analysis combined with ethnography provides a powerful methodology for investigating how children – in peer groups as well as families – become competent social actors by learning to use language appropriately within these settings.[20]

Transcripts of videotaped interaction provide ways of documenting the sequential organization of endogenous events in people's lives. Rather than relying on interview data alone to understand how children view their notions of culture and social identity,[21] we have access through videotape to the ways that children *with other children* build their phenomenal world and events that matter for them. We can document quite precisely both the linguistic resources (including grammatical structure) and the embodied practices through which stance and affect are displayed, positions are negotiated, and social identities are co-constructed. Combining close analysis of moment-to-moment interaction with ethnographic research allows us to understand the dynamics of social groups, and the ways that language can be deployed to build more enduring social identities (such as the marginal status of a child), or identities that shift with changing contexts (considering age, level of expertise, present alliances, gender group composition, etc.). We can ground our analysis of how identities of various sorts (not simply those specifically oriented to by participants as gendered)[22] are constructed in the details of the sequential organization of conversation.

While I have discussed these interactive practices by focusing on girls' groups, I am not claiming that they are unique to girls; ethnographic research among sixth graders in a Los Angeles middle school conducted by Cadigan (2003) has found practices of social exclusion in boys' and well as girls' groups. Nishina et al. (2005:37), in a study based on self reports of victimization and school functioning, found no sex or ethnic group differences in the models they proposed: "the indirect effect of perceived peer harassment on school functioning through psychosocial problems and physical symptoms was similar for African American, Latino, European American and Asian students" (Nishina et al. 2005:46). Nishina and Juvonen (in press) report that boys and girls were equally distressed regardless of the type of victimization they experienced.

By making explicit the structure of actions such as disagreement, insult, comparisons, stories, or assessments, I have rendered visible to others specific practices through which social dimensions, such as hierarchy, opposition, alliances, friendship, oppression, and so on, within any group might be constructed. Others can utilize these materials to make cross-gender and cross-cultural comparisons. The value of an approach combining ethnography with conversation analysis is that we have access to the lived experiences of children as they navigate multiple aspects of their world.

Beyond Dualisms in Studying Girls' Culture and Social Organization

Exploring how girls negotiate the rules of games, as in chapter 2, we find that across an array of different social groups, girls are extraordinarily adept and articulate in producing moves that explicate a sense of justice. Girls display intense engrossment in formulating logical proofs and demonstrations for their positions and exhibit determination in the pursuit of their positions. Such a portrait of girls' abilities contradicts stereotypes that have dominated studies of female moral development.

The work of Carol Gilligan has perpetuated dualistic ways of thinking about girls' and boys' development. Gilligan proposed that while males become autonomous, individuated beings, oriented to rules of abstract reasoning and principles of justice through their game playing, females premise their moral decision making on context-specific principles based on social relationships. While Gilligan sought to refute abstract, universalist schemes for moral development which privilege males, her work is itself open to criticism for perpetuating an ahistorical and essentialist notion of females (Scott 1988). As argued by Somers and Gibson (1994:55), Gilligan's notion of identity allows "no room to accommodate changing power relations or history itself as they are constituted and reconstituted over time." Contextual variation is absent as well in the Gilligan model.[23]

The ability of girls to pursue issues of fairness was explored in chapter 3. The fifth grade girls' rebellion against the boys' colonization of playground led to a revamping of the way in which the soccer field was utilized, and initiated a new rotational pattern which provided equal access to the playing field for both genders. During the next school year a new "Zero Tolerance" or "Safe School" policy was implemented at the school, to deter forms of discrimination or exclusion (primarily those based on gender, disability, or ethnicity). The girls' actions on the soccer field demonstrated their abilities to negotiate their social interactions; such forms of negotiation have been argued to provide a strong expression of children's sociality.[24]

Most models of female interaction, based primarily on white middle class participants, have proposed that male speakers are socialized into a competitive style of discourse, while women are socialized into a more cooperative style of speech.[25] Females are said to learn to value relational closeness, to want to "create and maintain good social relationships" (Coates 1998:250), and avoid acts that threaten the face of others. Coates (1998:245), for example, argues that women's cooperative style is displayed through using mitigated rather than bald forms to protect the face of the addressee, negotiating sensitive topics, and encouraging the participation of others through showing support. In her later work, when analyzing "backstage" behavior of women, Coates (2000:257) finds women can relax the form of self-presentation they are obliged to uphold in public, and display "bad behaviour." Backstage, females discuss taboo feelings or reveal instances of behaving badly. In this setting, however, women still adhere to community norms of femininity, and display ambivalence towards such behavior, considering it "alternative, subversive aspects of their identities."

Most research takes for granted the notion that the upholding of particular norms of politeness is important for performing female identity. Folklorist Susan Kalčik (1975:5), discussing members of a women's consciousness-raising rap group, argues that "women almost never gossiped about members who were not there, avoided direct criticism of each other, and tried to keep others from criticizing themselves." She states that women's speech and interaction is based on the "underlying aesthetic" or "organizing principle" of harmony" (Kalcik 1975:6). Similarly sociologists such as Adler et al. (1992), in their fieldwork study among middle class elementary school children, argue that girls are more concerned with intimacy and cooperation than with openly competing against others.[26]

In this book by exploring how relations of power are built interactively in female groups I call into question the generalizability of accounts of female same-sex talk that focus exclusively on "prosocial,"[27] cooperative,[28] or polite[29] interactive practices.[30] Examining how girls in a clique make comparisons (chapter 6) or orchestrate participation in storytelling or gossip (chapter 5), we find girls delineating social difference through the ways that they respond to their interlocutors or talk about absent parties. When we look at how girls organize activities such as jump rope (chapter 4) or dramatic play (chapter 3), we find that girls use directives to construct hierarchically organized and differentiated social relations in both same-sex and in cross-sex interaction. In cross-sex interaction where adults do not intervene on behalf of the boys, control may be contingent upon expertise as much as gender.

The finding that level of expertise, rather than gender per se, influences relations of power in the midst of some games (jump rope, for example) can be of value in entertaining possible reform measures resulting from my observations of interaction on the playground. We need to develop more playground activities in which girls' games – such as the highly competitive sport of Double Dutch,[31] which is featured in international athletic competitions and in 2004 became a new craze in San Francisco (Ahlin 2004) – are promoted. Such games increase opportunities for girls to interact in competitive ways that permit them to develop their abilities as powerful actors in cross-sex interaction (as seen in chapter 4). At the same time we need to provide equal opportunities for girls' involvement in team sports that they enjoy – games such as softball, volleyball, and soccer – in both same- and cross-sex configurations of play. More attention to how boys dominate the playing field and "play rough" needs to be addressed explicitly in classrooms and on playgrounds, with teachers, students, coaches, and playground aides, so that girls will more eagerly join in playing team sports.

Relative rank among the girls I have studied is negotiated in a host of activities – not only through positions one takes up in the midst of conflict during games, but also in sequences of comparisons when girls are assessing other girls or their friends' alignments to elements of popular culture (chapter 6) and events in storytelling (chapter 5). Psychologists have argued that girls develop interdependent self-construals in which they "define themselves on the basis of relationships, affiliations with groups, and maintaining harmony" (Underwood 2003:8). Gilligan (2003) argues that women's morality is based on connectedness and interdependence with others. Because girls value relationships so intensely, when they want to harm another they do so by damaging friendships and social standing.[32] While I take issue with the idea that maintaining harmony in their social relations operates as the major concern in girls' interactions, the girls at Hanley School, as well as the girls I studied on Maple Street in Philadelphia in the 1970s, and in downtown Los Angeles in the 1990s, were intensely concerned with defining who was included and excluded in the social group of the moment. All of these groups made use of evaluative commentary either to sanction someone who violated norms of the group or to position someone as deviant.

Indexing Social Class

Feminist scholars have argued that focusing exclusively on gender, without examining other facets of identity and difference, such as social class, oversimplifies our views of the important intersection of aspects of self that affect human experience.[33] Ortner (1991:186), in her plea for an anthropological examination of social class, has argued that anthropologists tend to "ethnicize" groups under study and "to treat them as if they were in effect separate tribes." bell hooks (2000:5) notes that historically racial solidarity has "been used to obscure class." She argues (hooks 2000:6),[34] "Both Whites and Blacks have been told that race supersedes issues of class. This is partially due to the fact that issues of class are not as clear-cut as the binary categories of white and black or male and female." hooks (2000:156) further notes that "Most American citizens do not acknowledge the reality of class difference, of class exploitation, and they continue to believe that this is a classless society."

Marxist social scientists have argued that schools contribute to the reproduction of class divisions through the ways they socialize future workers at various levels of the capitalist labor process; school curriculum, relations of authority, and classroom routines are all organized to keep working class children in their place.[35] In his ground-breaking book *Learning to Labor* Paul Willis (1981) provides an ethnographic examination of the processes through which "working class kids get working class jobs." Willis examines how boys' interaction with other boys reproduces working class values through resistance to school knowledge, opposition to authority, and maintaining an antagonistic relation to the dominant culture.

The middle and upper middle class children whose interactions are discussed in this book differ radically from working class children in Willis's studies of working class children, in that children at Hanley School embrace the academic culture of the school as well as values of consumerism of the dominant culture, heavily influenced by Hollywood values. Through a description of language practices entailed in activities such as assessments, stories, insults, and exclusionary practices, as well as practices involved in indexing social status, I have attempted to show how in moment-to-moment interaction middle class girls reproduce middle class values.

Ironically while the school with its progressive ideals and multi-class, multi-ethnic student population was envisioned as an institution where children of diverse social classes could meet to foster mutual understanding, it provides a site where middle and upper middle class children teach one another how to put children of the working class in their place.[36] The implicit social justice curriculum of the school deals openly with difference in terms of physical appearance, disabilities, race, and ethnicity. Social class is seldom acknowledged as a feature of difference and remains a source of "hidden injuries."[37] Forms of "unequal childhoods,"[38] have real consequences for those who do not have access to the social capital and differential advantages which privilege affords.

At Hanley, a progressive school with highly educated, upper middle class moms and dads, parents frequently are guest speakers (i.e., in a science lesson on the brain, a parent who was a brain specialist came to class) and donate gifts. One parent, for example, donated small manual animation booklets, commonly referred to as "flipbooks", while another presented the class with a color laser printer. Marquez (2004) documented how teachers treat the children of such donors in special ways. During show-and-tell exchanges, for example, children of the donors get selected in show-and-tell sessions to talk about products (such as laser pictures) that emanate from the objects their parents donate. When the donors visit the school and are publicly thanked for their gifts, the child who gets singled out to present the thank-you note on behalf of the class is usually the child of the donor. Such practices elevate the status of the children of donors, contribute to the construction of differences along class lines, and validate the status of children of the wealthy.

Differences among children at Hanley were most overtly articulated in terms of social class among preadolescent children.[39] Johnson (2004), however, observed four-year-olds at Hanley expressing difference in terms of ethnicity as well as social class.[40] This is in line with what Scott (2002, 2003) has observed in her investigations of interactions among middle class white and working class black first grade girls, where both race and social class constitute intersecting forces affecting group dynamics.[41]

Bullying as Social Practice

Frequently the playground is romanticized and overlooked as a place where social relationships based on power and status are played out.[42] Since the April 1999 Columbine High School massacre, however, bullying has become an important concern in contemporary society. Bullying is experienced by children throughout the world – in the United States, Canada, Japan, Australia, New Zealand, Germany, Belgium, Italy, Spain, Portugal, France, Switzerland, England, Ireland, and Finland (Sanders 2004:2). It constitutes the most predominant form of aggression in US schools.[43] A recent report of the *Journal of the American Medical Association*[44] states that in a survey using self-report data of 15,686 sixth through tenth graders in public and private schools throughout the United States, one-third of US schoolchildren report they had bullied other children or had been bullied.[45] Other survey data estimate that between 40 and 80 percent of all US school age children have been targets of peer harassment.[46] Among 558 middle school students surveyed in 1995 (in a major Midwestern metropolis with diverse socioeconomic groups), only 19 percent said that they had not been involved in bullying within a 30-day period.[47] Fears about bullying became so intense in 2005 that a public middle school in Culver City in Los Angeles County implemented a "no contact" rule that prohibits students not only from hitting, shoving, or pushing classmates, but also from holding hands, hugging or kissing on campus.[48]

Recently there has been considerable attention in the popular media to features of girls' social aggression. Psychologists debate the nature of girls' bullying and aggressive behavior, in particular what forms of behavior are associated with it, and how to classify it. With some exceptions[49] psychologists have tended to associate direct or overt aggression with boys, while girls have been associated with indirect, relational, and social forms, for example harming others through purposeful manipulation and damage of their peer relationships.[50] Nishina et al. (2005), however, report no sex or ethnic group differences in perceptions of peer victimization, psychosocial adjustment or physical symptoms. In a study of peer victimization in central Italy, Tomada and Schneider (1997) report that relational aggression is far more common among boys than girls.

The investigation of actual sequences of interaction in this book has shown that episodes of social aggression include both nonvocal behavior[51] as well as direct name calling, insults, verbal abuses, pejorative evaluations, and exclusion from games and activities. I find that direct and indirect forms are not mutually exclusive.[52] My earlier work among working class African American girls[53] showed that girls use indirect language practices to reconfigure alliances though storytelling behind someone's back, while accusation statements in a he-said-she-said confrontation may be presented directly to someone's face. Videotaped interaction of the popular girls' clique at Hanley School makes visible the fact that nonvocal collusive displays may accompany utterances that are intendedly quite direct.[54]

I have examined an array of oppositional sequences and social processes through which forms of relational aggression occur as girls delineate the boundaries of their group. Rather than relying on reports *about* experience, I have provided transcripts of the naturally occurring talk through which girls make comparisons with reference to features of difference.[55] I have also shown how through nonvocal collusive looks and byplay, girls sanction those within their friendship group who they feel put themselves above others. This is accomplished by countering attempts at one-upmanship through squelching storylines, issuing taunts from a distance, telling stories in someone's absence about plans of future exclusion, and prohibiting someone from playing games with the group.

In interaction with a "tag-along," girls construct degradation rituals in response to behavior they cast as socially inappropriate. In Angela's case, such acts included eating without a utensil and sitting on the lunch table. Often, however, victimization was unprovoked by Angela's own actions. Rather than talking about a girl obliquely, as occurred with members of their friendship group they wished to sanction, clique members instead quite openly humiliated the social outcast to her face; they issued imperatives and insulted her through deprecating reference to her social and economic situation and status as someone who lacked friends, in personal insults and stories. Acts of aggression among girls are thus built through verbal means that are both direct as well as indirect.

Towards New Methodologies for Studying Moral Behavior

Studying naturally occurring talk in context provides new ways of investigating moral behavior. Believing that "everyday moral discourse" has the power to "represent and transmit moral beliefs" (Shweder and Much

1987:198) psychologists[56] have argued that we should shift the focus from hypothetical explanations by individuals and instead study ongoing practical deliberation in naturally occurring interaction.[57] To date, however, most studies of moral development in psychology, psychological anthropology, and throughout the social sciences, have relied almost exclusively on interviews and questionnaires, conducted in laboratory settings.

Psychologists have stated that, "the more we structure a setting for the purposes of systematic observation, the more we risk losing the richness, complexity and spontaneity of natural children's interactions."[58] Yet psychologists are reluctant to move outside the laboratory or to use anything other than a controlled, experimental approach because ethnographic research with children is deemed too time consuming or unscientific. As Damon (1983:61) argues, "We cannot send researchers out all day looking for appropriate incidents; and even if we could, it would be impossible to analyze incidents in a comparable manner from a variety of real-life settings."

All too often the methodology used to study aggressive behavior, as in studies of gender-appropriate behavior and friendship,[59] assumes a traditional, individualistic rather than a socio-cultural or interpretive model of human development.[60] This is often true even among psychologists working within a constructivist paradigm who assume a more social view of the child. Many psychologists examining social aggression formulate the locus of behavior in the individual. In that this is so, the study of forms of social exclusion, like investigations of friendship,[61] often proceeds by looking at individual responses to questionnaires and clinical interviews about victimization.

In studies of peer victimization psychologists make use of peer evaluation techniques, self-reports, or combinations of both self and peer nomination reports. Underwood (2003:9) has argued that in order to adequately understand social aggression among girls, observational as well as questionnaire methods need to be used. Pellegrini (1998:171) has explicitly called for studies of peer victimization using "direct observation methods" involving videotaping, noting that "questionnaires limit our understanding events . . . to what respondents choose to tell us." Frequently, however, "the focus is on whether, how often, and in what form the individual behaved aggressively or not" and the context of aggression is largely ignored (Shantz and Hobart 1989). Rarely have psychologists (even those conducting naturalistic studies of children) investigated the actual discourse used during aggressive interactions.[62] Amazingly, with the exception of the work of Juvonen and her colleagues,[63] the role of the peer group[64] in peer victimization is seldom the object of study.

A focus on the individual and reliance on experiments has characterized anthropological studies of children's acquisition of racist attitudes as well because it is believed that "everyday behavior and speech provide little purchase on children's beliefs about race and ethnicity" (Hirschfeld 1996:198). In most studies of social exclusion and racial attitudes, as in studies of social class as a discursive practice, the actual social processes through which exclusion or the construction of social difference occurs are left unexplored.

An important alternative approach would view the activity of victimization as a social rather than an individual process, and locate values within interactive practice, adopting a Vygotskyian (1978) perspective. In this book by examining the actual exchanges that constitute bullying or exclusion, I have examined the interactive processes through which girls organize their social relations and delineate asymmetrical relations of power. Just such types of descriptions have been advocated by social psychologists; Jaana Juvonen and Sandra Graham (2004:231) in their work on "Research-Based Interventions on Bullying" state that children need concrete examples of bullying behavior rather than abstract definitions: "the many faces or forms of bullying (including ever-increasing cyber bullying)[65] need to be recognized and incorporated in school policies and for prevention and intervention purposes."[66] While it is easy to recognize physical aggression, forms of covert and indirect aggression are much less discernable, and often missed by teachers, aides, or other adults at the school.[67] Before bullying prevention projects can be effective adults need to recognize that bullying and aggression are not part of a "character forming experience" (Smith and Brain 2000), but rather a serious problem involving the individual rights of children.

Throughout the anthropological literature, female aggression is often dismissed as minimal and insignificant, behavior not worth theorizing (Burbank 1994a). Adults in the school situation acknowledge that males colonize the playing field and are fully aware that males practice aggressive behavior in the midst of games; however, they are oblivious to (or treat as inconsequential) girls' practices of exclusion or social aggression (which constitute 70 percent of the cases of female harassment (Crick et al. 2001).

Feminist primatologist Sarah Hrdy (1981) notes that social scientists have collected little information on the competitive features of feminine personalities. Jane Flax (1990) has argued that we need to avoid seeing women as totally innocent, acted upon beings; such a perspective prevents us from seeing the areas of life in which women have had an effect, are not totally determined by the will of the other, and the ways in which some women have and do exert power over others. In her recent book *Woman's Inhumanity to Woman* Phyllis Chesler (2001:7) expresses the hope that by acknowledging the "shadow side of female-female relationships" that "women can begin to transform envy into compassion, betrayal into cooperation." Rachel Simmons (2002:262) feels that by acknowledging the hidden culture of aggression, and by making girls aware that no friendships can survive without conflict, girls will be better prepared to deal with "girl bullying" "as a painful, but not earth-shattering event." Books such as Rachel Simmons' *Odd Girl Speaks Out: Girls Write about Bullies, Cliques, Popularity, and Jealousy* (2004) have allowed girls to describe experiences they have had being bullied or bullying other girls.

Carol Tavris (2002) critiques solutions to girl bullying based on individual psychology, and urges us to consider institutional changes. She states that while we cannot force someone to be accepted by unwelcoming peers, we can influence the kind of peer groups children belong to and work for programs that promote cooperation rather than competition among groups

(Tavris 2002:9). *Girl Wars: Twelve Strategies that Will End Female Bullying* (Dellasega and Nixon 2003) offers practical ideas about how to deal with hurtful practices of bullying and create environments where there is greater awareness of how to prevent it, how to intervene when it happens and how to foster caring environments that mitigate against it occurring. Brown et al. (2005:392) suggest educating elementary school and middle school teachers and principals, and recognizing the family, peer, school and societal influences that impact bullying. As they comment (2005:392), "This will truly take a coordinated effort among researchers, school professionals, parents, and communities with special emphasis on the perceptions of students."

Juvonen (2001) suggests that an effective anti-bullying approach consists of three interrelated components: school policy, instruction of all students about the meaning of the policy, and staff mediation that reinforces both school policy and instruction. The school must clearly delineate an explicit code of conduct, an anti-bullying and anti-harassment policy that specifies behaviors that are not to be tolerated. Students need to know how to deal with everyday disputes, and having clear guidelines will permit students to intervene. Bystanders too need to become aware that they are part of the problem. Awareness training should be extended beyond the classroom onto the schoolyard.

Effective bullying prevention and intervention programs will require an understanding of "the social ecology that establishes and maintains bullying and victimization behaviors" (Swearer and Espelage 2004:1). The school, peer group, family, community and culture all impact the encouragement or inhibition of bullying. Ideally data on bullying should be collected across settings of the home, school, community, and lab by multiple informants (observers, children, peers, parents, teachers), using multiple methods (home observations, lab tasks, classroom, playground, questionnaires, interviews) (Swearer and Espelage 2004:4). In his "call for research" on new methodologies for the study of peer victimization, Pellegrini (1998:166) has argued that "the time has come in our study of bully-victims relations to complement self report and laboratory methods with direct and indirect observational methods of youngsters functioning in the natural habitats in which these problems occur." In addition to accounts of girls' alternative aggressions obtained through interviews (i.e., Simmons 2002) and narratives (Simmons 2002; Dellasega and Nixon 2003), we need careful examination of the actual lived moments and practices that make up the life world of a particular group, so we can investigate how morality is lodged within the actions, and stances that children take up in interaction with their peers. Issues of social justice involve "the hidden injuries of class" as well as gender, ethnicity, race, and disability. Information about the specific behaviors and peer group dynamics of children's groups will not only provide us with a better picture of children's worlds, but also help guide policy and intervention strategies, including awareness training about children's indexing of social class status as a form of social aggression.

Often conversation analysis and critical discourse analysis are viewed as incompatible paradigms.[68] In this book I have attempted to show how a

focus on talk-in-interaction, explicating issues of importance to the participants themselves, rather than imposed by an analyst, need not be viewed as
incompatible with some traditional concerns in the social sciences. Specifically, I have examined conflict, the manifestation of power and inequality
in social relationships, and the articulation of difference based on features
of gender or social class, as children interact with one another. We have
looked at how asymmetrical gender relations are orchestrated not only in
cross-sex interaction, wherein relations of power are typically discussed with
respect to patriarchy, but also within same-sex all female interaction. In
examining actual examples of interaction on the playground I have avoided
a top-down or politically driven analysis of how institutional or patriarchal
power operates. While males could call upon a male aide ally (representing
the institution of the school) in their attempts to dominate the soccer field,
girls exhibited the power to negotiate their rightful position on the soccer
field and eventually restructure an implicitly sexist policy.

   With respect to examining the construction of culture in the midst of
talk,[69] I have analyzed the categorizations that children use to address one
another (for example, the term "tag-along") and the assessment adjectives
they use to categorize members of their playgroup and their activities. By
examining the structure and sequencing of complaints children lodge against
others in gossip sessions, we are privy to the ways in which children with
other children articulate their notions of culturally appropriate ways of
acting and being in the world; we can also look at the practices they utilize
to make one another accountable for their actions. By conducting long-
term fieldwork one has access to the lived experiences of participants occurring over time across a range of circumstances. Through sequential analysis of
the practices through which members of social groups produce their social
order we can merge concerns for methodological rigor, needed for producing
grounded observations about the social life of children, with concerns for
how relations of power are articulated in moment-to-moment interaction.

Appendix A

Transcription Symbols

From Marjorie Harness Goodwin's *He-Said-She-Said: Talk as Social Organization among Black Children* (1990) Bloomington: Indiana University Press, pp. 25–26.

Data are transcribed according to the system developed by Jefferson and described in Sacks et al. (1974:731–733). The following are the features most relevant to the present analysis.

Example Number 1 234 56 789 10

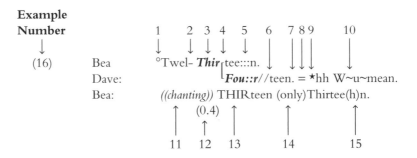

1. **Low Volume**: A degree sign indicates that talk it precedes is low in volume.
2. **Cut-off**: A dash marks a sudden cut-off of the current sound.
3. **Bold Italics**: Italics indicate some form of emphasis, which may be signaled by changes in pitch and/or amplitude.
4. **Overlap Bracket**: A left bracket marks the point at which the current talk is overlapped by other talk. Thus Dave's "*Fou::r*teen" begins during the last syllable of Bea's "*Thir*teen." Two speakers beginning to speak simultaneously are shown by a left bracket at the beginning of a line.
5. **Lengthening**: Colons indicate that the sound immediately preceding has been noticeably lengthened.
6. **Overlap Slashes**: Double slashes provide an alternative method of marking overlap. When they are used the overlapping talk is not

indented to the point of overlap. Here Bea's last line begins just after the "***Four***" in Dave's "***Four***teen."

7. **Intonation**: Punctuation symbols are used to mark intonation changes rather than as grammatical symbols:
    - A period indicates a falling contour.
    - A question mark indicates a raising contour.
    - A comma indicates a falling–rising contour.

8. **Latching**: The equal sign indicates "latching"; there is no interval between the end of a prior turn and the start of a next piece of talk.

9. **Inbreath**: A series of *h's* preceded by an asterisk marks an inbreath. Without the asterisk the *h's* mark an outbreath.

10. **Rapid Speech**: Tildes indicate that speech is slurred together because it is spoken rapidly.

11. **Comments**: Double parentheses enclose material that is not part of the talk being transcribed, for example, a comment by the transcriber if the talk was spoken in some special way.

12. **Silence**: Numbers in parentheses mark silences in seconds and tenths of seconds.

13. **Increased Volume**: Capitals indicate increased volume.

14. **Problematic Hearing**: Material in parentheses indicates a hearing that the transcriber was uncertain about.

15. **Breathiness, Laughter**: An *h* in parentheses indicates plosive aspiration which could result from events such as breathiness, laughter, or crying.

Appendix B

Jump Rope Rhymes

Hanley School Jump Rope Rhymes

Movements requiring athletic agility take place in the midst of some of the rhymes of jump rope. In the game entitled "Texaco Mexico" players must jump in the air while doing kicks, splits, turning around, touching the ground, "paying their taxes" (by slapping the hand of a turner), and "getting outa town" (jumping out of the rope) while the rope is in motion.

Texaco Mexico

Texaco Mexico	*Turners turn rope*
Went over the hill	*Jumper jumps into the moving rope*
Where far away	*Jumper jumps*
And they do some splits, splits, splits	*Jumper executes splits*
And they turn around round round	*Jumper turns around*
And they touch the ground, ground, ground	*Jumper touches the ground*
And they do some kicks, kicks, kicks	*Jumper does kicks*
And they pay their taxes, taxes, taxes	*Jumper slaps hand of turner*
And they get outa town, town, town	*Jumper moves out of the rope,*
And they jump back in, in, in	*Jumper jumps back into the rope*
And that's the end, end, end	*Jumper jumps out of the rope*

Teddy Bear

Teddy Bear Teddy Bear	*Turners turn rope*
Turn around	*Jumper turns around*
Teddy Bear Teddy Bear	*Jumper jumps*
Touch the ground	*Jumper touches the ground*
Teddy Bear Teddy Bear	*Jumper jumps*
Turn out the lights	*Jumper pantomimes turning out light switch*

Teddy Bear, Teddy Bear	*Jumper jumps*
Say Good night	
Teddy Bear, Teddy Bear	
Go upstairs	*Jumper pantomimes going up stairs*
Teddy Bear Teddy Bear	
Say your prayers	*Jumper folds hands*
Brush your hair	*Jumper pantomimes brushing hair*

Cinderella

Dressed in yalla
Sent upstairs to kiss a fella
Made a mistake
And kissed a snake
How many doctors did it take.

Ice Cream Soda

Vanilla berry punch
Tell me the name
of your honey bunch
Is it A, B, C, D

The letter that you miss on is the first initial of your boyfriend.

Jennifer Makofsky (1997) reports similar rhymes for the middle class Caucasian Northern California girls she studied.

The girls view this as a form of narrative about their social relationships with boys. Whereas in other rhymes the aim is to jump as long as possible, in this rhyme they sometimes intentionally miss on the initial of first name of a boy they like, and then girls squeal and yell the boy's name "S Sean." "D David. You like David!" The verse following the "ice cream soda" verse deals with the gender and configuration of children that will result from the marriage: "Boy, Girl, Twins or Triplets." Other four best verses are concerned with the outcome of the relationships (divorce or marriage) and the type of house (house, apartment, shack, mansion).

One boys' rhyme was:
I had a bird and it was Enza.
I opened the window and in flew Enza.

Rounds at the completion of rhymes

H-E-L-P
Some set rotations of are used at the completion of turns. For example, players recite the letters H-E-L-P until someone misses. The player must

then execute the move which the letter stands for H-E-L-P (turning the rope until the jumper misses on one of these letters).

Highwire   *The rope is turned a few inches off the ground so that it is difficult to maneuver*

Eyes closed *Jumper must jump with her eyes closed*

Leapfrog   *Jumper must jump from squatting position*

Peppers   *Red hot chili peppers (turning the rope very fast)*

Many rounds are based on explicit hetero-normal ideologies. For example, one round deals with what category of children one will have. One recites:

Boys, girls, twins or triplets

Others deal with how a marriage will result: marriage, divorce, etc.

When the jumper misses, the next round she jumps to reflects the epistemological status of the category: "Yes, no, maybe so."

M-A-S-H

Another round is M-A-S-H (mansion, apartment, shack, house). This is derivative of a game in which players fill out four choices for a number of categories including boys, car, job, husband's job, salary, husband's salary, place to live, honeymoon, and number of kids.

For each category the player chooses three things they would want and the judge fills in the fourth slot with what would be an undesirable choice. Then the judge makes marks on the paper in the corner until the player calls stop. The judge counts how many marks were made and that number is used to eliminate choices. After the judge is left with only one choice in each category the player's life is read. The objective is to live in the house with the guy you like, driving the car you desire, etc.

Jump Rope Rhymes in Downtown Los Angeles

Rhymes similar to those of the Hanley School were also sung in parts of downtown Los Angeles. However, in addition, there were themes of women's superiority to men in rhymes such as "Blueberry Street" and "My Mother Gave Me a Nickel."

Blueberry Street

My mother your mother lived across the street
Eighteen nineteen Blueberry Street
Everytime they had a fight
This is what they said

Boys are rotten
Made out of cotton
Girls are handy
Made out of candy
Boys go to Jupiter
'Cause they're more stupider

Girls go to college
To get more knowledge
Boys drink beer to get more fear
Girls drink Pepsi to get more sexy
Inky binky soda pop, inky binky boo
inky binky soda pop a boy loves you

My Mother Gave Me a Nickel

My mother gave me a nickel
My father gave me a dime
My sister gave me a boyfriend
His name is Frankenstein/to kiss him all the time.

He made me wash the dishes
He made me wash the floor
He made me wash his underwear
So I kicked him out the door.

I kicked him to Los Angeles
I kicked him to Japan
I also kicked him everywhere
without his underwear.

Notes

Preface

1 Studies by Maltz and Borker (1982) as well as Maccoby (1998) provide dualistic visions of girls' and boys' gendered play and gender-typed norms, and are often cited as foundational research upon which contemporary gender studies are based. See, for example, Leaper and Smith (2004:1018).
2 See Whiting and Edwards (1973).
3 See Maccoby (1986).
4 Baron-Cohen's article summarizes ideas in his 2003 book *The Essential Difference*.
5 In 1984 Carol Gilligan was named "Woman of the Year" by *Ms.* magazine.
6 The term "voice" for Gilligan means "something like what people mean when they speak of the core of the self" (Gilligan 1982:xvi).
7 See Boling (1996:69).
8 Gilligan (1982:173) provided an early version of cross-gender miscommunication, which she termed "a propensity for systematic mistranslation." She argued that "men and women may speak different languages that they assume are the same, using similar words to encode disparate experiences of self and social relationships" (Gilligan 1982).
9 For example, discussing gender differences in moral decision-making Brown et al. (1995:314) argue that while a justice orientation, characteristic of males, reflects "an ideal of equality, reciprocity, and fairness between persons," the care orientation, associated with females, reflects "an ideal of attachment, loving and being loved, listening and being listened to, and responding and being responded to."
10 See Talbot (2002:2).
11 See Belenky et al. (1986).
12 See Cameron (1998c) and Bucholtz (1999a) for a differentiation of deficit, dominance, and difference views of gender relations.
13 Henley and Kramarae (1991:19), for example, argue that gender-related language differences must necessarily be "viewed in the context of male power and female subordination." While researchers concerned with dominance relations seek to avoid the essentialist explanations often present in deficit and difference views, Stokoe (2000:554) notes they can unwittingly perpetuate dichotomized notions of male and female practices "blending a constructionist stance with cultural (essentialist) feminism."
14 See Maccoby (1986, 1990).
15 See Maltz and Borker (1982), Coates (1996, 1997, 1998).
16 See Holmes (1995) and Pilkington (1998).
17 Pellegrini and Blatchford (2000:86) argue that the best setting for observing forms of children's aggression is where children are minimally supervised by adults because "there are low costs and high benefits associated with committing these deeds."

18   Pellegrini and Blatchford (2000:86–87) make use of remote video cameras in conjunction with radio microphones to record children's behavior. They note that providing audio records of language is superior to observing or recording playground behavior from a car, but comment that children aged 11–12 are often reticent when wearing microphones.

1   Introduction

1   Data are transcribed according to the system developed by Gail Jefferson, outlined in Sacks et al. (1974:731–733). See Appendix A for the meaning of the transcription symbols. Important is that punctuation symbols are used to mark intonation changes rather than as grammatical symbols.
2   See, for example, Walkerdine (1985) and James (1993:200).
3   The entire transcript appears in Appendix 1.1 at the end of this chapter.
4   Belief that girls are not entitled to the same type of playing field as boys abounds in reports of the inequality in space allocated for girls. An August 9, 2001 *LA Times* article (Chavez 2001) reported that a Los Altos (northern California) high school soccer team maintains an "uneven playing field." The girls' field is marked with bumps and steep slopes at a middle school 20 minutes from the high school, while boys play on a nicer soccer field on the high school campus. While boys use campus bathrooms, the girls use a portable toilet. While the boys change in the locker room, girls often must form a circle on the field, hold up towels or t-shirts and change in the middle.
5   See chapter 4, Example 4.1.
6   I am using the historical present rather than past tense to introduce my examples to enable the reader to enter more directly into the scene.
7   For example, the statement "You're always get like- attitude when people are joking around" was said by an onlooker in the midst of a jump rope game when a turner defiantly put her hand on her hip and denied that she had any part in turning the jump rope irregularly.
8   See James et al. (1998:95).
9   Thornborrow (1998) argues that children's interaction can be highly constrained by the presence of adults on the scene.
10   See, for example, Pepler et al. (1995) and Craig et al. (2000).
11   See Pepler et al. (1995).
12   See Olweus (1991) and Pepler et al. (1995).
13   While Pepler et al. (1995) showed that aggression which was either physical or verbal happened once every 2.4 minutes on the playground, Roberts et al. (1999) found that in the classroom aggressive interactions occurred once every 37 minutes. Indeed, a study done at Hanley School by the school nurse showed that 90 percent of all problems occurred during lunchtime or when the children were on the playground.
14   Such an approach has resonances with theories of gender as "performance" as in work by Barrett (1999), Butler (1993), Hall (1997), and Cameron (2005).
15   See C. Goodwin (2000:1490).
16   Much of the work on language in the peer groups and identity construction has relied on data generated from interview situations. Edley and Wetherell's (1995, 1997) project analyzing identity construction among middle class white 18–19-year-old boys at a single sex independent school in the UK as well as Widdicombe and Woffitt's (1995) study of "the language of youth subcultures" in the UK are based largely on interview data, interaction between the research subjects and the

researcher. Similarly, in psychology, much of the work on peer aggression (Underwood 2003) is based on interviews or vignettes told to a researcher; consequently, we have no picture of what the actual activity of verbal bullying or social aggression looks like. As I have argued elsewhere (Goodwin 1997b:112), rather than accepting reports as instances of the events they describe, social science researchers need to seriously investigate the process of reporting itself as a situated conversational activity.

17 See also Schegloff (2002).

18 Garfinkel and Sacks (1970:342) argued that language occupies a central place in the organization of human social phenomena; they equate the basic social actor (member) with mastery of natural language.

19 See Heritage (1984b:242).

20 See Atkinson and Heritage (1984), Sacks et al. (1974), and Schenkein (1978).

21 Membership categories, as defined by Sacks (1995a:40–48), are classifications or social types that may be used to describe people. As discussed by Hester and Eglin (1997:3–4) "Membership categories may be interactionally linked together to form classes, collections or 'membership categorization devices' (MCDs) which Sacks (1974:218) defines as 'any collection of membership categories, containing at least a category, which may be applied to some population containing at least a member, so as to provide, by the use of some rules of application, for the pairing of at least a population member and a categorization device member. A device is then a collection plus rules of application.'"

22 See Goodwin and Goodwin (2000).

23 See Ochs and Schieffelin (1989).

24 With respect to games, Garfinkel (1963:190) argues that activities provide sites for the examination of rules and conduct seen in relation to them.

25 Recent social science research builds from work by Pierre Bourdieu (1977a, 1990), Anthony Giddens (1979, 1984), Garfinkel (1967), and Garfinkel and Sacks (1970). Hanks (1990:11) describes "practice" as "the point at which three things converge: the law of system, the quick of activity, and the reflective gaze of value." Opposing formalist descriptions of language he asks (Hanks 1990:13), "What if, instead of sharing a grammar, speakers shared routine ways of acting, similar perspectives, a sense of space, or common ways of evaluating speech?"

26 See Ortner (2003:13; 1999; in press).

27 Ortner (2001:12), drawing upon Bourdieu's notion of "habitus" is concerned with describing how "class" as a component of personal identity provides "an external world of cultural assumptions and social institutions that ordinary people inhabit without thinking very much about them" as well as an "internalized version of that world that becomes part of people's identities, generating dispositions to feel/think/judge/act in certain ways."

28 See, for example, the work of Kitzinger (2002), Speer (2005), and Stokoe and Weatherall (2002). Hutchby (1996a, 1996b) argues that conversation analysis can be used to show how power asymmetries in discourse arise in the midst of conversation and are not determined by macro features of the situation.

29 See Speer (2005).

30 For an analysis of this concept see Schegloff (1997).

31 For a review of the anthropological as well as conversation analytic notion of "practice" see Sidnell (2005).

32 See Goodwin (1990:75–108).

33 See Goodwin (1990:177–185).

34 See Pomerantz (1984) and Sacks (1987).

35 Goffman (1967:306) defines "face" as the "positive social value a person effectively claims for himself by the line others assume he has taken during a particular contact.

Face is an image of self delineated in terms of approved social attributes." See Heritage (1984b:265) regarding how talk is organized to maintain social cohesion.

36 See Bourdieu (1977a, 1977b, 1990), Foucault (1980), and Eckert and Mc Connell-Ginet (2003).

37 See, for example, van Dijk (1993).

38 See Atkinson and Heritage (1984); Goodwin and Heritage (1990), and Clayman and Maynard (1994).

39 See Garfinkel (1967) and Heritage (1984b) for discussions of ethnomethodology.

40 See also Sacks (1984).

41 In tune with arguments made by Schegloff (1997:166), Sidnell (2003b), Stokoe (2000:556), Speer (2005) and Kitzinger (2000:170), state that rather than uncritically linking particular patterns to gender, or presuming an a priori set of categories, we instead need to attend to the meanings, interpretations, and understandings of the participants themselves observable in the data.

42 See Sidnell (2003b), Kitzinger (2000; 2002:55–57), Stokoe (2000), Sunderland (2004), and Speer (2005).

43 See, for example, Schegloff (1997:174).

44 With respect to explicit commentary or orientation towards social categories, Kitzinger (2002:55–57) notes that acts of oppression may occur in the absence of participants explicitly orienting towards them as oppressive.

45 See chapter 3, Example 3.21 and examples in the section "Disputes in Cross-Sex Relations" for explicit mention of the categories "boy" and "girl" in talk; and chapter 4, Examples 4.20–4.22, 4.32 and 4.36 for mention of the terms "boy" and "girl" in the midst of a cross-sex contest of jump rope.

46 See Sperber and Wilson (1986).

47 For a review of the debates between Schegloff, Wetherell, and Billig regarding how gender relevance in interaction must be demonstrated in the participants' orientations see Stokoe and Weatherall (2002). See also Speer (2005) and Cameron (2005).

48 See Kitzinger (2002:49).

49 See Lakoff (1973, 1975), Thorne et al. (1983), Spender (1980), and Zimmerman and West (1975).

50 For a critique of work by cultural feminists see Hare-Mustin and Maracek (1990).

51 For a critique of work by eco-feminists see Tavris (1992).

52 See, for example, Chesler (2001).

53 See Weatherall (1998, 2002), Crawford (1995), Thorne (1993), Cameron (1998a), Gal (1995:171), Bucholtz and Hall (2004), Speer (2005), and Stokoe (2000).

54 See Weatherall (2002:85).

55 For critiques on difference theory see Weatherall (1998), Aries (1997), Cameron (1997b, 2005), and Crawford (1995).

56 See Antaki and Widdicombe (1998).

57 See Davies and Harré (1990), Edley and Wetherell (1997), and Widdicombe and Woffit (1995).

58 For a careful review of alternative paradigms in gender and language research see Speer (2005).

59 See Bucholtz (2002).

60 See Henley (1995), Mills (2003:181), Cameron and Kulick (2003), Eckert and McConnell-Ginet (1992), and Bucholtz (1999a).

61 See Weatherall (2000).

62 See Bettie (2003), Liechty (2003), and Ortner (2003).

63 However, see Rampton (2003) and Eckert (1987, 1997).

64 See Bing and Bergvall (1996) and Kyratzis (2001a, 2004).

65   As argued by Brown (1998:10) "there is little to be found in the psychological or feminist literature about girls' anger."

66   Leaper and Smith (2004:993–994) base their studies on works that have perpetuated essentialist views of girls and boys: "Narrative reviews of the research literature. Leaper (1994), Maccoby (1998), and Maltz and Borker (1982) suggest that girls are more likely than boys to use language to make connections with others. This may include greater talkativeness and the frequent use of affiliative speech acts. In contrast, boys appear more likely than girls to use assertive language to establish dominance or to achieve utilitarian goals.

67   See Ihinger-Tallman and Cooney (2005:118).

68   See, for example, Leaper and Smith (2004:1018).

69   See Whiting and Edwards (1973).

70   See Maccoby (1986).

71   See Collins (1990:8).

72   By way of contrast Lyn Mikel Brown (1998, 2003) studied girls of different economic, racial and geographic backgrounds.

73   See, for example, work by Kitzinger (1994), Turiel (1998), Walker et al. (1995), and Weisz and Black (2003).

74   Gilligan's initial study of care involved interviewing 24 women in the first trimester of their pregnancy who were planning or considering an abortion.

75   See Piaget (1965).

76   See Lee (1982:53–54).

77   See Goodwin (1990).

78   Brown herself has for some time distanced herself from this perspective in her books *Raising Their Voices: The Politics of Girls' Anger* (1998) and *Girlfighting: Betrayal and Rejection among Girls* (2003).

79   See Talbot (2002), and Meadows (2002).

80   See Brown (2003:15).

81   See Campbell (1982).

82   See Henley (1995).

83   See Goodwin (1980b, 1990).

84   Although Maltz and Borker (1982) is cited by most psychologists (i.e., Maccoby 1998; Underwood 2003) as the definitive review study based on ethnographic research showing gender difference, much of it is based on a highly selective reading of my own fieldwork.

85   See also Aries (1996, 1997) on exaggeration of sex differences.

86   See Goodwin (1990:ch. 7).

87   As stated by Roy Elveton (2005), *lifeworld* is a concept that originated in the phenomenology of Edmund Husserl (1859–1938). It emphasizes "the centrality of perception for human experience. This experience is multi-dimensional and includes the experience of individual things and their contextual/perceptual fields, the embodied nature of perceiving consciousness, and the intersubjective nature of the world as it is perceived, especially our knowledge of other subjects, their actions, and shared cultural structures."

88   See Harré (1964).

89   See Gilligan and Attanucci (1988) and Lyons (1988b).

90   See Langdale (1986) and Rothbart et al. (1986).

91   See Bjorkqvist et al. (1992a), Bjorkvist and Niemela (1992), Crick and Grotpeter (1995), and Olweus (1993).

92   For exceptions, see the work of Jaana Juvonen and Sandra Graham (2004), who examine the social matrix of peer victimization. Hepburn (1997) also argues against explaining bullying with reference to fixed personality traits, but her concern is with analyzing *accounts for* bullying behavior from the perspective of a postmodern discursive framework.

93 See also Fiske (1998:940).

94 See Packer (1985).

95 See also Corsaro and Maynard (1996), Dunn (1988), Cook-Gumperz (2001), and Best (1983) regarding forms of hurtful interaction among nursery school children and children in middle childhood.

96 See Olweus (1991).

97 See Mead (1933:8–9).

98 See anthropologists such as Scheper-Hughes and Sargent (1998a, 1998b), Stephens (1995), Reynolds (in press), de Leon (in press), Sirota (in press), Paugh (2003), Hirschfeld (2002); and sociologists of children such as Thorne (1993), Eder (1995), Corsaro (1990), Corsaro and Eder (1995), Alanen (1988), Ambert (1986), Boocock and Scott (2005). The new Rutgers Series on Childhood Studies, edited by Myra Bluebond-Langner provides rich ethnographic studies of the everyday lives of children.

99 Levi-Strauss (1936) wrote in his discussion of the Bororo, "The entire village left the next day in about 30 canoes, leaving us alone with the women and children in the abandoned houses." This quote is cited by Michard-Marshale and Ribery (1982:7) in Eichler and Lapointe (1985:1) and Conkey (1997:57). As Schlegel (1996) points out "the women and children are portrayed as not having the equivalent status as those who left them in the "abandoned" houses. Those who did the leaving were the true villagers, or rather, presumably, the men.

100 See James et al. (1998:94).

101 See Parsons (1951).

102 See Richards (1974).

103 See Hutchby and Moran-Ellis (1998:8).

104 This concept is developed in the work of Bucholtz (2002), Caputo (1995), Mackay (1991), Hardmann (1973), and Thorne (1987).

105 See Opie and Opie (1977:22).

106 See, for example, Wulff (1988), Amit-Talia and Wulff (1995), Berentzen (1984), Eckert (1987), Eder (1995), Evaldsson (1993), Evaldsson and Cosaro (1998), James and Prout (1990, 1997), Mayall (1994), Shuman (1986), Thorne (1993), Waksler (1991), Adler and Adler (1998), and Corsaro (1985).

107 See also James and Prout (1990), James et al. (1997), Waksler (1991), Mayall (1994), and Qvortrup et al. (1994).

108 See Caputo (1995:28) and James and Prout (1990:22–31).

109 See Speer and Potter (2002:156–157).

110 See Hutchby and Moran-Ellis (1998:10–13).

111 See Hutchby and Moran-Ellis (1998:8).

112 See Corsaro (1985, 1997), Corsaro and Eder (1990), and Eder (1995).

113 See Sheldon (1990).

114 See Evaldsson (1993) and Tholander (2002).

115 See Kyratzis and Guo (2001).

116 See Paugh (2003) and de Leon (1998a, 1998b).

117 See Whalen (1995), Maynard (1985a), and Corsaro (1979).

118 See Hutchby and Moran-Ellis (1998:22).

119 See Pellegrini and Blatchford (2000:86–87) regarding the importance of good sound for documenting children's language use, particularly during "bullying bouts."

120 See Goffman (1967).

121 See Goodwin and Goodwin (2004).

122 See C. Goodwin (2000).

123 "The Bedroom Song" appears in chapter 3.

124 See Goodwin and Goodwin (1987, 1992).

2   Multimodality, Conflict, and Rationality in Girls' Games

1   See Pomerantz (1984).
2   See Brown and Levinson (1987) and Lerner (1996).
3   See also Lakoff (1975) and Brown (1980, 1990).
4   Shantz and Hartup (1992:4) distinguish *aggression* – "behavior aimed at hurting another person or thing" – from conflict, defined as "a state of resistance or opposition between (at least) two individuals." For a discussion of conflict in social life see the collection edited by Briggs (1996) on "disorderly discourse."
5   For an analysis of the role of conflict in children's friendship development see Corsaro and Rizzo (1990), Corsaro and Eder (1990), and Maynard (1985b).
6   See Adger (1984), Corsaro and Rizzo (1990), Eder (1995), Genishi and Paolo (1982). Goodwin (1982b), Maynard (1985b), Sheldon (1992a, 1992b), Danby and Baker (2000, 2001), Kyratzis and Guo (2001), Evaldsson (2004), and Evaldsson and Corsaro (1998).
7   See, for example, Hartup and Laursen (1993).
8   See Rizzo (1992:94, 102), Corsaro (1990), Corsaro and Rizzo (1990), Eder (1995), Maynard (1985b), Shantz (1987), and Shantz and Hobart (1989).
9   See Hartup and Laursen (1993), Hartup et al. (1993).
10   See Maynard (1985b).
11   However, see Eder's (1993) analysis of conflict exchanges among working and lower class white adolescents in the Midwest, and Shuman's (1986) analysis of disputes among African American, white (Polish American and Irish American), and Puerto Rican inner city junior high school students in Philadelphia. When conflict in young girls has been examined, it has usually been in terms of face-saving strategies that young (white) socially advantaged girls utilize to mitigate conflict (Sheldon 1992a, 1992b).
12   See Borman (1982a, 1982b), Borman and Frankel (1984), Borman and O'Reilly (1987), and Lever (1976, 1978).
13   See Lever (1976, 1978).
14   For a critique of the binary thinking inherent in Gilligan's statements on games see Evaldsson (2004).
15   Broughton (1993) argues that both Gilligan and Kohlberg subscribe to dualistic psychologies; he feels that Gilligan subscribes to a "liberal romantic idealism" which is fundamentally Cartesian.
16   Even data used in "the first systematic, empirical test of Gilligan's theories" relies on "responses of thirty-six individuals to questions asked in open-ended interviews designed to draw out an individual's conception of self and orientation to morality" (Lyons 1988b:23).
17   Shweder et al. (1987:16) argue that Kohlberg "reduced the study of moral concepts to the study of verbal justification of moral ideas. The study of moral understanding has been narrowed, by methodological fiat, to the study of what people can propositionalize. That is dangerous because what people can state is but a small part of what they know. Kohlberg's interview methodology requires subjects to access verbally their moral concepts, produce moral arguments, and talk like a moral philosopher." What is talked about is what an individual person knows. What the girls I investigate know is how to manipulate the public semiotic materials that comprise the environment that they operate upon. Rather than dealing with an interior psychological knowledge we are investigating the public structure of the organization of knowledge.
18   See Brown and Gilligan (1992:8).

19 Studies by Stack (1993) and Harding (1987) find few differences in the kinds of morality displayed by African American women and men living in situations of poverty. Power rather than gender appears to be the important variable distinguishing orientations towards morality. Situational variables, ignored in Gilligan's model, have been found to be important in studies of moral reasoning by a number of researchers: Clopton and Sorell (1993), Hare-Mustin and Marecek (1990), and Garcia (1996). Enduring characteristics of the person rather than descriptions of how people navigate their way through situations are foregrounded in Gilligan's work. From such a perspective "the situation is only a vehicle for the expression for the reasoning personality, whether that be caring or abstract" (Luria 1993:202).

20 See discussion by Sidnell (2003a:431) regarding Garfinkel's use of the example of games as a site for examining rules and conduct.

21 Justification is defined as "evidence or reasons for one's beliefs, feelings, or actions" by Goetz and Shatz (1999:722). They (1999:744) note that conflict justifications "generally support statements which are somewhat 'objective' in comparison with those supported by self-expansions; the actions referred to are usually physically observable, the rules or standards have quite often been stated or presented as absolutes, and facts are by definition those statements that are putative and not presented as mere opinion." The conflict situation examined here resembles that discussed by Goetz and Shatz (1999:744), in that strong assertions are required. Notice that no causal connectives are used (something also observed by Goetz and Shatz 1999). The explanation occurs immediately following the *Out*-call.

22 See C. Goodwin (2000) on the notion of multiple semiotic fields.

23 See Bradac et al. (1995).

24 See Goodwin (1994).

25 See Sacks (1987) and Pomerantz (1984).

26 Norma Mendoza-Denton (personal communication, 1995) points out that this example shows how the bilingual phonology of the children operates, taking the English word "cheater" and code-switching in the middle of it at a morphological boundary by changing the /t/ of "cheat" to /r/. Although the vowel quality is primarily Spanish, the word has an English phonological process operating within it, with the intervocalic flapping of /t/.

27 I am indebted to Jack Sidnell (personal communication, 2004) for this observation.

28 Duranti (1984:278) argues that when subject pronouns are used in Italian, a pro-drop language, they work to define the role of a given character in a story and suggest particular attitudes and value judgments that the speaker is making about such a character. In particular, Duranti argues that personal pronouns are used to display empathy or positive affect towards the person described. Davidson (1996:543) argues that the use of subject pronouns in Spanish, another pro-drop language, signals that utterances are "more personally relevant"; they are used pragmatically to switch reference for purposes of emphasis and negotiating conversational turns. In the examples being analyzed, in the midst of a hopscotch contest, subject pronouns are used to accuse the current jumper that she has made an inappropriate move.

29 See Clark and Gerrig (1990) on the concept of *demonstration*.

30 The use of "*bim*" to indicate an "*out*" is perhaps unique to this group. No other Korean students I have asked over a ten-year period have heard of the term in the game. Several people have remarked that the sound may resemble a buzzer in a game show indicating someone's disqualification from the game.

31 See C. Goodwin (2000) for a discussion of the use of deictic stomps as resources in the construction of accounts in hopscotch.

32 See C. Goodwin (2003).

33 A similar perspective regarding the universality of game activity structure is argued by Sacks (1995:504).

34   See Tarone (1973). I am indebted to Christina Foreman (personal communication, 1999; 2000) and Andrea Kortenhoven (personal communication, 2000) for their interpretation of this pitch contour.
35   See C. Goodwin (2000).
36   See Goodwin et al. (2002).
37   See, for example, Lever (1978), Gilligan (1982), and Sutton-Smith (1979a, 1979b).
38   See, for example, Freed (1992), Henley (1995), Kramarae (1990), Houston and Kramarae (1991), and Morgan (1995).
39   See, for example, Anzaldúa (1987, 1990), Moore (1991), Orenstein (1994), Sadker and Sadker (1994).
40   See, for example, Lever (1978), Piaget (1965), Savasta and Sutton-Smith (1979), and Sutton-Smith (1979b).

3 Social Dimensions of a Popular Girls' Clique

1   Similar to what Thorne (1993) has described for the elementary school children she observed, the largest area of the playground, the playing fields, were occupied primarily by boys.
2   See Lareau (2003) and Wingard (in press) on scheduling of homework in families.
3   A clique has been defined as a group of several young people that remains small enough to enable its members to be in regular interaction with one another and to serve as the primary peer group (Brown and Klute 2003). Cole et al. (2005:597) state that most adolescents belong to several different cliques that are organized at different times of the day or in different settings.
4   See Willis (1981), Griffiths (1995), McRobbie (1978), Lees (1993), and Eckert (1987). Griffiths (1995:122), for example, argues that the adolescent girls she studied spent more time "getting on with each other than getting on with work." McRobbie (1978) discusses how working class high school girls in England are preoccupied with fashion, beauty, dating, and marriage rather than schoolwork.
5   Melissa, the most popular girl with the boys of her age cohort, was the exception; she had arrived only a year before the study began, and was considered by her teachers to have adapted very quickly to the school social environment.
6   In contrast to the primarily working class girls studied by Eckert (1996:185), fifth grade girls in this study enjoyed playing games as well as talking. Eckert (1996:184) argues that with increasing interest in boys and the development of the "hetero-sexual marketplace" girls rejected games as childish. However, among Hanley School girls, games such as jump rope, softball, or volleyball were enjoyed, in part because they could provide an opportunity for girls to interact with boys.
7   The names (pseudonyms) of other children who are included in the study appear in Appendix 3.1 at the end of this chapter.
8   See Appendix B for complete transcripts of the jump rope rhymes.
9   Evaluations were repetitively made in terms of popularity. See Eder (1995).
10 See Griswold (in press); Goodwin (1990).
11 The composition of the African American and Russian playgroups may have accounted for the desirability of the role of mom. In both the cases of African American girls (Goodwin 1990, with girls aged 4–10) and Russian girls (Griswold in press, ages 6–9) younger girls were members of the playgroups.
12 See Kyratzis and Wade (2002) on children's use of assertive control acts.
13 Wingard (1997) analyzed sequences of arm wrestling among third grade boys.
14 Thorne (1986) and Eckert and McConnell-Ginet (2003:24–25) view gender separation as one of the classic ways that children are arranged in institutional settings into groups.

15   See Kienpointner (1997:262–263).
16   Vanessa, an African American girl, shows considerable skill in arguing with her male counterparts. Schofield (1982) and Corsaro (1997) argue that African American girls are generally more assertive and independent in their relations with one another and with boys than white girls.
17   See Kienpointner (1997:262–263).
18   See Schofield (1981) and Best (1983).
19   The popular group thus differed from girls observed by Eckert (2003:317–318) who "replaced vigorous physical playground activity with observing, heckling, and occasionally disrupting boys' games, and with sitting or walking around in small and large groups."
20   Thorne (2002) cautions against deriving the structure of an ethnography from what she terms "theoretical imperatives."
21   Giddens' notion of "duality of structure" is compatible to Wetherell's ideas on the double sense of "positioning and being positioned" (Wetherell and Edley 1998:171; Wetherell 1998).
22   Both boys and girls discussed friendships with the other sex in terms of romantic relationships from the third grade onward. I concur with Eckert (1997:2) and Eckert and McConnell-Ginet (2003:25–27) that "the entire heterosexual enterprise at this point is about alignments within the cohort rather than about individual boy-girl relationships."
23   One girl, who was a star soccer player, came to school 45 minutes early so that she could play with a boy who was a neighbor who also attended the school because she refused to play soccer with the "rough" boys in her class at recess.
24   See Fishman (1978a, 1978b), Henley and Kramarae (1991), West (1979, 1992), West and Garcia (1988), West and Zimmerman (1983), Woods (1988), and Zimmerman and West (1975).
25   See Davis (1988).
26   However, note that Eckert and McConnell-Ginet (2003:88) argue that males may be licensed to be hierarchical, "to expose their hierarchical orientation to public view" but that females may in fact be as hierarchical as men. Eckert (1989) found that girls operate with respect to hierarchies of popularity; see discussions by Eder (1985) and Adler and Adler (1998) with respect to cycles of popularity.
27   My original analysis looked at gender differences in the construction of a task activity. In subsequent work I have looked at how expertise (Goodwin 2001) rather than gender provides a more appropriate way of analyzing what makes a difference in the use of more aggravated directive forms.
28   Working within an ethnomethodological framework, Danby and Baker (2000) examined how Australian inner-city boys aged 3–5 make use of threats inflicting personal injury ("smashing" down the block construction and "bashing" one of the boys) and introduce themes of terror and violence to create asymmetrical relationships.
29   See Pomerantz (1984) and Sacks (1987).
30   See Goodwin (1990).
31   Such a view contrasts with the perspective of elementary school girls studied by Eckert (1997) whose goal was to act "mature" and distance themselves from a "babyish" identity.
32   Note (in Example 3.8 of this chapter), however, in the midst of playing house how girls select the identity of teenager as the ideal role they want to play.
33   For a discussion of instigating see Goodwin (1990:258–279).
34   Girls use the adjective "rude" to define inappropriate behavior. In the following not wanting to turn the jump rope, but instead jump in the rope with other girls, is defined as "rude".

    Emi: You guys wait. Wait. Wait.
            I- I wanna say something.
            It's kinda rude for you guys not to do this
            Just because it was Lisa's turn and you wanted
            to take her turn.
    Sarah: I wasn't *tak*ing her turn.
    Emi: I know you guys all love to do this
            but you guys wanted to go with Lisa
            So you didn't wanna turn. It was *rude*.

35 Adler et al. (1992) in their three-year fieldwork study among middle class ele-
    mentary school children argue that girls derive status from success in grooming,
    clothes and other appearance-related variables, as well as romantic success with
    boys (Holland and Eisenhart 1990), measures of affluence, and academic success.
    Boys strive to distance themselves from deference to authority and investment in
    academic effort. See also Connell (1987:294), Jordan and Cowan (1995), Willis
    (1981:177–179), Eckert (1987), and Paley (1984:4–6).
36 See Goodwin (1990:84–85).
37 See Ervin-Trip (1976), Brown and Levinson (1978), and Goodwin (1990).
38 In his discussion of "territories of the self" Goffman (1971:29–30) notes that at the
    center of social organization is "the concept of claims" to various sorts of preserves,
    including forms of personal space: "the space surrounding an individual, anywhere
    within which an entering other causes the individual to feel encroached upon,
    leading him to show displeasure and sometimes to withdraw."
39 See Goodwin and Goodwin (1990:95–98).
40 On the concept of piggybacking onto someone else's move see Goodwin and
    Goodwin (1990:101–107).
41 Labov and Fanshel (1977:84) discuss the difference between aggravated (or baldly
    stated) and mitigated forms of directives.
42 See Scott (1985) concerning how powerless people protest or resist the actions of
    more powerful persons.

4 Social Organization, Opposition and Directives in the Game of Jump Rope

1   See Lever (1978).
2   See Goodwin (1990:39–42).
3   See Goodwin (1990:126–135).
4   See Goffman (1961:18).
5   See Goodwin (1985).
6   See Ahlin (2004).
7   See Burling (1966).
8   The motions and words for the rhyme for "Texaco Mexico" are described in
    Appendix B.
9   Appendix B contains the rhymes most frequently used by Hanley School and the
    downtown Los Angeles school.
10 The rhymes are in Appendix B.
11 See Goodwin (1982b:87).
12 See Halliday and Hasan (1976:178).
13 See Pomerantz (1975:26); Goodwin (1990:152–156).

14 Goffman (1971:107) states that the function of remedial work is to "change the meaning that otherwise might be given to an act, transforming what could be seen as offensive into what can be seen as acceptable." In Western society this is accomplished through accounts, apologies, and requests.

15 See Pomerantz (1975:26).

16 Example 4.5 is part of a longer sequence (4.6) to be discussed in more detail below.

17 See Goodwin (1990:177–185).

18 See, for example, Borman and Lippincott (1982), Borman and Frankel (1984), Borman and O'Reilly (1987), Lever (1976), and Piaget (1965).

19 See Goodwin (1990).

20 See Brown and Levinson (1987) and Bellinger and Gleason (1982).

21 See Goodwin (1990:316–317).

22 See Eisenberg and Garvey (1981:160).

23 See Goodwin (1990:63–137).

24 Not only did Tom have difficulties in sports, he also had problems participating in verbal duels with other boys and at points, according to the boys, was aggressive without provocation.

25 Among the African American children I studied in Philadelphia (Goodwin 1990) there were gender differences in types of accounts: boys' directives rather than girls' frequently dealt with personal desires rather than requirements of the activity.

26 See Ervin-Tripp (1982:35).

27 Modal verbs are verbs that, when used with other verbs, express ideas such as possibility, intention, obligation, and necessity. The main modal verbs in English are: may/might; can/could; shall/should; must. Palmer (1986:1) analyzes modality as a grammatical category. While English has a system of modal verbs (will, can, may, must, etc.), Latin has a system of mood: indicative, subjective, and imperative.

28 I learned in an interview with Reggie, the Coach, after the children had gone into class that he had counseled them that although Angela was "pushy," they should try to imagine what it would be like for themselves if they were trying to make friends and no one included them.

29 For discussion of context see Goodwin and Goodwin (1992), Goodwin and Duranti (1992).

30 See Douvan and Adelson (1966:100–202), Eder and Hallinan (1978), and Feshbach and Sones (1971).

31 See also Kyratzis (2001b).

32 See also Thorne (2002).

5   Language Practices for Indexing Social Status: Stories, Descriptions, Brags, and Comparisons

1 With regard to gender as a social construction see Blatchford (1998), Cook-Gumperz (2001), Cook-Gumperz and Szymanski (2001), Danby and Baker (1998, 2000), Davies (1989), Evaldsson (2002, 2003, 2004), Hey (1997), Jordan (1995), Jordan and Cowan (1995), and Thorne (1993). See Corsaro and Maynard (1996), Corsaro and Rizzo (1988, 1990), Sansone (1995), Kyratzis and Guo (2001), Kyratzis and Wade (2002), with respect to ethnicity. See Van Ausdale and Feagin (1996), Scott (2002, 2003), and Boocock and Scott (2005) with respect to race as a social practice. For literature on childhood itself as socially constructed see James (1993), James and Prout (1997), James et al. (1998), and Hutchby and Moran-Ellis (1998).

Ortner (2003:11) argues that "class is not some natural object lying around in the world, but is culturally or discursively constructed." She elaborates saying that "the view of class as a discursive construction argues that different rhetorics of class do different things for different purposes." Ortner (2003:12) feels that class is something akin to what Bourdieu (1977a, 1990) calls a "habitus," an external world of cultural assumptions and social institutions that ordinary people inhabit. Ortner's (2003) recent study *New Jersey Dreaming* has explored how the interviews she conducted with members of the class of 1958 at Weequahic High School show that social class is closely linked with race and ethnicity.

2　But see Eckert (1989, 1996), Bucholtz (2003), Bettie (2003), Eder (1995), and Proweller (1998).

3　Bettie (2003:5), in her ethnographic study of Mexican American and European American girls coming of age in a high school of the Central Valley of California argues that Gilligan's (1982) and Pipher's (2001) work showcases gender as the most significant dimension of girls' selves, while social class (in addition to ethnicity and sexuality) is left "analytically subordinate." She argues that we need to consider the multiple ways in which girls define themselves; citing Alarcón (1990:360) she argues that aside from relationships to males "one can 'become a woman' in opposition to other women" and discusses multiple social hierarchies that young girls embrace with respect to styles and consumer culture (Bettie 2003:42).

4　See also Ortner (1998).

5　Ortner (1991:186) argues that anthropologists tend to ethnicize "the groups under study" and "to treat them as if they were in effect separate tribes" (1991:186).

6　From a similar perspective Proweller (1998:69) argues that class is "a relatively unspoken descriptor."

7　See also Ehrenrich (1989).

8　Katherine Newman (1989) argues that "the middle class is a category so broad that it encompasses everyone from white collar executives to elite unionized labor, sometimes called the labor aristocracy."

9　With respect to the notion that brands constitute objects that "coproduce the social" see Lury (2004).

10　See Sacks and Schegloff (1979) on alternative preference organization in reference to persons.

11　Hot Rod Skateboard Shop in Westwood, Los Angeles, sells equipment for skateboarding and rollerblading.

12　A Zero Jacket is a brand name jacket that provides warmth in cold and wet conditions and cost $169 in 2005.

13　"Dope" means "cool" and provides a positive assessment of an object or event described.

14　Jamie Thomas is a professional cult skateboarding hero living in Encinitas, CA.

15　Cigar City is the name of a television show about mobs in Tampa.

16　See Goodwin (1990:39–42).

17　See Berentzen (1984).

18　See Danby and Baker (1998).

19　The digital pet appeared first in Japan in late 1996, was popular in the US in 1997 and disappeared in 1998 (superseded by *Tamagotchi Plus*).

20　See also Sidnell (2000, 2003b, 2005) with respect to how stories (in a Guyanese rumshop) provide rich contexts for understanding how identity (in the Guyanese case, gender identity) as well as exclusivity of a group is constructed and managed through talk-in-interaction.

21　See Goodwin (1983b), Goodwin and Goodwin (1986) for interactive features of word searches.

22　See Lerner (2004) on collaborative turn sequences.

23 Unfortunately the alliteration that occurred in the original transcript cannot be replicated accurately because Angela is a pseudonym, not her real name.

24 Bootie here means "butt."

25 Snickerdoodles are a form of sugar cookie.

26 The "oo" sound in "poppydoo," similar to that in "snickerdoodle," may act as a sound trigger for the telling. "Taboo," the word that Aretha talks about in her chained story, has a similar "oo" sound.

27 See Glenn (2003) regarding laughter in the midst of storytelling.

28 See Goodwin and Goodwin (1990).

29 Sacks (1995b:437–443) discusses the activity of reminiscing.

30 This is an important consideration, if we want to understand how participants themselves organize their social relations in real time, rather than relying on the reports given to a social science investigator about girls' lives.

31 Carolyn Steedman (1986:15) discusses clothes, shoes, and make-up as objects of women's experience of class identity. She describes them as important features of women's "culture of longing" and "politics of envy." Among the girls in downtown Los Angeles whom I studied, a "culture of longing" was invoked when a Chinese American girl was ridiculed for wearing second-hand clothing. This ridicule resulted in the Chinese American girl's stealing money from her mother to purchase clothing that was acceptable to the peer group's standards.

32 See Goodwin (1986) for a discussion of how story recipients may provide rival interpretations to those anticipated by story tellers and undercut expected next actions.

33 Ortner (2003:44) discusses how members of the Class of 1958 of Weequahic High School in New Jersey used location as a major marker of class difference. She argues that "grammar schools and their related subneighborhoods formed an extensively used code for reading and expressing class differences."

34 With respect to how comments on descriptions always display one's access to and knowledge about the topic at issue see Goodwin and Goodwin (1987). See also Heritage and Raymond (2005).

35 See Goodwin and Goodwin (1990) on the notion of topic-invoked participation framework.

36 Melissa (who, by comparison with Emi or Janis, is less likely to position herself in competition with others) responded by attempting to downplay the event (line 6), answering Sarah's plaintive "I wanna do Cotillion" with "Nope. You do not."

37 See Eckert and McConnell-Ginet (2003:317–318).

38 See Goodwin (1990:258–279).

39 See Goffman (1959).

40 Schegloff (1972:114–115), discussing place formulation, states that each "occasion of the use of a place formulation selected because of its presumed recognizability to a member of such a class is part of a never ending potential test in which persons can be shown to be inadequate members of the class, and thereby inadequate candidates for the activity."

41 See Goodwin (1990:243–257).

42 See Goodwin and Goodwin (1990).

43 See, for example, Edley and Wetherell (1997), Bamberg (2004), and Kiesling (2001).

44 See Goodwin (1990:177–185).

45 Proweller (1998:75) also found that brand name clothes from the Gap, DKNY, and Calvin Klein, along with jewelry such as sterling amethyst earrings were identified by the girls as types of "sorting mechanisms" within the professional middle class. Such girls were disliked for their assumptions of superiority. See also Bucholtz (2003) and Miller (1998) regarding the importance of material culture in defining social position.

46   See Davis (1992:21).
47   See Example 5.19, and lines 4–5, 6–8, 10, 14, 19, 22, 24–26, 27, 30, 35 of Example 5.20 below.
48   Formulations of car ownership, like place formulation recognition, provides for what Schegloff (1972:115) describes as a "never ending potential test in which persons can be shown to be inadequate members of the class."
49   According to the June 2002 *Consumers Reports* cars named in the playing house episode were valued as follows: a Miata was valued at $21,000; a Ford Mustang cost up to $30,000; a Porsche was listed at $42,000–$51,600; and a Chevrolet Corvette went for $41,000–49,000.
50   Schegloff (1972) in his article on "Formulating Place" examines the work that members need to engage in to produce or recognize a competent location formulation.
51   But see Ervin-Tripp et al. (1990), Kyratzis and Guo (2001), Kyratzis and Wade (2002), deHart (1996), Sheldon (1996) Evaldsson (2004), Goodwin (1990), and Eder (1990).
52   See Goodwin (1990:42–46).

6   Stance and Structure in Assessment and Gossip Activity

1   See for example work by Brenneis (1996), Evaldsson (2002), Cameron (1997a) and Johnson and Meinhof (1997).
2   Gossip is by no means the exclusive terrain of females. Gossip events are important for males because they provide an opportunity for sociability. Among men in a Fijian rural community Brenneis (1984a, 1984b, 1996) discusses how gossip in *talanoa* allows contributors to chain narrative utterances about an absent, offending, other. Gossip in Fiji can precede a formal mediation process.
3   See Coates (1989).
4   See Coates (2000).
5   See Blum-Kulka (2000).
6   See Eder (1995:110).
7   See Fine (1986:414, 419).
8   See Pilkington (1998:257).
9   See Eder (1995).
10   See Goodwin (1990).
11   See Coates (1989).
12   See Gluckman (1963).
13   See Coates (2000).
14   See Goodwin (1990).
15   See Wootton (1997:135–136).
16   See Pomerantz (1975:26) and Goodwin (1990:152).
17   See Sacks (1995a:716–721).
18   See Goodwin (1990:177–188).
19   See Pomerantz (1984) and Heritage and Raymond (2005).
20   See Jefferson (1985).
21   See Pomerantz (1984).
22   I am indebted to Mary Bucholtz (personal communication, 2004) for this observation of the use of "butt" as a compound collocation.
23   See Arlington (2003).

24 See Coates (1996).
25 See Pilkington (1998).
26 See Goodwin and Goodwin (1992:151).
27 The voice Angela makes use of has elaborate singsong intonation, with dramatic pitch contours. Note that here Angela utilizes the quotative "be like", a framing device Bucholtz (2005) associates with "popular girl" identity (contrasting with nerd, mainsteam youth, and hip hop fan identity) among California youth.
28 The magazine deals with problems at school, with family and friends, as well as personal hygiene; questions written into the "Help" column are posed by girls eight to nine years of age. Issues which are discussed include what a nine-year-old girl should do when her baby sister wants to follow her around all the time; when a friend is bragging about how her report card is much better than that of other girls; when one's teacher never calls on you in class; when your new science partner is not as smart as you; when you feel you're spending all of your time caring for your puppy; how to prepare for taking a test, etc. The categories under the "Help" column include "school smarts," "family matters," "the care and keeping of friends," "the care and keeping of you," "I'm scared," and more.
29 I am using the expression "second description" to refer to a format resembling second stories, discussed by Sacks (1995b).
30 See Wetherell (1998), Davies and Harré (1990), and Bamberg (2004).
31 See Goodwin (1990:260–261).
32 See also Thornborrow and Morris (2004:249) and Pilkington (1998:255) regarding gossip as a source of enjoyment and entertainment. Brenneis (1996:46) discusses a particular gossip activity called "talanoa" as not only useful for toying with people's reputations, but also providing for a good time. People enjoy both the lively interaction as well as the idea of having fun at someone else's expense.
33 See Coates (1996).
34 See Eder and Hallinan (1978), Eder and Enke (1991), and Goodwin (1990).
35 See Goodwin and Goodwin (1987, 1992).
36 See Jefferson (1979) and Glenn (2003).
37 In that children aged eight to ten grow rapidly, it is dubious that Sarah actually purchased her shirt three years ago. Stating that the shirt is three years old constitutes a form of hyperbole, one that contrasts her shirt with the trendy new shirt that Janis is wearing.
38 See Arlington (2003) and Holmes (1998).
39 See Goodman and Ben-Ze'ev (1994), Coates (1989), Jones (1990), Pilkington (1998), and Thornborrow and Morris (2004).
40 See Gluckman (1963), Eder (1988), Goodwin (1990), Shuman (1986), and Tholander (2002).

7 Constructing Social Difference and Exclusion in Girls' Groups

 1 See, for example, Keenan (1974), Kulick (1992, 1993), Goodwin (1980b), Brown (1990), Morgan (1999), and Burbank (1994b). Cultural anthropologists, by way of contrast, remained silent about features of female aggression until the work of Burbank (1994a) and Cook (1993), and the 1994 special issue of *Sex Roles* on "The Cultural Construction of Gender and Aggression" (Fry and Gabriel 1994).
 2 See Coates (1994:72).
 3 See Holmes (1995).

4   See Maltz and Borker (1982).
5   See Simmons (2002), Wiseman (2002), Chesler (2001), White (2002), and Lamb (2001).
6   See Olweus (1991:413). For a review of the literature on bullying see Pellegrini (2002).
7   See Rivers and Smith (1994).
8   See Olweus (1993).
9   See Owens et al. (2000) and Salmivalli (2001). However, see Cadigan (2003), who studied peer victimization ethnographically among sixth graders in a Southern California middle school.
10   See Bergvall et al. (1996) and Freed (1995).
11   See Simmel (1902:45−46), Caplow (1968), and Vinacke and Arkofff (1957).
12   See M. Goodwin (1985, 1998, 2000, 2001) and Goodwin et al. (2002).
13   See Lever (1978).
14   See Piaget (1965) and Brown et al. (1995:311−312).
15   See Goodwin (1990:143−225). See Evaldsson (2002) for a discussion of gossip among male peer groups.
16   See Goodwin (1990:39−44).
17   See Brown et al. (1995).
18   See M. Goodwin (1985, 1998, 2000, 2001).
19   See Gilligan (1982), Gilligan and Attanucci (1988); Gilligan et al. (1989:91).
20   See also Thompson et al. (2001).
21   For example, Van Ausdale and Feagin (1996, 2001) deal with issues of ethnicity and race in exclusion; Blatchford (1998), Jordan (1995), and Thorne (1993) discuss forms of discrimination in terms of gender. Other ways in which children are differentiated are in terms of disability and body type. Here I will be concerned with difference with respect to social class.
22   See Maltz and Borker (1982).
23   See Leaper (1991).
24   See Maccoby (1998).
25   See Adler and Adler (1998), Eder (1995), and Eder and Hallinan (1978).
26   See Crick (1996), Crick and Grotpeter (1995), and Crick et al. (1996, 1997, 1999).
27   See Chesler (2001), Dellasega and Nixon (2003), Simmons (2002), Talbot (2002), Wiseman (2002), and White (2002).
28   For an excellent review of the literature on gender differences in bullying, see Espelage et al. (2004).
29   See Feshbach (1969) and Lagerspetz et al. (1988).
30   See Crick and Grotpeter (1995).
31   See Cairns et al. (1989).
32   See Lagerspetz et al. (1988).
33   See Long and Pellegrini (2003:402).
34   See Craig et al. (2000:23).
35   According to Cairns and Cairns (1986:331) the socioeconomic and ethnic status represented persons living in that region of the country; the population was primarily white and African American.
36   See Olweus (1993).
37   See Bjorkquist (1994) and Pulkkinen and Pitkanen (1993).
38   See Crick et al. (1996, 1997), Crick and Grotpeter (1995), and Batsche and Knoff (1994).
39   See Rivers and Smith (1994).
40   See Owens (1996) and Rigby (1997).
41   For an excellent review of the Separate Worlds or Two Cultures perspectives see Kyratzis (2001a).

42 See Miller et al. (1986), Sachs (1987), Sheldon (1990), Leaper (1991), and Tannen (1990).

43 Indirect bullying is defined as "getting another person to assault someone, persuading another person to insult someone, spreading malicious rumors, and deliberate exclusion from a group or activity" (Rigby 1997:20). Sharp and Smith (1991), for example, report that girls were more likely to experience direct and indirect verbal aggression, while boys are more often the victims of direct physical aggression.

44 Peer nominations and peer ratings are different methods used in measuring relational aggression. In peer ratings every peer rates every other peer on a 1–5 scale, while in peer nominations every peer votes for only three people who engage in particular behaviors.

45 Studies of peer harassment have yielded different results, depending on their methodologies. Juvonen et al. (2001:105) report that "self-reports yield higher rates of victimization than do peer nominations."

46 Rigby (1998) and Knight et al. (2002).

47 Prinstein et al. (2001).

48 See Ochs et al.'s (2001) study of processes of exclusion towards children with autism in a school peer context.

49 See Underwood (2003:75).

50 See Espelage et al. (2004:17).

51 See Goodwin (1990) and Dellasega and Nixon (2003).

52 The work of Campbell (1993, 1995, 1999) among working class girls argues that girls who positively assess themselves or explicitly compare themselves with others are disliked.

53 See Sacks (1995b).

54 See Goodwin (1997a).

55 Bucholtz (personal communication, 2004) notes that with the term "lesbian" "we see a move not only into heteronormativity but homophobia." She notes that ritual insults such as "lesbian" and "whore" don't actually refer to specific attributes of targets but serve as generalized – and gendered – insult terms.

56 In part motivated by their peers' exclusionary practices, nerds perform their identity through the selection of superstandard and hypercorrect phonological forms, adherence to standard and superstandard syntactic forms, use of lexical items associated with the formal register, and orientation to parody and punning.

57 Regarding the concept of inequality see Ore (2000).

58 See, for example, Schegloff et al. (1977), Heritage (1984b), Lerner (1996).

59 See Goffman (1967:237–258) regarding character contests.

60 Kienpointner (1997:259) defines rudeness as "a kind of prototypically non-cooperative or competitive communicative behavior" characterized by "mutual irreverence and antipathy, which serves egocentric interests." Behaviors associated with rudeness include ignoring, or failing to acknowledge the other's presence, dissociating from the other (by avoiding sitting together), using a code known to others in the group, but not the target, using abusive or profane language, using derogatory names, emphasizing one's relative power, and invading the other's space (literally or metaphorically) (Kienpointner 1997:260–262). See also Beebe (1995, 1997). Invoking a psychological model Beebe (1995:154) views rudeness as a way the individual can achieve power and vent negative feelings while violating socially sanctioned norms of interaction (Beebe 1995:159).

61 In chapter 2 I analyze how friends deal with conflict.

62 See Adler and Adler (1998:95).

63 See Eder (1995:50–51).

64 See Bellmore et al. (2003:1159).

65   See Smith and Sharp (1994:2).
66   I am indebted to Lauren Mason for the phonetic transcription provided here.
67   On the concept of pollution see Douglas (1966).
68   See Goffman (1971:79).
69   See Holmes (1995) and Coates (1995).
70   See Goodwin (1990).
71   See Underwood (2003) and Rivers and Smith (1994). A study by Rivers and Smith (1994) in 23 schools in the UK found that direct verbal aggression occurred with similar frequency among girls as well as boys. Dunn (2001:62) cautions also that context plays a major role in how children behave. She feels that sex differences in aggressive behavior are more common in "public" settings (classrooms, playgrounds, neighborhood gangs) rather than in the home or family.
72   See Crick and Grotpeter (1995:711).
73   Crick and Grotpeter (1995) excluded discussions of nonvocal behavior from their classic definition of relational aggression.
74   See Goodwin (1980a, 1982a, 1990).
75   See chapter 3, Example 3.48; chapter 5, Example 5.12.
76   See also Underwood (2003:21–34).

8   Conclusion

1   See Pellegrini and Bohn (2005) and Pellegrini and Smith (1998), who argue that social skills increase with the frequency with which children enact different and varied social roles (particularly during recess).
2   See Pellegrini (2005).
3   See Blatchford (1998).
4   See Thorne (1993), Eder (1995), and Finnan (1982).
5   See Rampton (1995).
6   See Bucholtz (1999b) and van Ausdale and Feagin (2001).
7   See Scott (2002).
8   Recall the discussion in chapter 4 of the co-ed jump rope contest in which Janis prohibited boys from playing.
9   Backstage, however, Scott reports that African American girls gathered in a group to resist the imposition of the club's rules of excluding boys from play.
10   See Whiting and Edwards (1988).
11   See James and Prout (1997:243–244 quoting Harré 1979).
12   See Alanen (1988), Ambert, (1986), and Harris (1995).
13   See Bigelow et al. (1996:20–21).
14   See Shantz (1987:284).
15   See Sullivan (1953) and Youniss (1980).
16   See Piaget (1965).
17   See Sullivan (1953).
18   See Bigelow et al. (1996:156).
19   As argued by Gaskins et al. (1992:13), "Language is a key to understanding meaning because it is both the primary tool by which human beings negotiate divergent points of view and construct shared realities."
20   See M. Goodwin (2003) and Kyratzis (2004) for reviews of peer language socialization literature.
21   See, for example, studies by Bamberg (2004) and Widdicombe and Wooffitt (1995).
22   For discussions of how gender "creeps into talk" see Hopper and LeBaron (1998) or becomes relevant to talk (as something oriented to and invoked) as it unfolds

see Beach (2000), Hopper (2003), Kitzinger (2000), Sidnell (2005), Speer (2005), and Stokoe (2000).

23 In a study of "shifting moral stances" during the game of four square, Evaldsson (2004) found girls oriented towards different forms of ethos as participants in the game changed.

24 See Bigelow et al. (1996:20–21).

25 See Coates (1994:72; 1996), Maccoby (1986), and Jones (1990).

26 Boys, by way of contrast, are said to value "toughness, trouble, domination, coolness, and interpersonal bragging and sparring skills" (Adler et al. 1992:184). See also Berentzen (1984), Danby and Baker (1998, 2001), and Goodwin (1990). Among the children at Hanley School boys in second and third grade competed in arm wrestling matches and challenges to establish rank among the boys (Wingard 1997).

27 See Maccoby (1986, 1990).

28 See Maltz and Borker (1982) and Coates (1996, 1997, 1998).

29 See Holmes (1995) and Pilkington (1998).

30 See also Cook-Gumperz (2001), who shows that through oppositional stances three-year old girls explore and experiment with the "possibility of constructing opposition to their compliant, polite, and conciliatory selves" by rejecting stereotypical ways of interacting.

31 The San Francisco-based women's group Double Dutchess stresses that jumping rope provides both an inexpensive way to have fun as well as a good way of getting in shape (Ahlin 2004). Unfortunately some city schools (including the downtown school where I did research) have outlawed the playing of Double Dutch because the activity of twirling ropes is considered potentially dangerous.

32 See Crick and Grotpeter (1995), Galen and Underwood (1997), and Underwood (2003:8).

33 See hooks (1984), Jordan (1981), and Somers and Gibson (1994).

34 Zinn (1980:205) notes that W. E. B. Du Bois viewed the growth of American capitalism as contributing to the enslavement of whites as well as blacks.

35 See Bowles and Gintis (1977).

36 Recently (Finder 2005) benefits of integrating students economically have been reported, showing dramatic gains in test scores for lower-income students. I feel that such improvements in the life chances of lower-income students certainly provide a motivation for economic integration in schools, despite the social problems that arise from disparity in life experiences.

37 See Sennett and Cobb (1972:156).

38 See Lareau (2003).

39 This is similar to findings of Lareau (2003:140, 240–241, 306), in her study of the family and school lives of fourth grade working class, poor, and middle class elementary school children.

40 See Starr (2005) for a discussion of preschool queen bees in the article "Subadolescent Queen Bees." Burr et al. (2005) discuss forms of relational aggression among preschoolers.

41 Scott (2002) found that a predominantly African American environment resulted in girls supporting assertive and female group interdependence, and more equal relationships between girls and boys. Crothers et al. (2005) discuss the relevance of ethnicity for how girls are socialized to deal with oppression, prejudice, and discrimination through assertive or direct approaches when problem solving with peers.

42 See Blatchford and Sharp (1994:33) and Adler and Adler (1998).

43 See Ross (2002).

44 See Spivak and Prothow-Stith (2001).

45 Brown et al. (2005:384) report that one in five elementary school and one in ten middle school students in the United States is bullied. Their statistics are based on

studies by Pellegrini et al. (2001) and Pellegrini and Long (2002). In their study, Brown et al. (2005:385) report that one-third of the 9 to 13-year-olds reported being bullied "once in a while."

46 See Bonney-McCoy and Finkelhor (1995) and Hoover et al. (1992).
47 See Bosworth et al. (1999) and Juvonen and Graham (2004).
48 See Cho (2005:B1).
49 See Underwood (2003) and Rivers and Smith (1994), for example. One exception is a study by Rivers and Smith (1994) in 23 schools in Britain. This study found that direct verbal aggression occurred with similar frequency among girls as well as boys. Dunn (2001:62) cautions also that context plays a major role in how children behave. She feels that sex differences in aggressive behavior are more common in "public" settings (classrooms, playgrounds, neighborhood gangs) rather than in the home or family.
50 See, for example, Crick and Grotpeter (1995:711).
51 These were excluded from Crick and Grotpeter's (1995) classic definition of relational aggression.
52 See also Underwood (2003:21–34).
53 See Goodwin (1980b, 1982a, 1990).
54 See chapter 3, Example 3.48; chapter 5, Examples 5.6 and 5.14; and chapter 7, Examples 7.1 and 7.18, and Figure 7.2 for examples of collusive gestural displays.
55 Cadigan (2003) in an ethnographic study of peer victimization among sixth graders in a southern California middle school found that sixth graders rarely segregated themselves by ethnicity. Among the Hanley School children groups were multi-ethnic and social class was a more salient dimension for differentiating groups than ethnicity. Ortner (1998) and Eckert (1987) make use of extensive ethnographic research to discuss the relevance of social class for children in US high schools.
56 See, for example, Packer (1987) and Shweder and Much (1987:198, 231).
57 Walker et al. (1995) also argue that for the development of the field, moral psychology should be based on how people experience morality day by day, rather than on hypothetical dilemmas.
58 See Damon (1983:61).
59 See Damon (1977) and Selman (1980).
60 See Ambert (1995).
61 See Winterhoff (1997).
62 See the study by Tapper and Boulton (2000) using hidden cameras.
63 See Bellmore et al. (2004) and Nishina et al. (2005).
64 See Bulkowski and Sippola (2001) and Salmivalli et al. (1996).
65 As technology becomes more advanced increasingly children take their fights from schoolyards to the Internet. The *Dominion Post* (Fairfax, New Zealand) reported the children had gone beyond using text messaging and e-mail to "cyber bullying," by devoting a website to attacks on someone and encouraging people to join in the activity (Kay 2003).
66 In collaboration with a school psychologist, Juvonen and Graham developed "Cool Tools," a systemic bullying approach which provides children with specific strategies to respond to perceived or actual provocation (Juvonen and Graham 2004).
67 Scott (2002:406) reports that children on the playground of a middle income school considered supervising adults as "clueless" and lacking in understanding of the dynamics of their social world. She reports (Scott 2002:405) that adults who were supervising play "did not understand the process of ostracism" though they did know that minority girls were the excluded girls.
68 See Woffitt (2005:158).
69 See Hester and Eglin (1997) and Sacks (1995a; 1995b).

References

Adger, Carolyn Temple
  1984 Communicative Competence in the Culturally Diverse Classroom: Negotiating Norms for Linguistic Interaction. Unpublished Ph.D. Dissertation, Linguistics, Georgetown University.
Adler, Patricia A., and Peter Adler
  1998 Peer Power: Preadolescent Culture and Identity. New Brunswick, NJ: Rutgers University Press.
Adler, Patricia A., Steven J. Kless, and Peter Adler
  1992 Socialization to Gender Roles: Popularity among Elementary School Boys and Girls. Sociology of Education 65(3):169–187.
Ahlin, Elizabeth
  2004 In San Francisco, a New Twist on a Schoolyard Pastime. New York Times, August 16: A9.
Ahmad, Y., and P. K. Smith
  1994 Bullying in Schools and the Issue of Sex Differences. In Male Violence. J. Archer, ed. Pp. 70–83. London: Routledge.
Alanen, Leena
  1988 Growing Up in the Modern Family: Rethinking Socialization, the Family, and Childhood. In Growing into a Modern World: An International Interdisciplinary Conference on the Life and Development of Children in Modern Society. K. Ekberg and P. E. Mjaavatn, eds. Pp. 919–945. Trondheim: The Norwegian Centre for Child Research.
Alarcón, Norma
  1990 The Theoretical Subject(s) of This Bridge Called My Back and Anglo-American Feminism. In Making Face, Making Soul/Haciendo Caras: Creative and Critical Perspectives by Women of Color. G. Anzaldúa, ed. Pp. 356–369. San Francisco: Aunt Lute Foundation.
Ambert, Ann-Marie
  1986 Sociology of Sociology: The Place of Children in North American Sociology. In Sociological Studies of Child Development, vol. 1. P. Adler and P. A. Adler, eds. Pp. 11–31. Greenwich, CT: JAI Press.
  1995 Toward a Theory of Peer Abuse. Sociological Studies of Children 7:177–205.
Amit-Talia, Vered, and Helena Wulff
  1995 Youth Culture: A Cross-Cultural Perspective. New York: Routledge.
Antaki, C., and S. Widdicombe
  1998 Identity as Achievement and as a Tool. In Identities in Interaction. C. Antaki and S. Widdicombe, eds. Pp. 1–14. London: Sage.

Anzaldúa, Gloria
  1987   Borderlands/La Frontera: The New Mestiza. San Francisco: Spinsters/Aunt Lute.
Anzaldúa, Gloria, ed.
  1990   Making Face, Making Soul/Haciendo Caras. San Francisco: Aunt Lute.
Archer, John, and Sarah M. Coyne
  2005   An Integrated Review of Indirect, Relational, and Social Aggression. Personality and Social Psychology Review 9(3):212–230.
Aries, E.
  1996   Men and Women in Interaction: Reconsidering the Differences. New York: Oxford University Press.
  1997   Women and Men Talking: Are They Worlds Apart? *In* Women, Men, and Gender: Ongoing Debates. M. R. Walsh, ed. Pp. 91–100. New Haven: Yale University Press.
Arlington, Angela M.
  2003   Alliance Building in Girls' Talk: A Conversational Accomplishment of Playful Negotiation. Australian Review of Applied Linguistics 26: 38–54.
Atkinson, J. Maxwell, and John Heritage, eds.
  1984   Structures of Social Action. Cambridge: Cambridge University Press.
Bamberg, Michael
  2004   Positioning with Davie Hogan: Stories, Tellings, and Identities. *In* Narrative Analysis: Studying the Development of Individuals in Society. C. Daiute and C. Lightfoot, eds. Pp. 135–158. Thousand Oaks, CA: Sage.
Baron-Cohen, Simon
  2003   The Essential Difference. London: Penguin.
  2005   The Male Condition. New York Times. August 8: Op-Ed, A19.
Barrett, Rusty
  1999   Indexing Polyphonous Identity in the Speech of African American Drag Queens. *In* Reinventing Identities: The Gendered Self in Discourse. M. Bucholtz, A. C. Liang, and L. Sutton, eds. Pp. 313–331. New York: Oxford University Press.
Batsche, G. M., and H. M. Knoff
  1994   Bullies and Their Victims: Understanding a Pervasive Problem in the Schools. School Psychology Review 23:165–174.
Beach, Wayne A.
  2000   Inviting Collaborations in Stories about a Woman. Language in Society 29:379–407.
Becker, Judith
  1982   Children's Strategic Use of Requests to Mark and Manipulate Social Status. *In* Language, Thought and Culture. S. Kuczaj II, ed. Pp. 1–35. Hillsdale, NJ: Erlbaum:
Beebe, Leslie M.
  1995   Polite Fictions: Instrumental Rudeness as Pragmatic Competence. *In* Georgetown University Roundtable on Language and Linguistics, vol. 46. J. E. Alatis and C. Ferguson, eds. Pp. 154–168. Washington, DC: Georgetown University Press.
  1997   Rude Awakenings: Ways of Responding to Rudeness. Pragmatics and Language Learning 8:1–35.
Belenky, Mary Field, Blythe McVicker Clinchy, Nancy Rule Goldberger, and Jill Mattuck Tarule
  1986   Women's Ways of Knowing: The Development of Self, Voice, and Mind. New York: Basic Books.

Bellinger, David C., and Jean Berko Gleason
  1982 Sex Differences in Parental Directives to Young Children. Sex Roles 8:1123–1139.
Bellmore, Amy D., Melissa R. Witkow, Sandra Graham, and Jaana Juvonen
  2004 Beyond the Individual: The Impact of Ethnic Context and Classroom Behavioral Norms on Victims' Adjustment. Developmental Psychology 40(6):1159–1172.
Berentzen, Sigurd
  1984 Children Constructing Their Social World: An Analysis of Gender Contrast in Children's Interaction in a Nursery School. Bergen: Department of Social Anthropology, University of Bergen.
Berger, P., and T. Luckmann
  1967 The Social Construction of Reality. London: Allen Lane.
Bergmann, Jorg R.
  1998 Introduction: Morality in Discourse. Research on Language and Social Interaction 31(3/4):279–294.
Bergvall, Victoria L., Janet M. Bing, and Alice F. Freed, eds.
  1996 Rethinking Language and Gender Research: Theory and Practice. London and New York: Longman.
Best, Raphaela
  1983 We've All Got Scars. Bloomington: Indiana University Press.
Bettie, Julie
  2003 Women without Class: Girls, Race, and Identity. Los Angeles: University of California Press.
Bigelow, Brian J., Geoffrey Tesson, and John H. Lewko
  1996 Learning the Rules: The Anatomy of Children's Relationships. New York: The Guilford Press.
Bing, Janet M., and Victoria L. Bergvall
  1996 The Question of Questions: Beyond Binary Thinking. *In* Rethinking Language and Gender Research: Theory and Practice. V. Bergvall, J. Bing, and A. Freed, eds. Pp. 1–30. London: Longman.
Bjorkquist, Kaj
  1994 Sex Differences in Physical, Verbal, and Indirect Aggression. Sex Roles 30:177–188.
Bjorkqvist, Kaj, and P. Niemela
  1992 New Trends in the Study of Female Aggression. *In* Of Mice and Women: Aspects of Female Aggression. K. Bjorkqvist and P. Niemala, eds. Pp. 1–15. San Diego: Academic Press.
Bjorkqvist, Kaj, Kirsti M. J. Lagerspertz, and Ari Kaukiainen
  1992a Do Girls Manipulate and Boys Fight? Developmental Trends in Regard to Direct and Indirect Aggression. Aggressive Behavior 18:117–127.
Bjorkqvist, Kaj, Karin Osterman, and Ari Kaukiainen
  1992b The Development of Direct and Indirect Aggressive Strategies in Males and Females. *In* Of Mice and Women: Aspects of Female Aggression. K. Bjorkqvist and P. Niemala, eds. Pp. 51–64. San Diego: Academic Press.
Blatchford, Peter
  1998 Social Life in School: Pupils Experience of Breaktime and Recess from 7 to 16 Years. London: Falmer Press.
Blatchford, Peter, and Sonia Sharp
  1994 Breaktime and the School: Understanding and Changing Playground Behaviour. London: Routledge.
Bluebond-Langner, M.
  1978 The Private Worlds of Dying Children. Princeton: Princeton University Press.

Blum, Larry, Marcia Homiak, Judy Housman, and Naomi Scheman
    1976   Altruism and Women's Oppression. *In* Women and Philosophy: Towards a Theory of Liberation. C. Gould and M. Wartofsky, eds. Pp. 222–247. New York: G. P. Putnam's Sons.
Blum-Kulka, Shoshana
    2000   Gossipy Events at Family Dinners: Negotiating Sociability, Presence and the Moral Order. *In* Small Talk. J. Coupland, ed. Pp. 213–240. London: Longman.
Boling, Patricia
    1996   Privacy and the Politics of Intimate Life. Ithaca: Cornell University Press.
Bonney-McCoy, S., and D. Finkelhor
    1995   Psychosocial Sequelae of Violent Victimization in a National Youth Sample. Journal of Consulting and Clinical Psychology 63:726–785.
Boocock, Sarane Spence, and Kimberly Ann Scott
    2005   Kids in Context: The Sociological Study of Children and Childhoods. Lanham, MD: Rowman and Littlefield Publishers.
Borman, Kathryn M.
    1982a   Children's Interpersonal Relationships: Playground Games and Social Cognitive Skills. Final Report: National Institute of Education Education, Washington.
Borman, Kathryn M., ed.
    1982b   The Social Life of Children in a Changing Society. Hillsdale, NJ: Lawrence Erlbaum Associates.
Borman, Kathryn M., and Judith Frankel
    1984   Gender Inequities in Childhood: Social Life and Adult Work Life. *In* Women in the Workplace: Effects on Families. K. M. Borman, D. Quarm, and S. Gideonse, eds. Pp. 113–135. Norwood, NJ: Ablex.
Borman, Kathryn M., and Nancy T. Lippincott
    1982   Cognition and Culture: Two Perspectives on "Free Play". *In* The Social Life of Children in a Changing Society. K. M. Borman, ed. Pp. 123–142. Hillsdale, NJ: Lawrence Erlbaum.
Borman, Kathryn M., and Patricia O'Reilly
    1987   Learning Gender Roles in Three Urban U.S. Kindergarten Classrooms. Child and Youth Services 8(3–4):43–66.
Bosworth, Kris, Dorothy L. Espelage, and Thomas R. Simon
    1999   Factors Associated with Bullying Behavior in Middle School Students. Journal of Early Adolescence 19(3):341–362.
Bourdieu, Pierre
    1977a   Outline of a Theory of Practice. Richard Nice, trans. Cambridge: Cambridge University Press.
    1977b   The Economics of Linguistic Exchanges. Social Science Information XVI(6):645–668.
    1984   Distinction: A Social Critique of the Judgment of Taste. Cambridge, MA: Harvard University Press.
    1990   The Logic of Practice. Cambridge: Polity Press.
    1991   Language and Symbolic Power. John B. Thompson, ed. and intro. Raymond Gino & Matthew Adamson, trans. Cambridge, MA: Harvard University Press.
    1993   The Field of Cultural Production: Essays on Art and Literature. Cambridge: Polity Press.
Bowles, Samuel, and Herbert Gintis
    1977   Schooling in Capitalist America. New York: Basic Books.
Bradac, James J., Anthony Mulac, and Sandra A. Thompson
    1995   Men's and Women's Use of Intensifiers and Hedges in Problem-Solving Interaction: Molar and Molecular Analyses. Research on Language in Social Interaction 28(2):93–116.

Brenneis, Donald
  1984a Gossip as Dialogue: Complicitous Coperformance in a Fiji Indian Village.
  1984b Grog and Gossip in Bhatgaon: Style and Substance in Fiji Indian Conversa-
          tion. American Ethnologist 11:487–506.
  1996   Telling Troubles: Narrative, Conflict and Experience. *In* Disorderly Discourse:
          Narrative, Conflict and Inequality. C. L. Briggs, ed. Pp. 41–52. Oxford:
          Oxford University Press.
Briggs, Charles L.
  1996   Disorderly Discourse: Narrative, Conflict, and Inequality. Oxford: Oxford
          University Press.
Briggs, Jean L.
  1992   Mazes of Meaning: How a Child and a Culture Create Each Other. Interpre-
          tive Approaches to Children's Socialization 58:25–48.
Broughton, John M.
  1993   Women's Rationality and Men's Virtues: A Critique of Gender Dualism in
          Gilligan's Theory of Moral Development. *In* An Ethic of Care: Feminist and
          Interdisciplinary Perspectives. M. J. Larrabee, ed. Pp. 112–139. New York:
          Routledge.
Brown, B. B., and C. Klute
  2003   Friendships, Cliques, and Crowds. *In* Blackwell Handbook of Adolescence,
          Blackwell Handbooks of Developmental Psychology. G. R. Adams and
          M. D. Berzonsky, eds. Pp. 330–348. Malden, MA: Blackwell Publishers.
Brown, Lyn Mikel
  1994   Standing in the Crossfire: A Response to Tavris, Gremmen, Lykes, Davis,
          and Contratto. Feminism and Psychology 4(3):382–398.
  1998   Raising Their Voices: The Politics of Girls' Anger. Cambridge, MA: Harvard
          University Press.
  2003   Girlfighting: Betrayal and Rejection among Girls. New York: New York
          University Press.
Brown, Lyn Mikel, and Carol Gilligan
  1992   Meeting at the Crossroads: Women's Psychology and Girls' Development.
          Cambridge, MA: Harvard University Press.
  1993   Meeting at the Crossroads: Women's Psychology and Girls' Development.
          Feminism and Psychology 3(1):11–35.
Brown, Lyn M., Carol Gilligan, and Mark B. Tappan
  1995   Listening to Different Voices. *In* Moral Development: An Introduction.
          W. M. Kurtines and J. L. Gewirtz, eds. Pp. 311–335. Boston: Allyn and Bacon.
Brown, Penelope
  1980   How and Why Are Women More Polite: Some Evidence from a Mayan Com-
          munity. *In* Women and Language in Literature and Society. S. McConnell-
          Ginet, R. Borker, and N. Furman, eds. Pp. 111–149. New York: Praeger.
  1990   Gender, Politeness and Confrontation in Tenejapa. Discourse Processes 13:123–
          141.
Brown, Penelope, and Stephen C. Levinson
  1978   Universals of Language Usage: Politeness Phenomena. *In* Questions and
          Politeness Strategies in Social Interaction. E. N. Goody, ed. Pp. 56–310.
          Cambridge: Cambridge University Press.
  1987   Politeness: Some Universals in Language Usage. Cambridge: Cambridge
          University Press.
Brown, Stephen L., David A. Birch, and Vijaya Kancherla
  2005   Bullying Perspectives: Experiences, Attitudes, and Recommendations of
          9–13 Year-Olds Attending Health Education Centers in the United States.
          Journal of School Health 75(10):384–392.

Bucholtz, Mary

    1999a Why Be Normal?: Language and Identity Practices in a Community of Nerd Girls. Language in Society 28:203–223.

    1999b You da man: Narrating the Racial Other in the Production of White Masculinity. Journal of Sociolinguistics 3(4):443–460.

    2002 Youth and Cultural Practice. Annual Reviews in Anthropology 31:525–552.

    2003 Shop Talk: Gendered Discourses of Class, Consumption, and Style among American Youth. Paper presented at Words, Worlds, and Material Girls: A Workshop on Language, Gender, and Political Economy. Department of Anthropology, University of Toronto, October 17, 2003.

    2005 Styling, Quoting, and California Youth Identities in Interaction. Center for Language, Interaction and Culture, UCLA, November 2, 1005.

Bucholtz, Mary, and Kira Hall

    2004 Language and Identity. In Companion to Linguistic Anthropology. A. Duranti, ed. Pp. 369–394. Oxford: Blackwell.

Bulkowski, William M., and Lorrie K. Sippola

    2001 Groups, Individuals, and Victimization: A View of the Peer System. In Peer Harassment in School: The Plight of the Vulnerable and Victimized. J. Juvonen and S. Graham, eds. Pp. 355–377. New York: Guilford Press.

Burbank, Victoria K.

    1994a Cross-Cultural Perspectives on Aggression in Women and Girls: An Introduction. Sex Roles 30(3/4):169–176.

    1994b Fighting Women: Anger and Aggression in Aboriginal Australia. Berkeley: University of California Press.

Burling, Robbins

    1966 The Metrics of Children's Verse: A Cross-Linguistic Study. American Anthropologist 68:1418–1441.

Burr, Jean E., Jamie M., Ostrov, Elizabeth A., Jansen, Crystal Cullerton-Sen, and Nicki R. Crick

    2005 Relational Aggression and Friendship during Early Childhood: "I Won't Be Your Friend!" Early Education and Development 16(2):161–183.

Butler, Judith

    1993 Bodies that Matter: On the Discursive Limits of "Sex". New York: Routledge.

Cadigan, R. Jean

    2003 Scrubs: An Ethnographic Study of Peer Culture and Harassment among Sixth Graders in an Urban Middle School. Ph.D. Dissertation, Department of Anthropology, UCLA.

Cairns, Robert B., and Beverly D. Cairns

    1986 The Developmental-Interactional View of Social Behavior: Four Issues of Adolescent Aggression. In Development of Antisocial and Prosocial Behavior: Research, Theories and Issues. D. Olweus, J. Block, and M. Radke-Yarrow, eds. Pp. 315–342. New York: Academic Press.

    1994 Lifelines and Risks: Pathways of Youth in Our Time. New York: Cambridge University Press.

Cairns, R. B., B. D. Cairns, H. J. Neckerman, L. L. Ferguson, and J. Gariepy

    1989 Growth and Aggression: 1. Childhood to Early Adolescence. Developmental Psychology 25:941–951.

Cameron, Deborah

    1997a Performing Gender Identity: Young Men's Talk and the Construction of Heterosexual Masculinity. In Power and the Language of Men. S. Johnson and U. H. Meinhof, eds. Pp. 47–64. Cambridge, MA: Blackwell.

    1997b Theoretical Debates in Feminist Linguistics: Questions of Sex and Gender. In Gender and Discourse. R. Wodak, ed. Pp. 21–36. London: Sage Publications.

    1998a Gender, Language, and Discourse: A Review Essay. Signs 23(4):945–967.

1998b "Is there Any Ketchup, Vera?": Gender, Power, and Pragmatics. Discourse and Society 9(4):437–455.

1998c Why Is Language a Feminist Issue? *In* The Feminist Critique of Language. D. Cameron, ed. Pp. 1–20. New York: Routledge.

2005 Relativity and Its Discontents: Language, Gender, and Pragmatics. Journal of Intercultural Pragmatics 6(3):321–334.

Cameron, Deborah, and Don Kulick
2003 Language and Sexuality. Cambridge: Cambridge University Press.

Campbell, Anne
1982 Female Aggression. *In* Aggression and Violence. P. Marsh and A. Campbell, eds. Pp. 135–150. Oxford: Basil Blackwell.

1993 Men, Women and Aggression. New York: Basic Books.

1995 A Few Good Men: Evolutionary Psychology and Female Adolescent Aggression. Ethology and Sociobiology 16:99–123.

1999 Staying Alive: Evolution, Culture, and Women's Intra-Sexual Aggression. Behavioural and Brain Sciences 22(2):203–252.

Canaan, Joyce
1987 A Comparative Analysis of American Suburban Middle Class, Middle School, and High School Teenage Cliques. *In* Interpretive Ethnography of Education at Home and Abroad. G. Spindler and L. Spindler, eds. Pp. 385–406. Hillsdale, NJ: Lawrence Erlbaum Associates.

Caplow, Theodore
1968 Two against One: Coalitions in Triads. Englewood Cliffs, NJ: Prentice-Hall.

Caputo, Virginia
1995 Anthropology's Silent "Others": A Consideration of Some Conceptual and Methodological Issues for the Study of Youth and Children's Cultures. *In* Youth Culture: A Cross-Cultural Perspective. V. Amit-Talia and H. Wulff, eds. Pp. 19–42. New York: Routledge.

Chavez, Stephanie
2001 Girls' Team's Goal: Even Playing Field. Los Angeles Times. August 9:B1.

Chesler, Phyllis
2001 Woman's Inhumanity to Woman. New York: Thunder's Mouth Press/Nation Books.

Chesney-Lind, Meda, and Katherine Irwin
2004 From Badness to Meanness: Popular Constructions of Contemporary Girlhood. *In* All About the Girl: Culture, Power, and Identity. A. Harris, ed. Pp. 45–56. New York: Routledge.

Cho, Cynthia
2005 "No Contact" a Touchy Issue in Middle School. Los Angeles Times. December 27:B1. http://www.latimes.com/news/local/la-me-contact27dec27, 1,3084827.story, B1.

Clark, Herbert H., and Richard J. Gerrig
1990 Quotations as Demonstrations. Language 66(4):764–805.

Clayman, Steven E., and Douglas W. Maynard
1994 Ethnomethodology and Conversation Analysis. *In* Situated Order: Studies in the Social Organization of Talk and Embodied Activities. P. ten Have and G. Psathas, eds. Pp. 1–30. Washington DC: University Press of America.

Clopton, N. A., and G. T. Sorell
1993 Gender Differences in Moral Reasoning: Stable or Situational? Psychology of Women Quarterly 17(1):85–101.

Coates, Jennifer
1989 Gossip Revisited: Language in All-Female Groups. *In* Women in Their Speech Communities: New Perspectives on Language and Sex. J. Coates and D. Cameron, eds. Pp. 94–122. New York: Longman.

1994   The Language of the Professions: Discourse and Career. *In* Women and Career: Themes and Issues in Advanced Industrial Societies. J. Evetts, ed. Pp. 72–86. London: Longman.

1995   Language, Gender and Career. *In* Language and Gender: Interdisciplinary Perspectives. S. Mills, ed. Pp. 13–30. London: Longman.

1996   Women Talk: Conversation between Women Friends. Cambridge, MA: Blackwell.

1997   Women's Friendships, Women's Talk. *In* Gender and Discourse. R. Wodak, ed. Pp. 245–262. London: Sage.

1998   Gossip Revisited: Language in an All-Female Group. *In* Language and Gender: A Reader. J. Coates, ed. Pp. 226–253. Oxford: Blackwell.

2000   Small Talk and Subversion: Female Speakers Backstage. *In* Small Talk. J. Coupland, ed. Pp. 241–263. Harlow, England: Longman.

Cole, Michael, Sheila R. Cole, and Cynthia Lightfoot

2005   The Development of Children. 5th edition. New York: Worth Publishers.

Collins, Patricia Hill

1990   Black Feminist Thought. New York: Routledge.

Conkey, Margaret W.

1997   Men and Women in Prehistory: An Archaeological Challenge. *In* Gender in Cross-Cultural Perspective. 2nd edition. C. Brettell and C. F. Sargent, eds. Pp. 57–66. Upper Saddle River, NJ: Prentice Hall.

Connell, Robert W.

1987   Gender and Power. Stanford, CA: Stanford University Press.

Cook, H. B. Kimberly

1993   Small Town, Big Hell: An Ethnographic Study of Aggression in a Margariteño Community. Volume Fundación la Salle. Caracas: Instituto Caribe de Antropología y Sociología.

Cook-Gumperz, Jenny

2001   Girls' Oppositional Stances: The Interactional Accomplishment of Gender in Nursery School and Family Life. *In* Gender in Interaction: Perspectives on Femininity and Masculinity in Ethnography and Discourse. B. Baron and H. Kotthoff, eds. Pp. 21–49. Amsterdam: John Benjamins.

Cook-Gumperz, Jenny, and Margaret Szymanski

2001   Classroom "Families": Cooperating or Competing – Girls' and Boys' Interactional Styles in a Bilingual Classroom. Research on Language and Social Interaction 34(1):107–130.

Corsaro, William A.

1979   "We're Friends, Right?": Children's Use of Access Rituals in a Nursery School. Language in Society 8:315–336.

1985   Friendship and Peer Culture in the Early Years. Norwood, NJ: Ablex.

1990   The Underlife of the Nursery School. *In* Social Representations and the Development of Knowledge. G. Duveen and B. Lloyd, eds. Pp. 11–28. Cambridge: Cambridge University Press.

1997   The Sociology of Childhood. Thousand Oaks, CA: Pine Forge Press.

Corsaro, William A., and Donna Eder

1990   Children's Peer Cultures. Annual Review of Sociology 16:197–220.

1995   The Development and Socialization of Children and Adolescents. *In* Sociological Perspectives on Social Psychology. K. Cook, G. Fine, and J. House, eds. Pp. 421–451. Needham Heights, MA: Allyn & Bacon.

Corsaro, William A., and Douglas W. Maynard

1996   Format Tying in Discussion and Argument Among Italian and American Children. *In* Social Interaction, Social Context, and Language. D. I. Slobin, J. Gerhardt, A. Kyratzis, and J. Guo, eds. Pp. 157–174. Mahwah, NJ: Lawrence Erlbaum.

Corsaro, William A., and Thomas A. Rizzo
  1988   Discussion and Friendship: Production and Reproduction within the Peer
         Culture of Italian Nursery School Children. American Sociological Review
         53:879–894.
  1990   Disputes and Conflict Resolution among Nursery School Children in the
         U.S. and Italy. *In* Conflict Talk. A. Grimshaw, ed. Pp. 21–66. Cambridge:
         Cambridge University Press.
Craig, Wendy M., Debra Pepler, and R. Atlas
  2000   Observations of Bullying in the Playground and in the Classroom. Social
         Psychology International 21:22–36.
Crawford, Mary
  1995   Talking Difference: On Gender and Language. London: Sage.
Crick, Nicki R.
  1996   The Role of Overt Aggression, Relational Aggression, and Prosocial Behavior
         in the Prediction of Children's Future Social Adjustment. Child Development
         67:2317–2327.
Crick, Nicki R., Maureen A. Bigbee, and Cynthia Howes
  1996   Gender Differences in Children's Normative Beliefs about Aggression: How Do
         I Hurt Thee? Let Me Count the Ways. Child Development 67:1003–1014.
Crick, Nicki R., Juan F. Casas, and Monique Mosher
  1997   Relational and Overt Aggression in Preschool. Developmental Psychology
         33(4):579–588.
Crick, Nicki R., and J. K. Grotpeter
  1995   Relational Aggression, Gender, and Social-Psychological Adjustment. Child
         Development 66:710–722.
Crick, Nicki R., David A. Nelson, Julie R. Morales, Crystal Cullerton-Sen,
Juan F. Casas, and Susan Hickman
  2001   Relational Victimization in Childhood and Adolescence: I Hurt You Through
         the Grapevine. *In* Peer Harassment in School: The Plight of the Vulnerable
         and Victimized. J. Juvonen and S. Graham, eds. Pp. 196–214. New York:
         Guilford Press.
Crick, Nicki R., Nicole E. Werner, Juan F. Casas, Kathryn M. O'Brien,
David A. Nelson, Jennifer K. Grotpeter, and Kristian Markon
  1999   Childhood Aggression and Gender: A New Look at an Old Problem. *In*
         Nebraska Symposium on Motivation, vol. 44. D. Bernstein, ed. Pp. 75–142.
         Lincoln: University of Nebraska Press.
Crothers, Laura M., Juliane E. Field, and Jered B. Kolbert
  2005   Navigating Power, Control, and Being Nice: Aggression in Adolescent Girls'
         Friendships. Journal of Counseling and Development 83(Summer):349–354.
Damon, William
  1977   The Social World of the Child. San Francisco: Jossey-Bass.
  1983   The Nature of Social-Cognitive Change in the Developing Child. *In* The
         Relationship between Social and Cognitive Development. W. F. Overton,
         ed. Pp. 103–141. Hillsdale, NJ: Lawrence Erlbaum.
Danby, Susan, and Carolyn Baker
  1998   How to be Masculine in the Block Area. Childhood 5(2):151–175.
  2000   Unraveling the Fabric of Social Order in Block Area. *In* Local Educational
         Order: Ethnomethodological Studies of Knowledge in Action. S. Hester and
         D. Francis, eds. Pp. 91–140. Amsterdam: Benjamins.
  2001   Escalating Terror: Communicative Strategies in a Preschool Classroom
         Dispute. Early Education and Development 12(3):343–358.
Davidson, Brad
  1996   Discourse Uses of "Tú" and "Yo" in Spoken Madrid Spanish. Journal of
         Pragmatics 26:543–565.

Davies, Bronwyn
    1989   Frogs and Snails and Feminist Tales. Boston: Routledge and Kegan Paul.
Davies, Bronwyn, and Rom Harré
    1990   Positioning: The Discursive Production of Selves. Journal for the Theory of
            Social Behaviour 20:43–63.
Davis, Kathy
    1988   Paternalism Under the Microscope. *In* Gender and Discourse: The Power of
            Talk. A. D. Todd and S. Fisher, eds. Pp. 19–54. Norwood, NJ: Ablex.
    1994   What's in a Voice? Methods and Metaphors. Feminism and Psychology
            4(3):353–361.
Davis, Mike
    1992   City of Quartz: Excavating the Future in Los Angeles. New York: Vintage.
DeHart, Ganie B.
    1996   Gender and Mitigation in 4-Year Olds' Pretend Play Talk with Siblings.
            Research on Language and Social Interaction 29(1):81–96.
de Leon, Lourdes
    1998a   Mu Me Majeluk, Mu Me uteluk, Not with Hitting, Not with Scolding:
            Socializing Emotion and Moral Agency in Tzotzil (Mayan) children. *In* Paper
            Presented at the 97th Annual Meeting of the American Anthropological
            Association, December 5, Philadelphia, at the session "Talk, Emotion, and
            Social Activity in the Socialization of Agency", organized by Lourdes de
            Leon and Marjorie H. Goodwin.
    1998b   The Emergent Participant: Interactive Patterns in the Socialization of Tzotzil
            (Mayan) Infants. Journal of Linguistic Anthropology 8(2):131–161.
    In press   Subverting Asymmetries: Humor and Interactive Unfolding of Verbal Play
            in (Tzotzil) Mayan Children. Research on Language and Social Interaction.
Dellasega, Cheryl, and Charisse Nixon
    2003   Girl Wars: Twelve Strategies that Will End Female Bullying. New York:
            Simon and Schuster.
Douglas, Mary
    1966   Purity and Danger: An Analysis of Concepts of Pollution and Taboo.
            Baltimore, MD: Penguin.
Douvan, Elizabeth, and Joseph Adelson
    1966   The Adolescent Experience. New York: Wiley.
Du Bois, Barbara
    1983   Passionate Scholarship: Notes on Values, Knowing and Method in Feminist
            Social Science. *In* Theories of Women's Studies. G. Bowles and R. D. Klein,
            eds. Pp. 105–116. Boston: Routledge and Kegan Paul.
Dunn, Janet S.
    2001   The Development of Children's Conflict and Prosocial Behavior: Lessons for
            Research on Social Aggression and Gender. *In* Conduct Disorders in Child-
            hood and Adolescence. J. Hill and B. Maughan, eds. Pp. 49–66. New York:
            Cambridge University Press.
Dunn, Judy
    1988   The Beginnings of Social Understanding. Cambridge, MA: Harvard Univer-
            sity Press.
Duranti, Alessandro
    1984   The Social Meaning of Subject Pronouns in Italian Conversation. Text
            4(4):277–311.
    1997   Linguistic Anthropology. Cambridge: Cambridge University Press.
Eckert, Penelope
    1987   Jocks and Burnouts: Social Categories in a US High School. New York:
            Teachers University Press.

1989   The Whole Woman: Sex and Gender Differences in Variation. Language Variation and Change I:245–267.

1996   Vowels and Nail Polish: The Emergence of Linguistic Style in the Preadolescent Heterosexual Marketplace. *In* Gender and Belief Systems: Proceedings of the Fourth Berkeley Women and Language Conference. N. Warner, J. Ahlers, L. Bilmes, M. Oliver, S. Wertheim, and M. Chen, eds. Pp. 183–190. Berkeley, CA: Berkeley Women and Language Group.

1997   Gender, Race, and Class in the Preadolescent Marketplace of Identities. Paper presented at the 96th Annual Meeting of the AAA, Washington, DC.

Eckert, Penelope, and Sally McConnell-Ginet

1992   Communities of Practice: Where Language, Gender and Power All Live. *In* Locating Power: Proceedings of the Second Berkeley Women and Language Conference. K. Hall, M. Bucholtz, and B. Moonwomon, eds. Pp. 89–99. Berkeley, CA: Berkeley Women and Language Group.

2003   Language and Gender. Cambridge: Cambridge University Press.

Eder, Donna

1985   The Cycle of Popularity: Interpersonal Relations among Female Adolescents. Sociology of Education 58:154–165.

1988   Building Cohesion through Collaborative Narration. Social Problems Quarterly 51:225–235.

1990   Serious and Playful Disputes: Variation in Conflict Talk among Female Adolescents. *In* Conflict Talk: Sociolinguistic Investigations of Arguments in Conversations. A. D. Grimshaw, ed. Pp. 67–84. Cambridge: Cambridge University Press.

1993   "Go Get Ya a French!": Romantic and Sexual Teasing among Adolescent Girls. *In* Gender and Conversational Interaction. D. Tannen, ed. Pp. 32–62. Oxford: Oxford University Press.

1995   School Talk: Gender and Adolescent Culture. New Brunswick, NJ: Rutgers University Press.

Eder, Donna, and Janet Enke

1991   The Structure of Gossip: Opportunities and Constraints on Collective Expression among Adolescents. American Sociological Review 56:494–508.

Eder, Donna, and Maureen T. Hallinan

1978   Sex Differences in Children's Friendships. American Sociological Review 43:237–250.

Eder, Donna, and David A. Kinney

1995   The Effect of Middle School Extracurricular Activities on Adolescents' Popularity and Peer Status. Youth and Society 26(3):298–324.

Eder, Donna, and S. Parker

1987   The Cultural Production and Reproduction of Gender: The Effect of Extracurricular Activities on Peer Group Culture. Sociology of Education 60(3):200–213.

Edley, N., and M. Wetherell

1995   Men in Perspective: Practice, Power and Identity. Hemel Hempstead: Prentice-Hall/Harvester Wheatsheaf.

1997   Jockeying for Position: The Construction of Masculine Identities. Discourse and Society 8:203–217.

Ehrenreich, Barbara

1989   Fear of Falling: The Inner Life of the Middle Class. New York: Pantheon Books.

Eichler, Margrit, and Jeanne Lapointe

1985   On the Treatment of the Sexes in Research. Ottawa: Social Sciences and Humanities Research Council of Canada.

Eisenberg, Ann R., and Catherine Garvey
    1981   Children's Use of Verbal Strategies in Resolving Conflicts. Discourse Processes 4:149–170.
Elveton, Roy
    2005   Lebenswelt [Lifeworld]: The Literary Encyclopedia [online database].
Ervin-Tripp, Susan M.
    1976   "Is Sybil There?": The Structure of Some American English Directives. Language in Society 5:25–67.
    1982   Structures of Control. *In* Communicating in the Classroom. L. C. Wilkinson, ed. Pp. 27–47. New York: Academic Press.
    1986   Activity Structure as Scaffolding for Children's Second Language Learning. *In* Children's Worlds and Children's Language. J. Cook-Gumperz, W. A. Corsaro, and J. Streeck, eds. Pp. 327–357. Berlin: Mouton de Gruyter.
Ervin-Tripp, Susan M., J. Guo, and M. Lampert
    1990   Politeness and Persuasion in Children's Control Acts. Journal of Pragmatics 14:195–219.
Espelage, Dorothy L., Sarah E. Mebane, and Susan M. Swearer
    2004   Gender Differences in Bullying: Moving Beyond Mean Level Differences. *In* Bullying in American Schools: A Socio-Ecological Perspective on Prevention and Intervention. D. L. Espelage and S. M. Swearer, eds. Pp. 15–35. Mahwah, NJ: Lawrence Erlbaum.
Evaldsson, Ann-Carita
    1993   Play, Disputes and Social Order. Linköping: Department of Communication Studies, Linköping University, Linköping Studies in Arts and Sciences #93.
    2002   Boys' Gossip Telling: Staging Identities and Indexing (Unacceptable) Masculine Behavior. Text 22(2):199–225.
    2003   "Throwing Like a Girl?": Situating Gender Differences in Physicality across Game Contexts. Childhood: A Global Journal of Child Research 10(4):475–497.
    2004   Shifting Moral Stances: The Situational Relevance of Rules in Same Sex and Cross Sex Games. Research on Language and Social Interaction 37(4):331–363.
Evaldsson, Ann-Carita, and William A. Corsaro
    1998   Play and Games in the Peer Cultures of Preschool and Preadolescent Children: An Interpretative Approach. Childhood 5(4):377–402.
Farr, Marcia
    1994   Echando Relajo: Verbal Art and Gender among Mexicanas in Chicago. *In* Cultural Performances: Proceedings of the Third Berkeley Women and Language Conference, April 8–10. Pp. 168–186. Berkeley: Berkeley Women and Language Group.
Feshbach, Norma
    1969   Sex Differences in Children's Modes of Aggressive Responses toward Outsiders. Merrill Palmer Quarterly 15:249–258.
Feshbach, Norma, and Gittelle Sones
    1971   Sex Differences in Adolescent Reactions toward Newcomers. Developmental Psychology 4:381–386.
Finder, Alan
    2005   As Test Scores Jump, Raleigh Credits Integration by Income. New York Times, Education Section. September 25: 1, col. 5.
Fine, Gary Alan
    1980   The Natural History of a Preadolescent Male Friendship Group. *In* Friendship and Social Relations in Children. H. C. Foot, A. J. Chapman, and J. R. Smith, eds. Pp. 293–320. New York: John Wiley and Sons.

1986   The Social Organization of Adolescent Gossip: The Rhetoric of Moral Evaluation. *In* Children's Worlds and Children's Language. J. Cook-Gumperz,
W. A. Corsaro, and J. Streeck, eds. Pp. 405–423. Berlin: Mouton de Gruyter.
Finnan, Christine Robinson
1982   The Ethnography of Children's Spontaneous Play. *In* Doing the Ethnography of Schooling: Educational Anthropology in Action. G. Spindler, ed.
Pp. 356–380. New York: Holt, Rinehart and Winston.
Fishman, Pamela
1978a   Interaction: The Work Women Do. Social Problems 25:397–406.
1978b   What Do Couples Talk about When They're Alone? *In* Women's Language
and Style. D. Butturff and E. L. Epstein, eds. Pp. 11–22. Akron, OH: L. and
S. Books.
Fiske, Alan Page, Shinobu Kitayama, Hazel Rose Markus, and Richard E. Nisbell
1998   The Cultural Matrix of Social Psychology. *In* The Handbook of Social Psy-
chology. D. T. Gilbert, S. T. Fiske, and G. Lindzey, eds. Pp. 915–981.
Boston: McGraw-Hill.
Flax, Jane
1990   Thinking Fragments: Psychoanalysis, Feminism, and Postmodernisn in the
Contemporary West. Berkeley, CA: University of California Press.
Foreman, Christina Gayle
2000   Identification of African-American English from Prosodic Cues. Texas
Linguistic Forum 43:57–66.
Foucault, Michel
1980   Power/Knowledge: Selected Interviews and Other Writings 1972–1977.
C. Gordon, trans. New York: Pantheon.
1984   The Birth of the Asylum. *In* The Foucault Reader. P. Rabinow, ed.
Pp. 141–168. New York: Pantheon Books.
Freed, Alice
1992   We Understand Perfectly: A Critique of Tannen's View of Cross-Sex
Communication. *In* Locating Power: Proceedings of the Second Berkeley
Women and Language Conference. K. Hall, M. Bucholtz, and B. Moonwomon,
eds. Pp. 144–152. Berkeley: Berkeley Women and Language Group, Depart-
ment of Linguistics, University of California, Berkeley.
1995   Language and Gender: Review Essay. *In* Annual Review of Applied Lingui-
stics, vol. 15. W. Grabe, ed. Pp. 3–22. Cambridge: Cambridge University Press.
Fry, D., and A. H. Gabriel
1994   Preface: The Cultural Construction of Gender and Aggression. Sex Roles
30:177–188.
Gal, Susan
1995   Language, Gender, and Power: An Anthropological Review. *In* Gender
Articulated. K. Hall and M. Bucholtz, eds. Pp. 169–182. New York:
Routledge.
Galen, B. R., and M. K. Underwood
1997   A Developmental Investigation of Social Aggression among Children.
Developmental Psychology 33:589–600.
Galindo, D. Letticia
1992   Dispelling the Male-Only Myth: Chicanas and Calo. Bilingual Review 17(1):3–
35.
1994   Capturing Chicana Voices: An Interdisciplinary Approach. *In* Cultural
Performances: Proceedings of the Third Berkeley Women and Language
Conference. M. Bucholtz, A. C. Liang, L. A. Sutton, and C. Hines, eds.
Pp. 220–231. Berkeley: Berkeley Women and Language Group, University
of California.

1999   Caló and Taboo Language Use among Chicanas. *In* Speaking Chicana: Voice, Power, and Identity. D. L. Galindo and M. D. Gonzales, eds. Tucson: University of Arizona Press.

Garcia, Angela
1996   Moral Reasoning in Interactional Context: Strategic Uses of Care and Justice Arguments in Mediation Hearings. Sociological Inquiry 66(2):197–214.

Garcia, Linda, and J. B. Orange
1996   The Analysis of Conversational Skills of Older Adults: Current Research and Clinical Approaches. Journal of Speech-Language Pathology and Audiology 20(2):123–138.

Garfinkel, Harold
1956   Conditions of Successful Degradation Ceremonies. American Journal of Sociology 61:240–244.
1963   A Conception of, and Experiments with, "Trust" as a Conception of Concerted Stable Actions. *In* Motivation and Social Interaction: Cognitive Determinants. O. J. Harvey, ed. Pp. 187–238. New York: Roland Press.
1967   Studies in Ethnomethodology. Englewood Cliffs, NJ: Prentice-Hall.
1991   Respecification: Evidence for Locally Produced, Naturally Accountable Phenomena of Order, logic, Reason, Meaning, Method, etc. in and as of the Essential Haecceity of Immortal Ordinary Society (I) – an Announcement of Studies. *In* Ethnomethodology and the Human Sciences. G. Button, ed. Pp. 10–19. Cambridge: Cambridge University Press.

Garfinkel, Harold, and Harvey Sacks
1970   On Formal Structures of Practical Actions. *In* Theoretical Sociology. J. D. McKinney and E. A. Tiryakian, eds. Pp. 337–366. New York: Appleton-Century Crofts.

Gaskins, S., P. J. Miller, and W. A. Corsaro
1992   Theoretical and Methodological Perspectives in the Interpretive Study of Children. *In* Interpretive Approaches to Children's Socialization. W. A. Corsaro and P. J. Miller, eds. Pp. 5–24. San Francisco: Jossey-Bass.

Genishi, Celia, and Marianna di Paolo
1982   Learning through Argument in a Preschool. *In* Communicating in the Classroom. L. C. Wilkinson, ed. Pp. 49–68. New York: Academic Press.

Giddens, Anthony
1979   The Central Problems of Social Theory. London: Macmillan.
1984   The Constitution of Society: Outline of the Theory of Structuration. Berkeley, CA: University of California Press.

Gilligan, Carol
1982   In a Different Voice: Psychological Theory and Women's Development. Cambridge, MA: Harvard University Press.
1987   Moral Orientation and Moral Development. *In* Women and Moral Theory. E. F. Kittay and D. T. Meyers, eds. Pp. 19–33. Totowa, NJ: Rowman and Littlefield.
1988   Remapping the Moral Domain: New Images of Self in Relationship. *In* Mapping the Moral Domain: A Contribution of Women's Thinking to Psychological Theory and Education. C. Gilligan, J. V. Ward, J. M. Taylor, and B. Bardige, eds. Pp. 3–20. Cambridge, MA: Harvard University Press.
2003   The Birth of Pleasure: A New Map of Love. New York: Random House.

Gilligan, Carol, and J. Attanucci
1988   Two Moral Orientations: Gender Differences and Similarities. Merrill-Palmer Quarterly 34:451–456.

Gilligan, Carol, Nona P. Lyons, and Trudy J. Hanmer
1989   Making Connections: The Relational Worlds of Adolescent Girls at Emma Williard School. Troy, NY: Emma Willard School.

Glenn, Phillip J.
  2003   Laughter in Interaction. Cambridge: Cambridge University Press.
Gluckman, Max
  1963   Gossip and Scandal. Current Anthropology 4:307–315.
Goetz, Peggy J., and Marilyn Shatz
  1999   When and How Peers Give Reasons: Justifications in the Talk of Middle
         School Children. Journal of Child Language 26:721–748.
Goffman, Erving
  1959   The Presentation of Self in Everyday Life. Garden City, NY: Doubleday.
  1961   Encounters: Two Studies in the Sociology of Interaction. Indianapolis:
         Bobbs-Merrill.
  1963   Behavior in Public Places: Notes on the Social Organization of Gatherings.
         New York: Free Press.
  1967   Interaction Ritual: Essays in Face to Face Behavior. Garden City, NY:
         Doubleday.
  1971   Relations in Public: Microstudies of the Public Order. New York: Harper
         and Row.
  1977   The Arrangement between the Sexes. Theory and Society 4:301–331.
  1978   Response Cries. Language 54:787–815.
  1979   Footing. Semiotica 25:1–29 (reprinted in Erving Goffman's *Forms of Talk*,
         1981, Philadelphia: University of Pennsylvania Press, Pp. 124–159).
  1981   Footing. *In* Forms of Talk. E. Goffman, ed. Pp. 124–159. Philadelphia:
         University of Pennsylvania Press.
Goodenough, Ward H.
  1981   Culture, Language and Society. 2nd edition. Menlo Park: Benjamin Cummings.
Goodman, Robert, and Aaron Ben-Ze'ev
  1994   Good Gossip. Lawrence, KA: University of Kansas Press.
Goodwin, Charles
  1981   Conversational Organization: Interaction Between Speakers and Hearers.
         New York: Academic Press.
  1986   Audience Diversity, Participation and Interpretation. Text 6(3):283–316.
  1994   Professional Vision. American Anthropologist 96(3):606–633.
  2000   Action and Embodiment within Situated Human Interaction. Journal of Prag-
         matics 32:1489–1522.
  2003   Pointing as Situated Practice. *In* Pointing: Where Language, Culture and
         Cognition Meet. S. Kita, ed. Pp. 217–241. Hillsdale, NJ: Lawrence Erlbaum
         Associates.
  In press (a)   Interactive Footing. *In* Voicing: Reported Speech and Footing in
         Conversation. E. Holt and R. Clift, eds. Cambridge: Cambridge University
         Press.
  In press (b)   Retrospective and Prospective Orientation in the Construction of
         Argumentative Moves. Text and Talk.
Goodwin, Charles, and Alessandro Duranti
  1992   Rethinking Context: An Introduction. *In* Rethinking Context: Language
         as an Interactive Phenomenon. A. Duranti and C. Goodwin, eds. Pp. 1–42.
         Cambridge: Cambridge University Press.
Goodwin, Charles, and Marjorie Harness Goodwin
  1987   Concurrent Operations on Talk: Notes on the Interactive Organization of
         Assessments. IPrA Papers in Pragmatics 1(1):1–52.
  1990   Interstitial Argument. *In* Conflict Talk. A. Grimshaw, ed. Pp. 85–117. Cam-
         bridge: Cambridge University Press.
  1992   Assessments and the Construction of Context. *In* Rethinking Context:
         Language as an Interactive Phenomenon. A. Duranti and C. Goodwin, eds.
         Pp. 147–190. Cambridge: Cambridge University Press.

2004   Participation. *In* A Companion to Linguistic Anthropology. A. Duranti, ed. Pp. 222–243. Oxford: Blackwell.

Goodwin, Charles, and John Heritage
1990   Conversation Analysis. Annual Reviews of Anthropology 19:283–307.

Goodwin, Marjorie Harness
1980a   Directive/Response Speech Sequences in Girls' and Boys' Task Activities. *In* Women and Language in Literature and Society. S. McConnell-Ginet, R. Borker, and N. Furman, eds. Pp. 157–173. New York: Praeger.
1980b   "He-Said-She-Said": Formal Cultural Procedures for the Construction of a Gossip Dispute Activity. American Ethnologist 7:674–695.
1980c   Processes of Mutual Monitoring Implicated in the Production of Description Sequences. Sociological Inquiry 50:303–317.
1982a   "Instigating": Storytelling as a Social Process. American Ethnologist 9:799–819.
1982b   Processes of Dispute Management Among Urban Black Children. American Ethnologist 9:76–96.
1983a   Aggravated Correction and Disagreement in Children's Conversations. Journal of Pragmatics 7:657–677.
1983b   Searching for a Word as an Interactive Activity. *In* Semiotics 1981. J. N. Deely and M. D. Lenhart, eds. Pp. 129–138. New York: Plenum Press.
1985   The Serious Side of Jump Rope: Conversational Practices and Social Organization in the Frame of Play. Journal of American Folklore 98:315–330.
1990   He-Said-She-Said: Talk as Social Organization among Black Children. Bloomington, IN: Indiana University Press.
1997a   By-Play: Negotiating Evaluation in Story-telling. *In* Towards a Social Science of Language: Papers in Honor of William Labov 2: Social Interaction and Discourse Structures. G. R. Guy, C. Feagin, D. Schriffin, and J. Baugh, eds. Pp. 77–102. Amsterdam: John Benjamins.
1997b   Toward Families of Stories in Context. Journal of Narrative and Life History 7:107–112.
1998   Games of Stance: Conflict and Footing in Hopscotch. *In* Kids' Talk: Strategic Language Use in Later Childhood. S. Hoyle and C. T. Adger, eds. Pp. 23–46. New York: Oxford University Press.
2000   Morality and Accountability in Girls' Play. Texas Linguistic Forum 43 (Proceedings of the Seventh Annual Symposium about Language and Society, Austin): 77–86.
2001   Organizing Participation in Cross-Sex Jump Rope: Situating Gender Differences within Longitudinal Studies of Activities. Special issue "Gender Construction in Children's Interactions: A Cultural Perspective". Research on Language and Social Interaction 34(1):75–106.
2003   Gender, Ethnicity and Class in Children's Peer Interactions. *In* The Handbook of Language and Gender. J. Holmes and M. Meyerhoff, eds. Pp. 229–251. Oxford: Blackwell.

Goodwin, Marjorie Harness, and Charles Goodwin
1986   Gesture and Coparticipation in the Activity of Searching for a Word. Semiotica 62(1/2):51–75.
2000   Emotion within Situated Activity. *In* Communication: An Arena of Development. N. Budwig, I. C. Uzgiris, and J. V. Wertsch, eds. Pp. 33–54. Mawah, NJ: Lawrence Erlbaum.

Goodwin, Marjorie Harness, Charles Goodwin, and Malcah Yaeger-Dror
2002   Multi-modality in Girls' Game Disputes. Journal of Pragmatics 34:1621–1649.

Gordon, David, and Susan Ervin-Tripp
  1984 The Structure of Children's Requests. In The Acquisition of Communic-
        ative Competence. R. L. Schiefelbusch and J. Pickar, eds. Pp. 298–321.
        Baltimore, MD: University Park Press.
Griffiths, V.
  1995 Adolescent Girls and Their Friends: A Feminist Ethnography. Aldershot:
        Avebury.
Griswold, Olga
  In press Achieving Authority: Discursive Practices in Russian Pre-Adolescent Girls'
        Pretend Play. Research on Language and Social Interaction.
Gumperz, John J.
  1972 Introduction. In Directions in Sociolinguistics: The Ethnography of Com-
        munication. J. J. Gumperz and D. Hymes, eds. Pp. 1–25. New York: Holt,
        Rinehart and Winston.
Hall, Kira
  1997 "Go Suck Your Husband's Sugarcane!": Hijras and the Use of Sexual Insult.
        In Queerly Phrased: Language, Gender, and Sexuality. A. Livia and K. Hall,
        eds. Pp. 430–460. New York: Oxford University Press.
Halliday, M. A. K., and Ruqaiya Hasan
  1976 Cohesion in English. London: Longman.
Hanks, William F.
  1990 Referential Practice: Language and Lived Space among the Maya. Chicago:
        University of Chicago Press.
Harding, S.
  1987 The Curious Coincidence of Feminine and African Moralities: Challenges
        for Feminist Theory. In Women and Moral Theory. E. F. Kittay and D. T.
        Meyers, eds. Pp. 296–315. Totowa, NJ: Rowman and Littlefield.
Hardman, C.
  1973 Can There by an Anthropology of Children? Journal of the Anthropological
        Society of Oxford 4(11):85–99.
Hare-Mustin, R. T., and J. Maracek, eds.
  1990 Making a Difference: Psychology and the Construction of Gender. New
        Haven: Yale University Press.
Harré, Rom
  1979 General Editor's Preface. In Nicknames: Their Origin and Social Con-
        sequences. J. E. A. Morgan, ed. London: Routledge and Kegan Paul.
  1964 The Language of Morals. Oxford: Oxford University Press.
Harris, Anita
  2004 Introduction. In All About the Girl: Culture, Power, and Identity. A. Harris,
        ed. Pp. xi–xxv. New York: Routledge.
Harris, Judith Rich
  1995 Where is the Child's Environment? A Group Socialization Theory of
        Development. Psychological Review 102(3):458–489.
Hart, H. L. A.
  1951 The Ascription of Responsibility and Rights. In Essays on Logic and Language.
        A. Flew, ed. Pp. 145–166. New York: Philosophical Library.
Hartup, Willard W., D. D. French, B. Laursen, M. K. Johnston, and J. R. Ogawa
  1993 Conflict and Friendship Relations in Middle Childhood: Behavior in a Closed-
        Field Situation. Child Development 64(2):445–454.
Hartup, Willard W., and Brett Laursen
  1993 Conflict and Context in Peer Relations. In Children on Playgrounds:
        Research Perspectives and Applications. C. H. Hart, ed. Pp. 44–84. Albany,
        NY: State University of New York Press.

Henley, Nancy M.
　1995　Ethnicity and Gender Issues in Language. *In* Bringing Cultural Diversity to Feminist Psychology: Theory, Research, and Practice. H. Landrine, ed. Pp. 361–396. Washington, DC: American Psychological Association.
Henley, Nancy M., and Cheris Kramarae
　1991　Gender, Power and Miscommunication. *In* "Miscommunication" and Problematic Talk. H. G. Nikolas Coupland, and John M. Wiemann, ed. Pp. 18–43. Newbury Park: Sage.
Hepburn, Alexa
　1997　Teachers and Secondary School Bullying: A Postmodern Discourse Analysis. Discourse and Society 8:27–48.
Heritage, John
　1984a　A Change-of-State Token and Aspects of Its Sequential Placement. *In* Structures of Social Action. J. M. Atkinson and J. Heritage, eds. Pp. 299–345. Cambridge: Cambridge University Press.
　1984b　Garfinkel and Ethnomethodology. Cambridge: Polity Press.
Heritage, John, and Geoffrey Raymond
　2005　The Terms of Agreement: Indexing Epistemic Authority and Subordination in Talk-in-Interaction. Social Psychology Quarterly 88(1):15–38.
Hester, S., and P. Eglin, eds.
　1997　Culture in Action: Studies in Membership Categorization Analysis. Boston: International Institute for Ethnomethodology and University Press of America.
Hey, Valerie
　1997　The Company She Keeps: An Ethnography of Girls' Friendships. Buckingham: Open University Press.
Hirschfeld, Lawrence A.
　1996　Race in the Making: Cognition, Culture and the Child's Construction of Human Kinds. Cambridge, MA: MIT Press.
　2002　Why Don't Anthropologists Like Children? American Anthropologist 104(2):611–627.
Holland, Dorothy C., and Margaret A. Eisenhart
　1990　Educated in Romance: Women, Achievement, and College Culture. Chicago: University of Chicago Press.
Holmes, Janet
　1995　Women, Men, and Politeness. London: Longman.
　1998　Complimenting – A Positive Politeness Strategy. *In* Language and Gender: A Reader. J. Coates, ed. Pp. 100–119. Oxford: Blackwell.
hooks, bell
　1984　Feminist Theory: From Margin to Center. Boston: South End Press.
　2000　Where We Stand: Class Matters. New York: Routledge.
Hoover, J. H., R. Oliver, and R. J. Hazler
　1992　Bullying: Perceptions of Adolescent Victims in Midwestern USA. School Psychology International 13:5–16.
Hopper, Robert
　2003　Gendering Talk. East Lansing: Michigan State University Press.
Hopper, Robert, and C. LeBaron
　1998　How Gender Creeps into Talk. Research on Language and Social Interaction 31(1):59–74.
Houston, M., and C. Kramarae
　1991　Speaking from Silence: Methods of Silencing and of Resistance. Discourse and Society 2:387–399.
Hrdy, Sarah Blaffer
　1981　The Woman That Never Evolved. Cambridge, MA: Harvard University Press.

Hutchby, Ian
    1996a Power in Discourse: The Case of Arguments on Talk Radio. Discourse and
        Society 7(4):481–497.
    1996b Power in Discourse: The Case of Arguments on a British Talk Radio Show.
        Discourse and Society 7(4):481–497.
Hutchby, Ian, and Jo Moran-Ellis
    1998 Introduction. *In* Children and Social Competence: Arenas of Action. I. Hutchby
        and J. Moran-Ellis, eds. Pp. 1–25. London: Falmer Press.
Ihinger-Tallman, Marilyn, and Teresa M. Cooney
    2005 Families in Context: An Introduction. Los Angeles: Roxbury Publishing
        Company.
James, Allison
    1993 Childhood Identities. Edinburgh: Edinburgh University Press.
James, Allison, and Alan Prout
    1990 Constructing and Reconstructing Childhood: Contemporary Issues in the
        Sociological Study of Childhood. London: Polity Press.
    1997 Constructing and Reconstructing Childhood: Contemporary Issues in the
        Sociological Study of Childhood. London: Falmer Press.
James, Allison, Chris Jenks, and Alan Prout
    1998 Theorizing Childhood. Oxford: Polity Press.
Jefferson, Gail
    1979 A Technique for Inviting Laughter and its Subsequent Acceptance/
        Declination. *In* Everyday Language: Studies in Ethnomethodology. G. Psathas,
        ed. Pp. 79–96. New York: Irvington Publishers.
    1985 On the Interactional Unpackaging of a "Gloss". Language in Society 14:435–466.
Johnson, Nastassia Isis
    2004 Constructing Social Difference in the Everyday Lives of Children. Honors
        Thesis. Department of Anthropology, UCLA.
Johnson, S., and U. Meinhof, eds.
    1997 Language and Masculinity. Oxford: Blackwell.
Jones, Deborah
    1990 Gossip: Notes on Women's Oral Culture. *In* The Feminist Critique of
        Language: A Reader. D. Cameron, ed. Pp. 242–250. London: Routledge.
Jordan, E.
    1995 Fighting Boys and Fantasy Play: The Construction of Masculinity in the
        Early Years of School. Gender and Education 8(3):311–321.
Jordan, E., and A. Cowan
    1995 Warrior Narratives in the Kindergarten Classroom – Renegotiating the Social
        Contract. Gender and Society 9(6):727–743.
Jordan, E., A. Cowan, and J. Roberts
    1995 Knowing the Rules – Discursive Strategies in Young Children's Power
        Struggles. Early Childhood Research Quarterly 10(3):339–358.
Jordan, June
    1981 Civil Wars. Boston: Beacon.
Juvonen, Jaana
    2001 School Violence Prevention Testimony. June, CT-178. Santa Monica: RAND
        Health.
Juvonen, Jaana, and Sandra Graham
    2004 Research Based Interventions on Bullying. *In* Bullying, Implications for the
        Classroom: What Does the Research Say? C. E. Sanders and G. D. Phye,
        eds. Pp. 229–255. San Diego: Academic Press.
Juvonen, Jaana, Adrienne Nishina, and Sandra Graham
    2001 Self-views versus Peer Perceptions of Victim Status among Early
        Adolescents. *In* Peer Harassment in School: The Plight of the Vulnerable and

Victimized. J. Juvonen and S. Graham, eds. Pp. 105–124. New York: Guilford Press.

Kalčik, Susan
    1975   ". . . Like Anne's Gynecologist or the Time I Was Almost Raped": Personal Narratives in Women's Rap Groups. Journal of American Folklore 88:3–11.

Kay, Martin
    2003   Cyber Bullies Prey on Girl. The Dominion Post. November 20. www.dompost.co.nz.

Keenan, Elinor Ochs
    1974   Norm-Makers, Norm-Breakers: Uses of Speech by Men and Women in a Malagasy Community. *In* Explorations in the Ethnography of Speaking. R. Bauman and J. Sherzer, eds. Pp. 125–143. Cambridge: Cambridge University Press.

Kendon, Adam
    1977   Spatial Organization in Social Encounters: The F-formation System. *In* Studies in the Behavior of Social Interaction. A Kendon, ed. Lisse, Holland: Peter DeRidder Press.

Kienpointner, Manfred
    1997   Varieties of Rudeness: Types and Functions of Impolite Utterances. Functions of Language 4(2):251–287.

Kiesling, Scott Fabius
    2001   "Now I Gotta Watch What I Say": Shifting Constructions of Masculinity in Discourse. Journal of Linguistic Anthropology 11(2):250–273.

Kitzinger, Celia
    1994   Sex Differences Research: Feminist Perspectives. Feminism and Psychology 4(2):330–336.
    2000   Doing Feminist Conversation Analysis. Feminism and Psychology 10(2):163–193.
    2002   Doing Feminist Conversation Analysis. *In* Talking Gender and Sexuality. P. McIlvenny, ed. Pp. 49–77. Amsterdam: John Benjamins.

Knight, G. P., I. K. Guthrie, M. C. Page, and R. A. Fabes
    2002   Emotional Arousal and Gender Differences in Aggression: A Meta-Analysis. Aggressive Behavior 28: 266–393.

Kohlberg, Lawrence
    1976   Moral Stages and Moralization: The Cognitive-Developmental Approach. *In* Moral Development and Behavior: Theory, Research, and Social Issues. T. Lickona, ed. Pp. 31–53. New York: Holt, Rinehart, and Winston.

Kramarae, Cheris
    1990   Changing the Complexion of Gender in Language Research. *In* Handbook of Language and Social Psychology. H. Giles and W. P. Robinson, eds. Pp. 346–361. New York: John Wiley and Sons.

Kulick, Don
    1992   Anger, Gender, Language Shift and the Politics of Revelation in a Papua New Guinean Village. Pragmatics 2(3):281–296.
    1993   Speaking as a Woman: Structure and Gender in Domestic Arguments in a New Guinea Village. Cultural Anthropology 8(4):510–541.

Kyratzis, Amy
    2001a   Children's Gender Indexing in Language: From the Separate Worlds Hypothesis to Considerations of Culture, Context, and Power. Research on Language and Social Interaction 34(1):1–13.
    2001b   Constituting the Emotions: A Longitudinal Study of Emotion Talk in a Preschool Friendship Group of Boys. *In* Gender in Interaction: Perspectives

on Femininity and Masculinity in Ethnography and Discourse. B. Baron and H. Kotthoff, eds. Pp. 51–74. Amsterdam: John Benjamins.

2003   Peer Language Socialization: Talk and Interaction among Children and the Co-construction of Peer Culture. *In* Annual Reviews of Anthropology.

2004   Talk and Interaction among Children and the Co-construction of Peer Groups and Peer Culture. Annual Review of Anthropology 33:625–649.

Kyratzis, Amy, and Jiansheng Guo

2001   Preschool Girls' and Boys' Verbal Conflict Strategies in the U.S. and China: Cross-Cultural and Contextual Considerations. Special issue, "Gender Construction in Children's Interactions: A Cultural Perspective". Research on Language and Social Interaction 34:45–74.

Kyratzis, Amy, and Evelyn Reder Wade

2002   American and Austrian Preschool Girls' Linguistic Practices for Enactment Power in Friendships. *In* Paper Presented at the American Anthropological Association Annual Meeting, New Orleans, November.

Labov, William

1972   Rules for Ritual Insults. *In* Language in the Inner City: Studies in the Black English Vernacular. Pp. 297–353. Philadelphia: University of Pennsylvania Press.

Labov, William, and David Fanshel

1977   Therapeutic Discourse: Psychotherapy as Conversation. New York: Academic Press.

Lagerspetz, Kirsti M. J., Kaj Bjorkqvist, and Tarja Peltonen

1988   Is Indirect Aggression Typical of Females? Gender Differences in Aggressiveness in 11- to 12-Year Old Children. Aggressive Behavior 14:403–414.

Lakoff, Robin

1973   Language and Women's Place. Language in Society 2:45–80.

1975   Language and Women's Place. New York: Harper.

Lamb, Sharon

2001   The Secret Lives of Girls. New York: Free Press.

Langdale, C. U.

1986   A Re-vision of Structural-Developmental Theory. *In* Handbook of Moral Development: Models, Processes, Techniques, and Research. G. L. Sapp, ed. Pp. 15–54. Birmingham: Religious Education Press.

Lareau, Annette

2003   Unequal Childhoods: Class, Race, and Family Life. Berkeley, CA: University of California Press.

Leaper, Campbell

1991   Influence and Involvement in Children's Discourse: Age, Gender and Partner Effects. Child Development 62:791–811.

1994   Exploring the Consequences of Gender Segregation on Social Relationships. New Directions for Child Development 65(Fall):67–86.

Leaper, Campbell, and Tara A. Smith

2004   A Meta-Analytic Review of Gender Variation in Children's Language Use: Talkativeness, Affiliative Speech, and Assertive Speech. Developmental Psychology 40(6):993–1027.

Lee, Richard B.

1982   Politics, Sexual and Non-sexual, in an Egalitarian Society. *In* Politics and History in Band Societies. E. Leacock and R. B. Lee, eds. Pp. 37–59. Cambridge: Cambridge University Press.

1986   Eating Christmas in the Kalahari. *In* Anthropology 86/87: Annual Editions. E. Angeloni, ed. Pp. 17–20. Guilford, CT: Dushkin (Reprinted from Natural History, 1969).

Lees, Sue
1993 Sugar and Space: Sexuality and Adolescent Girls. Harmondsworth: Penguin.
Lerner, Gene H.
1996 Finding "Face" in the Preference Structures of Talk-in-Interaction. Social Psychology Quarterly 59(4):303–321.
2004 Collaborative Turn Sequences. *In* Conversation Analysis: Studies from the First Generation. G. H. Lerner, ed. Pp. 225–256. Amsterdam: John Benjamins.
Lever, Janet Rae
1976 Sex Differences in the Games Children Play. Social Problems 23:478–487.
1978 Sex Differences in the Complexity of Children's Play and Games. American Sociological Review 43:471–483.
Levi-Strauss, Claude
1936 Contribution a l'Etude de l'Organization Sociale des Indiens Bororo. Journal de la Societe des Americanistes de Paris 28:269–304.
Liechty, Mark
2003 Suitably Modern: Making Middle-Class Culture in a New Consumer Society. Princeton, NJ: Princeton University Press.
Long, Jeffrey D., and Anthony D. Pellegrini
2003 Studying Change in Dominance and Bullying with Linear Mixed Models. School Psychology Review 32(3):401–417.
Luria, Zella
1993 A Methodological Critique. *In* An Ethic of Care: Feminist and Interdisciplinary Perspectives. M. J. Larrabee, ed. Pp. 199–203. New York: Routledge.
Lury, Celia
2004 Brands: The Logos of the Global Economy. New York: Routledge.
Lyons, Nona Plessner
1988a Listening to Voices We Have Not Heard: Emma Willard Girls' Ideas about Self, Relationships, and Morality. *In* Making Connections: The Relational Worlds of Adolescent Girls at Emma Willard School. C. Gilligan, N. P. Lyons, and T. J. Hanmer, eds. Pp. 30–72. Troy, NY: Emma Willard School.
1988b Two Perspectives: On Self, Relationships, and Morality. *In* Mapping the Moral Domain: A Contribution of Women's Thinking to Psychological Theory and Education. C. Gilligan, J. V. Ward, J. M. Taylor, and B. Bardige, eds. Pp. 21–48. Cambridge, MA: Harvard University Press.
Maccoby, Eleanor E.
1986 Social Groupings in Childhood: Their Relationship to Prosocial and Antisocial Behavior in Boys and Girls. *In* Development of Antisocial and Prosocial Behavior: Theories, Research and Issues. D. Olweus, J. Block, and M. Radke-Yarrow, eds. Pp. 263–284. San Diego: Academic Press.
1990 Gender and Relationships: A Developmental Account. American Psychologist 45(4):513–520.
1998 The Two Sexes: Growing Up Apart, Coming Together. Cambridge, MA: Harvard University Press.
Mackay, Robert W.
1991 Conceptions of Children and Models of Socialization. *In* Studying the Social Worlds of Children: Sociological Readings. F. C. Waksler, ed. Pp. 23–37. London: Falmer Press.
Makofsky, Jennifer
1997 "And That Is All I Know": Folkloric Speech in the World of Children. Paper presented for completion of Linguistics 246, Meryl Seigel, UC-Berkeley.
Malinowski, Bronislaw
1959 [1923] The Problem of Meaning in Primitive Languages. *In* The Meaning of Meaning. C. K. Ogden and I. A. Richards, eds. Pp. 296–336. New York: Harcourt, Brace & World.

Maltz, Daniel N., and Ruth A. Borker
   1982   A Cultural Approach to Male-Female Miscommunication. *In* Language and Social Identity. J. J. Gumperz, ed. Pp. 196–216. Cambridge: Cambridge University Press.

Marquez, Jason
   2004   Struggle for Status: A Study into the Quest for Status among First Graders. Independent Study. Department of Anthropology, UCLA.

Mayall, B.
   1994   Children's Childhoods: Observed and Experienced. London: Falmer Press.

Maynard, Douglas W.
   1985a   How Children Start Arguments. Language in Society 14:1–29.
   1985b   On the Functions of Social Conflict among Children. American Sociological Review 50:207–223.

McNamara, Mary
   2003   90049 is the Recall's Hip Zip: Brentwood Has Become Hyannis Port West. Los Angeles Times. August 5.

McRobbie, A.
   1978   Working Class Girls and the Culture of Femininity. *In* Women Take Issue: Aspects of Women's Subordination. Women's Studies Group, ed. Pp. 96–108. London: Hutchinson.

Mead, Margaret
   1933   More Comprehensive Field Methods. American Anthropologist 35:1–15.

Meadows, Susannah
   2002   Meet the Gamma Girls. Newsweek. June 3:44–50.

Mendoza-Denton, Norma
   1996   "Muy Macha": Gender and Ideology in Gang-Girls' Discourse about Makeup. Ethnos 61:47–63.
   1999   Turn-Initial No: Collaborative Opposition among Latina Adolescents. *In* Reinventing Identities: The Gendered Self in Discourse. M. Bucholtz, A. C. Liang, and L. A. Sutton, eds. Pp. 273–292. New York: Oxford University Press.
   Forthcoming   Homegirls: Symbolic Practices in the Making of Latina Youth Styles. Oxford: Blackwell Publishing.

Michard-Marshale, Clare, and Claudine Ribery
   1982   Sexisme et Science Humaine. Lille: Presses Universitaires de France.

Miller, Daniel
   1998   A Theory of Shopping. Ithaca, NY: Cornell University Press.

Miller, P. M., D. L. Danaher, and D. Forbes
   1986   Sex-Related Strategies for Coping with Interpersonal Conflict in Children Aged Five and Seven. Developmental Psychology 22:543–548.

Mills, Sara
   2003   Gender and Politeness. Cambridge: Cambridge University Press.

Moerman, Michael
   1988   Talking Culture: Ethnography and Conversation Analysis. Philadelphia: University of Pennsylvania Press.

Moore, Joan W.
   1991   Going Down in the Barrio: Homeboys, Homegirls in Change. Philadelphia: Temple University Press.

Morgan, Marcyliena
   1995   No Woman No Cry: The Linguistic Representation of African American Women. *In* Cultural Performances: Proceedings of the Third Berkeley Women and Language Conference. M. Bucholtz, A. C. Liang, L. A. Sutton, and C. Hines, eds. Pp. 525–541. Berkeley: Berkeley Women and Language Group, University of California.

1999   No Woman No Cry: Claiming African American Women's Place. *In* Reinventing Identities: The Gendered Self in Discourse. M. Bucholtz, A. C. Liang, and L. A. Sutton, eds. Pp. 27–45. New York: Oxford University Press.

Newman, K.
1989   Falling from Grace: The Experience of Downward Mobility in the American Middle Class. New York: Vintage Books.

Nishina, Adrienne, and Jaana Juvonen
In press   Daily Reports of Witnessing and Experiencing Peer Harassment in Middle School. Child Development.

Nishina, Adrienne, Jaana Juvonen, and Melissa Witkow
2005   Sticks and Stones May Break My Bones, but Names Will Make Me Feel Sick: The Psychosocial, Somatic, and Scholastic Consequences of Peer Harassment. Journal of Clinical Child and Adolescent Psychology 34(1):37–48.

O'Barr, W., and S. Atkins
1980   "Women's Language" or "Powerless Language"? *In* Women and Language in Literature and Society. S. McConnell-Ginet, R. Borker, and N. Furman, eds. Pp. 93–110. New York: Praeger.

Ochs, Elinor, Tamar Kremer-Sadlik, Olga Solomon, and Karen Gainer Sirota
2001   Inclusion as Social Practice: Views of Children with Autism. Social Development 10(3):399–419.

Ochs, Elinor, and Bambi Schieffelin
1989   Language Has a Heart. Text 9(1):7–25.

Okin, Susan Moller
1992   Women in Western Political Thought. Princeton, NJ: Princeton University Press.

Olweus, Dan
1991   Bully/Victim Problems among Schoolchildren: Basic Facts and Effects of a School-based Intervention Program. *In* The Development and Treatment of Childhood Aggression. D. Pepler and K. Rubin, eds. Pp. 411–448. Hillsdale, NJ: Erlbaum.
1993   Bullying at School: What We Know and What We Can Do. Cambridge, MA: Blackwell.

Opie, Iona, and Peter Opie
1959   The Lore and Language of School Children. Oxford: Clarendon Press.
1969   Children's Games in Street and Playground. Oxford: Clarendon Press.
1977   The Lore and Language of Schoolchildren. London: Paladin.

Ore, Tracy
2000   The Social Construction of Difference and Inequality: Race, Class, Gender, and Sexuality. Mountain View, CA: Mayfield.

Orenstein, Peggy
1994   Schoolgirls: Young Women, Self-Esteem and the Confidence Gap. Garden City, NY: Doubleday.

Ortner, Sherry B.
1991   Reading America: Preliminary Notes on Class and Culture. *In* Recapturing Anthropology: Working in the Present. R. G. Fox, ed. Pp. 163–189. Santa Fe: School of American Research Press.
1998   Identities: The Hidden Life of Class. Journal of Anthropological Research 54:1–17.
1999   Generation X: Anthropology in a Media-Saturated World. *In* Critical Anthropology Now. G. Marcus, ed. Pp. 55–87. Santa Fe: School of American Research Press.

2003   New Jersey Dreaming: Capital, Culture, and the Class of '58. Durham: Duke University Press.

2006   Anthropology and Social Theory: Rethinking Culture and the Acting Subject. Durham: Duke University Press.

Owens, L.
1996   Sticks and Stones and Sugar and Spice: Girls' and Boys' Aggression in Schools. Australian Journal of Guidance and Counseling 6:45–57.

Owens, L., R. Shute, and P. Slee
2000   "Guess What I Just Heard?": Indirect Aggression among Teenage Girls in Australia. Aggressive Behavior 26(1):67–73.

Packer, Martin J.
1985   The Structure of Moral Action: A Hermeneutic Study of Moral Conflict. Basel: Karger.

1987   Social Interaction as Practical Activity: Implications for the Study of Social and Moral Development. *In* Moral Development through Social Interaction. W. Kurtines and J. Gewirtz, eds. Pp. 245–277. New York: John Wiley & Sons.

Paley, V. G.
1984   Boys and Girls: Superheroes in the Doll Corner. Chicago: Chicago University Press.

Palmer, F. R.
1986   Mood and Modality. Cambridge: Cambridge University Press.

Parsons, Talcott
1951   Towards a General Theory of Action. Cambridge, MA: Harvard University Press.

Parsons, T., and R. F. Bales
1955   Family, Socialization, and Interaction Process. Glencoe, IL: Free Press.

Paugh, Amy
2003   Multilingual Play: Children's Codeswitching, Role Play, and Agency in Dominica, West Indies. Language in Society 34(1):63–86.

Pellegrini, Anthony D.
1998   Bullies and Victims in School: A Review and Call for Research. Journal of Applied Developmental Psychology 19(2):165–176.

2002   Bullying, Victimization, and Sexual Harassment during the Transition to Middle School. Educational Psychologist 37:151–163.

2005   Recess: Its Role in Education and Development. Mahwah, NJ: Erlbaum.

Pellegrini, Anthony D., M. Bartini, and F. Brooks
2001   School Bullies, Victims, and Aggressive Victims: Factors Relating to Group Affiliation and Victimization in Early Adolescence. Journal of Educational Psychology 91:216–224.

Pellegrini, Anthony D., and Peter Blatchford
2000   The Child at School: Interactions with Peers and Teachers. New York: Oxford University Press.

Pellegrini, Anthony D., and Catherine M. Bohn
2005   The Role of Recess in Children's Cognitive Performance and School Adjustment. Educational Researcher 34(1):13–19.

Pellegrini, Anthony D., and J. D. Long
2002   A Longitudinal Study of Bullying, Dominance and Victimization During the Transition from Primary School through Secondary School. British Journal of Developmental Psychology 20:259–280.

Pellegrini, Anthony D., and P. K. Smith
1998   Physical Activity Play: The Nature and Function of a Neglected Aspect of Play. Child Development 68:577–598.

Pepler, D. J., and W. M. Craig
    1995   A Peek behind the Fence: Naturalistic Observations of Aggressive Children
            with Remote Audiovisual Recording. Developmental Psychology 31:548–553.
Pepler, D. J., W. M. Craig, and W. R. Roberts
    1995   Aggression in the Peer Group: Assessing the Negative Socialization Process.
            In Coercion and Punishment in Long-term Perspectives. J. McCord, ed.
            Pp. 213–228. New York: Cambridge University Press.
Piaget, Jean
    1965 [1932]   The Moral Judgment of the Child. New York: Free Press.
Pilkington, Jane
    1998   "Don't Try and Make Out that I'm Nice!": The Different Strategies Women
            and Men Use when Gossiping. *In* Language and Gender: A Reader.
            J. Coates, ed. Pp. 254–269. Malden, MA: Blackwell.
Pipher, Mary Bray
    2001   Reviving Ophelia: Saving the Selves of Adolescent Girls. New York:
            Ballantine.
Pomerantz, Anita
    1975   Second Assessments: A Study of Some Features of Agreements/
            Disagreements. Unpublished Ph.D. dissertation, Division of Social Sciences,
            University of California, Irvine.
    1984   Agreeing and Disagreeing with Assessments: Some Features of Preferred/
            Dispreferred Turn Shapes. *In* Structures of Social Action: Studies in
            Conversation Analysis. J. M. Atkinson and J. Heritage, eds. Pp. 57–101.
            Cambridge: Cambridge University Press.
Potter, J.
    1996   Representing Reality: Discourse, Rhetoric, and Social Construction.
            London: Sage.
Prinstein, M., J. Boergers, and E. M. Vernberg
    2001   Overt and Relational Aggression in Adolescents: Social-Psychological
            Adjustment of Aggressors and Victims. Journal of Clinical Child Psychology
            30:479–491.
Proweller, Amira
    1998   Constructing Female Identities: Meaning Making in an Upper Middle Class
            Youth Culture. Albany, NY: State University of New York Press.
Pulkkinen, L., and T. Pitkanen
    1993   Continuities in Aggressive Behavior from Childhood to Adulthood. Aggres-
            sive Behavior 19:249–263.
Qvortrup, Jens, Marjatta Burdy, Tiovanni Sgritta, and Helmut Wintersberger
    1994   Childhood Matters: Social Theory, Practice, and Politics. Vienna: European
            Centre.
Rampton, Ben
    1995   Crossing: Language and Ethnicity among Adolescents. New York: Longman.
    2003   Hegemony, Social Class, and Stylisation. Pragmatics 13(1):49–84.
Reynolds, Jennifer
    In press   "Buenos Días:" The Natural Life History of Coined Ritual Insults and
            Verbal Duels in Antonero Maya Households. Research on Language and
            Social Interaction.
Richards, Martink P. M., ed.
    1974   The Integration of a Child into a Social World. Cambridge: Cambridge
            University Press.
Rigby, Ken
    1997   Bullying in Schools – And What to Do about It. London: Jessica Kingsley.
    1998   Gender and Bullying in Schools. *In* Children's Peer Relations. P. T. Slee and
            K. Rigby, eds. Pp. 47–59. London: Routledge.

Rivers, I., and P. K. Smith
    1994   Types of Bullying Behavior and Their Correlates. Aggressive Behavior 20:359–368.
Rizzo, Thomas A.
    1992   The Role of Conflict in Children's Friendship Development. New Directions for Child Development 58(Winter):93–111.
Roberts, W. R., D. J. Pepler, and W. M. Craig
    1999   Naturalistic Observations of Aggressive and Nonaggressive Children in the Classroom and on the Playground. Ms.
Ross, D. M.
    2002   Bullying. *In* Handbook of Crisis Counseling, Intervention, and Prevention in Schools. J. Sandoval, ed. Pp. 105–135. Mahwah, NJ: Erlbaum.
Rothbart, M. K., D. Hanley, and M. Albert
    1986   Gender Differences in Moral Reasoning. Sex Roles 15:645–653.
Sachs, Jacqueline
    1987   Preschool Boys' and Girls' Language Use in Pretend Play. *In* Language, Gender and Sex in Comparative Perspective. S. Philips, S. Steele, and C. Tanz, eds. Pp. 178–188. Cambridge, MA: Cambridge University Press.
Sacks, Harvey
    1984   Notes on Methodology. *In* Structures of Social Action. J. M. Atkinson and J. Heritage, eds. Pp. 21–27. Cambridge: Cambridge University Press. (Edited by Gail Jefferson from various unpublished lectures).
    1987 [1973]   On the Preferences for Agreement and Contiguity in Sequences in Conversation. *In* Talk and Social Organisation. G. Button and J. R. E. Lee, eds. Pp. 54–69. Clevedon, England: Multilingual Matters.
    1995a Lectures on Conversation I. Cambridge, MA: Blackwell.
    1995b Lectures on Conversation II. Cambridge, MA: Blackwell.
Sacks, Harvey, and Emanuel A. Schegloff
    1979   Two Preferences in the Organization of Reference to Persons and Their Interaction. *In* Everyday Language: Studies in Ethnomethodology. G. Psathas, ed. Pp. 15–21. New York: Irvington Publishers.
Sacks, Harvey, Emanuel A. Schegloff, and Gail Jefferson
    1974   A Simplest Systematics for the Organization of Turn-Taking for Conversation. Language 50:696–735.
Sadker, Myra, and David Sadker
    1994   Failing at Fairness: How America's Schools Cheat Girls. New York: Charles Scribner's Sons.
Salmivalli, Christina
    2001   Group View on Victimization: Empirical Findings and Their Implications. *In* Peer Harassment in School: The Plight of the Vulnerable and Victimized. J. Juvonen and S. Graham, eds. Pp. 398–419. New York: Guilford Press.
Salmivalli, Christina, Kirsti Lagerspetz, Kaj Bjorkqvist, Karin Osterman, and
Ari Kaukiainen
    1996   Bullying as a Group Process: Participant Roles and Their Relations to Social Status within the Group. Aggressive Behavior 22:1–5.
Sanders, Cheryl E.
    2004   What is Bullying? *In* Bullying: Implications for the Classroom. C. E. Sanders and G. D. Phye, eds. Pp. 2–19. New York: Academic Press.
Sansone, Livio
    1995   The Making of a Black Youth Culture: Lower-Class Young Men of Surinamese Origin in Amsterdam. *In* Youth Cultures: A Cross-Cultural Perspective. V. Amit-Talia and H. Wulff, eds. Pp. 114–143. London: Routledge.

Savasta, M. L., and Brian Sutton-Smith
    1979   Sex Differences in Play and Power. *In* Die Dialektk des Spiels. B. Sutton-Smith, ed. Pp. 143–150. Schorndoff: Holtman.
Schatzki, Theodore R.
    2001   Introduction: Practice Theory. *In* The Practice Turn in Contemporary Theory. T. R. Schatzki, K. Knorr Cetina, and E. von Savigny, eds. Pp. 1–14. London: Routledge.
Schatzki, Theodore R., Karin Knorr Cetina, and Eike von Savigny
    2001   The Practice Turn in Contemporary Theory. London: Routledge.
Schegloff, Emanuel A.
    1972   Notes on a Conversational Practice: Formulating Place. *In* Studies in Social Interaction. D. Sudnow, ed. Pp. 75–119. New York: Free Press.
    1997   Whose Text? Whose Context? Discourse and Society 8(2):165–187.
    1998   Reply to Wetherell. Discourse and Society 9(3):413–416.
    2002   Conversation Analysis, Then and Now. *In* Paper prepared for the Inaugural Session of the Section-in-Formation on Ethnomethodology and Conversation Analysis of the American Sociological Association, Chicago, IL, August 19.
Schegloff, Emanuel A., Gail Jefferson, and Harvey Sacks
    1977   The Preference for Self-Correction in the Organization of Repair in Conversation. Language 53:361–382.
Schenkein, Jim
    1978   Studies in the Organization of Conversational Interaction. New York: Academic Press.
Scheper-Hughes, Nancy, and Carolyn Sargent
    1998a Introduction: The Cultural Politics of Childhood. *In* Small Wars: The Cultural Politics of Childhood. N. Scheper-Hughes and C. Sargent, eds. Pp. 1–34. Berkeley, CA: University of California Press.
    1998b Small Wars: The Cultural Politics of Childhood. Berkeley, CA: University of California Press.
Schlegel, Jennifer
    1996   Re-visioning Children as Agents: Problematizing Peer. Paper presented at the 95th Annual Meeting of the American Anthropological Association, San Francisco.
Schofield, Janet
    1981   Complementary and Conflicting Identities: Images and Interaction in an Interracial School. *In* The Development of Children's Friendships. S. R. Asher and J. M. Gottman, eds. Pp. 53–90. Cambridge: Cambridge University Press.
    1982   Black and White in School: Trust, Tension, or Tolerance? New York: Praeger.
Schwartzman, Helen B.
    2001   Introduction: Questions and Challenges for a 21st Century Anthropology of Children. *In* Children and Anthropology: Perspectives for the 21st Century. H. B. Schwartzman, ed. Pp. 15–56. Westport, CT: Bergin and Garvey.
Scott, James C.
    1985   Weapons of the Weak: Everyday Forms of Peasant Resistance. New Haven: Yale University Press.
Scott, Joan Wallach
    1988   Gender and the Politics of history. New York: Columbia University Press.
Scott, Kimberly Ann
    2002   "You Want to be a Girl and Not My Friend": African American Girls' Play with and without Boys. Childhood 9:397–414.
    2003   In Girl, Out Girl, and Always Black: African-American Girls' Friendships. Sociological Studies of Children and Youth 9:211–227.

2004 African-American-White Girls' Friendships. Feminism and Psychology 14:383–388.

Selman, Robert L.
1980 The Growth of Interpersonal Understanding. New York: Academic Press.

Sennett, Richard, and Jonathan Cobb
1972 The Hidden Injuries of Class. New York: Vintage.

Shantz, Carolyn Uhlinger
1987 Conflicts between Children. Child Development 58:283–305.

Shantz, C. U., and W. W. Hartup
1992 Conflict in Child and Adolescent Development. Cambridge: Cambridge University Press.

Shantz, C. U., and C. J. Hobart
1989 Social Conflict and Development. In Peer Relationships in Child Development. T. J. Berndt and G. W. Ladd, eds. Pp. 71–94. New York: John Wiley.

Sharp, S., and P. K. Smith
1991 Bullying in UK Schools: The DES Sheffield Bullying Project. Educational and Child Psychology 12(2):81–88.

Sheldon, Amy
1990 Pickle Fights: Gendered Talk in Preschool Disputes. Discourse Processes 13:5–31.
1992a Conflict Talk: Sociolinguistic Challenges to Self-Assertion and How Young Girls Meet Them. Merrill Palmer Quarterly 38:95–117.
1992b Preschool Girls' Discourse Competence: Managing Conflict. In Locating Power: Proceedings of the Second Berkeley Women and Language Conference. K. Hall, M. Bucholtz, and B. Moonwomon, eds. Pp. 529–539. Berkeley: University of California.
1996 You Can Be the Baby Brother, But You Aren't Born Yet: Preschool Girls' Negotiation for Power and Access in Pretend Play. Research on Language and Social Interaction 29(1):57–80.

Shuman, Amy
1986 Storytelling Rights: The Uses of Oral and Written Texts by Urban Adolescents. Cambridge: Cambridge University Press.

Shweder, Richard A., Manamohan Mahapatra, and Joan G. Miller
1987 Culture and Moral Development. In The Emergence of Morality in Young Children. J. Kagan and S. Lamb, eds. Pp. 1–98. Chicago: University of Chicago Press.

Shweder, Richard A., and Nancy C. Much
1987 Determinations of Meaning: Discourse and Moral Socialization. In Moral Development Through Social Interaction. W. Kurtines and J. Gewirtz, eds. Pp. 197–244. New York: John Wiley & Sons.

Sidnell, Jack
2000 Primus Inter Pares: Story-telling and Male Peer Groups in an Indo-Guyanese Rumshop. American Ethnologist 27(1):72–99.
2003a An Ethnographic Consideration of Rule-Following. Journal of the Royal Anthropological Institute 9:429–445.
2003b Constructing and Managing Male Exclusivity in Talk-in-interaction. In The Handbook of Language and Gender. J. Holmes and M. Meyerhoff, eds. Pp. 327–352. Malden, MA: Blackwell.
2005 Talk and Practical Epistemology: The Social Life of Knowledge in a Caribbean Community. Amsterdam: John Benjamins.

Silverman, David
1998 Harvey Sacks: Social Science and Conversation Analysis. New York: Oxford University Press.

Simmel, Georg
  1902   The Number of Members as Determining the Sociological Form of the Group. American Journal of Sociology 8:158–196.
  1950   The Sociology of Georg Simmel. Translated by Kurt Wolff. Glencoe, IL: Free Press.
Simmons, Rachel
  2002   Odd Girl Out: The Hidden Culture of Aggression in Girls. New York: Harcourt.
  2004   Odd Girl Speaks Out: Girls Write about Bullies, Cliques, Popularity, and Jealousy. San Diego: Harcourt, Inc.
Sirota, Karen
  In press   Habits of the Hearth: Children's Bedtime Routines as Relational Work. Text.
Smith, P. K., and P. Brain
  2000   Bullying in Schools: Lessons from Two Decades of Research. Aggressive Behavior 26:1–9.
Smith, Peter K., and Sonia Sharp, eds.
  1994   School Bullying: Insights and Perspectives. New York: Routledge.
Somers, Margaret R., and Gloria D. Gibson
  1994   Reclaiming the Epistemological "Other": Narrative and the Social Constitution of Identity. In Social Theory and the Politics of Identity. C. Calhoun, ed. Pp. 37–99. Oxford: Blackwell.
Sosa, Juan Manuel
  1991   Fonética y Fonología de la Entonación del Español Hispanoamericano. Ph.D. Dissertation in Spanish and Portuguese, University of Massachusetts.
Speer, Susan A.
  2005   Gender Talk: Feminism, Discourse, and Conversation Analysis. London: Routledge.
Speer, Susan, and Jonathan Potter
  2002   From Performatives to Practices: Judith Butler, Discursive Psychology and the Management of Heterosexist Talk. In Talking Gender and Sexuality. P. McIlvenny, ed. Pp. 151–206. Amsterdam: John Benjamins.
Spender, Dale
  1980   Man Made Language. London: Routledge and Kegan Paul.
Sperber, Dan, and Deirdre Wilson
  1986   Relevance: Communication and Cognition. Cambridge, MA: Harvard University Press.
Spivak, Howard, and Deborah Prothow-Stith
  2001   The Need to Address Bullying – An Important Component of Violence Prevention. Journal of the American Medical Association 285(16):2131–2132.
Stack, Carol B.
  1993   The Culture of Gender: Women and Men of Culture. In An Ethic of Care: Feminist and Interdisciplinary Perspectives. M. J. Larrabee, ed. Pp. 108–111. New York: Routledge.
Starr, Alexandra
  2005   Subadolescent Queen Bees. New York Times Magazine. December 11. http://www.google.com/search?client=safari&rls=en&q=subadolescent+queen+bee&ie=UTF-8&oe=UTF-8.
Steedman, Carolyn
  1986   Landscape for a Good Woman: A Story of Two Lives. New Brunswick, NJ: Rutgers University Press.
Stephens, Sharon, ed.
  1995   Children and the Politics of Culture. Princeton, NJ: Princeton University Press.

Stokoe, Elizabeth H.
   2000   Toward a Conversation Analytic Approach to Gender and Discourse.
           Feminism and Psychology 10(4):552–563.
Stokoe, Elizabeth H., and Ann Weatherall
   2002   Gender, Language, Conversation Analysis and Feminism. Discourse and
           Society 13(6):707–713.
Strayer, F. F., and Janet Strayer
   1980   Preschool Conflict and the Assessment of Social Dominance. *In* Dominance
           Relations: An Ethological View of Human Conflict and Social Interaction.
           D. R. Omark, F. F. Strayer, and D. G. Freedman, eds. Pp. 137–157. New
           York: Garland STPM Press.
Sullivan, H. S.
   1953   The Interpersonal Theory of Psychiatry. New York: Norton.
Sunderland, Jane
   2004   Gendered Discourses. Basingstoke: Palgrave Macmillan.
Sutton-Smith, Brian
   1979a   Play and Learning. New York: Gardner Press.
   1979b   The Play of Girls. *In* Becoming Female. C. B. Kopp and M. Kirkpatrick, eds.
           Pp. 229–257. New York: Plenum.
Swearer, Susan M., and Dorothy L. Espelage
   2004   Introduction: A Social-Ecological Framework of Bullying among Youth. *In*
           Bullying in American Schools: A Socio-Ecological Perspective on Prevention
           and Intervention. D. L. Espelage and S. M. Swearer, eds. Pp. 1–12. Mahwah,
           NJ: Lawrence Erlbaum.
Talbot, Margaret
   2002   Girls Just Want to Be Mean. New York Times Magazine, February 24,
           Section 6: 24–65.
Tannen, Deborah
   1990   You Just Don't Understand: Women and Men in Conversation. New York:
           William Morrow and Co.
Tapper, Katy, and Michael Boulton
   2000   Social Representations of Physical, Verbal, and Indirect Aggression in
           Children: Sex and Age Differences. Aggressive Behavior 26:442–454.
Tarone, Elaine
   1973   Aspects of Intonation in Black English. American Speech 48:29–36.
Tavris, Carol
   1992   The Mismeasure of Woman: Why Women are Not the Superior Sex, the In-
           ferior Sex or the Opposite Sex. New York: Simon and Schuster/Touchstone.
   2002   Are Girls Really as Mean as Books Say They Are? Chronicle of Higher
           Education 48 (Section: The Chronicle Review): B7, http://chronicle.com/
           free/v48/i43/43b00701.htm.
Tholander, Michael
   2002   Doing Morality in School: Teasing, Gossip and Subhteaching as Collabor-
           ative Action, Linkoping University.
Thompson, Michael, Catherine Grace O'Neill, with Lawrence J. Cohen
   2001   Best Friends, Worst Enemies: Understanding the Social Lives of Children.
           New York: Ballantine Books.
Thornborrow, Joanna
   1998   Children's Participation in the Discourse of Children's Television. *In*
           Children and Social Competence: Arenas of Action. I. Hutchby and
           J. Moran-Ellis, eds. Pp. 134–153. London: Falmer.
Thornborrow, Joanna, and Deborah Morris
   2004   Gossip as Strategy: The Management of Talk about Others on Reality TV
           Show "Big Brother". Journal of Sociolinguistics 8(2):246–271.

Thorne, Barrie
   1986   Girls and Boys Together . . . But Mostly Apart: Gender Arrangements in
          Elementary School. *In* Relationships and Development. W. W. Hartup and
          Z. Rubin, eds. Pp. 167–184. Hillsdale, NJ: Erlbaum.
   1987   Re-visioning Women and Social Change: Where are the Children? Gender
          and Society 1:85–109.
   1993   Gender Play: Rutgers University Press.
   2002   Gender and Interaction: Widening the Conceptual Scope. *In* Gender in Inter-
          action: Perspectives on Femininity and Masculinity in Ethnography and Dis-
          course. B. Baron and H. Kotthoff, eds. Pp. 3–18. Amsterdam: John Benjamins.
Thorne, Barrie, Cheris Kramarae, and Nancy Henley
   1983   Language, Gender and Society. Rowley, MA: Newbury House.
Tomada, Giovanna, and Barry H. Schneider
   1997   Relational Aggression, Gender, and Peer Acceptance: Invariance across
          Culture, Stability over Time, and Concordance among Informants. Develop-
          mental Psychology 33(4):601–609.
Turiel, E.
   1998   The Development of Morality. *In* Handbook of Child Psychology,
          vol. 3: Social, Emotional, and Personality Development. W. Damon and
          N. Eisenberg, eds. Pp. 863–932. New York: Wiley.
Underwood, Marion K.
   2003   Social Aggression in Girls. New York: Guilford Press.
van Ausdale, Debra, and Joe R. Feagin
   1996   Using Racial and Ethnic Concepts: The Critical Case of Very Young
          Children. American Sociological Review 61:779–796.
   2001   The First R: How Children Learn Race and Racism. Landham, MD: Rowman
          and Littlefield.
van Dijk, Teun A.
   1993   Principles of Critical Discourse Analysis. Discourse and Society 4(2):249–283.
Vinacke, W. Edgar, and Abe Arkoff
   1957   An Experimental Study of Coalitions in Triads. American Sociological
          Review 22:406–414.
Vygotsky, Lev S.
   1978   Mind in Society: The Development of Higher Psychological Processes. Cam-
          bridge, MA: Harvard University Press.
Waksler, Francis Chaput
   1991   Beyond Socialization. *In* Studying the Social Worlds of Children: Sociolo-
          gical Readings. F. C. Waksler, ed. Pp. 12–22. London: Falmer Press.
Walker, L. J., R. C. Pitts, K. H. Henning, and M. K. Matsuba
   1995   Reasoning about Morality and Real-Life Moral Problems. *In* Morality in
          Everyday Life: Developmental Perspectives. M. Killen and D. Hart, eds.
          New York: Cambridge University Press.
Walkerdine, Valerie
   1985   On the Regulation of Speaking and Silence: Subjectivity, Class, and
          Gender in Contemporary Schooling. *In* Language, Gender, and Childhood.
          C. Steedman, C. Urwin, and V. Walkerdine, eds. Pp. 203–241. London:
          Routledge and Kegan Paul.
Weatherall, Ann
   1998   Re-visioning Gender and Language Research. Women and Language
          21(1):1–9.
   2000   Gender Relevance in Talk-in-Interaction and Discourse. Discourse and
          Society 11(2):286–288.
   2002   Gender, Language, and Discourse. New York: Routledge.

Weisz, A. N., and B. M. Black
  2003   Gender and Moral Reasoning: African American Youths Respond to Dating Dilemmas. Journal of Human Behavior in the Social Environment 6(3):17–34.
West, Candace
  1979   Against Our Will: Male Interruptions of Females in Cross-Sex Conversation. Annals of the New York Academy of Sciences 327:81–97.
  1992   Rethinking "Sex Differences" in Conversational Topics. Advances in Group Processes 9:131–162.
West, Candace, and A. Garcia
  1988   Conversational Shift Work: A Study of Topical Transitions between Women and Men. Social Problems 35:551–575.
West, Candace, and Don Zimmerman
  1983   Small Insults: A Study of Interruptions in Cross-Sex Conversations between Unacquainted Persons. *In* Language, Gender, and Society. B. Thorne, C. Kramarae, and N. M. Henley, eds. Pp. 103–118. Rowley, MA: Newbury.
Wetherell, Margaret
  1998   Positioning and Interpretive Repertoires: Conversation Analysis and Post-Structuralism in Dialogue. Discourse and Society 9(3):387–412.
Wetherell, Margaret, and Nigel Edley
  1998   Gender Practices: Steps in the Analysis of Men and Masculinities. *In* Standpoints and Differences: Essays in the Practice of Feminist Psychology. K. Henwood, C. Griffin, and A. Phoenix, eds. Pp. 156–173. London: Sage Publications.
Whalen, Marilyn R.
  1995   Working toward Play: Complexity in Children's Fantasy Activities. Language in Society 24:315–348.
White, Emily
  2002   Fast Girls: Teenage Tribes and the Myth of the Slut. New York: Scribner.
White, Geoffrey M., and Karen Ann Watson-Gegeo
  1990   Disentangling Discourse. *In* Disentangling: Conflict Discourse in Pacific Societies. K. A. Watson-Gegeo and G. M. White, eds. Pp. 3–49. Stanford: Stanford University Press.
Whiting, Beatrice Blyth, and Carolyn Pope Edwards
  1973   A Cross-Cultural Analysis of Sex Differences in the Behavior of Children Aged Three through Eleven. Journal of Social Psychology 91:171–188.
  1988   Children of Different Worlds: The Formation of Social Behavior. Cambridge, MA: Harvard University Press.
Widdicombe, S., and R. Woffitt
  1995   The Language of Youth Subcultures: Social Identity in Action. London: Harvester Wheatsheaf.
Williams, Raymond
  1977   Marxism and Literature. Oxford: Oxford University Press.
Willis, Paul
  1981   Learning to Labor: How Working Class Kids Get Working Class Jobs. New York: Columbia University Press.
Wingard, Leah
  1997   Lunchtime Wrestling: An Analysis of Boys' Ranking during Arm Wrestling. *In* Paper written for Anthropology 242, the Ethnography of Communication.
  In press   Mentioning Homework First in Parent–Child Interaction. Text.
Winterhoff, Paul A.
  1997   Sociocultural Promotions Constraining Children's Social Activity. Comparisons and Variability in the Development of Friendships. *In* Comparisons in

Human Development: Understanding Time and Context. J. Tudge, M. Shanahan, and J. Valsiner, eds. Pp. 222–251. New York: Cambridge University Press.

Wiseman, Rosalind
  2002   Queen Bees and Wannabees: Helping Your Daughter Survive Cliques, Gossip, Boyfriends, and Other Realities of Adolescence. New York: Crown.

Wittgenstein, Ludwig
  1958   Philosophical Investigations. G. E. M. Anscombe and R. Rhees, eds. G. E. M. Anscombe, trans. 2nd edition, Oxford: Blackwell.

Woffitt, Robin
  2005   Conversation Analysis and Discourse Analysis: A Comparative and Critical Introduction. London: Sage.

Woods, Nicola
  1988   Talking Shop: Sex and Status as Determinants of Floor Apportionment in a Work Setting. *In* Women in Their Speech Communities. J. Coates and D. Cameron, eds. Pp. 141–157. London: Longman.

Wootton, Tony
  1997   Interaction and the Development of Mind. Cambridge: Cambridge University Press.

Wulff, Helena
  1988   Twenty Girls: Growing Up, Ethnicity and Excitement in a South London Microculture. Stockholm: University of Stockholm.

Youniss, James
  1980   Parents and Peers in Social Development: A Sullivan-Piaget Perspective. Chicago: University of Chicago Press.

Zimmerman, Don H., and Candace West
  1975   Sex Roles, Interruptions and Silences in Conversation. *In* Language and Sex: Difference and Dominance. B. Thorne and N. Henley, eds. Pp. 105–129. Rowley, MA: Newbury House.

Zinn, Howard
  1980   A People's History of the United States. New York: Harper and Row.

Author Index

Subject Index

absent parties, assessments about, 196–206

access rituals, 229

accounts, 12
  in boys' jump rope, 135–6
  in girls' jump rope, 128–35

accusations, 118
  accusation/counter accusation sequences, 129–31
  direct, 134
  he-said-she-said, 7

activities
  regulation through directives, 136–8
  situated activity systems, 7, 10–13
  speech events, 7–8
  as unit of analysis, 5, 7

address terms, 44, 178

adjacency pair, 117

adornment, 183–4

adult-centered socialization model, 22

adverbial intensifiers, 197–8

affective alignments and displays, 4, 40–2, 43

age, and asymmetrical relations, 107–19

agency of children, 21–4, 119, 245

aggravated correction, 42

aggression, 214–16
  direct verbal, 215, 216, 240
  female, 214–16, 250–1, 253
  indirect, 214–15, 216, 240
  male, 214–16, 250–1
  micro-aggression, 225
  physical, 214–15
  relational, 214, 215, 216, 251
  social, 20, 214, 215, 216, 240, 250–1
  verbal, 214, 215, 216, 240, 251
  see also bullying

agreement, preference for, 32, 107–8, 192

alignment
  forms of, 171, 194
  of participants in storytelling, 171–5

alliances
  formation, 206–8
  quick-changing nature, 221

animation of voices, 165, 168

apparatus, 12

argumentative actions, 117

argumentative stances in games, 71–2

assessments
  about absent parties, 199–206
  assessment adjectives, 195, 198, 218
  differentiated participation and alliances in, 206–8
  divergent and congruent perspectives, 193
  evaluation in assessment sequences, 191–5
  grammatical resources and stance construction, 195–9
  ironic positive, 159
  negative, 192, 218, 230
  overlapping talk, 202
  positive, 159
  second, 192, 201, 202
  stance and structure in, 190–209

asymmetrical relationships
  and age, 107–19
  among girls, 15–16, 106–19
  and directive use, 141–4
  and gender, 98–106

"at least," use of, 233–4

attentiveness, structure of, 68–71

audiotape use, 4, 25

autonomous morality, 17–18